TO
LUKE
IT WAS SUCH A
PLEASURE SHARING
THE STAGE WITH
AT THE DANCTEACHER-
I'M A BIG FAN.
HUGS
Da/A RAB

TOUGH GUYS
DO DANCE

TOUGH GUYS DO DANCE

DAVID WINTERS

Indigo River Publishing

Indigo River Publishing
3 West Garden Street Ste. 352 M
Pensacola, FL 32502
www.indigoriverpublishing.com

Editors: Whitney Evans, Justyn Newman, Jordan Thames, and Regina Cornell
Cover Designer: Larry Barsky
Interior Design: mycustombookcover.com

Ordering Information: Quantity sales: Special discounts are available on quantity purchases by corporations, associations, and others. For details, contact the publisher at the address above.

Orders by U.S. trade bookstores and wholesalers: Please contact the publisher at the address above.

Printed in the United States of America

Library of Congress Control Number: 2018944660

ISBN: 978-1-948080-27-9

First Edition

With Indigo River Publishing, you can always expect great books, strong voices, and meaningful messages. Most importantly, you'll always find ... words worth reading.

TABLE OF CONTENTS

QUOTES

The following quotes were collected recently and over the years, and I am very excited to share them with you.

"I met David Winters when I took his jazz class in L.A. I knew then that he was truly talented and would be a great choreographer. He was soft-spoken, sensitive, funny, and humble, but also, when he moved, he was like a panther: dangerous, strong, and cunning. David did all the musical numbers in *Viva Las Vegas.*" He also directed and choreographed my first headlining show at the Rivera Hotel, did my first television special, and received an Emmy nomination. He has been a wonderful friend through all these years."

—Ann-Margret, 5 time Golden Globe Winner, Emmy Award Winner, and 2 time Academy Award Nominee

"I LOVE you in *"West Side Story"* David.
I watch it every week of my life, it's my favorite movie....I know every step from it, I wish I was in it.
You in that movie...... inspired me so much"

—Michael Jackson ....World #1 SuperStar

"David Winters is one of the most interesting and talented people I know. His ability to 'think outside the box' inspired me to take chances in my own musical career. He was a great friend to me in the earliest stages of my career and remains a friend to this day. That, above all else, speaks to his character. Oh my...is he one talented guy! "

—Lynda Carter, The Original Wonder Woman and Singing Star of her own TV Specials

"When you look at the men who have inspired boys to dance—Fred Astaire, Gene Kelly, Sammy Davis Jr.—David Winters's name is high on that list. He was certainly my inspiration. Watching him dance in *"West Side Story"* changed my life. When I began dancing I soon realized, if you want to be a dancer, you need to be *tough!*"

—Nigel Lythgoe, OBE (Order of the British Empire), Producer and Owner of *"American Idol"* and *"So You Think You Can Dance"*

"The first time I saw David Winters was in 1957 or '58 when my mother and I went to the Winter Garden Theatre in New York to see *"West Side Story."* David played Baby John in the original production, and later he played A-rab in the film. I never forgot his performance. He was strong, energetic, and sexy. Years later when I was producing my TV special, *"Movin' With Nancy,"* I knew I had to ask David to do the choreography. He created and performed an extremely athletic number all around the run-down Pacific Ocean Park with a group of dancers that made the lifeless pier live again—and won himself an Emmy in the process! That was in 1967. After all these years, I still treasure our friendship and always hold him close to my heart."

—Nancy Sinatra, top-selling recording artist

"David Winters, I just want to shake your hand. When I was a kid growing up I wanted to be an actor and a dancer. Everyone told me not to, it was too difficult, and I wouldn't be a success, but when I saw you in *"West Side Story"* you inspired me to do it. I just want to shake your hand and thank you for the inspiration! Thank you, David!"

—Henry Winkler (The Fonze), Golden Globe- and Emmy-winning actor

"I know David from our working experience on the film *"West Side Story."* David's sheer presence gave the Jets the strength so important to "the gang"—who they are and what they feel, the important word being *feel*—very important to the story. His talent as an actor makes everything very real. Humor, pathos, strength, and a wonderful imagination—he has them all. I have great admiration for David! David is the best!"

—George Chakiris, Academy Award- and Golden Globe-winning actor

"David Winters has been one of the most important people in my professional life. He not only gave me my first dancing job on television and my first dancing job in a film, but his encouragement gave me the confidence I needed to continue pursuing a career. He was my first mentor, and I am forever grateful. Thank you, David!"

—Donna McKechnie, Tony Award, Drama Desk Award, and Theater World Special Award-winning star of "*A Chorus Line*"

"David Winters is a RHAPSODY!!"

—Burt Reynolds, Golden Globe and Emmy Award winning actor

"David Winters has excelled in every aspect of the entertainment world—from dancer to studio head. He is an innovator. He has worked with and influenced some of the biggest names in show business for nearly 60 years. His new book, *Tough Guys Do Dance*, is a must read. You will be enthralled!"

—Robert Davi, multi-award-winning actor and current star of the TV series *"Paper Empire"*

"Little did I know that taking David Winters's dance classes at the Coronet Theatre in LA would launch my career as a dancer, choreographer, director, and producer. I had never seen anyone dance like David—WOW! David was my mentor, and my first TV series for David was *"Shindig,"* and then *"Hullabaloo,"* with films to follow. I owe him more than words can possibly say. Thank you, David. I am forever grateful!"

—Anita Mann, five-time nominee and one-time winner of the Emmy Award

Announced to the audience every night at Universal's Amphitheatre and NYC's Radio City Music Hall: "There is a little guy backstage who never sleeps, who's responsible for all of this. He is my amazing director and producer, and his name is David Winters. Please give him a really big round of applause! David, come out here and take a bow!"

—Diana Ross, all-time–best-selling female recording artist in the world

"David Winters is my favorite choreographer. We did four films together, starting with *"Viva Las Vegas,"* then *"Girl Happy," "Tickle Me,"* and *"Easy Come, Easy Go."* I love working with him, and he makes it so much fun. It's not like work at all."

—Elvis Presley, the King of Rock and Roll

"David Winters is one of the most talented film industry professionals that I've had the pleasure to work with. He is a genius choreographer and a very talented director. I worked with him on "*Dancin': It's On!*" where we applied technology to enhance the surround sound. David is also a wonderful person to work with and has always been open to new ideas."

—Tony Bongiovi, award-winning music producer of over 40 Platinum and Gold records

"Thank you David for your AMAZING work on Nancy's Special. You made her look terrific and your solo dance number was wonderful. I am very proud of her and as her father I wish to simply say a big THANK YOU!" *Signed, Nancy's Dad.*

—Frank Sinatra, known as the greatest singer of the 20th century and winner of The Academy Award and The Golden Globe

"I'm so happy David chose to share his interesting life which I am apart of. David, as Baby John, was wonderful in the original "West Side Story". An artist in every way and now an author. Thank you David."

—Chita Rivera, 2018 Tony Lifetime Achievement Award winner, 2 time Tony Award winner and 10 time nominee, awarded the Kennedy Center Presidential Award, and holds the all time record for the most Tony nominations earned by a single performer.

"David is an icon! His dancing and choreography are as good as it gets. Working with him in *"West Side Story"* was an absolute delight! Just don't play gin rummy with him. You'll lose all your money!"

—Russ Tamblyn, Oscar nominee and Golden Globe-winning actor

"West Side Story," the original cast and Jerome Robbins, is the reason I became an actor. I idolized David Winters in the show and had a huge crush on him. Over the years, watching shows he choreographed with Ann-Margret and the movies with Elvis mesmerized me. He produced me in a wonderful role in a movie called *"Double Threat."* I had a blast with him. His book, *Tough Guys Do Dance*, promises to be a classic experience in reading."

—Sally Kirkland, Academy Award nominee and Golden Globe winner as Best Actress in the film *"Anna"*

"David Winters has chronicled a huge career within this book! And let's not forget he started as a child star! What a gift to the world David is! He's an amazing man, producer, director, choreographer… and a great dancer! David has worked with all the major stars of our time, and you will love reading all about his journey in *Tough Guys Do Dance*! David Winters is a great talent! An amazing life, a spectacular book! Get it! Read it! You will be happy you did! Tough guys do dance!"

—Joe Tremaine, President of Tremaine Dance Convention, attended by over two-million dance students and teachers and teacher of Paula Abdul, Cher, and Diana Ross

"What an insightful look into the amazing life of David Winters— dancer, actor, singer, choreographer, director, and producer. The depth of David's formidable talent leaps off the pages of this book and offers performers and non-performers alike a view into the incredible and often insane world of the entertainment industry. On a personal note, I would like to thank David for taking a chance on an unknown ballet/ jazz dancer in 1975 for Alice Cooper's *"Welcome to My Nightmare."* It worked out well."

—Sheryl (Mrs. Alice) Cooper, famous dancer and actress

"Just watch David's incredible 20-second solo from *"West Side Story*'s" "Cool." He takes dance steps, turns them into raw emotion, and tells a story. It was the aha! moment when I understood what dance should be about.

"I became his assistant in 1963, at his legendary dance class above the Coronet Theater, where not only the greatest dancers in Hollywood came to train, but so did television and movie stars. I remember Elvis Presley leaning against the open door of the studio to check out Sue Lyon. It was the place to be!

"He knew how to merge traditional jazz dance and the go-go dancing exploding in the clubs onto film and television.

"He took me along for an amazing ride, choreographing groundbreaking TV like *"Shindig"* and the iconic *"T.A.M.I. Show"* and films like *"Pajama Party, Beach Blanket Bingo,"* and *"Viva Las Vegas,"* to name just a few. It was the jumping-off point of my solo career. Thanks, David…"

—Toni Basil, award-winning producer, director, choreographer, and singer of the multimillion-selling worldwide hit "Mickey"

"David Winters was the brilliant director, choreographer, and the most essential part of my highly successful world tour and movie *"Welcome to My Nightmare,"* and nearly killed me—okay, beat me to death—getting me dancing.
"Tough guys do dance, and he's one of the toughest, STILL one of the toughest! Wouldn't mess with him! (said with a smile.) When you're talking show biz, you're talking David. He has worked with everyone. David could call anyone in show biz and they would pick up the phone. That's a pretty good reputation when you can span ballet to Broadway to punk."

—Alice Cooper, world-famous, best-selling recording artist considered the "Father of Shock Rock"

"David Winters was the idol of any young male dancer, and all wanted to be him—the cool vulnerability and strength. As a choreographer, every young male dancer wanted to do his steps, including me!"

—Dennis Grimaldi, three-time–Tony Award-winning Broadway producer, and Pulitzer Prize winner

"One of the greatest influences on my life as an entertainer was the film, *"West Side Story."* And David Winters as, A-Rab, was a monster entertainer in my eyes. Fast forward a few years and suddenly he is introduced to me as one of the Directors of the *"Monkees TV Series"* and the stage director of the first MONKEES WORLD TOUR. As he guided and rehearsed me through that intense process, it was all I could do to not ask for his autograph. There wasn't much choreography in our show, per say, but David brought to the staging of our show his inimitable style, essence, and joy de vive that is what David Winters is all about."

—Micky Dolenz, member of The Monkees and star of the Emmy Award winning TV series of the same name

"David Winters is an inspiration to everyone, whether in the entertainment industry or any other walk of life. He has had success throughout his life as a dancer, choreographer, director, film producer, and now author because he never gives up, he constantly re-creates himself and pushes himself. He has overcome cancer operations and heart transplants and just keeps on succeeding. The man has the spirit of a warrior that just never quits! David, it has been a pleasure and an honor to be a small part of your journey."

—Gary Daniels, world-champion martial artist

"Doing *"Once Upon a Wheel"* with director/producer David Winters was a terrific experience. I loved the special so much it was my idea to expand it into a film. We bought two racing cars and had a blast doing the race circuit. A once-in-a-lifetime experience, AND we became great friends."

—Paul Newman, Academy Award-, Golden Globe-, BAFTA-, and Emmy-winning actor

Your *"Raquel"* Special was terrific! A wonderful special David. Congratulations on a great show.

—Fred Astaire, known as one of the greatest dancers ever who also won The Academy Award, The Golden Globe, and the Emmy.

"West Side Story!" *"Shindig!"* *"Hullabaloo!"* Nancy Sinatra! *"The T.A.M.I. Show!"* *"Viva Las Vegas"* starring Elvis and Ann-Margret! "The Monkees!" David Winters is responsible for entertaining my entire youth! And he was just getting started!"

—Stevie Van Zandt, star of *"The Sopranos"* and *"Lilyhammer"* TV series and the lead guitar player of Bruce Springsteen's E Street Band

"David Winters, a bona fide dance icon, was and will always be recognized as a very special creative force in Hollywood and the entertainment industry as a whole, having worked with all of the greatest legends to ever exist, such as Elvis Presley, Barbra Streisand, and Diana Ross! David possesses the unique ability to encourage and instill in artists, both amateurs and seasoned professionals, the confidence to see the hope and artistic voice inside themselves—two necessary things most certainly needed to succeed."

—Shabba-Doo, star of *"Breakin'"* and *"Breakin' 2"*

"I met David Winters when I was a young woman living in London and working for MCA Universal Pictures as a personal assistant. David was there to direct Alice Cooper's *"Welcome to My Nightmare."* I had adored *"West Side Story"* and was enthralled to be meeting someone so talented and charismatic. David offered me a job as his assistant on a movie he was directing in Hollywood—I couldn't believe my luck. I arrived in LA and never left. He was the first person to tell me I was smart and could do anything I wanted. I have been a producer for the past 32 years, and I am forever grateful to him and his inspiration. I cannot wait to read his book."

—Victoria Pearman, Producing Partner with Mick Jagger, at Jagged Films, for 25 years and a Grammy nominee

"David is inspirational…He had a lot to do with inspiring me!"

—Dionne Warwick, three-time Grammy Hall of Famer and award-winning singer

"David is a winner! He was born with all the tools and knows how to use them. His book puts them where they belong—right in your hands. Go ahead, let him sing to you!"

—Grover Dale, two-time Tony Award nominee and Drama Desk Award winner and owner of Answers 4 Dancers

"While directing *"The Steve Allen Show"* in Hollywood and, at the time, offered my first feature film, *"The T.A.M.I. Show,"* I asked around as to who was the hottest choreographer in town, and the answer was unanimous: DAVID WINTERS. I went to the Coronet Theater on La Cienega Blvd. to watch one of his dance classes, and it was the experience of a lifetime. We've not only remained good friends ever since, but [this meeting] led to a fantastic [working] relationship, not only on *"T.A.M.I."* but on *"Hullabaloo"* and *"Lucy in London,"* and with Diana Ross and The Dave Clark Five, and being given the opportunity to work with his incredible assistant choreographers and dancers enriched my life beyond words. Working with David was an experience I shall never forget, and needless to say, to this day, I am still a David Winters fan...and friend!"

**—Steve Binder, Emmy- and ACE
Award-winning director**

"David Winters gave me my first job in Hollywood dancing in the Ann-Margret, Elvis Presley film *"Viva Las Vegas."* After, I worked for David on every television network in town and with every big star there was. At the time, David was the most sought-after choreographer in Hollywood. While working with David, I learned what it meant to be a professional dancer and especially about how to choreograph. I watched him create dance number after dance number. I gained valuable experience and the confidence to try new things, new challenges, with my dancing and more importantly my choreography. David was my mentor and "teacher by example" the whole time I worked with him. Thank you, David ....I'm so grateful for all you taught me."

**—Walter Painter, award-winning choreographer
with 3 Emmy wins and 4 more nominations**

"Working for David as a dancer was always a real privilege and a joy. He was talented and compassionate with the dancers. You always wanted to do your very best for David. A talented performer as well as choreographer, director, and producer, he has the background as well as the raw talent to make magic happen on the screen. I have only happy memories of working for David! Great guy. (Great sense of humor, too! Gypsy humor, that is...)"

—Pete Menefee, award-winning costume designer with 3 Emmy wins

"David, Elvis loved and respected your extraordinary talent, and considered you a good friend. When you choreographed his films and were there on the set with him he felt more at ease and secure."

—Larry Geller, Hair Stylist to Elvis Presley

FOREWORD

Breathing in a scenario of great anticipation, David Winters takes a giant step forward in a new venture...that of author. His life has been a tale of emotion; a journey thru the arts – a royalty of riches bestowed.

Amazing is this man who conquered our hearts in *"West Side Story"* as Baby John in the original Broadway production and Arab in the award winning film, among countless of other projects as an actor, producer, director and choreographer to such stars as Elvis, Ann-Margret, Barbra Streisand, Alice Cooper, Diana Ross, Raquel Welch, Lucille Ball, Nancy Sinatra, Michael Jackson, Kenny Rogers and others too numerous to mention.

And now, as he ventures into that new entertainment plateau in his autobiography *Tough Guys Do Dance,* you can't help but realize, the power of dreams and the power of soul within that is like a rapidly moving escalator fulfilling a magical trend-setting life indeed for all to enjoy.

Get ready for David's breath-taking journey. Mesmerized you will become. Escapades are numerous from infancy, escaping death by fire, being shot at by German commandos, meeting his father for the first time at age 7, arriving in the US at age 9 to his first and subsequent Broadway/film/television ventures, his many loves, the mafia, to his fight for life.

What you will come to realize in reading *Tough Guys Do Dance,* is that David Winters is a risk-taker. He's a sensitive soul. His courage and stamina to control what is before him defies his lust for life; the dreams of what was yesterday to the dreams of tomorrow's to come. His talents are epic. Small in stature...he's larger than life...brilliant is the mind, yet childlike. He's his own sonnet. To quote Burt Reynolds, "David Winters is like a rhapsody." Ain't that the truth!!!

Although David lets you into his private world, there's so much left unsaid. He hasn't hardened with time…or has he! His emotions run deep; deeper than most. Like Hercules, he's stronger than most, yet there's that childlike vision that has lasted thru time. Like Moses he can move mountains. But here within lies a silent wanderer. And so the story begins in *Tough Guys Do Dance*.

He began writing this "diary" 15 years ago on paper – many memories of course were lost; still more were uncovered as he dug deep into the centerfolds of his life. Raindrops of tears flooding the pages – happy times were recovered, with blazing impact as he, at times, ran for the danger zone.

With 90% percent burns to his body, the toddler began his 9-lives conquest for life through the years. Today, at 79, his focus is to just make it thru to the next day and hopefully give guidance to those who yearn to achieve. David Winters danced into our lives at a young age. He still dances in our hearts to the melody of "don't give up!"

To reveal all that is the nature of *Tough Guys Do Dance* chapter to chapter, would be an injustice to the author and to his many fans. There's just too much to relate and take in. To say one would be shocked by the "personal" of it all is a complete understatement, as David in reality, is a very private person. In today's world, he does not take kindly to crowds or to blasts of noise. When he speaks, he speaks in whispers at times until drama takes its course. Then watch out for the sound explosion.

Tough Guys Do Dance is a testimonial; David's private and luxurious testimonial. What person doesn't like a bit of drama in their lives! The rush for acceptance sometimes takes its toll.

All of the Hollywood Royalty are featured. And so, this story has to be told and the one who reads *Tough Guys Do Dance*, becomes a moving participant, feeling every heartbeat emotion and drama; drama definitely.

Picture this: THE CANNES ESCAPE: the bodyguard draws a gun out of his jacket. …oh my God - they're chasing me. ..I was also expecting a bullet at any second. My heart is beating so fast, what can I do? I see a closet so I quickly close the door and hide in it, hoping I've lost them. Like a bad French farce, my foot is caught in a washerwoman's pail. Now I'm stuck and I couldn't move if I wanted to.

Now picture this if you can: DANGER TIME IN VEGAS – A drug bust with Linda Lovelace where Elvis, Liza and Sinatra come to the rescue. ..door bursts open and in a couple of seconds a flood of about seventeen heavy guys, shouting and pointing guns storm into our suite. Two of them grab me and throw me to the ground, face down, pressing guns to my temple and screaming "Don't move and you won't get hurt".

Or this…David Winters takes on the role of sleuth in the apparent Bangkok suicide of actor/friend David Carradine and told in no uncertain terms not to express his thoughts. Get the picture!!!

Don't think for a moment there's drama all the way…there's funny episodes too…plenty of them as David has written. Forever the jokester, David's imagination is one to be reckoned with and I for one, putting them in print would do an injustice.

Why stop here as the rollercoaster ride of David Winters hits many a curve along the way – up and down; round and round you spin with winning many an honor and nominations plenty!!!

"We are excited about working with David Winters," says Dan Vega, Founding Partner and President of Indigo River Publishing. "He is truly an icon in the film and dance community, and the perception of jazz and ballet would be very different without his influence. David's autobiography is a testament for the life he has lived and the thousands of entertainers that he personally guided and developed. He shares many humorous and fascinating behind the scenes stories regarding his associations with some the biggest names in show-business. Working with him is an amazing pleasure. Whether you are a student of dance or film, or just looking to take an amazing journey, his book will be one of the most captivating books you will ever read…."

It's always rewarding when "star" personalities come together to honor their own with wings spread far and wide, encircling with love for a friend, a mentor, a teacher, a fellow performer. So beholding are these written or recorded sentiments that acknowledge feelings shared about that one certain individual that has come into their world and influenced their achievements; giving credit where it is due and so heartily earned.

David Winters, through the years and many a sleepless night has achieved more than one could ever dream of fulfilling. Long live the applause and become a part of the luster of Hollywood and International fame. Enjoy!!!

—Dona Kay, Journalist and Reporter

PREFACE

Fade up from black...

I'm sitting here on my balcony in Fort Lauderdale, Florida, looking at the beautiful view of the river and boats below and the ocean straight ahead. I'm thinking about the last few years of my life, when I've been making a film in Florida, *"Dancin'—It's On!"* At the same time, I have undergone thirteen heart operations, four of them open-heart surgeries, as well as two procedures for cancer in my ear and another cancer operation extremely close to my left eye and brain.

There were so many times during this period that I thought I would die. In fact, I was once told that I had just twenty-five seconds to live, but I pulled through because I still have lots to accomplish in my life, including writing this book.

I've had the most amazing life, and I've been fortunate to work with so many superstars, such as Michael Jackson, Elvis, Alice Cooper, Barbra Streisand, Paul Newman, Diana Ross, Josh Brolin, Ann-Margret, Frank Sinatra, Lucille Ball, John Wayne, Sonny & Cher, Bobby Darin, Liza Minnelli, Simon & Garfunkel, Rudolph Nureyev, Dennis Hopper, Burgess Meredith, Kirk Douglas, Pamela Anderson, Nancy Sinatra, Tom Jones, Sammy Davis Jr., James Dean, Mel Brooks, and Dean Martin—the list goes on and on.

It's taken me over fifteen years to write this story, as every day I remember things that I had forgotten from my past. I would like other people to read it and share with me and enjoy both the highs and the lows, the ups and the downs.

Since I naturally see everything like a film, let's flash back to...
The beginning...

Lights...Camera...Action...

My Roots in England

It all started in London, England, where I was born on the 5th of April 1939, which incidentally is the very same birthdate as three of my all-time favorite movie stars, Spencer Tracy, Bette Davis, and Gregory Peck. I was born the first son of Samuel and Sadie Weizer, and arrived just in time for a world war, the number-two edition, which started just five months after my entry onto this planet.

My father was a furrier by profession and had joined the British army to fight the Nazi filth at the outset of hostilities when I was one year old. Consequently, I didn't get to see him again until 1946 when I was seven years old. During those war years, my mother rarely heard from my father and at times didn't know whether he was alive or dead.

As an Aries, a fire sign, I have always been fascinated with fire, and as a one-and-a-half-year-old, I began my interest in a very dramatic fashion. It was a cold late-winter morning, and my nanny had positioned me in my highchair in front of the fireplace to make sure I didn't get too cold from the bitter English weather. She added more coals to the fire and stoked the glowing embers to encourage the blaze, then wandered off to the kitchen. As the flames crackled and licked around the hearth, I leaned forward, with childlike fascination, towards the flames and tumbled, soundlessly, headlong out of my highchair, straight into the raging fire. At that moment, the nanny returned to see me cradled in the flames and let out a piercing scream, unable to move.

We are shooting the next shot from inside the fireplace to give the audience the maximum effect of the burning baby.

My mother, who had been in the study writing a letter to my father, came running into the room past the motionless but screaming nanny, grabbed the coal tongs, hooked them to my tiny leg, and yanked me out of the hearth. She raced to the kitchen and turned the faucet on to douse my smoldering clothes and body. Apparently, through all this, I didn't make a sound. I must have been in shock. I was rushed to hospital with burns to ninety percent of my little body, but at least I was still alive.

So traumatized was I by this horrible experience that I remained silent through the whole ordeal. It would be another eighteen months before I uttered another sound. The scars have since faded, but I still have one scar on the outside of my left arm and a small one under my chin as permanent reminders of that awful day.

My mom told me that whenever she took me to the hospital to see the doctor, which was once a week, I would cry soundlessly. She never knew whether I would ever talk or utter another sound again. At three years old, I did finally talk, thank God.

The next scene is shot with a handheld camera to add to the horror.

One afternoon, during the Blitz days of 1940–41, my mom had taken me up to Hampstead village, not far from the center of the city, to visit my grandparents when an air raid started.

Hear the sound of a wailing banshee as the air-raid sirens kick in.

I can clearly remember being terrified as the bombs began falling all around us. Dodging falling masonry, my mom ran along with me under her arm trying to make it to an air-raid shelter. Buildings were spitting out burning embers like confetti. How we survived I'll never know. It was like being in a raging hell.

Even though I was just a little baby on my mother's arms, the awful stench of burning buildings and flesh is fresh in my mind, just as clear as childhood smells like Mother's cooking, fairground popcorn and hotdogs, or the distinct smell of burning leaves in autumn.

Some aromas just stay with you, deep in the subconscious, conjuring up otherwise forgotten events.

Whip pan to establishing shot of the Isle of Wight.

In the summer of 1942, when I was just over three years old, my mother moved us to the Isle of Wight, on the south coast of England, thinking it would be safer for us, which for a while it was. But one cloudless, sunny morning, as two of my nanny's children and I were peeking into a Rolls Royce parked next door, we heard the unmistakable sound of an airplane. We stopped what we were doing and looked up into the clear blue sky to see a German plane heading towards us. We had no idea that it was a German plane, so it held no fear for us. We stopped what we were doing and simply watched it, totally fascinated as it got nearer and nearer.

Then, without warning, it began shooting at us. Bullets kicked up the dirt all around me and the other children, and we all simply froze. Why the German pilot would want to shoot at three harmless children I can't imagine, but that's exactly what he did.

My nanny came running out onto the veranda and screamed, followed seconds later by my frantic mother, while, out of nowhere, two unarmed American GIs came running from around the corner, right towards us.

Fast cuts between the plane, me and the kids, the nanny screaming, the GIs, my crying mother, us, the plane, the GIs, etc.–again and again!

Now swell the music as the GIs gather us up in their arms and run with us, full speed, across the lawn to the house, a distance of about fifty yards.

The plane could have shot at us more, but for some reason it didn't. With us in their arms, the GIs dove headfirst under the veranda, quickly followed by my terrified mother and equally terrified nanny. In the arms of the GIs, we could see the German plane as it flew towards us once more. Then it dipped its wings in a gesture of arrogance and flew off back from whence it had come. I can only assume that the plane had run out of ammunition, but as a child, I believed that the brave, unarmed American GIs had frightened him off. It makes a great scene for a movie, but not for real life, especially if you're the kid. As far as I was concerned, those heroic GIs won the day. From that moment on, I decided that I wanted to go to America and be an American, all because of those two big GI Joes who, I was convinced, had saved our lives, and all without guns, just like my comic hero, Superman. Just three years old, and I'd had two dramatic and narrow escapes from death. (This could definitely be viewed as an action movie.)

Following that incident, my mother decided to leave the Isle of Wight and move us to Enfield, a suburb of London, figuring we might be safer. The Germans were dropping bombs on us all the time. It almost seemed like some sort of sick game, called Kill the English in Their Houses. Almost every night we would hear the wail of the banshee, that's the air-raid sirens to you and me.

As young as I was, I can clearly remember the screaming of the bombs as they came hurtling down, followed by a deep, thunderous rumble as they smashed into the buildings and exploded, sending flames and debris high into the sky. This was followed by the staccato clatter of the yak-yak guns (anti-aircraft guns) pumping their responses into the night sky. You never forget the sound of those bombs—ever. I couldn't understand it as a young kid: Why did they want to kill me? What did I ever do to them?

Sometimes Mom and I had to travel up to the city, and the air-raid sirens would sound off. The air-raid wardens would herd everybody on the streets towards the underground subway stations, where we had to stay until the all-clear was sounded. We sometimes spent the entire night sleeping underground with hundreds of other mothers and children. The government had provided bunk beds along the platforms for this purpose, and the trains would run as usual, with commuters coming and going as we slept, or tried to sleep, at any rate. It was a lot safer than being above ground. Mothers would tie string leashes around their children so as not to lose them in the confusion and hysteria.

During air raids, the city of London was completely blacked out, and sometimes I would open the blackout curtain at home just a sliver and look up into the sky. There were bangs and flashes everywhere from the anti-aircraft guns and shafts of light from the searchlights picking out the invading aircraft. It was amazing, an awesome sight for a young child to behold, and although it was extremely scary, it was also very exciting.

Every once in a while, I would see a parachute open in the middle of all this and a man come falling towards the ground. Maybe the parachutist was one of ours; maybe it was one of theirs—I never knew. I remember thinking that if it was a German, his war was over and that was a good thing for us.

Underscore the next scenes with music.

Despite the general hatred for Hitler and the Nazis, in Britain there was still an undercurrent of anti-Semitism rife throughout British society, which added insult to injury for Jews who were born and bred in the British Isles. My mom had a millinery shop in Cockfosters, the borough where we lived, and every now and again a local racist hooligan would throw a brick through the shop window or daub the walls with anti-Semitic slogans, like "Get out of here, Jew," which, given that my father was away fighting the war like so many other British Jews, was particularly upsetting for my mother.

I remember when my grandfather and grandmother took me to see a famous Jewish singer, Sophie Tucker. She was known as "the last of the red-hot mamas." She was adored by the British public and the armed forces alike, for her earthy performances and morale-lifting songs. On the way home, we were riding on a trolley bus and I was sitting next to Grandma, holding a red balloon that she and Grandpa had bought for me outside the theatre. My grandpa was speaking Yiddish to my grandma, enthusing about Sophie Tucker's performance, when a young man standing next to him, vindictively and for no apparent reason, stubbed his burning cigarette straight into my balloon, causing it to burst loudly and giving me a huge fright. As a young child, I was naturally distraught and burst into tears.

I can remember my grandpa getting into an argument with this horrible man and saying to him, "If you have a problem with my being Jewish, then take it out on me, not my little grandson." Everyone in the trolley car looked at us like we were the bad guys, instead of the nasty piece of work who burst my balloon. After that incident my mother and grandparents decided that it would be better for me to get out of the big city and sent me away to a Jewish boarding school, Aryeh House, not far from London on the south coast near Brighton Beach. Every day, the class would take a walk en masse for our daily exercise, but whenever we passed by a certain Catholic school, they would pour out of the school gates and jeer and throw insults and stones at us.

Cue sound effects of rocks hitting little bodies.

We wanted to pick up the stones and throw them back, but our schoolmasters wouldn't allow us to confront them. They ordered us to ignore them and keep walking, which for feisty young boys was very hard to do. When I told my mom about it, she was furious and decided to remove me from that establishment and enroll me in a Catholic school further along the coast, under the principle "If you can't beat 'em, join 'em." However, I wasn't allowed to tell anyone there that I was Jewish; otherwise, they would have thrown me out. Even so, it wasn't so bad, and I liked singing the hymns in church, mainly because they were in English and I was able to understand them.

Many people in England blamed the war on the Jewish people. The Jews seemed to be everyone's scapegoat. My parents were not particularly religious, so I never understood why being Jewish was such a bad thing to other religions and why we were so persecuted. My religion might have been Judaism, but I was English and so were my parents. My father was like thousands of other North Londoners: he supported his local football team, Tottenham Hotspurs; he voted for the Conservatives in the elections and loved the king and the royal family. So what was the problem?

World War II affected my entire life in a way that I have never been able to get over. To this day I won't buy a German car or go to Germany, other than on necessary business, yet I have many German friends. I am obsessed with the Second World War unlike anything else in my life, and constantly tell my children all about it. They listen politely, but I know they're not really interested, and maybe that's a good thing, who knows? What I do know is that I never want anyone to forget what happened to so many good and innocent people. War brings out the worst and the best in people, and I'm sure there are thousands of stories of unsung heroes from WWII yet to be told.

Fast forward to 1945–1948. The war has ended, and thankfully we won.

I remember my mother packing a suitcase, taking us to King's Cross station in London, and getting on a steam train bound for Leeds in the north of England. Having done the rounds of my dad's family, which included ten brothers and sisters, we were going to spend a few days with my mom's family.

Like most children, I loved steam trains. I can remember the huge plumes of steam bellowing out from the engine as we chugged along rhythmically through the beautiful English countryside. Everyone was celebrating the end of the war. Flags and balloons festooned the stations and houses everywhere. People were singing and dancing on the platforms and in the streets as we puffed by. At each stop, people would wish us well, laughing and smiling, and offer us food and drink.

After so much darkness, it was magical. Suddenly, the world was bright, and in one fell swoop, the gloom had gone. It seemed like the whole world was celebrating, which of course it was. My aunt and my grown-up girl cousins were there to meet us at Leeds station, screeching excitedly and talking with funny northern accents as they hugged and kissed us. It's hard to imagine what it was like to feel that rush of joy that accompanied the end of hostilities. No more bombs, no more blackouts, and, most importantly, no more fear. Everyone was happy to be alive, and we felt like we all belonged to one big happy family.

I remember the street parties that took place across the entire country. Tables would be laid out along the whole street, and everyone who lived on that street attended the party. In my aunt's street, they had set up stages for entertainment at both ends of the block. There were spam-and-cheese sandwich triangles, hot sausages, iced buns, fairy cakes, bread-and-butter pudding, jelly and Carnation milk, custard pies, lemonade, and orange squash—what a feast for a small boy to behold. They must have used up all their food quotas for months to come, as rationing was still very much in force, but nobody cared. They just wanted to have fun. After everybody had their fill, various entertainers danced and sang, did conjuring tricks, and told jokes. People fell around laughing and carrying on. I didn't understand the jokes, but I laughed along with everybody else, regardless. It was magical. Somebody had made an effigy of Hitler and had hung it from a pole with a rope attached to its neck and then set fire to it. We all cheered at this sight, and the whole block burst into dance. They carried on dancing long into the night, which was also a first for me, being only six years old and being allowed to stay up late. What bliss. From that time on, I always associated dance with joy, happiness, enthusiasm, and, most of all, freedom. The only downside to our celebrating was, despite the fact that the war had ended, my father had still not come home.

My mom and dad, Sadie and Samuel

Then, in 1946, with my seventh birthday soon approaching, my mom woke me up early one morning and said, "Time to wake up, Putchkey (my mom's love name for me). I've got a surprise for you downstairs." Naturally, I thought it was a birthday present, albeit a little early.

I wiped the sleep from my eyes and jumped out of bed excitedly. I ran down the stairs, straight into the living room; and, lo and behold, there was my mother standing by the window next to a big man dressed in a khaki soldier's uniform. Mom had been contacted by the Home Office. It seems that at the end of the war my daddy had been in a hospital, with shell blast from a grenade that was thrown at him, and he had trouble remembering the simplest of things, like his family and our address. When she met my dad at the train station, he walked right past her. He didn't even recognize her at first, but she ran to him, and like a scene out of a war movie, she hugged and kissed him many times over.

Backlight the scene and bring in the hero theme music.

The morning sun was streaming through the window, putting them in semi-silhouette and making it hard for me to see his face clearly. "Putchkey," said my mother, beaming a broad smile, "say hello to your father." He moved towards me, and as his face came into focus, I recognized him as the man in the picture I had kept on my sideboard for six years. To me, he looked like one of the heroes in the movies that my grandpa had taken me to see. I'd dreamed of this moment, what I'd say and what I'd do, but I did nothing, I just stood there frozen to the spot. He bent over me and swept me up into his big arms and held me out in front of him. He just stared at me without saying a word and then pulled me to his chest and hugged me so hard I could barely breathe.

"Are you my daddy?" I wheezed, struggling for breath.

"That's right, son," he said in a booming voice. "I'm yer dad."

Then Mom joined us, and the three of us just stood there for what seemed like hours, holding on to each other, with Mom sobbing quietly. As for me, I'd never been so happy in all my young life. My daddy was back from the war at long last, my mom was smiling constantly, and we could leave all the lights on with the curtains open without being scared of German bombers. Life was good at last. And I finally had a daddy.

It was kind of strange, having a man in the house, even though he was my father, given that I had never had the experience before, other than visiting my uncles for short periods. Also, Dad didn't say much, if he spoke at all. I wanted him to talk to me so badly, but he never really did. Mom told me to be patient, as Dad had had a hard time during the war and it would take a bit of time to adjust. Even though I was only seven, I could relate to that and settled for just having him back with us.

A couple of days after he got back, my dad came into my bedroom where I was reading a story book, and without any explanation, he said, "This is for you, son," and handed me a German dagger. I put down the book and took the dagger from him. I remember it being very heavy and big in my small hand, but it was an awesome sight to behold. It was black with a diamond-shaped white inlay. Inside the inlay was a bright-red Nazi swastika. He said that he'd taken it off a German soldier after a battle somewhere, but never elaborated. In fact, he never talked to me about it again. I often speculated to myself on the fate of the German who had owned the dagger, about whether my dad had taken it from him in hand-to-hand fighting in a life-or-death struggle or after he was already dead. Either way, my dad was always a war hero to me. Later I discovered that he was one of the soldiers who landed on the beach on D-Day and that he had been in communications and was always behind enemy lines, the most dangerous place to be. He was later awarded two medals, which my younger brother, Marc, still has.

Years later my mom confided in me that Daddy was a very different person from the man who'd left and that even though she loved him dearly, she missed her pre-war husband, who was supposedly more gregarious and fun-loving and who loved to dance. God only knows what he must have gone through and experienced. He was always very quiet and introverted, and I found it hard to imagine him as a happy-go-lucky kind of guy. I always wondered what went on in his mind when he thought about the war. He didn't talk much, but when he did everyone would listen because he wasn't the kind of man to waste words.

As a young man, my father had been a boxer, and during his short but illustrious career, he won twenty-two fights in a row and never lost a fight. But coming from a respectable middle-class Jewish family, boxing was not considered an acceptable pastime. His family made him feel guilty about it and encouraged him to quit, feeling that it was beneath his station to indulge in such a low-class sport.

I remember many occasions when Dad would endeavor to teach me boxing with real boxing gloves. Thinking back, those were the times when he spoke to me the most and when I felt the closest to him. He seemed to come alive at these moments. To this day, I still love to watch boxing matches, especially world championships.

During one of these sparring sessions, my dad told me a story that has stuck with me all these years. He told me that I was actually named after his oldest sister, Davora. Years earlier, when he had been working in his fur factory, he heard somebody calling his name. He asked the other workers who were in the same room, "Who called my name? Which one of you called me?" Everyone just looked at him like he was crazy. Although he thought it was strange, he returned to his job, nailing a fur skin to a wooden table to stretch it out. Again, he heard his name called and asked who had called him. Everyone thought he was joking and ignored his question. A third time he heard his name being called. At this point, he stopped what he was doing, put on his coat, and went to his parents' home, where his older sister, Davora, was bedridden with cancer. As he walked into her bedroom, she looked at him, smiled, and died. He was told that Davora had been calling his name all afternoon. They were very close, as she was the oldest sister and he was the youngest brother, the child in the family. She had known she was going to die and wanted to see him before she passed. Miraculously, he had heard her voice. When he told me this story he still seemed very touched by it, and I was glad that he shared it with me. It was one of the few times he actually opened up to me.

As my family settled into life after the war, my mom and dad and I loved to go to my grandparents' house every Sunday for family lunches. It was bang in the middle of Hampstead Heath, surrounded by woodland and wildlife. Their spacious house always seemed to be full of my aunts, uncles, and cousins, and rang out with loud, booming classical music, which put everyone in a great mood and made our Sunday lunches joyous affairs.

My grandfather would make great ceremony of carving the Sunday roast, and my uncles would tell funny stories while my aunts would pretend to be outraged, filling the dining room with shrieks of laughter. After lunch, all the younger kids would flood out onto the heath and run through the woods and up to the pond at the top of the heath to look at the model boats that people would sail every Sunday. After running ourselves ragged playing "catch," we would head back to the house for a traditional English meal of cucumber sandwiches, various buns and cakes, and, of course, a nice pot of tea. After tea we would all settle down in the big, comfortable living room filled with soft, lumpy sofas and easy chairs; and my grandmother, Jenny, would play one of her favorite operas on the gramophone. We would all sit back and listen respectfully as she sang along. Unlike my cousins, who thought it was a terrible bore, this was the part of Sundays that I loved the most. While they fidgeted, I would listen, enraptured by the beautiful vocal strains and orchestral music filling the large room. This didn't go unnoticed by my grandmother.

Grandma Jenny surprised me by taking me to visit a synagogue. We weren't really a religious family and rarely, if ever, went to synagogue, except every once in a while on the high holidays. Shortly after we entered the synagogue, a large man stood up and started singing with great power. He had the most beautiful voice I had ever heard. My grandma told me that he was my great-grandpa and he was a cantor at this synagogue. He was amazing. When he stopped singing, we left.

Grandma was a wise woman, and when she saw my reaction to her father's singing she decided to take me to the theatre. My first experience at a theatre was with her when she took me to the Covent Garden Opera House, a famous theatre in the heart of London's West End, to see the opera *Faust*, written by the German composer Charles Gounod. We arrived at the theatre at seven thirty in the evening and joined the long queue reaching halfway around the block. A troop of Cockney Pearly Kings and Queens in their sparkling costumes appeared on the street to entertain us. Every part of their attire was sequined with glistening pearl buttons laid out in lace-like patterns. They looked beautiful. They tap danced and sang for us, with their chirpy cockney voices, and when they finished they came around with the hat to collect money. This was my first encounter with live entertainers, and I loved every second of it. I remember Grandma giving me a whole penny to give to them. The Pearly King called me his "old cock sparrow," and I was thrilled.

We eventually made our way through to the grand entrance, up some equally grand stairs, and out into what seemed like Aladdin's cave. We were high up in what the English call the "Gods," the upper balcony of the theatre, with a perfect view of the stage. I remember the vast auditorium filled with elegant men and women, plush red seats with gold fittings, and the moldings and carvings on the walls and ceilings. The grandness of the decoration was like something out of a fairytale for a young, impressionable boy, and I was stunned by it all.

We found our way to our seats, and no sooner had we sat down than the lights began to dim, the orchestra struck up the intro, and the curtain started to lift. Suddenly, the stage was flooded with light and filled with colorful characters singing at the top of their voices. I thought my heart would pop out of my mouth with excitement, and I sat there spellbound throughout the entire performance. After the show, I left the theatre in a daze, my mind dancing with the sounds and images I'd just experienced. We got on the trolley bus in Charing Cross Road and headed back to Grandma's home. Sitting there in the dull lights, as we rumbled through the foggy streets of a perpetually grey London, it seemed to me like it had all been a dream, such was the reality shift. It was on that ride back, with my grandmother humming the tunes from *Faust*, that I decided, at the ripe old age of seven, what I wanted to do when I grew up.

Cue applause. Cross-fade audience clapping.

I wanted my grey world to be filled with color. I wanted the bright lights and the applause.

Cross-fade to a future me taking a bow on a brightly lit stage.

Me at 7 years of age

On many occasions, I would stay over with my grandmother and sleep with her in her big, soft, warm bed. I would snuggle up to her, and she would send me to sleep with stories from all the various operas that she knew. It was magical, a great way for a kid to go to sleep, and it fired up my imagination. I would conjure up vast landscapes filled with people singing and dancing, just like at the opera. I pictured myself amongst them, dancing and singing. I guess I got that from my mother, who had begun a stage career only to be pulled off the stage, quite literally, in the middle of a performance, by her father when she was just seventeen years old. It's funny how things work out. Being deprived of her youth and her husband for almost seven years took its toll on my mother, who felt that her best years had been stolen from her by the war.

The years following the war were called the Austere Years, and, my God, were they austere. Although there were no bombs or fear of the postman bringing bad news, there was still wartime rationing, which meant luxuries of any kind were few and far between. I guess the austerity got to Mom, and she wanted to leave England and all those bad memories behind her and move to a brand-new country. My dad just wanted a quiet life, so South Africa was chosen as the likely place to emigrate to because of the weather. Also, there was reportedly a good fur trade there so my father could make us a good living. Two weeks before we were to sail, my mom decided it would be America instead, so on April 5, 1948, my ninth birthday, we set sail from Southampton on the SS *Aquitania* bound for New York City and America.

The Cunard Lines' *Aquitania* was one of the top ships of its day. It was the third-largest and second-fastest ship afloat and was more like a floating city than any ship I'd ever seen, and living on the Isle of Wight, I'd seen a few. Bands were playing, and there was a tremendous, infectious excitement in the air as thousands of people pushed to get aboard. Balloons were flying everywhere, and people were shouting "Bon Voyage." As I stood on the afterdeck, staring down at all the merriment happening on the dock, I tearfully thought to myself, "Will I ever see England again?" Mom said we had over a hundred cousins in America, and I couldn't wait to visit them all. Couple that with the fact that it was the land of those fantastic G.I. Joes who saved my life that unforgettable day on the Isle of Wight, and it was: yippee, America, here I come!

Helicopter shot of boat leaving and at sea.

It was dark when the SS *Aquitania* finally slipped anchor and steamed out into the strait of Solent, heading for the vast reaches of the Atlantic. Since it was dark, I didn't get to see dear old England for the last time, and that made me tearful all over again. The following morning, I woke up very early, and I could see the sun glinting sharply through the porthole. I hopped out of my bunk, dressed in my warmest clothes, and slipped out of my cabin, heading for the back of the boat. I had hoped to see England far in the distance, but as in the lyrics "What did I see? I saw the sea," there were no green hills and no white cliffs, just endless boring sea, but as I looked over the side, I saw a large school of dolphins breaking the surface alongside the ship. There must have been at least twenty or more swimming a little faster than the ship. It was the first of many beautiful things I would witness in my life, but remains, strangely, one of the most memorable.

My mom learned that a young Scottish man in third class had died suddenly, leaving a wife and child to fend for themselves. On arrival in America, the wife would not be able to afford a funeral for her unfortunate husband, so the captain had offered to bury him at sea. If we wanted to pay our respects, the burial ceremony would be held at 9:00 a.m. the next day. A collection was being organized to help the widow and her daughter with their expenses, to which my mother and grandmother gave generously. The next morning, as we made our way to the back of the lower deck for the ceremony, we could feel the ship slowing under our feet as we stepped out into a miserable grey morning. It could not have been more depressing. It was cold and damp, with a chilly mist hanging in the air like a shroud. The ship eventually came to a complete standstill, and the crew and others attending the ceremony crowded onto the decks above the burial point. The widow and young daughter looked pitiful standing in the grey mist next to the body that was covered with a Union Jack flag. A lone piper in full Scottish regalia walked slowly around the deck, making that mournful and haunting sound that only bagpipes can make. The sight and sound of all this served to make me extremely sad, and my lip started to quiver as I fought back the tears. Then the captain gave a eulogy that had everybody reaching for their hankies, while the ships bugler played "The Last Post" as two crewmen stepped forward and tilted the board on which the body was resting, and it slid out from beneath the flag into the icy Atlantic waters below. I can still feel the icy chill of that sad occasion whenever I think about it.

Also on our crossing to America, we stopped to help a man whom the ship's captain had spotted in a dinghy floating in the middle of the ocean. He had some disease, and the cargo ship he had been on did not have a doctor or a nurse. Knowing that our ship would be passing that way in a couple of days, they had set him adrift. As crazy as that sounds, it was a fact and one that we all witnessed, as the ship actually stopped right in the middle of the open ocean to pick him up.

My family was pretty well off, so we travelled on the ship in first class, but I liked to sneak down to third class, where all the Scottish and Irish people sang and danced all night. They knew how to have fun, not like first class, which to me was very boring. The rich people would just sit around and gamble all the time and never seemed to smile very much.

Extreme wide shot of New York City... Helicopter shot of the Statue of Liberty. (It's quite a sight when you see the Statue of Liberty and New York City for the first time.)

As the *Aquitania* pulled in, the air was filled with excitement and anticipation. We had heard about it, but had never before seen a skyscraper like the Empire State Building. We weren't allowed to stay in the USA, so we moved on to Toronto, Canada, where we lived for a while.

A film montage showing passage of time... Dissolve to...

Four years later we returned, and not knowing where we wanted to live, we took a bus tour of thirty-six American states. Miami Beach, Florida, was chosen as our new home, but the humidity wasn't comfortable for my mom, so we moved to Brooklyn, New York, where Dad bought a luncheonette on the corner of Ave. U and East 21st Street. Mom enrolled me in PS 234 Cunningham JHS, nearby. What I remember most from that school was when we were all herded into the hallways by our teachers during the air-raid drills and made to sit up against the wall till the drill was over. All the other kids used to joke around and enjoyed the break from classes, but for me it was different, as I recalled the London bombings and it brought back the horror of the war. I would sit against the wall and cry as the other kids made fun of me. They had no idea what I was going through mentally. It was pure torture. I was also admonished by my teachers, who were not aware of my background. At times, people can really be cruel.

While watching TV in those early days, I used to get up and dance alongside all the performers on the tube. I was especially inspired by Gene Kelly and Fred Astaire. But whereas Fred Astaire was smooth and sophisticated, Gene Kelly was more athletic and wore street wear with his muscles showing, so I could relate to Gene Kelly easier. Like all Jewish mothers, my mom wanted me to become a lawyer or a doctor. No way, Jose. My mind was made up. The only thing I had to do was figure out a way to realize my dream. According to my mom, I had been dancing since I was two years old. She would look at me in amazement, as she had no idea where I was getting the steps I used to do. She had never taught me any dances at all. She always told me my dancing talent was God-given, but both my mom and dad were wonderful dancers and used to dance together socially. So, obviously, it was in my genes, and I was more and more determined to find a way to accomplish my dream.

We were living close to the Coney Island boardwalk, so I used to watch the local black kids shine shoes with a rag and a little spit and polish. I studied how they snapped the rag, making this wonderful sound. I found myself an old orange crate and rebuilt it into a shoeshine box. After I mastered snapping the rag, I was ready to start my first business venture, but I couldn't tell Mom because I knew she didn't want me to go into show business. Anyway, as well as shining shoes, I would dance and sing and tell jokes. That went down really well with the customers, and the first day I worked I made five dollars, which was a lot of money in those days for a twelve-year-old kid. I immediately enrolled in a dance school near us called Mac Levy's. After my second tap class, they put me on a local TV show and told me that they had nothing more to teach me, that I was a natural dancer and should really take professional lessons in New York City.

Whenever I shined shoes, I would find out the entire plot of a film currently showing in the cinemas; then I would tell my mom all about the movie, thus covering for the time I was shining shoes. One day, after telling her about a film I had supposedly just seen, she said to me, "Okay, now tell me the truth. What were you doing today?" This time I told her the truth, that I was on the boardwalk shining shoes, and asked her how she knew I wasn't at the cinema. She said my aunt had seen me, and that this was not acceptable for members of our family. She said if I really wanted it that badly, she would take me to the city for lessons on one condition: that I had a bar mitzvah on my thirteenth birthday, which was coming up in three weeks. We shook on it. I didn't know how to read Hebrew, so I memorized the entire book in the short time I had left. I also sang it instead of reading it, making it feel a little more like showbiz. I was a boy soprano, and the reaction was wonderful. In fact, the synagogue offered me a job singing on the high holidays for $250, a huge amount of money. My dad and my mom were beaming. When I reminded Mom of our handshake deal, she stood by it and enrolled me in a New York City theatrical school for children, Charlie Lowe's.

CHAPTER 2

New York City and Show Business

Extended-tracking shot along the tracks of the BMT subway in Brooklyn... Dissolve to shot of subway car arriving at the 49th Street and 7th Ave. station in NYC...

The Academy Award-nominated actor, singer, and dancer Elliott Gould and I first met in 1952 when we were both about thirteen years of age. Now many decades later, we're still friends. We were both attending classes at Charles Lowe's School of the Performing Arts, run by a lovely old Vaudevillian, Charles Lowe, and his wife, Kasha. Their school was different from all the others, as they taught their students to have personality when they performed, not just dance steps. Charlie was famous for this. Some parents would take their shy kids to Charlie just to loosen them up, without any thought of their going into show business. He was incredible at bringing out these inhibited kids. Charlie liked to have us perform even in class so that we got used to an audience. This was a great idea. Even after all these years, I still remember some of his songs and routines. Charlie developed a lot of kids who went into show business. The atmosphere was like a social club. We all were friends with each other, as were the mothers. We rooted for each other, and it was like a second family. In addition to Elliott, Christopher Walken, then called Ronny, and his brothers Ken and Glen were also classmates of mine. The Walkens were professional and worked all the time.

Whenever a young kid was needed for some engagement, the agents would always call Charlie first. I got a lot of jobs thanks to

Charlie. My first was as an extra in the film *"The Clown,"* starring actor and comedian Red Skelton. I'll never forget the placard that was on the casting director's desk at MGM Studios when I went to audition for that job: "IT TAKES 20 YEARS OF HARD WORK TO BECOME A STAR OVERNIGHT." So true!

The school was located in the basement of 1650 Broadway, on 51st Street near the famous Brill Building at 1619 Broadway and 49th Street. Totally devoted to show business, mainly the music business, the Brill Building was filled with music publishers, agents, songwriters, record companies, and production companies. Almost everyone who went in and out of that building was in show business: song writers such as Burt Bacharach, Neil Sedaka, Carol King, Gene Pitney, Buddy Holly, and Neil Diamond—you name 'em. Likewise, 1650 Broadway was filled with showbiz companies and music industry people.

Next door to the school was Hanson's Drugstore, a legendary combination luncheonette and makeup store, where everyone in the industry would hang out and where all the Broadway performers and chorus girls would come to buy their makeup. It was a bustling, energized place, and I loved it. Hanson's would be a part of my life for many years to come.

I was interested in taking some Afro/Cuban jazz classes, so I also joined the Savilla Ford Dance Studios on Broadway and 44th Street in NYC. In my class, I noticed a stunning girl named Joyce Livingstone. She had a beautiful body and was a terrific dancer. She noticed me, too, and we found ourselves looking at each other quite a lot. After class one day, we started talking to each other about dancing, and she told me she was twenty-one years old. When I told her I was thirteen, she said that I seemed older when I spoke. One thing led to another, and we wound up having a soda together. Then she invited me to her apartment and introduced me to some great music. This became a regular thing, and she taught me a lot about music and rhythms. In fact, she taught me a lot about a lot of things. The inevitable happened: we kissed, and that led to making love. What an experience, what an explosion! And what a physical relief. That day changed my life forever. It was so beautiful with Joyce. She was so gentle, so sensual, so careful to make it right for me. She knew how impressionable I was, and she didn't want to ruin it in any way. We knew that it wouldn't lead to anything, so we enjoyed it for what it was: a beautiful meeting of the minds and bodies.

One day I got a chance to perform at Zimmerman's Hungarian Restaurant on 46th Street when a talent scout from NBC-TV came up to me and asked if I'd be interested in being on TV. A few days later, I was in his office and got the leading role in a segment of the TV series *"The Big Story."* Was I excited! So was my mom. She was so happy for me. Mom even arranged for me to get my first four-picture composite as a dancer made. After this show, and because of its exposure, I got a lot more roles on TV shows and then my first Broadway show.

My first dancing composite

My favorite acting shot from when I was 13 years old

My first award, at 13 as Brooklyn Star of the Week, presented to me from Namm-Loeser's Department Store

"On Your Toes," My First Broadway Show

I auditioned for the 1953 revival of *"On Your Toes,"* and I was chosen to play the part that Donald O'Connor played in the film version. I was over the moon, and so was Mom. The show, written by Richard Rodgers and Lorenzo Hart, would be choreographed by the great George Balanchine and directed by the even greater George Abbott. I would only be in the first two scenes because my character in the play grew up. Bobby Van would play the older me in the show, the part that Ray Bolger played in the film.

I showed up for rehearsals and met Mr. Balanchine, Mr. Abbott, and Mr. Rodgers. Three legends in my first show—wow, I was so nervous. Mr. Balanchine and I went off with the two actors who played my parents. Mr. Balanchine explained to us that he was not a tap dancer, so we would have to choreograph our song-and-tap-dance number ourselves. And where I had my solo parts, it would be up to me to do whatever tricks I thought were my best ones. I was stunned. My first Broadway show, and I was just fourteen years old and would have to choreograph my own dancing. As they say, necessity is the mother of invention, so I did it.

Getting dressed for the show was a problem as there were not enough dressing rooms at the 46th Street Theatre to go around, so they put me in with all the chorus girls. I must say that getting ready for the show was almost the best part of the job.

Also featured in the show was the brilliant Elaine Stritch, whom I used to watch in awe every night as she controlled the stage. She was the winner of numerous Tony Awards, Drama Desk Awards, and the Laurence Olivier Award. Sadly, she recently passed away. You may be gone, Ms. Stritch, but you are *not* forgotten! Thank you for all the lessons you never knew you gave me.

For my first-ever Broadway show, my number "Two a Day for Keith and Three a Day for Lowe" opened the show and got a fabulous reaction from the crowd. But the rest of the show was a bit too old fashioned for the critics, and the reviews were not what we call "money" reviews.

Our next shot is of an empty theater from the audience's point of view.

At the first matinee, there were more people on stage than in the audience—definitely a bad sign, I'd say. That night my stage parents and I were given two-week's notice. I was really distraught, and I cried and cried. Joshua Shelley, an actor in the show, comforted me. He said, "David, when one door closes a thousand others open up." What he said made a lot of sense, so I went out into the world to find those other thousand doors. And you know what? He was right.

Years later, I found out that I was the first performer to ever be recorded tap dancing, on the original cast album that we made for Decca Records prior to the opening night of *"On Your Toes."* I had no idea at the time that I was making history. Too cool!

After *"On Your Toes,"* I got many jobs on TV, one after another, mostly through my agent Archer King. Through the years I met lots of actors in Archer's office, people like Peter Falk, James Dean, Jason Robards, Martin Sheen, Elizabeth Montgomery, Tommy Tune, John Cassavettes, Bette Midler, and Ron Howard. I would eventually audition for actor/director Burgess Meredith. I didn't know it at the time, but this would become a lifelong friendship. He became like a second father to me and was one of my mentors.

"On Your Toes" had closed, but I was still working. I was very short for my age, so when the casting agents needed a young kid of eleven, I would be called to read for the part. The eleven-year-olds found it hard to compete with me, as my mind and ability were that of a fourteen- or

fifteen-year-old. I think that's the reason I got a lot of the parts that were on offer. I was also very good at accents, which helped a lot. I got a lead on *"The Naked City"* TV series because I was good with a yo-yo. You never know, huh?

My first acting composite used by my agent, Archer King

Co-starring on the TV series *"The Naked City"*

When I went to rehearsals to meet the director of a new B'way play called *"See the Jaguar,"* I saw this very interesting young actor, whom I had previously seen in my agent's office, on stage in a cage. The director introduced me to him. His name was James Dean. He was kind of shy, but very friendly. He was extremely respectful to me, even though I was just a kid. We talked about Archer King, acting, and cars, and we quickly developed a camaraderie. He told me I reminded him of his favorite book, *The Little Prince* by Antoine de Saint-Exupery, and said I could play the leading character. He wanted to put a long cape on me. He was like a playful kid. He expressed his sensitivity to all things beautiful in life. I was quite impressed with him, but as his break was over, he had to go back to work. I hated to see him go. He said to me, kind of yelling, "Hey, my little prince, I'll see you in the movies." Interestingly enough, we did hang out together years later. By that time, I had read *The Little Prince*. It gave me great insight into James Dean's thought processes. Since the day I first read it, *The Little Prince* became my favorite book. It is the most socially significant work I have ever read. Here's a quote: *And now here is my secret, a very simple secret: It is only with the heart that one can see rightly, what is essential is invisible to the eye.*

By the time I was seventeen I had acted in over 150 television shows. I regularly appeared on such shows as *"The Jackie Gleason Show," "The Milton Berle Show," "Mr. Peepers," "The Philco-Goodyear Television Playhouse," "The United States Steel Hour," "Studio One in Hollywood," "Your Show of Shows," "The Dick Powell Theatre," "Perry Mason," "Love of Life,"* and *"The Red Buttons Show."* This time period has been called by many the Golden Age of Television. I guess my timing was perfect!

During this time, I also appeared on Broadway in numerous productions as well as in a few motion pictures, and I sang lead vocal on some records. I was rarely out of work the entire time I lived in New York City. Amazingly, three weeks is the longest I remember being out of work. I honed my craft as I worked with some of the best actors and directors that New York City had to offer. When I wasn't working, I went to dance classes six days a week for sometimes ten hours a day studying my craft. I felt that this was the only way to become truly great at anything. I was determined to be a great dancer at least, and possibly a great actor. Every time I worked I learned so much from all the other actors, singers, and dancers. I also studied the directors and choreographers because I knew I wanted to eventually do that, as well.

Me and Uncle Miltie on "THE MILTON BERLE SHOW"

Me with Academy Award Winner Walter Matthau

I co-star in the movie "ROOGIE'S BUMP" with Michael Mann

Me on "77 SUNSET STRIP" with Efrem Zimbalist Jr.

Myself and Eliot Feld in the stage show "SANDHOG"

I appeared in the stage production of "THE CLIMATE OF EDEN"

Above are a few pictures from the more than 150 television shows, movies, and stage shows I acted in from 13 to 17 years of age

Top left: Me and Uncle Miltie on *"The Milton Berle Show"*
Top right: Me with Academy Award-winner Walter Matthau
Middle left: I co-star in the movie *"Roogie's Bump"* with Michael Mann
Middle right: Me on *"77 Sunset Strip"* with Efrem Zimbalist Jr.
Bottom left: With Eliot Feld in the stage show *"Sandhog"*
Bottom right: In the production of *"The Climate of Eden"*

My dance photo at age 15 taken by the famous
Bruno of Hollywood, who was known in those days as "the Photographer to the Stars."
My costume was made of orange-colored velvet with sea shells sewn onto it.

Another photo by the great Bruno of Hollywood, of me and partner Joy Ciro.

I'm 14 and in my first Broadway show, *"On Your Toes."*

CHAPTER 4

"Shinbone Alley," My Second Broadway Show

As I look back at it, being in live theatre on Broadway was the best time of my life.

I was sixteen years old when I got the role of Shorty in the Broadway musical *"Shinbone Alley,"* starring Eartha Kitt and Eddie Bracken. Eddie was a famous motion picture star, and Eartha was famous as a unique kind of singer, with this sexy, seductive voice. Eartha was also a very beautiful woman and was always being photographed and in the papers and magazines a lot. The show was based on a famous syndicated cartoon, *Archie and Mehitabel*, which ran in over a hundred American newspapers. It was about the adventures and romance of a cockroach named Archie and a cat named Mehitabel. I got to play a cat in the show...what fun! In one of my numbers, I danced with Jacques D'Amboise and Allegra Kent, both premiere dancers with George Balanchine's New York City Ballet. The show played at the Broadway Theatre.

Chita Rivera, an unknown at the time, had been hired as Eartha Kitt's understudy. Chita and I became friends, and we're still good friends today. I love her! She is so amazingly talented, the greatest. I call her Chita-Bita. She, of course, went on to become a great Broadway star. She's an American treasure.

One of the writers of *"Shinbone Alley"* was Mel Brooks. I remember him well because of one particular incident. It was opening night, and as usual, all the creative people involved with the production were out in the front of the house, ready to watch the show. They were all dressed up in their tuxedos waiting to be congratulated and pawed over by their friends and acquaintances in the business—and ready, of course, to go to the opening night party. The work had been done, and now it was massage-the-ego time.

During the show, I had to quickly run under the stage to make my entrance on the other side; it was the only way for me to get there. As I ran through the basement of the theatre, there was one of the writers, Mel Brooks, with his jacket off, sleeves rolled up, busy doing rewrites for a show that he knew needed them. I remember being so impressed with him, thinking, here's a guy who really cares about the work. He's not out there with the rest of them listening to all the bullshit; he's back here with us continuing the work. I took note of this and followed his career all through the years. I had worked with Mel previously as a child actor on the classic Sid Caesar show *"Your Show of Shows."* The writers on this TV show were Mel, Woody Allen, Neil Simon, and Carl Reiner, all just beginning their careers. Can you imagine being in one room with all this talent? No wonder the show's a classic. I was, and still am, humbled by these oh-so-talented gentlemen.

One morning the phone rang at my New York apartment on the West Side. I picked it up, wiping the sleep from my eyes, and a woman's voice on the other end said, "David Winters?"

"Yeah," I replied, stifling a yawn.

"Hi, I'm Jerome Robbins's secretary. Mr. Robbins saw you in *"Shinbone Alley"* last night, and he'd like you to audition for his new Broadway show."

"Yeah right," I said. "Come on, quit kidding me," and I hung up the phone.

The phone rang again, and it was the same voice at the other end. "Like I said," continued the voice at the other end, "I'm Mr. Robbins's secretary, and he wants you to audition for his new show called *"West Side Story."* We're looking for young actors, dancers, and singers, so do you want to audition or what? Mr. Robbins saw you last night in the Broadway show *"Shinbone Alley"* and thought you might be good for a role in his new show." Her tone convinced me, to my shock, that she wasn't kidding, and I went along at the appointed hour.

Over-the-shoulder shot from behind me looking into an almost empty theater with only six people seated in the audience.

Sure enough, I found myself singing and dancing for the great, most famous and respected Jerome Robbins; the creator, director, and choreographer of the new show-to-be and the hottest and most sought-after talent on Broadway. With Jerry was the incredible Leonard Bernstein, writer Arthur Laurents, producers Hal Prince and Bobby Griffith, and the then little-known and very young lyricist Steven Sondheim. Wow!

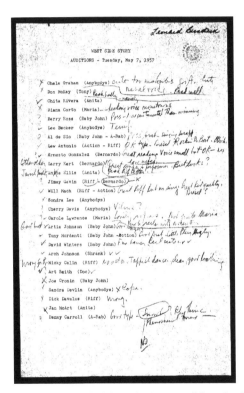

Leonard Bernstein's notes from the May 7th, 1957, auditions for *"West Side Story."* Mine is the ninth name from the bottom. Beside my name Mr. Bernstein wrote, "Fine dancer, Real cute" with two check marks. Thanks, Lenny!

The show sounded very exciting to me, a new musical based on Shakespeare's *"Romeo and Juliet,"* all about gangs on the streets of New York City. As I auditioned I felt very nervous and thought that my first audition was terrible, but to my surprise, I was called back for another audition. As luck would have it, I was called back several times to audition, increasing my chances of landing a roll.

One night backstage at *"Shinbone Alley,"* I was sitting outside the dressing rooms, hanging with Chita Rivera, when she told me that she had also auditioned for a part in the same show. I was delighted and told her I was sure she'd get a part because of her incredible talent. We fantasized about what would happen if we both made it to the new show and how we would become big stars. We laughed and kidded about it, never knowing that this show would actually change both our lives forever. After many more auditions for Mr. Robbins and company, I was told one auspicious day that I had been given the part of the character Baby John, the youngest kid in the street gang called The Jets, and that I was the very first actor to be cast in the show. I was thrilled to bits that they had chosen me from the hundreds who had auditioned. I was told to wait around for a bit to speak to the stage manager, and I overheard Mr. Robbins and Mr. Bernstein discussing who would play the part of the character Anita. I heard them say my friend Chita's name. Needless to say, I was thrilled, so that night I got to the theatre early and let Chita know that she'd been picked for *"West Side Story"* along with me. As you can imagine, she was beside herself with joy. Our dream that we had dared to dream a week or so earlier had actually come true! We hugged each other and screamed and jumped around like crazy kids until we were out of breath, then sat back in a daze, filled with excitement for the future. Little did Chita and I know how much the new show, *"West Side Story,"* would dramatically change our lives, how big a hit it would be, and how much that show would mean to millions of people throughout the world.

I will never forget the lyrics of a song that Eartha Kitt sang in *"Shinbone Alley";* they have affected me for the rest of my life. The song is called "Toujours Gai," and the lyrics are:

I'll sing 'neath a bleary eyed moon
A rousing and rollicking tune,
For no time for sleeping have I;
I'll sleep long enough when I die.

When I first heard these lyrics, as Eartha sang the song in rehearsals, they had an effect on me unlike any other song I had ever heard before. As I thought about the words, I realized that if I slept like many suggest, eight hours a night, by the time I was sixty I would have slept twenty years. Sleeping—what a waste of twenty years. I have a love of life, which I inherited from my mom, and I love the action, just like her as well. She only slept around three hours a night, and I have done likewise. I'm lucky that it has never affected my work or my life in any negative way that I can see. For sure, I have lived a very full life so far, and I continue to do so. I've lived that philosophy ever since hearing those lyrics. I rarely get more than a few hours of sleep.

Once in Vegas, with my dear buddy Marco Derhy, I was directing a film, *"Racquet,"* and never slept the entire week we were shooting. He was so amazed. The crazy thing is, it doesn't bother me at all. At one time I looked around and I was the only one standing on the set. Everyone else was lying on the floor trying to get some sleep. Maybe I sometimes push my co-workers too hard. My mind is always working, and it's hard to turn it off. My mom's was the same. She died, God rest her sweet soul, at the age of eighty-eight, and she was still performing every day till she died, God bless her. I talk to her every day, and I know she is up there dancing with the angels. Wherever I travel, I take her framed pictures and candle with me. I miss her so! She is my guardian angel, and I feel her presence around me at all times.

During rehearsals for *"Shinbone Alley,"* I experienced my one and only Bob Fosse moment. I got an unexpected chorus call for a play called *"New Girl in Town."* This musical comedy was being choreographed by renowned Bob Fosse for the talented red-headed dancer and actress Gwen Verdon, who would be his second wife. She had just played the critically acclaimed role of Lola, in the Broadway musical *"Damn Yankees"* and had received a Tony Award for her performance.

While I planned to audition with the knowledge that I was way too young—not yet seventeen—for this show, the opportunity to dance before B'way legend Bob Fosse was a once-in-a-lifetime opportunity I was not going to miss. I got on stage with several dozen other older and taller dancers, and I did two routines with every ounce of energy

I could muster. After being saved from elimination twice, Fosse asked me to step forward. I knew not what to expect.

"Son, what are you doing here?" said Fosse.

"Mr. Fosse, I know I might be way too young for this show, but I just thought that if I auditioned for you today, you might possibly remember me in the future for another role!" I responded.

Bob Fosse cracked a slight, knowing smile and said, "Thank you, young man. I really enjoyed your dancing." And we never saw each other again. Hearing those words from Bob Fosse was one of the highlights of my young life and made that audition really worth the effort.

CHAPTER 5

"West Side Story," the Broadway Show

We had a really good feeling about *"West Side Story."* After all, other than Steven Sondheim, who was a relative newcomer, all the other contributors were already famous and extremely talented. Very quickly the word spread on the theatrical grapevine that there was to be a very special new show coming to town. Everyone that was anyone in New York was talking about it because the concept was so contemporary and different, and Leonard Bernstein's music was so stunningly original, more so than any musical in the history of Broadway.

To stage a musical about two street gangs, the Jets and the Sharks, that took place on the mean streets of the west side of Manhattan Island was very avant-garde for its day. Racial conflict between Anglo-Saxon Americans (the Jets) and Latino Americans (the Sharks) was considered unlikely material for a musical play. That coupled with the fact that it was an adaptation of Shakespeare's *"Romeo and Juliet"* caused great consternation among the showbiz crowd and really blew everyone's minds. But given that it was being staged by Jerome Robbins, responsible for a host of Broadway award-winning hits, such as *"The King and I," "Pajama Game," "On the Town,"* and others too numerous to mention, and considered one of the best balletic choreographers in the world—well, they had to take it seriously, didn't they?

I found out from Mr. Robbins himself that he had created the show ten years earlier, in 1947, and the story had originally been about the Catholics and the Jews on the lower east side of NYC. The brilliant actor Montgomery Clift gave Jerry the germ of the idea at a party, and Jerry ran with it. In Jerry's earlier incarnation, the show was called *"East Side Story,"* but at that time Cheryl Crawford, the producer, couldn't raise the money for the production because no one thought it would work. A musical about two gangs of kids on the streets of New York? Nah! By the time Hal Prince and Bobby Griffith became the producers, ten years had passed, it was 1957, and the social problems of the past had shifted to the Upper West Side and were no longer between Catholics and Jews, but Latinos from Puerto Rico and Anglo-Saxon Americans. So the creators made the appropriate changes, and the rest is, as they say, history.

Eventually, all the parts were cast, *"Shinbone Alley"* had closed, and rehearsals for *"West Side Story"* were scheduled to start. Just before they did, though, on July 16, 1957, I received another present, one I am so proud of. I became an American citizen. It had been five years since I had applied for citizenship, and it was finally the day, and I took my oath of allegiance. What an exciting day that was for me!

So now back at *"West Side Story"*... The big day came when the entire cast was to meet for the first time. We were all young and unknown and very excited about the prospects for the show. This was obviously the crème de la crème of the young dancers, singers, and actors available at this time in New York City, and we all knew it. We were all proud to have been chosen for this amazing show, and Jerry knew it, so right away he took control of the situation and played us like we were pawns in his chess game.

This man taught me more than anyone I ever met before or after him. He is honestly responsible for almost all that I have done in my life since that first day of rehearsals. I thank Jerry for all of it. More than anyone in my life, he was my mentor. I was lucky enough to perform in three stage productions and one film under his guidance. As they say, "In life, timing is everything," and I am so thankful to have been at the right place at the right time to meet and work with such a true genius.

We all showed up to start rehearsals in a huge studio situated on the west side of New York City on 56th Street and 7th Avenue. I only knew a few of the dancers. I knew Chita, of course, and singer Reri Grist, as well as another dancer and singer from *"Shinbone Alley,"* Elizabeth

Taylor. Not the movie star; this Elizabeth Taylor was a dancer married at different times to the great jazz musician Miles Davis.

Most of the other cast members were dancers with ballet backgrounds, with the exception of Mickey Callan and myself, which, I have to say, made us feel a bit insecure to start with. Plus, everyone else was older than I. At seventeen, I was the youngest member of the cast. Mickey and I started out in show business as hoofers (tap dancers); and even though I was studying jazz dancing, which was pretty strenuous, we weren't used to the discipline and athleticism of ballet dancers, which was extremely arduous, to say the least. I had taken a few ballet classes, but not many. And we were a touch worried because we'd heard through the grapevine that Robbins was a bit of a taskmaster, bordering on the sadistic, and that he was really tough with his dancers, and he was.

To start with, he gave us a long speech about how this show was going to be very different from anything else that had ever been done before—and was he ever right about that one—and that we had to approach the show as actors, not singers and dancers. He wanted it to be very real, very stark, and very shocking. To be fair to him, he did warn us that he would be tough on us. Boy, was that an understatement. All through rehearsals he would tell us that we had to find ways to make the experience personal to each of us, to feel our characters, to actually be them, which we did. In dragging the performances out of us, many of the cast were reduced to tears, but that made no difference to Jerry. He just kept pushing harder and harder. I was thrilled because they were approaching the production more like a play than a musical, which made a lot of sense to me, given the kind of performances we were being called on to deliver. In many ways it was easier for me, despite my young age. I had been working for years as an actor and had appeared in many TV shows as an actor, but almost everyone else had only worked as dancers or singers, so it was a unique experience for them.

We started rehearsals every day at the ballet bar and then moved on to some center-floor work, which is actual dancing. Either Jerry would teach the class himself or his assistant, Howard Jeffrey, would do it. We rehearsed the dance numbers for only eight weeks, which might seem like a lot of time, but with the amount of routines we had to learn, it didn't seem nearly long enough. We followed that up for a further five weeks or so with the dialogue scenes and songs. Most shows don't rehearse that long, but there was so much dancing to be learned that we needed every minute we could find; plus, it was exceptionally tough dancing.

Jerry brought in the wonderful and famous choreographer Peter Gennaro to help with certain numbers in the show, which pleased me because I had actually taken some of Peter's jazz classes before. It was Peter who choreographed and staged the show-stopping "America" number, which would dazzle audiences worldwide and is still one of the best numbers in the show and the movie.

Peter Gennaro rehearsing me and others for "the dance at the gym"

Jerry would bring in clippings from the NYC papers where the headlines were always about some gang members going to jail or a rumble between them, in which kids were killed. These pics and articles were put up on the board for everyone to see and to get us into the mood of the piece. I must say, they were totally depressing and had the desired effect on all of us. I watched how Jerry manipulated all of us to get exactly what he wanted. He was a brilliant master, and he did whatever it took to get what he wanted, without much consideration for our feelings. I realized I was the luckiest guy in the world to be working with him, on what would be the first Broadway hit show of my young life.

Myself and the other Jets rehearsing for the number *Cool*

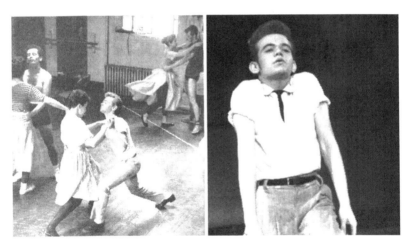

Rehearsing for *"West Side Story"*

Finally we finished rehearsing the show, and we all trucked off down to Washington, D.C., where the show was to open. Not knowing how the show was going to be received was pretty nerve-racking to us all.

It was now opening night, and the show started without a hitch until, during the scene with the knife fight at the end of the first act, a member of the audience died of a heart attack right there in his seat. You can imagine how the cast felt. Our first show, and an audience member dies. We couldn't believe it and thought it was a bad omen for the show. Knowing that someone had died during the show would prove very difficult for us all during the second act. We all somehow felt responsible, like somehow it was our fault.

At the end of the second act, the closing curtain came down and there was nothing. No clapping, no coughing, no shuffling, nothing but dead silence for about twenty seconds, which felt more like twenty minutes. Nothing, just stony silence. The audience simply sat there, stunned, not even moving. Later, we learned that they were so moved by our show that they couldn't clap. We all thought they hated it. But then, just like in the movies, one person clapped and then two and then twenty, and then the whole place just erupted with hysterical applause. The entire audience stood up, and the curtain rose again for bows. I just watched them in awe. My eyes filled up with tears, and I started to cry, such was the emotional release. They were yelling bravo and screaming. It was truly fantastic. This conservative group of politicians and Washington highbrows was telling us, in no uncertain terms, that they loved the show. We were all overcome with emotion as well as a great deal of relief. I realized for the first time that night that I was part of something very special. The cast couldn't help looking at each other on stage during the bows, we were all so happy. The hard work had paid off. We had done it.

Still, the death affected us, and the opening party was a little depressing, until the reviews came out, and then we started to party. The reviews said that Jerry was a genius—what else was new? They said it was an important piece of theatre, as it dealt with a real social problem that was actually taking place on the streets of New York City: gang warfare.

We sold out for the entire run in Washington. The legend had begun. From Washington, the show moved on to Philadelphia and played to packed houses for its entire run. In fact, we sold out every performance in advance, which was a big surprise to everybody involved. However, this made no difference to Jerry, who, as a perfectionist, meticulously and mercilessly carried on his regime of hardnosed rehearsals. In fact, as the reputation for the show grew, the rehearsals got harder and harder. He was one tough cookie, but we all loved him in spite of his harsh treatment. There's a great quote found in an article published in *Vanity Fair* magazine, attributed to Mel Tomlinson, who was a soloist with the NYC Ballet: "If I go to Hell I will not be afraid of the Devil because I have worked with Jerome Robbins." And I thought I was the only one who knew his secret identity.

For example, one morning we were rehearsing at a small downtown theatre that was not a regular musical house; in other words, it wasn't designed for professional dance rehearsals, so the floor wasn't in the best shape. There were slivers of wood and nails sticking up all over it. Unfortunately, two of the dancers came in a few minutes late. Jerry turned and looked at them as though they had just murdered his grandmother, and then turned back and shouted to everyone to stop. He turned back to the hapless latecomers and shouted over his shoulder to the rest of us to relax; he was going to run over one of the dance sequences with the two late-birds. They were both part of a section in the opening prologue of the show where they had to slide across the floor on their stomachs and grab an opposing gang member. He made them rehearse it on this terrible rough surface; none of us could believe it, but like I said, Jerry could be cruel, like a drill sergeant. We all cringed as we heard the horrible sound of their clothing being ripped by the splinters. Of course, the guys were in terrible pain, but to their credit, like good soldiers, they took it and carried on rehearsing. Jerry showed no sympathy whatsoever and had them do it over and over, and when he'd finished rehearsing the prologue with them, he insisted they carry on the rehearsals with the rest of us. Dancing is a tough business. I've often heard it said that to be a dancer you have to be a masochist. I don't know about that, but it sure could help.

Tony Mordente, who played the roll of A-rab in the original Broadway show and Action in the motion picture version, and I used to know instinctively when Jerome was going to get angry. We knew it was going to happen when he began to kick cigarette butts around and move chairs from one position to another. If he was really pissed, he would move them back again, scraping and scratching and getting more agitated in the process. So when we saw him start to do that, we would say to each other, "It's time to move to the back of the stage," and we would surreptitiously creep to the back of the stage, and then some other poor sap would end up getting it.

On one occasion, during the Philadelphia tryout, he had us all stand in a semi-circle at the rear of the stage, and he got up from his chair and started walking slowly backwards towards the edge of the stage, spitting insults at one or another of us as he went. We all watched intently without saying a word, willing the bastard on in the hope that the tyrant would tumble back into the orchestra pit and get his comeuppance. He backed up, tantalizingly, right to the edge; and if he had taken one more step, just one, he would have fallen backwards into the orchestra pit. But, no, somehow his instincts stopped him and he froze. He slowly turned, looked down at the pit, and turned back around. He looked at each of us in turn, slowly and deliberately, with a thin Mona Lisa smile on his lips, as if to say "f**k you." He was telling us that he knew we all wanted him to fall in, but he didn't give a shit. All of us had this love/hate thing with Jerry, but we all respected his incredible talent, which is why we allowed him to be so abusive. He was a true dance genius, and he never let up on us for a second.

Philadelphia was our second tryout city. It worked out amazingly well, and we ended our run with critical approval. Next came the Mecca of musical theatre, Broadway in New York City, the Big Apple. The show was booked into the Winter Garden Theatre at 1634 Broadway, between 50th and 51st Streets, and opened on September 26, 1957, to incredible media attention and excitement. There were lines of people five deep around the block clamoring for tickets for shows months in advance. We were a smash hit even before we opened. People were saying it was the best musical of all time. It was dizzying. I was just seventeen years old and had a leading part in what the critics and the public were calling the best stage musical ever. My mom and dad, grandmother and grandfather were bursting with pride. They came to see the show on opening night, and I introduced them to all the cast. Opening night on Broadway—what a night. The show went off without a hitch, with everybody giving outstanding performances, particularly Chita, who danced her perfectly formed butt off.

When the curtain fell after the finale, it seemed like the audience would never stop clapping. What a triumph. God only knows how many curtain calls we must have had; I lost count after a while. It was unlike any Broadway curtain call I—or anyone else, for that matter—had ever witnessed. Carol Lawrence reportedly said that it was eighteen curtain calls.

That night at the opening party, we all waited with unbridled confidence for the first review to hit the streets. I can remember the stage manager, Ruth Mitchell, sweeping into the room, excitedly waving a New York rag in the air. "I got it, I got it," she yelled. We all grabbed for it and began to read hungrily, but instead of the whoops and yee-haws you might have expected to hear, the room got quieter until it was eventually like a morgue. The first review was not a rave as we had all expected, but was in fact a bit of a put-down. The critic Walter Kerr had nitpicked and found small faults with the show to complain about. We were all so young and thought, "That's it. It's all over. The show's a flop in the only place that counts, New York City." Disappointed and stunned, we hugged each other for support. We couldn't understand. Had this critic been at the same theatre as us? Did he hear all the cheers and whistles? Evidently not. At that low moment the next review arrived, and it was an ecstatic rave.

Our spirits began to pick up again. Then the next arrived and the next and the next. They were unanimous in their opinion that the show was a smash. And with that, the party gained its momentum again, and we were dancing and singing and laughing for the rest of the night.

Chita Rivera was singled out as a star born overnight. It was just like we had fantasized months before when we were still playing in "Shinbone Alley." Chita-Bita was born to play Anita, and when the critics praised her to the heavens, everyone connected to the show agreed. Boy, did she deserve it. She was and is the best ever! As proof, she has ten Tony nominations, holding the all time record for the most Tony nominations earned by a single performer, 2 wins, as well as the Kennedy Center Presidential Award.

The Jets hold down Chita Rivera and put me on top of her

Standing room only crowds, outside The Winter Garden Theater, waiting to get in.

So we all settled into life on Broadway in a smash hit and soaked up the adulation that went with a successful show. Compliments rained down on us like manna from heaven, filling us with confidence and pride. It was fabulous. Remember, I'm a young boy of seventeen years of age, acting, singing, and dancing in a hit show in my hometown. Life couldn't have been sweeter.

The Jets singing the "Jet Song." I'm fourth from the left.

When you're in a long-running show, no matter how good you are, it gets harder and harder to make it appear real and fresh night after night. I managed to keep my performance snappy and sharp by making a special piece of the stage, a 3'x3' area, my personal turf. Every time a Puerto Rican stepped onto my turf, I would take it to heart. I'd go crazy inside, for real, like I really meant it. This process worked extremely well for me and kept my performances fresh, so to all you young performers out there who are going to be in any kind of production of *"West Side Story,"* try it and see if it works for you.

The entire cast of the original Broadway production of *"West Side Story"* recording the cast album, led by Mickey Callan who played "Riff," the leader of the Jets

Three days into the Broadway run, September 29, 1957, we recorded the original cast album of the show, which was a new experience for most, if not all, of us. By this time, I felt like an old hat at it, having previously recorded the cast album for *"On Your Toes"* at the tender age of fourteen. The album was recorded at the Columbia Records studio on 30th Street, known as "the Church," and was produced by the "Godfather of Show Albums," Mr. Goddard Leiberson, who just happened to be born on the same day as I was. Mr. Bernstein personally handled the vocal arrangements and directed us through the process of singing for the purpose of recording, which is subtly different from singing on stage. I can remember all of us crowding into the studio to sing our numbers and then crowding into the control room to listen back to them. It was truly fantastic because we had never heard ourselves sing the songs from the show before. We were always too busy *doing* the show to stop and listen, so this was a real treat for all of us.

Here I am with Grover Dale, Lowell Harris, Mickey Callan, Hank Brunjes, Al De Sio, and Jamie Sanchez listening to a playback of the "Quintet" and loving what it sounded like.

I remember one very auspicious rehearsal. It was a run-through for the special Sunday-night performance for the actors' union, Actors' Equity. This was the only time other performers could come and see our show since they were generally working to the same schedule as we were, making it virtually impossible for them to see other shows. Every show on Broadway did this one performance as a benefit for Actors' Equity.

What made this rehearsal extra special was that Leonard Bernstein himself conducted the run-through of the entire show, and needless to say, it was incredible. We sounded better than we ever had—or would. He had a certain infectious magic and strength and knew how to get the best out of his performers. So dynamic was his conducting that we surprised ourselves with the depth of sound he managed to squeeze out of us. I remember watching him in awe. He was so animated, jumping up and down, never relaxing for a moment. His energy was simply inspirational, and all of the cast were mesmerized by him. He was the epitome of a Svengali.

Singing and dancing in front of your peers is a daunting experience because you know they are watching and waiting for you to make mistakes, but we were all still high from Mr. Bernstein's run-through and gave the performances of our lives in the special benefit for actors equity. Every number we did became a show-stopper. The audience went wild, which was impressive, given that they were all seasoned entertainers themselves and we were all still very young and relatively inexperienced. Other performers are the toughest critics of all, and we had bowled them over with what was arguably the best performance of *"West Side Story"* ever staged. It was pure magic.

Because of the publicity surrounding us, after every performance huge crowds would be waiting at the stage door for our autographs. As the reputation of the show grew, so did our personal reputations, to the point that all the other dancers in the city, from all the other shows, looked at us with total respect. It was important to us, as dancers, to gain recognition from our peers. When we attended dance classes, the other students would stare at us when we danced. Lots of people would recognize me in the streets and invite me to parties and functions. It was fabulous and I loved it. We had all been in lots of shows before, but this was different. This was special— truly special! We were *the* show on Broadway that season and maintained that rep from opening day throughout the entire run.

During the year and a half I was in the show, I shared a dressing room with three other guys, all in the Jet gang of course. My roommates were Tony Mordente (A-rab), Grover Dale (Snowboy), and Eddie Roll (Action). In fact, Tony sat right next to me and so we became very close buddies. To this day, he calls me "Betta Saint John" and I call him "A-rabina", because I was playing Baby John and he was playing A-rab. Our dressing room was directly across the hallway from Chita Rivera and just down the hall from Larry Kert, who played Tony, the leading male role. Because of our close proximity to each other, we all became very good friends and hung out in each other's dressing rooms when we had some free time. We also drove Ruth Mitchell, our stage manager, nuts. We were flying high, and our egos were somewhat exaggerated,

I must say. Because of that, really crazy things happened on our floor. Our floor became *the* place to be, especially because Tony and I were partners in crime, you might say; in fact, we still are today. Tony was my closest buddy in the show and also in the film, and we loved to play gags. I remember when Rock Hudson, the number-one leading man in the world in movies, came to see the show. He came backstage to congratulate us and we all got up from our chairs, screaming "Rochelle Hudson—oh no!" at the top of our voices, and pretended to faint as we fell to the floor and lay there. Many in the industry knew that Rock was gay, but in those days it would have lost him millions of his fans if the public had known. We had rehearsed this gag ahead of time, knowing he was coming. Well, Rock had a good sense of humor and took it very well. He laughed and actually seemed to enjoy our crazy prank. We all had a giggle, even Rock Hudson.

In the last scene of the play, my character, Baby John, has compassion for Maria (played by Carol Lawrence) and carefully places a shawl on her head.

During the run of the show, my mother became pregnant and my brother Marc was born. I couldn't believe it because after seventeen years of being an only child, the idea of having a brother came as a bit of a shock. I had no idea that my folks were planning to have another child until it became obvious as my mother gained weight. Only then, a few short months before the big event, did they spring it on me. But I couldn't have been more delighted. I was going to be a big brother, and that was the icing on the cake for me.

During the run of *"West Side Story,"* I decided to capitalize on its popularity by teaching dance classes at the Dance Center on the eighth floor of Carnegie Hall on Saturdays between shows. Many of the actors in other Broadway shows came to my classes, including Rip Torn, Madeleine Sherwood, and Tammy Grimes. It gave them another faculty to work with: their bodies.

The Dance Center was famous in those days because Marlon Brando, the biggest star in Hollywood, used to sit in on Frank Wagner's dance class and play conga drums with Dean Sheldon, who taught him how to play in his drum class. Before *"West Side Story,"* I had been taking jazz classes with Frank, and remembered Marlon's drumming during many of my classes. Marlon would show up with makeup on his face and a boat-neck shirt when he played for us. In those days that was far-out, to say the least. There was always a large crowd pretending to watch our dance class when Marlon showed up, since he was already a huge star, following *"The Wild One"* and *"On the Waterfront."* He was the biggest male sex symbol in the world at that time. Marlon had studied conga drums with Dean, as had I, but I never got to play with him, which I will always regret. Even today I love to play whenever I get the opportunity. I always have a conga drum wherever I'm living just in case I get the chance to play.

Another young actor who used to hang around the Dance Center was Steve McQueen, who also studied drums with Dean Sheldon. He was a nice-enough guy, but everyone kind of laughed at him behind his back because it was so obvious to everyone that he was trying to be a Marlon clone. He bought a motorcycle just like Marlon, he played drums like Marlon, and he also kinda dressed like Marlon and took on Marlon's attitude. Steve was seeing a friend of mine, Neile Adams.

She was a Broadway dancer who was also in Frank's jazz class and was really doing well. Steve eventually got a role in *"A Hatful of Rain,"* with Ben Gazzara, on Broadway, and to his credit, he received some very good reviews and, as we all know, went on to become a superstar. Long before his fame and fortune, he married Neile, and they moved to Hollywood, where she landed a leading role in the film *"This Could Be the Night,"* co-starring with Anthony Franciosa and Jean Simmons. For quite a while, she was the breadwinner in that relationship. She had the greatest faith in Steve and would constantly reassure him that he would be a big success one day. She sure was right about that.

As most people know, Steve was into cars and motorbikes in a big way and collected many classic cars. It was after talking with Steve about cars that we became friends and I bought the first of my many exotic automobiles, a white 1953 Chevrolet Corvette, the first Corvette GM ever made. It looked just like a rocket—too cool! That car is worth a fortune today—if you can find one! I recently read about one that sold for $600,000 at auction.

The Accidental Drug Bust...

I met Carole Marcus, a very beautiful girl who lived in Brooklyn. She and her older sister were both actresses. Carole was very different from all the other girls I knew. She was very sensitive and esoteric, and that appealed to me. We started seeing each other almost every day. Carole and I went out to lots of parties and clubs, and spent a lot of time in the Village. I loved Greenwich Village because I could play my conga drums in clubs there and I could get up and dance whenever I felt like it. I used to have a real live monkey named Baby John. He was a white-faced ringtail capuchin. Baby John would sit on my shoulder and go everywhere with me. Sometimes I pretended that I was a broke beatnik, and my artist friends in my entourage would do drawings of tourists who would give us money or buy us food and drinks. It was a carefree time, and the world was our oyster.

Carole and I had a lot in common, as neither of us smoked or did drugs, which was rare in the Village, and our industry, in those days. I liked to talk to her, and she amused me. She was exotically sexy, with long black hair and the sexiest lips as well as an amazing body. She also had a terrific personality, and we laughed a lot.

One night we were out at a party and I met a guy named Richard Marxhausen. I hung out with him a few times, and one Saturday he called me up and asked me what I was doing after that evening's performance of *"West Side Story."* I told him that Carole was coming by the theatre and we were going to go to a party in the village. He asked if he could join us, and I said sure. The plan was that he would come by the theatre and follow us to the party since my Corvette had only two seats. When he arrived at the theatre, he asked me to follow him for a minute, as he had to pick up something he had lost in a taxi at the police station on West 48th Street. In front of the station, he got out of the cab, leaned in my car, and asked me to hold a Murray Lee tie bag for him while he went into the precinct for a minute. Murray Lee was a trendy tie store at that time in New York, and I didn't think anything of it. I took the bag, and he went inside. We waited and waited, but no Richard.

Eventually, two men came out of the precinct and headed right to my car. They asked me what I was doing there, and I said I was waiting for Richard. Wow, was that ever a mistake, one of the biggest in my life. They immediately produced their police badges and asked Carole and myself to come with them into the station and not to throw anything out of our pockets. I didn't understand what was happening, but I wasn't about to argue.

In the station, we were escorted to a counter where we were asked to place everything we had on us other than our clothes. I emptied my pockets and put the tie bag and my car keys on the counter, and Carole did the same. As they went through everything, they opened the tie bag and looked inside; then they asked if I knew what was in it. I said no, that Richard had just given it to me and I presumed there was a tie inside. They told me there was marijuana inside and asked me whose it was. I told them that neither of us did drugs and that Carole had just witnessed him giving me the bag. Then they put us in a room and left us alone for a while. When they came back, they said Richard had denied giving me the bag and that he denied even knowing me. We were both in a state of shock. The police explained to Carole that she was fine, but because the bag had been in my possession, I had a really big problem. I was flabbergasted. A couple of minutes ago, we were sitting in my car, on top of the world, and now I was to be charged with possession of drugs. This was 1957. And in 1957, possession of marijuana or any drug was an extremely serious crime. I could see my life starting to slip away. The police were very understanding. They knew that Richard had given me the tie bag, but they couldn't prove it, and more importantly, neither could I.

Although Carole was free to go, she wanted to stay with me. They explained to her that they were going to have to book me for possession of drugs and I would be held in a jail cell, so she would have to leave pretty soon. They explained that when my case went to trial she would have an opportunity to testify as to what she had witnessed. She was crying, and I felt like doing likewise. I could see my career going down the toilet. I wanted to kill this Richard character.

The police came up with a plan. They would put me in a cell with Richard, with no one else around, just long enough for him to acknowledge to me that the bag was his. The cell came with a one-way mirror in it. They tried this, but he kept denying that he even knew me. I really wanted to strangle him, but I had to bite my tongue. I said to him, "Okay, Richard, I understand that you're scared and you're trying to protect yourself. And, okay, I know I'm gonna take the rap, but just as a man, between us, why don't you at least admit to me that it's your dope?"

He said, "I don't know you."

I felt real rage inside, then. This good-for-nothing asshole party person was ruining my life. I started to think of my family and everyone in the show. The kids knew I didn't do any drugs, because some of them did and when I was offered some, I always turned them down.

The police realized this piece of shit wasn't going to say a word until his lawyer arrived. The cops even said to him, "You're ruining this kid's life. Why don't you tell the truth?" He just stared off into space. They had to book me, and I was moved several times during the night. Eventually, I called Jerry Robbins and Arthur Laurents and told them of my plight. I apologized to each of them for calling so late on a Saturday night. They were very understanding and assured me that they would get me a lawyer, who would be in court in the morning when I was formally charged. I was distraught and confused. I tried to get some sleep, but the police kept moving me. I was told they were taking me downtown to the "Tombs." In one cell with a lot of rough guys, they asked me what I was in for, and I told them. When I asked the same question in return, one guy said, "Murder, man." This was crazy, like a Federico Fellini movie.

On Sunday morning, when I walked into that courtroom, I must've looked like I was strung out on dope. I hadn't shaved, and my hair was all messed up, and I had a long overcoat on, trying to keep warm in the cold jail cells. I looked over and saw my mother and father and Carole. I truly wanted to kill myself at that moment. Our eyes met. My mom was crying, and my father had this "you piece of shit" look on his face. I agreed with him. The lawyer got me out on bail, but not before the photographers, who had heard that I was the youngest star of Broadway's *West Side Story,* took loads of photos of me looking deranged. The newspaper reporters were all over me, like bees to honey. All I could think about was Mom; everything else seemed to be in slow motion. We tried to get away from the press, but they were taking pictures, nonstop. I tried to explain to Mom, and she was great. She never questioned me. She said she would always be there for me, no matter what. Pure, unconditional love—for sure, a hard thing to find.

Well, Monday came, and it was all over every NYC paper: "Young Baby John from *West Side Story"* arrested with drugs," or "Youngest star of *West Side Story"* a druggie" and so on. The pictures of me from the show and from court looked like two different people. I went to the theatre early so as not to be caught by the press, who of course also showed up at the backstage door early that night. More pictures and more questions. To tell the truth, it was all a big blur to me.

The cast was wonderful. No one said a word; they were so cool, like it had never happened. Tony Mordente said, "If you want to talk about it, OK. If not, OK." He hugged me, realizing I needed a lot of support, that night especially. When the opening curtain went up and we were sitting on the steps of a building, you could hear the audience whispering "That's him, the little one," or "Are you sure that's him?" I could see people pointing at me. My concentration was non-existent. I was about to cry when Tony said to me, "Keep it together, Baby John." Boy, did that come at the right time. Then Mickey Callan said, "Are you alright, Baby John?" and I said, "Yeah, Riff." These lines certainly weren't part of the show, but keeping in the characters of our gang, the guys all helped me overcome this horrible moment.

Left to right: Carole D'Andrea, Wilma Curley, Mickey Callan, and me doing the number "Cool"

As the show progressed, I was able to forget my reality for a second or two, but then I would hear a whisper from the audience and need the gang's help again. Even during curtain calls that night, and every night that followed for many months, I could see and hear people pointing me out to the people seated next to them. The same thing happened every night at the stage door. All of a sudden, everyone wanted my autograph. I could see that some of the fans felt for me, while others looked at me like I was some sort of freak. I know it's hard to imagine now, but in 1957 marijuana was a much bigger deal.

There is a line in the comedy song "Gee, Officer Krupke" that says "With all my marijuana, they won't give me a puff!" One night on stage when that line was sung, I broke, I went crazy. It was all pent up inside of me, and I had to get it out. I started screaming and tearing out my hair. I didn't know what I was doing, I was so distraught, and I totally lost it. Thank goodness for Tony Mordente. He punched me in the face, and I fell to the floor. When I opened my eyes, he was standing over me, looking down at me with real concern in his eyes. He said, "David, are you alright?" and I said, "Yeah, I think so. Thanks, Tone." I got up, continued with the song, and I don't know to this day whether that audience thought that Tony's punching me out was supposed to be in the show or not.

Regarding the charges: My lawyer told me that he had previously worked in the D.A.'s office, and he said that half of the people they sent to jail were innocent. Most were poor and just couldn't afford good lawyers. His conscience had bothered him, so he changed sides, and I was his first defense case. As it turned out, Richard Marxhausen had left his wallet in a cab three days before, and the cab driver had turned it in to the police lost and found. In the wallet, the police found a formula for some kind of drug, and that was what he had gone to the police station to reclaim. The weird thing was, out of 21,000 cabs in New York City, the one he got in was being driven by a friend of mine, Chad Block, who was a cabbie in the daytime and worked at night in the show "Li'l Abner." What a fluke, what a million-to-one shot. Chad testified on my behalf, and Carole and the police gave their evidence, and I was let off. Eventually things calmed down and I could get back to my life. Naturally, the newspaper article that announced my innocence was about one inch long, compared to the numerous articles about my arrest that filled whole pages.

David, far left, and The Jets performing the comical "Officer Krupke" number

Just recently, one of my old dressing-room buddies, Grover Dale, gifted me the only remaining poster from the original Broadway show of *"West Side Story"* that was signed by the entire cast. There is no other poster like it on the planet, and because so much of my life was devoted to *"West Side Story,"* it is a priceless treasure to me. What an incredible gift, Grover! I will cherish it forever. You have honored and humbled me, and I am at a loss of words for your generosity, your kindness, and your friendship for these last six decades. I'm so proud of what you are doing with your Answers4Dancers agency. You are making a huge difference in the lives of so many young and aspiring dancers by breaking down doors that have existed for too long against them. Dancers everywhere should erect a statue in your honor.

CHAPTER 6

Bobby Darin, a True Friend

I first met Bobby Darin in New York City at Hanson's Drugstore, which was in a building next to the backstage door of the Winter Garden Theatre where I was performing in *"West Side Story."* This building, like the famous Brill Building, was an industry landmark. Lots of music people hung out in the coffee shop inside Hanson's since it was a convenient location, right in the middle of the theatre district. Called Tin Pan Alley in those days, the building was well known, with all of the record companies and music promoters and agents having offices there. Full of showbiz people coming and going, the energy was magnetic. I loved it, as it was all about showbiz.

I met Bobby Darin through a singer/writer I knew from Brooklyn named Al Schwartz. I liked Bobby as soon as I met him. He was a real down-to-earth guy who was just trying to get discovered, like all the other musical talent hanging around Hanson's. Bobby told me he was going to be recording soon, and he was especially excited about one song, "Splish Splash." I asked him to sing it for me, but he declined, saying it was sort of a silly, funny song. I didn't push him on it, but as Bobby and I hung out together so much, we eventually became good friends. His recording session for this song got put off a few times, and sometimes he got depressed about it. I always tried to give him positive energy and lift his spirits.

Over time I came to realize that Bobby was a very loyal friend. He had a big heart and was only too happy to help others in need.

He was a good and gentle man, an incredibly special person, and I am proud to have known him and to have been his friend. We would just sit and have a soda and sandwich and talk about the business for hours at a time. We would talk about some of the people who had made it from the Brill Building, like Neil Sedaka, Carole King, Connie Francis, Buddy Holly, and Neil Diamond. Bobby and I were on the same wavelength, so we talked about the thing we loved most: show business. We talked about our dreams and people like Frank Sinatra and Elvis. Who knew I would one day work with both of them?

Later on, Bobby got me a part in the film he was starring in, *"Captain Newman,, M.D."* He was nominated for an Academy Award and won a Golden Globe for his performance in this film. But what was most special to me was that I eventually got to produce Bobby's own TV special, *"The Darin Invasion,"* with guest stars Linda Rondstadt and George Burns. Life is such a wonderful surprise sometimes!

One day Bobby was talking to me about "Splish Splash," and then he started singing it to me. I thought it was great and told him it would be a big hit and make him a big star. We laughed about it because it was so different and the lyrics were so silly. He was very excited about it, and I was excited for him. I liked the song so much that when I went backstage that night to do the show, I sang it for Chita. I also sang it for Larry Kert and my dressing-roommates. Everyone I sang it to loved it. "Splish Splash"—what a crazy name. Soon, we were singing it all the time backstage at the show. Then one day during curtain calls I started singing it on stage and everyone joined in. By this time, the whole cast had heard the song, and for a while it became our backstage and curtain-call anthem. When it was finally released, we all went crazy because we had known it beforehand, and we all knew it would be a big hit. It was like we were a part of its success, and Bobby's too. I always believed "Splish Splash" would be a huge hit. I assured him all the time that it would be a smash hit, and it was—a huge hit! Along with it came stardom for Bobby, just like I had predicted. But he never changed because, with him, it was all about the work, and he was just so thankful for his success that he never took it for granted, not for a second. He was a true artist, much like the singers in the old days. He was happy to "sing for his supper," so to speak. He became my generation's Frank Sinatra, as he was also a fabulous live performer. That surprised a lot of people in the business. Although Bobby went on to become a superstar and have many hits and win many awards, he always stayed the same down-to-earth Bobby, the same sweet guy I met in Hanson's luncheonette. We stayed friends for many years and shared lots of experiences together, worldly ones and personal ones.

My buddy Bobby Darin's album of his TV special that I produced, *"The Darin Invasion,"* guest starring Linda Ronstadt and George Burns

Sharry Rubin, My First Love

During *"West Side Story,"* I met a lovely girl whom I liked very much, and I started seeing her on a regular basis. Her name was Sharry Rubin. She lived on Long Island and was a model, an actress, and a dancer. I grew very attached to Sharry. My mom and dad and I got along well with her whole family, and I think that everyone thought we would marry one day. I know the two of us did.

After our second show on Saturday nights, I would stay at her house. We were falling in love. I was now eighteen years old, and with no fear in those days of AIDS/HIV, it was a crazy time to be a young heterosexual male.

One night, while I was playing drums in a club in Greenwich Village, without Sharry, I was introduced to this extraordinarily beautiful and exotic-looking girl. We talked all evening. Then she said that she wanted to take me to her apartment, give me a massage and bath, and make me feel good all over. It sounded like it would be an interesting and exciting experience, so I went with her. She was into Eastern philosophies and believed in making sure her man—or woman—was happy. Until then, I had never had such an experience, and it blew my young mind and body away. It was fantastic. I saw her a few more nights and started to become attached to her. I still loved Sharry, but I was getting confused. I had to get my mind back on my work and career and *"West Side Story."*

I had always said that the only way I would go to Hollywood was if they called me and paid me to go. I never wanted to be an actor walking the streets of L.A. looking for work. My best friend, Sal Mineo, had been called to Hollywood when he was on Broadway in *"The King and I,"* and Mickey Callan (Columbia Studios changed his name to Michael) had made the move during *"West Side's"* run. Now I was also thinking about films and Hollywood.

Sally Perle, a casting agent who liked me a lot and had given me work in the past, put together a deal for me to appear in Columbia Studios' *"The Last Angry Man,"* starring Paul Muni and David Wayne. Columbia was talking to me about a multiple-picture contract. The problem was I would have to leave the cast of *"West Side Story"* right away. I talked with Jerry Robbins and Hal Prince, and they agreed and wished me luck. I had been in the show for fifteen months. I was torn, as leaving the show was like leaving my new family. Tony, Chita, Larry, Grover—I loved them all; we had this special unspoken bond between us. Yet Hollywood was beckoning me. Maybe I would be a big movie star one day, like my buddies Sal and Mickey before me. Sometimes I was so happy thinking about it, but at other times I almost cried. It was a very strange time for me, but I knew I had to move on.

Left to right: Godfrey Cambridge, Sally Perle, and me on the set of
"The Last Angry Man"

Sitting in Hanson's Drugstore one day, Sharry and I started to talk about serious stuff. I wanted to be totally honest with her. I told Sharry that I had met this girl in Greenwich Village and that I was confused and needed a week or two to sort out my feelings and consider our future together. I told her to come see me in two weeks at the Winter Garden. I was leaving the show that Saturday. She was saddened by what I told her, but she wished me luck in the new film and said that she hoped I would come to my senses and realize that we were made for each other. She reminded me of how beautiful our relationship had been and how even our families loved one another.

We talked for hours, and I realized again what an incredible girl she was and how lucky I was to have her love. Being with Sharry seemed so pure, unlike with anyone else I had ever met before her—or, for that matter, after her. I feel like it was at this juncture in my life that I truly lost my innocence. For good. I've tried many times to regain it, but it has never been the same since that day in Hanson's with Sharry.

During the next two weeks, I experienced true ecstasy, and, selfishly, I did not want to give it up. My new bisexual friend pampered me like I was a king in a fairy tale. But I was still deeply in love with Sharry. With my movie career about to take off, I wasn't ready for marriage at that particular moment, so what was I to do?

When Sharry came to see me after two weeks apart, I tried to explain my thoughts to her and ended up telling her I had to keep seeing this new girl to see where it led. I told Sharry that I loved her and that I hoped she would wait for me. We talked about love between men and women. We talked about the fact that we were so young, that I was only eighteen and had a lot to learn and a lot of living to do before either of us could make a serious commitment. We talked for hours about everything. She said she thought that she had lost me and started to cry. I held her in my arms and told her she was wrong. I didn't want to leave her, but I had to go and do the evening show, my final performance of *"West Side Story."* She was extremely unhappy and hurt. I felt truly bad and sorry as we parted.

That evening I had to get my head back into work. And that evening was a wild one, with all the kids playing jokes on me, on and off the stage. They had a going-away party for me, full of many tearful goodbyes. Leaving the show was a very emotional experience for me. It had been my whole life for almost two years.

The strangest thing happened, though, as I was leaving my dressing room for the last time and taking my pictures off the mirror in front of me. Of course I had Sharry's picture there right in front of me so I could look at her every day and night when we performed the show. I had other pics stuck up on the mirror as well, but hers was an 8x10 showbiz shot of her beautiful face, and I can still see it in front of me like it was yesterday. I took down all the other pictures and packed them away, but when I took her picture down, I sat and stared at it for the longest time. I wasn't even aware of this until the guys in the dressing room asked me what was wrong and why I was staring at Sharry's picture like that. It was like I had spaced out, and when I heard their voices, it seemed like the volume was getting turned up and I was coming back from a dream of sorts. I had no explanation for my behavior and simply shrugged it off. If only I had been more in touch with my emotions then, I would have realized that there was something about to happen to Sharry and someone was trying to tell me. But with all the excitement and craziness of my leaving, I was blinded by my own ego and the commotion around me. To be honest, I wouldn't have been able to hear anything that night, even if you had screamed it at me.

I had performed on the Broadway stage for the last time as Baby John in *"West Side Story,"* and I left the show with great anticipation of what the future had in store for me.

We are now shooting in the NYC subway on a train going from Brooklyn to the city. The subway car is very crowded and extremely hot.

It was Monday, the first day of shooting for *"The Last Angry Man."* I had been to rehearsals and costume fittings, but today was the day, and I was so excited. I couldn't wait to get to the set and start filming. I was on my way to the city on the subway when I happened to look over the passenger's shoulder next to me and noticed a newspaper story he was reading. It was about a young girl who had not eaten much of anything for the two previous weeks. That Sunday she'd had a meal that had been the equivalent of three or four regular meals, and her stomach and intestines had burst and she died. The article said this case was so rare it would more than likely go down in the medical books. The girl's name was Sharry Rubin. I couldn't believe it. I was about to vomit. I couldn't take my eyes off the page. I didn't want to believe what I had just read. I remember thinking, "Nobody in this subway car knows or cares what I am going through right now. I am in such pain; I don't want to be here." I jumped out of my seat as the train pulled into DeKalb Station and ran out of the subway car and vomited. Then I immediately bought a newspaper hoping that story wouldn't be there and that I was just hallucinating. But no such luck. I read that story over and over and over, till I almost memorized it. I wanted to jump in front of the next train—but, no, I'm not a coward. Still, I felt so guilty because I felt that her death was perhaps because of my refusal to give up the other girl I had gotten involved with.

I called the production people at Columbia and told them what had just happened and that I could not show up for work. I said I understood if they wanted to fire me, but I was incapable of acting or even talking to anyone at that time. I must have been rambling on and on, because they asked me to stay where I was and not do anything foolish; they would send a limousine to pick me up and take me to the set, where I could lie down in the back of the limo all day, and the nurse on the set would take care of me. They offered to rearrange the scenes so that I didn't have to shoot that day. I don't remember much of the rest of that day because I was given a tranquilizer and I was out for most of it. I just remember feeling so guilty, like I had killed her myself.

I went over and over our conversation in my mind, wondering if Sharry might still be with us had I said things differently. She was so lovely, and I was such an ass. I truly hated myself at that moment and many times thereafter. I called her family, and all we could do was cry. Sharry's parents tried to make me feel less guilty, even as I tried to console them.

Even now, the pain and guilt are still present; I have just hidden them away with a lot of other things. I can never erase the feeling that I may have been at least partially responsible for Sharry's death. How can I say I'm sorry to someone who is gone? Why didn't I stay with her? I've been married four times, and here I am alone, seventy-nine years old, and still haunted by the memory of Sharry Rubin. Life is so complex.

Something else occurred later on, for which I have no explanation. Just before I left *"West Side Story,"* I had updated my address book, as I needed more space for my new contacts. It wasn't until after filming the movie that I noticed that Sharry's name was missing from my new book. I went through it, over and over, checking every name. All the others had been transferred except for Sharry's. That was so weird, like I'd had a premonition or something. Why would I not transfer her name, of all people? As I've said before, I will never fully understand life!

On the set of *"The Last Angry Man,"* everyone was very understanding, and Billy Dee Williams and Godfrey Cambridge, two unknown actors at the time, worked with me in all of my scenes and really helped me regain my energy. My contract with Columbia never happened, and they apologized, but I was now out of work.

After completing *"The Last Angry Man,"* I needed to get Sharry out of my mind. I tried to get busy, very busy, and get my mind back on my work. I did some TV shows, and I was offered and accepted the role of Yonkers in the new Jerome Robbins, Jule Styne, Arthur Laurents, and Stephen Sondheim Broadway musical *"Gypsy,"* starring the incredible Broadway superstar Ethel Merman. I also starred in another off-Broadway stage production, *"Half-past Wednesday,"* at the Orpheum Theater on Manhattan's Lower East Side. It was a musical version of the Brothers Grimm fairy tale *"Rumpelstiltskin."* I played Rumpelstiltskin, and the great comic Dom DeLuise played the silly, evil king. I loved doing that show because I got to sing some songs by myself and they had trampolines on the set for me so that it looked like I was flying as I jumped on stage. Even though it wasn't a big hit, Columbia Records recorded all the musical numbers from the show. Mr. Goddard Lieberson, the musical show recording guru, produced the recording. Although the show didn't run very long, it was fun while it lasted.

Poster for *"Half-past Wednesday,"* with my character, Rumpelstiltskin, swinging on a time pendulum

I had a ball recording the album for this off-Broadway show, *"Half-past Wednesday,"* with my good pal, the mad Dom DeLuise.

But no matter what I did or how I filled my days and nights, Sharry was always there in my mind. I never got over her. These are the lyrics of a song I wrote and recorded with Paul Simon. I called it "Dori Anne," but it's actually about Sharry Rubin.

"Dori Anne"
I'm all by myself,
But I'm not alone, you see.
Dori Anne, Dori Anne,
Dori Anne, Dori Anne,
You're always with me.
The rest of my life,
My love will be true.
Dori Anne, Dori Anne,
Dori Anne, Dori Anne,
I will always love you.

Paul Simon & Art Garfunkel

During the run of *"West Side Story,"* I met many people from all walks of life. Two guys I liked very much were Paul Simon and Art Garfunkel. They were a singing and writing team who were then going by the name of Tom and Jerry. They had a local New York hit with a song called "Hey, Schoolgirl in the Second Row," which was a mindless teenage song of its time. Their next record flopped, so they decided to break up, and Artie went to Europe.

It was towards the end of my run in *"West Side Story"* that Paul Simon and I met again and decided to join forces and create a singing group called *"David Winters and the West Siders."* We became partners and teamed up with a guy named Rod McKuen, who became famous later on as a writer, poet, and singer. He peddled our material around town and tried to get us deals. Rod was always meeting with the powers that be in the Brill Building, as he had a lot of contacts in the music business.

Paul and I wrote songs that we thought would be commercial, stuff like "Sloppy Lizzy from the Black Lagoon," I'm sure you get the idea—generally crap stuff. We would make demos of our songs, with me singing the lead and both of us doing the background voices. We also played all or most of the instruments ourselves. I played all the percussion parts and some guitar, and Paul played the rest. He was some talented guy! I also did some live appearances to promote our music, but nothing important came of it. So we ended our partnership, parted ways, but remained friends. We did work together again, much later, after many years apart.

During our partnership, Paul and I recorded a few songs, one being *Dori Anne*. We wrote the music and the lyrics together, with me singing the lead. It was made for a company called Rori Records. For some reason known only to him, Paul used the name Jerry Landis on the album. (His girlfriend at the time was named Susan Landis.) Don't ask me why. I didn't understand it then, and I sure don't now. Another friend of mine, teen heartthrob Teddy Randazzo, produced the record *Dori Anne* along with us. I had worked with Teddy earlier in a film he starred in, *"Rock, Rock, Rock!"* in which I played the part of Melville and got to act in a scene with my dear friend, the gorgeous Tuesday Weld, and the hit singer Fran Manfred. Another friend of mine, Valerie Harper, made her debut in this film. Valerie was a dancer in those early days, but she became a wonderful actress and comedienne years later. Before her success on both *"The Mary Tyler Moore Show"* and *"Rhoda,"* she worked for me in a TV series I produced called *"Story Theatre,"* which was a highly imaginative Broadway show created and directed by Paul Sills of Chicago's Second City and produced by the masterful impresario Zev Bufman. Zev was a good friend of mine, and because of him I went to see the show and loved it, so I bought the TV rights to it. The show was based on the Brothers Grimm fairy tales. It starred an amazing group of actors and actresses, who all had their own illustrious careers later on: Alan Alda, Valerie Harper, Paul Sand, Avery Schreiber, Tom Skeritt, Melinda Dillon, Bob Dishy, Peter Bonerz, Richard Libertini, Hamilton Camp, Richard Schaal—all talented performers.

But getting back to *"Rock, Rock, Rock!"* ... The star of this film was the number-one deejay of the day, Alan Freed, who was famous for his live rock-and-roll shows at the Paramount Theatre in Brooklyn. They were always sold out, and Alan was the voice of rock and roll in the '50s. Every major recording artist appeared in Alan Freed's shows and films. My friends and I went to the live shows and danced in the aisles of the theatre. It was such fun. The '50s were a wonderful time to be young. Everyone seemed truly happy, and life was great!

...

One beautiful, sunny but cold day in Brooklyn, I was driving my Corvette and came upon what looked like a long stretch of icy road in the distance. I thought I had plenty of time before I got to the ice, but it turned out my calculations were off—way off!

Before I knew it, I hit the ice, and the car skidded. I tried with all my strength to keep control of it, but my efforts were in vain. The Corvette was totally out of my control and heading towards a large semitruck parked on the side of the street. It all happened so fast, but I remember ducking my head so as not to be decapitated as I saw the bottom of the truck approaching. When I came to, I found myself under the truck, holding on to the steering wheel with the rest of the car smashed up, lying all around me in pieces below the parked truck.

It was just me, the steering wheel, the axle, and four tires; the rest of the car was totally demolished. To tell you the truth, I was just thankful and happy to be alive. But that was the end of my beautiful 1953 Chevy Corvette, and another close brush with death for me.

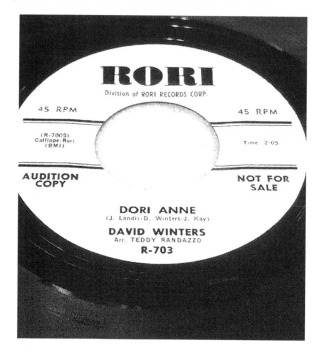

Paul Newman

"Gypsy," based on the life story of Gypsy Rose Lee, the famous stripper, starred Ethel Merman, the biggest star of Broadway at the time. We all knew this one would be a huge hit. And of course it was!

That's me on the right-hand side of Ethel Merman with my mouth open...as usual.

There were some very young boys in the show; and I noticed one of them, a kid named Bobby Brownell, kind of looking up to me since I was older, with my motorcycle, my girls, and my monkey on my shoulder or on my scooter. He was a nice kid, and I thought he was very talented. Later on in my career, Bobby and I worked together quite a few times in the TV and film business. When I became a choreographer, Bobby, who changed his name to Alan Roberts, was one of my dancers. We both changed careers again, and in fact he was my director of photography and editor on my latest film, *"Dancin'–It's On!,"* some fifty-seven years later. It was the third film we made together. On our first, *"Young Lady Chatterley"* Alan was the director and I was the producer. On our second, *"Racquet,"* I was the director, both Alan and I were producers, and he was the director of photography. Alan won an award at AMC's WideScreen Film Festival as best editor for his work on *"Dancin'–It's On!"* I was hoping he would also win best cinematography because his camera work on my film was excellent, but, alas, that was not to be. Sadly, Alan passed away last year. We were friends for fifty-eight years.

After *"West Side Story,"* *"Gypsy"* was quite a letdown for me, and I stayed in the show for just under a year. I loved to play baseball, so during that year, I formed the Gypsy baseball team, and we joined the Broadway Show League. Unbeknownst to most people, every Tuesday and Thursday, you can see all the B'way actors playing one another in this league in Central Park. I liked to play second base, and that is how I first met Paul Newman.

I'm on second base as Paul Newman guards the base and tries to tag me out.

He was starring on Broadway in the Tennessee Williams drama *"Sweet Bird of Youth,"* opposite eight-time Academy Award nominee Geraldine Page. When our teams met, on his first time at bat, he hit a double and landed on second base where I was playing. We kibitzed around and hit it off. I tried to tag him off base but missed. Another time, I landed on second base, and Paul and I joked with one another again.

After the game, we all had some sodas on the playing field, and Paul and I seemed to get along really well and continued the kibitzing that had begun on second base. Many of his co-stars—Rip Torn, Madeleine Sherwood, etc.—had told Paul about my dance class, which they attended on Saturdays between the matinee and evening shows. Paul told me he had heard good things about it and that he was seriously thinking of coming. I saw him many more times backstage at his show when I would pick up my pal Madeleine Sherwood after the performance. Many years later, Paul and I became partners in a racing film, *"Once Upon a Wheel,"* as well as in some racing cars, which was fabulously exciting. At this time, though, I had to stop giving dance classes as a new opportunity arrived.

"Oliver," the London Musical

I met the prolific multiple-award-winning British songwriter Lionel Bart during the run of *"West Side Story."* Until Sir Andrew Lloyd Webber, more recently, Lionel Bart was the only English writer to ever have four shows running at the same time in the West End in London. Now he was about to do a new show, a musical version of the classic story *"Oliver,"* and he wanted me to be a part of it. *All right!* How exciting, I thought, to go back to my country of birth, and in a Lionel Bart show, no less—incredible! *"Oliver"* would star Georgia Brown, who was a big stage performer in London, and Lionel asked me to come to England to play the part of the Artful Dodger in the show. It was a wonderful part, really well written. So he sent me a ticket, and when I arrived, he, Georgia, and I worked on the songs I would sing in the production. The music was great, and I knew it would be a big hit. I was excited about this show. Because it was new, I would be creating another original part in another original show. What a way to return to London!

So I started rehearsals with Georgia Brown, and during our rehearsals, I received a call from Jerry Robbins telling me that he wanted me to appear in the movie version of *"West Side Story."* They were about to shoot it, which meant I couldn't do both *"Oliver"* and the film *"West Side Story,"* so I had to make a choice. Truthfully, I needed a moment or two to think it over, so right away I called my mom in the US. She had received calls from Jerry and co-director

Robert Wise asking her where I was and telling her they had this great opportunity for me. But for me it was not an easy choice. Mom recommended that I come back to the US and do the film, and eventually I did, but only after I had negotiated an agreement with both Jerome and Robert that guaranteed me one of the three major parts in the Jets gang—either Baby John, the role I had created on Broadway; A-rab; or Action. I figured I was too young for the role of Action, but either of the other parts was fine with me. *"Oliver"* was great, but who knew, maybe I was wrong and it wouldn't be a hit. And even if it was, it was just on the London stage and I would probably grow out of the part very quickly, whereas *"West Side Story,"* as a film, would be seen all over the world, and I knew it would probably win an Academy Award. (I was wrong; it won ten Academy Awards, including Best Picture.)

I had always wanted to go to Hollywood, and here was my chance, staring me in the face. And I had many friends already there. Teenage idols of the time Sal Mineo, Michael Callan, Jimmy Darren, and Tommy Sands were just some of my friends out in L.A. So I thanked Lionel for the opportunity and said I hoped we'd work together again sometime in the future, which it turns out we did. He said to me, "We'll always stay friends," and we did till the day he died. He said he understood and wished me lots of luck. I immediately jumped on a plane back to New York, and then to Hollywood.

In New York, my Mom was so excited, but also scared. Just like all Jewish moms, she told me to be careful, eat well, and get plenty of rest.

She cried, I cried; she was going to miss me, and I her. She made me promise to write and call, and then she told me to save my money and not to call—such a Jewish mother. I loved her to pieces. She always thought of me as her baby, even to the day she died. But here I was, just nineteen, and leaving her. I had never lived in a city without my parents, and she was worried about me getting involved with the wrong people, like I had in the past. Marc, my little brother, was getting older, and I knew I would miss his growing up, and my being in Hollywood would probably affect our relationship somehow. I'm happy to say it didn't that much, and we're still very close. But this was an opportunity of a lifetime and one I had been dreaming about now for quite some time. So off I went, with my head flying in the clouds.

Whip pan to the Hollywood sign...

CHAPTER 11

"*West Side Story,*" the Movie

We are now shooting from a helicopter as it passes by the homes of the movie stars who live in the Hollywood Hills above Sunset Boulevard.

My best friend, Sal Mineo, was now a major star and teenage idol because of his performance alongside James Dean and Natalie Wood in the now classic film *"Rebel without a Cause."* Sal invited me to stay at his house in the Hollywood Hills overlooking Sunset Boulevard, and I was happy to take up his offer.

One day he loaned me his little classic Ford Thunderbird convertible. As I was driving down the hill, the brakes gave out, and I crashed into a wall, and the car was left dangling as if on a string. I thought, if I move, it will topple over and kill me. The woman who owned the house came running out and never asked me if I was okay; she just told me not to move and scolded me for losing control of the car. She also complained about my ruining her garden and flowers. Oh my God, she was a nutcase! She eventually called the police; then a fire engine arrived, and the firemen got me out safely. Jeez, I thought, Sal's gonna be pissed with me. But he was more concerned about me than he was about the car. He was a great guy and a true friend.

Now the time had come to rehearse at Samuel Goldwyn Studios before shooting there, as well as on the streets of NYC. Samuel Goldwyn Studios had the largest soundstage in Hollywood. It was actually two sound stages joined together with a huge door in the middle. For some of our street scenes, they needed a studio that large. Years later, it was the only studio big enough for the *"Donny and Marie Show"* since we needed a huge indoor skating rink.

Left to right: Jay Norman, Russ Tamblyn, and me goofing off during ballet class

Jerry Robbins, on the left, with a megaphone, giving us a ballet class before rehearsals and filming begins in New York City

And so we began. I met Rita Moreno, Natalie Wood, Richard Beymer, and Russ Tamblyn—all from Hollywood, none of whom had ever done the show on stage. The six of us from the original stage production who made it into the film were artistic snobs, and we resented these "Hollywood" actors. They had to work extra hard to gain our respect. Tony Mordente and I gave Rita, especially, a hard time because we were upset that Chita-Bita didn't get the role. Rita had been in many movies, and the executives were afraid that the movie-going public might not respond well to this unique film, with all of us in gangs, singing and dancing on the big screen. They wanted as much protection as they could get, but we weren't into the business of it; we just wanted our original mates to be with us. I must give Rita credit, though. She was great in the film and won the Academy Award for best supporting actress. She won us all over, and we became great friends.

First, they took stills and publicity shots of the entire cast. Then rehearsals began, and we rehearsed for what seemed forever. During rehearsals, I met a cute, sweet, young dancer named Taffy Paul. Since I didn't have a car, she used to drive me to work sometimes, and she showed me some of the city, too. It turned out that Taffy was under eighteen years of age, and the producers did not want a problem with scheduling time off the set for her studies, leaving only a few hours a day for work. So they let her go, which was sad, but she became a famous actress and still is. Her name is Stefanie Powers. You might have seen her in *"Hart to Hart," "The Man from U.N.C.L.E.,"* or one of the many films she's been in. She sure was a helpful and very giving person, and she made me feel at home in my new surroundings.

Left to right: Tony Mordente, Tucker Smith, me, Eliot Feld, and Russ Tamblyn rehearsing for the opening prologue

Left to right: me, Jay Norman, David Bean, and Tony Mordente

Although we rehearsed *"West Side"* for many months, I didn't find out what part I was going to play until we were close to filming. Eventually, Jerry called me into his office and told me I would be playing A-rab, but I would still be dancing and singing the solos I had created as Baby John in the original show. I was ecstatic with this decision, to say the least. Jerry decided to dye my hair strawberry blonde, so I had to go to Cinema Hairstylists on Sunset Boulevard every three weeks to have it colored. I hated this because I got scabs on my scalp, and it hurt whenever I combed my hair.

Here I am as A-rab, dancing the solo from the number "Cool", in the film that I originally did as Baby John in the Broadway show.

Me dancing the Baby John solo, "Cool" in the film as A-rab

Us guys from New York City, we were all wise guys, especially Tony and I. We knew it all. I was nineteen going on forty. I don't think the Hollywood set was expecting anything quite like us. Even Jerry was surprised by our antics on the set. There was no controlling us; it was like the inmates taking over the asylum. For instance, after we finished filming the grueling number "Cool," we put our kneepads into some trash cans and set them on fire. The studio had to call the fire department to put out the fire, as we hid, laughing. We heard that they were really pissed at us about that. Then, one day, we were in Natalie's dressing room when they called her to the set. We put ketchup on Natalie and ourselves, then we threw the furniture every which way and then laid down on the floor pretending to be dead. The assistant director, Robert Relyea, came to get her for her scene. He couldn't believe his eyes and got really scared and went back to the set crying and screaming that we had all been stabbed and murdered. This set off a rumor that lasted for days. It was so funny, although it stopped production for a few hours while we all had to clean up, get new costumes, and get made up again. Somehow the story got out to the press and, boy, was that a giggle. We absolutely drove them crazy.

We created so much havoc, it's a wonder they didn't fire us.

In between all this craziness, while we were waiting to shoot our scenes, Russ Tamblyn and I used to play cards. I'm very good with numbers, so through the years I've won a lot of money this way. And Russ was no different, he was an easy mark for me. Everyone on the set told him to stop, but he never did. Months later he finally got the message, but by that time I had already won a fortune from him.

One of my favorite stories from the filming of *"West Side"* comes from when we were shooting on location in New York City, and it was so hot and humid that it was impossible to stay dry or cool. There wasn't a cloud in the sky, so Tony Mordente said to me, "Hey, David, get me

God on the telephone, please," so I pretended to be a switchboard operator and dial God for him.

"What does God have to say, Tony?" I asked.

"God says to do a rain dance," he answered.

So I got all the other guys together, and we did an American Indian rain dance. Well, five minutes later it started pouring. Robert Wise was so mad that he made all the Jets involved in the rain dance rehearse all afternoon, and as he was leaving he said, "And by the way, there will be no more rain dances." We had a great laugh that afternoon, but we were also pissed that we had to rehearse since we already knew what we had to shoot. As it turns out, Bobby Banas filmed this whole scene, and I've heard that some of the rain dance appears in the latest MGM video put out about the film.

I became very friendly with Natalie Wood, and I recall her telling me that she was terribly afraid of water and that she used to dream about drowning. In fact, she did die by drowning. How prophetic and strange that turned out to be. She was such a sweet and unassuming girl. Just before she died, Robert Wagner, Natalie, my girlfriend, and I were sitting in the lounge of Caesar's Palace in Las Vegas and Nat and I were singing the score from *"West Side Story."* Natalie liked to drink, and she was feeling no pain. Robert came up and whispered in my ear, asking me to finish singing with Natalie; he could see that Nat was going downhill. I said sure, and we planned to meet in the morning. I never saw Natalie Wood again.

I had brought my pet monkey with me from New York. Well, one day, while we were out, he jumped off my shoulder and ran into a synagogue, of all places. Man, was I embarrassed. There I was, running all over the synagogue chasing my monkey, but no one else could see the monkey, so they thought I was some kind of nut, just running wildly and yelling through their synagogue. That was until the monkey scared the shit out of the head rabbi by jumping on his head and screaming in monkey talk. The rabbi went nuts, but after much coaxing, Baby John finally came to Daddy's shoulder. That rabbi was sure scared.

We went to New York City for a week to shoot some location scenes, but a guy got knifed where we were filming, and it ended up taking a month to do our scenes. Actually, we never finished all the scenes they had planned to shoot in New York. Jerome Robbins was a perfectionist, and he kept coming up with these brilliant ideas that took time to set up and film.

I worked on the film of *"West Side Story"* for a year and a half—longer than anyone else.

During the time we were in New York, we really got into our parts. We used to go through the halls of the hotel we were staying in, looking for guys from the other gang. When we found them we would jump them, and they did likewise. We had lots of fights in the hallways, and when Tucker Smith, who played Ice, got a cut on his nose the night before his big close-up, we were banned from any more of this type of behavior.

Jerome Robbins was pure genius, but because of his creativity, the film was way over budget, and the powers that be were getting nervous. Every day for weeks on end, we heard rumors about Jerry getting fired. He was co-directing the film with Robert Wise. Robert had started as an editor with Orson Welles and was a brilliant editor, working on such films as *"Citizen Kane"* and *"The Magnificent Ambersons,"* and had become one of the top-five film directors in the world, with Academy Awards for *"The Sound of Music"* and *"I'll Cry Tomorrow."* The idea was that Jerry would put his magical creative touch on the musical sequences and then kind of co-direct, in second position, with Robert when it came to the dramatic scenes.

Well, eventually the unthinkable happened. The Mirisch brothers fired Jerry. They actually fired the genius who created the entire project and was responsible for making the film a masterpiece. I then found out that, from the start, the Mirisch brothers had never wanted Jerry as the director. They had only offered him the position of choreographer, but he'd turned them down because he wanted to direct the film. They wouldn't let him direct it, so they compromised and got Jerry to choreograph by letting him co-direct with Robert. We were all so mad. How could you fire the man who had created, directed, and choreographed this one-of-a-kind masterpiece? Only in Hollywood, I tell you.

The production budget had doubled with Jerry at the helm, and he never made films in Hollywood again. In a quiet moment, he once said to me, "David, if you put an artist in a factory, he will go crazy"—a statement never so true as with Jerome Robbins and Hollywood. They were not meant for each other, and Jerry knew it! In what seemed like an instant, he was gone, and subsequently, it was never the same. Inspiration left all of us, and I can tell the difference when I look at the different scenes in the film. Even so, because of Jerry's touch, "West Side Story" won ten Academy Awards. Robert Wise was a lovely man, and certainly not without a great deal of talent, but when it came to musicals, he and Jerry were worlds apart. Jerry was the master, but I must say that Robert gave him the respect he so rightly deserved.

As it turned out, I liked making films and was enjoying myself in Hollywood, so I decided to stay and try to get more work after the film was finished. However, staying in Hollywood meant I had to have a car, as it is so spread out and there was no public transport at the time. So I moved into a house in Laurel Canyon, just off the Sunset Strip, and bought my second car, a 120 XK Jaguar convertible. Wow, was it a beauty! I loved it to death. Such a great feeling—driving it in the open air.

I loved cars, and through the years I wound up buying many expensive and exotic ones, including seven more Jaguars, ten Rolls Royces, an Austin Healy, and an Excalibur. Since I didn't drink or smoke or do drugs, cars and girls were my only two vices. When I had time, I'd go to London, buy a Rolls Royce, and ship it back to LA, as it was a lot cheaper to buy there. You might say I had a love affair with exotic cars.

After filming *"West Side,"* Jerry decided to direct his first drama, back in New York City, and he asked me to act in it. It was very interesting for me because Jerry, who was the master of dance, was now in an area he didn't feel as confident in—a straight drama. He was actually much easier to work with, and I saw a totally different human being. For whatever reason, even in *"West Side Story,"* Jerry was never mean to me; and, surprisingly, during this dramatic production, he was really open and understanding, friendly and kind. What a change from the monster I had seen come out and strike at many of the dancers during those tough days of *"West Side Story."*

The play was actually two plays by the very talented and now famous American writer Arthur Kopitt. *"Oh Dad, Poor Dad, Momma's Hung You in the Closet and I'm Feeling so Sad"* was the first, and *"Sing to Me through Open Windows,"* the play I was to act in, was the second. I would also understudy the lead actor, Austin Pendleton, in the first play, and vice versa. It was a wonderful opportunity for me, since once I came on stage I never left for the entire play. I played a ten-year-old boy who became a forty-five-year-old man right before your eyes. I kept switching between them on stage. It was a fabulous part and a terrific, uplifting experience. Too bad the play I was in got cut from the program. The producers felt that, with both plays, it was just an interesting evening in the theatre, not the kind of smash hit they were looking for. But the other play was so way-out that they felt they might get incredible reviews and it would be a smash hit. So there I was, cut again, for the second time in my career. Oh well, I thought, now you're an adult, and you must take the good with the bad. I was very grateful to Jerry for hiring me for this project and for his belief in me through all these years and through all these productions. Who knows? Maybe I hold the record for the actor appearing in the most Jerome Robbins productions. Even with all his craziness, there was never anyone like Jerome Robbins. Thanks, Jerry. I am truly honored to have worked with you. You were the biggest creative influence in my life.

Since I was now back in New York, I decided to go back to dance class with a vengeance. I returned to my old ten hours a day, six days a week, with every teacher possible. I even went to ballet class and wore tights. Some of my teachers were the great Eugene Louis "Luigi" Facculto, Rod Alexander, Arleigh Peterson, Matt Maddox, Mr. Dugodofsky, Frank Wagner, and Peter Gennaro. I also went back to tap class to brush up my technique as a hoofer, with Danny Hoctor, my teacher when I was young. Being in tap class brought back so many memories of Charlie Lowe and my classes at thirteen years of age with Elliott Gould and Christopher Walken. These are things that stay with you all of your life, and in many ways, the memories are much sweeter than the reality.

That's me third from the front as we do a ballet bar before shooting on the streets of New York City

The cool Jets showing everyone who owns the street as they snap their fingers and dance along the sidewalk

Shots from the Prologue of *"West Side Story"*

The Jets dancing down the street in the prologue, with the local people watching and cheering us on, New York style
This sequence was filmed on West 68th Street where they had torn down all the tenements to get ready for the construction of Lincoln Center.

Left: My character, A-rab, having fun at the expense of Anybodys, the tomboy who desperately wants to be a part of our gang, the Jets
Right: A picture of me from the Officer Krupke song

My First Cannes Film Festival

The sequence begins with a soaring plane ride high in the sky through the clouds, and goes from New York City to Paris.

Thomas Quinn Curtiss, a friend of mine and the drama critic for *The Paris Herald Tribune,* a position he kept for forty years, asked me if I would like to be a special guest of the Cannes Film Festival. What a question! "Of course" was my answer, without missing a beat. *"West Side Story"* had opened in France at the George V Cinema. It eventually became the longest-running film in the history of France at 249 weeks straight, a record that still stands today!

Thomas lived in Paris and was one of the very few Americans—I think there have been three—who have received the French Legion of Honour, the highest award given by France. He was also famous for taking beautiful movie stars, such as Marlene Dietrich and Paulette Goddard, to dinner at the world-class restaurant La Tour D'Argent in Paris. If you ever get a chance to eat in this restaurant, please do yourself a favor and go. It has been in the same location since 1582—over 436 years. That alone boggles the mind. Thomas lived on the second floor of this fantastic restaurant. He had a dumbwaiter that went directly from La Tour D'Argent's kitchen to his dining room. Having eaten this way on numerous occasions, I can vouch for the dumbwaiter's existence. In fact, in those days, if you ordered scrambled eggs at La Tour D'Argent, the menu referred to them as *Oeufs Brouille le Thomas Quinn Curtiss.*

The amazing view from the La Tour D'Argent restaurant, showing the Notre Dam Cathedral on the left hand side, with the Seine river running in the center

He knew everyone in Paris, so he pulled some strings and got me invited to the Cannes Film Festival as a special guest. The festival coincides with the Grand Prix de Monaco, so everyone from the festival goes to Monaco to watch this world-famous race. It's an exciting time to be there, for sure!

We are now soaring over the magnificent yachts that populate the marinas in the South of France, in such famous resorts as St. Tropez, Cannes, Juan-Les-Pins, Antibes, and Nice.

Landing at the Côte d'Azur Airport in Nice, I was picked up by one of the festival's own personal limousines reserved for the stars and taken directly to my suite at the Martinez Hotel in Cannes, a few miles down the coast—pretty cool. I was totally impressed with myself! The Martinez, one of those grand European hotels, sits right across from the beach in the middle of Cannes, placing it right in the center of the festival. They say that if you just sit on the terrace of the Martinez or the Carlton Hotel, you will see everyone who is at the festival. Marcel, a Frenchman in his early thirties, was assigned to be my interpreter for the duration of my stay. He would get me anything I wanted and make sure that everything was OK. He was an easy-going guy who made me feel comfortable whenever he was around.

The festival was a blast—lots of film premieres, lots of parties, and lots of beautiful women from all over the world, most of them actresses and models, of course. One day I wanted to go water skiing right in front of the hotel. Marcel arranged everything, and while we were out at sea, just off shore, I saw a fabulous-looking girl lying on the pier. By now, Marcel and I had become bosom buddies, and I asked him if he would see if she spoke English, because I'd love to invite her out with me that evening. He obliged and came back to the boat to tell me she did not, but he had learned that she was an Italian starlet brought to the festival by a well-known producer from Italy. She had also seen me and wanted to invite me to her suite tomorrow at 3:00 p.m. Who was I to say no?

Tomorrow took too long to come, but at exactly 3:00 p.m. I knocked on her suite door. She was stunning, dressed wild, just like a cheetah; and even if I had spoken her language, I would have been at a loss for words. It was like I was in a film: this wasn't real. We tried to communicate, but our attempts always ended up in laughs. The last laugh became a kiss and then love-making. There I was, just a young boy, making love with an Italian movie star! It was two hours of heaven on earth. Then she looked at her watch, and a worried look came over her face. She had lost track of time, just like I had. She motioned and spoke very quickly in Italian, and I got the message, loud and clear. Someone was expected, and they wouldn't be happy to find me there. She helped me get my clothes on, and kissy-kissy, before you could count to ten, I was almost literally thrown out of the suite into the hallway. And wouldn't you know it, as I landed in the hallway there was "the someone" at the other end, a short, bald Italian-producer type with a big bodyguard, who resembled a Mac truck. The producer type yelled at me, and I don't think it was a compliment, as I saw the bodyguard draw a gun out of his jacket. I couldn't believe this was happening to me. I turned tail and ran as fast as I could down the stairs. I gave a quick look around and—oh my God, they're chasing me. Where the f**k is Marcel when I need him? I ran down to another floor, and as I snuck a peek, they were still on my trail, still with gun in hand, and still cursing me in Italian. Somehow I was learning Italian very quickly.

Another stairway, another, another, and another—I was getting dizzy because the stairways in the Martinez are all circular. I was also expecting a bullet at any second. My heart was beating so fast. What could I do? I saw a closet in the hallway and quickly hid in it, hoping I had lost them. Like a bad French farce, my foot caught in a washerwoman's pail. Now I was stuck and couldn't move if I had wanted to. Steady with the breathing, I told myself as I heard them in the hallway. Eventually, their voices faded to nothingness, but I was afraid to step out. I waited for hours until I saw darkness under the crack of the door and then hall lights being turned on. I peeked out and saw lots of pairs of shoes left in the hallway to be shined for the morning. I carefully snuck down to the second floor and looked into the lobby, and I saw the little, bald producer talking to my love (I never did get her name) in a very animated way, with his arms flailing around all over the place (you know emotional Italians), with the bodyguard looking all around, I think, for me. She seemed to have weathered the storm, and they all went off to see the movie premiere. I ran to my room, called the concierge, and asked, "When does the next train leave for Paris?" After he told me 9:00 p.m. I booked a ticket on the SNCF train (Couchette) to Paris—I couldn't get out of there soon enough. I didn't even have time to say goodbye to Marcel or Thomas, and we didn't have mobile phones in those days.

The train was an uncomfortable overnight journey, but I was lucky to be alive. The next morning in Paris, I called everyone to explain. There were howls of laughter on the other end of the phone, and eventually on my end also, as I started to see the humor of it all. And so ended my first trip of many to the Cannes Film Festival.

Years later I shot a film in Cannes, and many of the shots filmed during a chase sequence at the Martinez Hotel were copies of my real adventure. I never knew for sure who that actress was, but I saw pictures on an Italian film poster of a movie star who looked exactly like my first Cannes lover. I've never told anyone her name. Now don't you be rude and ask me!

Because of "*West Side Story*'s" being the most successful and popular film in the history of France, even to this day, whenever I visit Cannes or Paris I have many fans who want my autograph, time and time again. I just sign and smile. It is a great feeling to have been a part of something so creative and lasting. As everyone now says, it's a classic!

CHAPTER 1 3

Bobby, Elliott & Barbra, and Andy, Circa 1962

By this time, my buddy Bobby Darin had become one of the top stars in the music industry—on records, in live concerts, and on film. He deserved it, for he was an extremely talented guy, a true musical genius. He had many number-one hits, like *"Mack the Knife"* from *"The Threepenny Opera,"* *"Beyond the Sea,"* and *"Splish Splash."* He was also nominated for an Academy Award for best supporting actor as well as two Golden Globe Awards, winning one of them, for his first films *"Captain Newman,, M.D."* and *"Pressure Point."* I was so pleased for him. He was married to America's sweetheart of films, Sandra Dee, and they were America's favorite couple. There were stories about them in every magazine. He had come a long way since we used to hang out at Hanson's Drugstore. I guess we both had, but Bobby was really riding high on top of a wave!

"Sunday Kind of Love" was a song I really loved back then; I used to sing it all the time. I created my own up-tempo version, which I sang to Bobby, and he seemed to like it. One day he told me he really loved my version of it, and he said, "Let's record it. I've just started a new record label called Addison Records. I'll sign you to my new label as a singer/writer." Man, I was so honored to get the offer from him. It was so easy between us; I totally trusted Bobby and knew he would always be honest and straight with me. And what could be better than recording with my buddy? The idea of not signing with him never entered my mind. Of course I would—happily!

We signed the necessary business documents and set a date to go into the studio to record both that song and another song, "Princess," as the B side. This was so exciting for us both. When the time came, Bobby worked hard to produce this recording. By this time, Bobby was a real pro and knew all the tricks about recording. I was really in awe and felt so lucky to have him backing me. Before, we had just been friends, but now we were business partners, and I was so glad it had happened, no matter what the results. I was also very proud that Bobby believed in my singing talent enough to spend the money and the time on me. To top it off, it was great fun.

In 1962 the A side, "Sunday Kind of Love," made some noise but never reached the top ten, so unfortunately I decided to leave Addison Records as an artist because I didn't think they really had the distribution thing together yet, and I didn't want to spend my and Bobby's time working so hard without getting the desired result. I thought that my recording of "Sunday Kind of Love" with another record company distributing it would have gone all the way—well, at least into the top ten. Bobby and I talked about it and he agreed, so there were no hard feelings between us, as we both had tried our best.

Bobby Darin and I stayed friends and worked together again many times. Bobby was a true friend and came to my rescue on more than one occasion. Bobby was a rare human being, and I consider myself extremely lucky to have been his friend. He was only with us for a short time, and I know many of his fans would agree with me when I say that he died way too young.

My dear pal Elliott Gould became a big star on Broadway. In 1962, he was starring in a Broadway musical called *"I Can Get It For You Wholesale."* There was a young girl in the show named Barbra Streisand. He introduced her to me, unaware that I already knew her. I had met Barbra when she was younger and wanted to be an actress, but she couldn't get a job, so she became a singer. She was around eighteen or twenty when I first met her, when she was performing at small clubs in New York City, and then I saw her at the Blue Angel on the Upper East Side of Manhattan, which was a very popular place.

She sat on a stool as she performed, and I remember thinking, wow, what an incredible voice. But she moved her arms and her hands and fingers in a very distracting way, kind of like Judy Garland did but even more so. She was so theatrical. I thought if she just toned down her gestures a little, it would be great and she would become a big star. I also loved the way she treated some of the well-known older songs that she sang. She was different and exciting, and her voice was truly amazing! I wanted to tell her that she didn't need those crazy movements, that her voice was magic all by itself, but I never did, though; I felt like she might take it the wrong way and feel like I was insulting her.

In Elliott's show, she played Miss Marmelstein and had just one song in the entire show. The show got horrible reviews, but everyone was ecstatic about Barbra. She got rave reviews and became a Broadway star overnight. She was then offered the lead in the new Jule Styne Broadway musical *"Funny Girl"* about the life of Fanny Brice, the famous singer. It was a huge hit, and she was asked to do the movie version of the same show with Omar Sharif. The rest is history.

...

While hanging out in the coffee shops of Greenwich Village, I met Paul Morrissey. He used to spend a lot of time in a loft owned by a guy named Andy, and he told me there were a lot of very bohemian types with a lot of creativity who came and went there all the time, and invited me up. I went with him and was introduced to Andy, who turned out to be Andy Warhol, a young up-and-coming artist. I saw his Campbell's soup can painting, his Marilyn Monroe, and many other paintings just sitting around indiscriminately leaning against the wall. God, what are they worth today?

I went to Andy's loft quite a few times after that, as the girls who came and went were amazing characters and way-out dressers. I loved the girls' names, too, like Candy Darling, Velvet Underground, and Ultra Violet. I must say, it was a highly visual place. In this large space, you could just do what you wanted. Andy always looked strange to me, with his blond hair and the way it was combed. He was an incredibly laid-back kind of guy. I always thought he was asexual because he never seemed to be with anyone. He was always either sitting around quietly doing nothing or having intellectual conversations. He seemed an extremely quiet, almost submissive, person, kind of a voyeur. He liked having all these people around him to watch them, I think. I found him very insecure, whereas Paul seemed to be on the ball and always made things happen. Paul eventually directed several films that Andy produced or financed. I remember a film they made about someone who was asleep. The film was fifteen or twenty minutes long, and all the person did was sleep. It was totally boring; nothing else happened. They liked making these avant-garde films that made a statement, but no money. I don't think they cared about commercial success at all, although later on they made a Dracula film that was a commercial film.

My impression of Andy? He was a nice, very pleasant bore!

Elvis & Ann-Margret in *"Viva Las Vegas"*

We are now in a large rehearsal studio, shooting a wide shot from behind a drummer and piano player. A jazz dance class is in session, with many students filling the studio.

It was now 1964, and I was teaching the most successful dance class in L.A. at the time, at the Coronet Theatre on La Cienega Boulevard, between Melrose Avenue and Beverly Boulevard, in a very large studio. Every day about forty to sixty people took my jazz class. I think one of the things that made my class so popular was that I was the only one in L.A. who had live drums and a piano in my classes. Everyone else used taped music, which wasn't nearly as exciting. Some of my students were famous actors, such as Richard Chamberlain, Raquel Welch, and Dennis Waterman. Maggie Banks was a terrific dancer and a very sweet person, who had been an assistant choreographer on *"West Side Story"* and had also worked on *"Bye Bye Birdie,"* where she became Ann-Margret's good friend.

Ann-Margret, the star of *"Bye Bye Birdie,"* was a very beautiful, hot young singer and actress who originally came from Sweden. She had created a sensation when she made an appearance on the Academy Awards show. Based on that appearance, the famous director George Sidney hired her for the film version of *"Bye Bye Birdie."* He was truly smitten with her, and the walls of his dressing-room trailer were completely covered with photos of her. He even created a special opening for the film of Ann-Margret on a treadmill with wind blowing her hair as she sang the title song. The film was fantastic and became a big hit, and Ann stole the show. From this film, she became a major film star in America. She was on every cover of every major magazine. Ann-Margret was very sexy but also all-American clean, if you know what I mean.

MGM Studios decided to team up the two sex symbols of the day, Elvis Presley and Ann-Margret, in a film called *"Viva Las Vegas"* to be shot in Los Angeles and Las Vegas. Meanwhile, back at my studio, Maggie called to say she wanted to bring Ann in to meet me and possibly study with me privately. So Ann came by to see my class. I'll never forget the first time I saw her; she was like a breath of fresh air. She was charming and gorgeous, and she had a great personality. She and I hit it off really well, so she started studying privately with me whenever she had the time. We got on beautifully because she and I were very much alike. She took the movements and steps I gave her and made them her own. Ann couldn't help it: whatever she did became sexy. It was so easy to work with her because we were so in tune.

We became good friends and phoned each other sometimes at night when we were alone. One particular night, when I was feeling down and depressed, I called Annie up, and she asked me what was bothering me. She could hear it in my voice. I told her I was wasting my life just teaching; I wanted to be out there choreographing, producing, and directing. I told her that I thought I was more talented than a lot of the people who were currently working in Hollywood. Then she sang a song to me, "I Believe in You" from a Broadway show called *"How to Succeed in Business without Really Trying."* She sang the whole song to me and lifted my spirits; and I thought, wow, what a beautiful person you are, Miss Margret, and how happy I am to be your friend.

A few days later, Annie called me and said that the studio had already hired a choreographer for *"Viva Las Vegas,"* but she had told Mr. Sidney that she wanted me because I knew her and knew what steps looked best on her and that my dance steps were new, exciting, and contemporary, whereas the guy they had hired was kind of old hat. She wanted all of the dance and music sequences to sizzle. She thought that she and Elvis could make a terrific film together. She had arranged for Mr. Sidney to come to my class to see what she was raving about. She couldn't promise anything, but she really wanted it to happen.

When Mr. Sidney came to watch my class, he seemed to be impressed. Then he brought back the producer, Jack Cummins, and they both seemed thrilled. So they fired the other choreographer and hired me. Annie and I were over the moon, like two little kids. She said, "We did it, we did it." And, wow, was I happy and ever so thankful to this gorgeous red-haired Swedish girl.

What I loved about Ann was that she used to act like a little kid all the time. She put on no airs; she was so pure and simple, just like her mom and dad, whom I had the pleasure of meeting later on—such sweet people. It made me want to visit Sweden to see the country and meet the people there for myself. Whatever I went on to do in my life after this, I owe much of it to Ann-Margret and her belief in my talent. I always wanted to thank her, and I guess this is as good as any place to do it. Thank you so much, Annie. I love you and always will!

I've always tried to help others, to give back at least as much as I have received, but I've found that it's impossible to weigh these things and know quite whether I am carrying my share of the load. I wound up concluding that all we can do is our best, and let it go at that. Still, gratitude is a powerful incentive for us to carry our share of the load.

I was so excited about this assignment, my first choreography job! I asked Maggie to assist me on the film, and she agreed. Now all I had to do was figure out a way to get my kids, my dance students who knew my style, into the film.

Five of my kids, in particular, went on to achieve much success. Teri Garr was an unknown then, but she became famous as the star of *"Tootsie,"* co-starring Dustin Hoffman, for which she received an Academy Award nomination for best actress, and *"Close Encounters of the Third Kind,"* directed by Steven Spielberg, with Richard Dreyfuss. Toni Basil became a famous singer with her number-one hit *Hey Mickey.* Anita Mann won an Emmy and received four more nominations for best choreography as well as being named one of America's top-five contemporary choreographers by the Academy of Television Arts and Sciences. She is also the producer/director/choreographer of *"Fantasy,"* the show that has been running for over nineteen years at the Luxor

Hotel in Las Vegas. Another one of my dancers, Pete Menefee, later went on to become a three-time Emmy-winning costume designer; and Walter Painter, also one of my dancers, won three Emmy Awards and has been nominated an amazing seven times as a choreographer.

I had to prove to the powers that be in Hollywood, and specifically MGM Studios, that the other dancers who were working on films couldn't do my specific style. Fortunately for me, George Sidney backed me up because it was going to cost a lot of money to prove my point. I had to sit through hundreds of dancers, auditioning them and paying all of them according to union rules, to be able to show the union heads the difference and how my steps should look. I won my case and was allowed to hire my people. I was very excited, as were my dancers, of course. Some of the many dancers I got to hire were Jimmy Hibbard, Sharon Garret Brooks, Ralph Garret, Lorene Yarnell, Raul Ciro, Joy Ciro, Steve Ciro, Sonja Haney, Erwin Marcus, Harod Sanders, Roberta Tennis Doitch, Carol Birner, Drew John, and Jim Bates. I apologize to any I may have left out.

It goes without saying that all of my female dancers went bonkers when they found out they were going to meet the King of Rock 'n' Roll. I was given a huge rehearsal hall, and the work began. We started working with Annie first, and then the day arrived. You'd have thought the dancers were getting ready for a date, the way they were primping and making themselves up. It was really cute. And when he walked in the room for the first time, they looked like they were going to faint.

Elvis entered with a huge entourage of the Memphis Mafia and came right up to me, and—can you believe this?—he actually introduced himself to me! Like I didn't know who he was! But seriously, I could see right off that he was a humble, sincere, and down-to-earth guy. He then introduced me to his boys. Little did I know that this would be the beginning of a long working relationship and, more importantly, a longer friendship with the King of Rock 'n' Roll. Elvis and I worked very well together and would have long talks on our breaks. Ann and he got along like a house on fire, and my dancers all thought he was a terrific guy. (That's an understatement.) He never played the star; same with Annie. It was a joy, a dream, as everyone left us alone to do our work, and we all felt we were doing something really good, like we were involved in something special. I guess we were right, because *"Viva Las Vegas"* is considered one of Elvis's best films, and the theme song is still popular.

As the movie progressed, Elvis, Annie, and I got closer and closer, and I could see a spark between Elvis and Annie on a personal level that really worked for the film and for their numbers every time they performed together. It was like watching a mutual respect as well as love grow. They never let on, but it seemed obvious to me, and I was so happy for them both.

He and I had many private conversations during and after work about love and romance and finding the right girl. I thought, for once he's met his match. I was hoping it would be a relationship that would continue on after the film. I was totally discreet, as there were so many times, when just the three of us were sitting around on a break or waiting for the next scene, that the air was filled with this combustible static. I always felt that Elvis and Ann just wanted to say "the Hell with it" and grab each other. They could have, for I knew what was happening, and they knew that I knew. But they were always totally professional and kept it all inside. Whatever may have happened was done in private, behind closed doors. And I am sworn to secrecy!

Elvis and I were getting on so well that he asked me to do his next film and to be his own personal choreographer. I was so excited and said yes right away, without even thinking about it. Wow! And he asked me himself! What a high!

We shot a lot of "Viva Las Vegas" in and around Las Vegas, and it turned out that my buddy Elliott Gould and Barbra Streisand, who were married by this time, were also in town. Elliott told me that Barbra had just been signed to open for Liberace at the main showroom of the Riviera Hotel for $5,000 a week. I was thrilled for Barbra. What a great thing for her and Elliott. But think about this: the last time she sang in Vegas, she was paid $20 million for one show, and her show was only about a two-hour performance. That is the highest price ever paid in the history of show business! Barbra came a very long way, huh?

Elliott and Barbra invited my first wife-to-be, Anita Kay Sutton, who was Miss Dallas, Texas, and me to have dinner in their suite. When we arrived for dinner, Barbra wanted to play her new album for me; she was so excited about it. She kept saying, "David, you gotta listen to this song," and "David, you gotta listen to this other song." She was so cute. I told her, "Barbra, we came to eat, not to listen to your album. Let's eat first, and then I'll be more than happy to listen," which we did, and it was beyond fantastic. (By the way, she cooked a wonderful meal for all of us.) Barbra is still my favorite female singer. Her voice is an amazing instrument. I didn't know it that night, but she and I would work together on a film much later on.

Eventually, all of us on "Viva Las Vegas" went back to L.A. for the studio shots. Many nights after shooting, Elvis would say he wanted to talk to me, so he would drive me back to my dance school, while one of his guys drove my car back for me. Inevitably, every time he took me back, we would park in front of my school, and I would tell Toni Basil, my assistant, to start class for me, that I would join later, which I rarely did. Elvis and I would just talk for hours. He and I had this terrific relationship that had developed as we worked together on the film. He reached out to me so many times, wanting to exchange thoughts so much, that I realized he had no one else to talk to about deep issues—emotions, politics, philosophies, etc. When my students came out after class, they would giggle and peek in Elvis's Rolls Royce

Phantom, which we were sitting in. I would get embarrassed, but Elvis took it with a grain of salt and even smiled and waved at some of the kids, which made them go nuts. A lot of my students weren't working on the film, so they had never seen him before.

Elvis, unlike most Hollywood stars, never went to the Hollywood parties; in fact, he never went out. He had a mystique about him, and the only way to see him was to buy a ticket to one of his movies. Colonel Tom Parker, his manager, who received fifty percent of all Elvis's income, kept him under wraps. Nobody ever got to see him in person in those days. He was almost like a living god. But I found out he was a lonely man who missed his home and family very much, especially his mother. Sometimes we would drive to his house in Beverly Hills and sit in his living room and talk for hours about everything. He loved to talk to me, and this made us even closer friends. We kept our friendship quiet, and I never mentioned it to anyone, knowing how he loved and cherished his privacy.

He was also one of the most giving people I have ever met. Sometimes he would give someone he liked the keys to one of his cars and tell them to keep it. He loved giving. I had a similar experience with him myself. One day, at MGM Studios, he had just bought a new ring. He showed it to me, and I said I liked it very much. He then took it off, handed it to me, and said, "It's yours." I said, "El, I'm just saying that I think it's a beautiful ring, that's all. I'm not saying I want it. Please keep it." And when I tried to give it back to him he refused to take it. He said, "David, you said you like it, and so I want you to have and enjoy it." I tried and tried, but it was useless; he had his mind made up, and that was that. He would not take it back. So I eventually had to accept it, and of course I thanked him for it. He was happy to be able to give me something I liked. Such a gracious and giving person, a one-of-a-kind gem, for sure!

When Elvis and I were talking together, his guys knew never to interrupt us. They only reacted if one of us told a joke or something. I said to him one day, "El, all these guys you have with you, except for Joe Esposito (his assistant), they're like sponges. When you laugh, they laugh; when you are upset, they are upset. They just soak up your energy, and they give you nothing back in return. They never contribute to a conversation, they never forward an opinion—why do you have them with you all the time? What's the point?"

"David, I trust them," Elvis answered, "and I don't trust anybody else in Hollywood. I've known them for most of my life. I understand what you're saying, but when we go home we have a good time. They're out of their element in this town, and to tell you the truth, so am I."

I heard what he was saying, but I felt sorry for him being caged up with all these Memphis guys who couldn't really relate to him in a way that he so obviously was reaching out to me for. He and I respected each other, and that had a great deal to do with it also.

I went on to make four films with Elvis: *"Viva Las Vegas," "Girl Happy," "Easy Come, Easy Go,"* and *"Tickle Me."* So I hold the record as the choreographer with the most films with Elvis. Then Annie also asked me to become her personal choreographer, and we made five films together, another record: *"Viva Las Vegas," "Made in Paris," "Kitten with a Whip," "Bus Riley's Back in Town"* and *"The Swinger."* Can you imagine how I felt? The two biggest young musical stars in the industry, both hiring me to be their personal choreographer? I was on cloud nine!

One day when we were filming an Elvis movie at Paramount Studios, I was walking to my car when I heard a voice behind me yelling my name. "David? David Winters?" I thought to myself, 'What did I do wrong?' and I started walking faster. I had no idea who it was that was calling me. The voice got closer and seemed more intent on getting my attention. The voice said stop, and so I did and turned around, and it was none other than Henry Winkler, the actor who was co-starring as the Fonz in the hot TV sitcom *"Happy Days"* with Tom Bosley and Ron Howard. Henry caught up with me and extended his hand. As we shook hands, he said, "I can't believe it's you, David Winters. I just want to thank you because you were my inspiration to become an actor." I had no idea what he was talking about, and I guess he could see that from the questionable expression on my face. He proceeded to explain: "When I was a young boy, I always wanted to be in show business as an actor, dancer, and singer, but everyone used to tell me that guys in musicals are mostly gay. But when I saw you in *"West Side Story,"* I knew you were not gay, you were definitely straight, and that made me not listen to anyone else but myself and go into show business, so I just want to shake your hand and thank you." We shook hands and I told Henry what a big fan I was of his, and we parted and went our separate ways. So many similar things happened to me because of my appearing in the film *"West Side Story."* It had such a strong effect on so many young people.

As I look back at *"Viva Las Vegas,"* it was a great experience. We were happy, we did excellent work, and I became close friends with two very special, kind, and loving people who would be a large part of my life in the coming years. And they happened to be the two hottest young musical icons at the time. Thinking back to that phone conversation when Annie sang "I Believe in You" to me—she did, and she proved she meant it, too. Annie made it all happen for me, and I can never repay her for this, as it changed the direction of my life forever after. I love you, Annie!

I know Annie has since talked publicly about her romance with Elvis, but I gave El my word, so I'm still sworn to secrecy!

Top left: I was interviewed in Elvis's quarterly magazine.
Top right: Talking with Elvis during the filming of *"Girl Happy"*
Bottom left: Me and Elvis during the shooting of *"Girl Happy"*
Bottom right: Pictures of me in El's Japanese fan club magazine

My dear, dear friend El, you are gone but certainly never forgotten.

"Shindig" and *"Hullabaloo"*

Cut to a concert audience of screaming young girls.

In 1964, an English producer named Jack Good was hired by ABC-TV to produce a rock-and-roll show called *"Shindig"* for the tube. Mr. Good called me up and asked me to choreograph the show. L.A. deejay Jimmy O'Neill was hired as the host, and guest acts like The Beatles, The Beach Boys, The Rolling Stones, Jerry Lee Lewis, Sam Cooke, Chuck Berry, Tina Turner, and The Everly Brothers appeared on the show. Unknown acts such as Bobby Sherman, The Righteous Brothers, Jackie DeShannon, Leon Russell, Darlene Love, and Billy Preston, who all went on to become household names and number-one-hit recording artists, also appeared on *"Shindig."* I hired ten girls who would be called the Shindig Dancers and would appear on every show of the series.

The original dancers: Teri Garr, Anita Mann, Carolyne Barry, Diane Stuart, Gina Trikonis, Laurine Yarnell, Maria Ghava, Pam Freeman, Virginia Justus, and my assistant Toni Basil

Right from the first show, we got terrific ratings and became a big, overnight success. Everything was going along fine until the rehearsal for one particular show. The singer Round Robin was going to be a guest, and I was called into the executive producer's office and told, "Your dancers can touch his clothes, but don't let them touch his skin." This was obviously because Round Robin was black, and in those days, a lot of America was still segregated. All the white TV execs were afraid of losing the southern viewers as well as sponsors. What bullshit, I thought. I told the executive that I would do no such thing, and that he was lucky I didn't call a press conference. And I quit the show then and there. I couldn't get out of his office fast enough. I actually felt sick to my stomach.

Soon after this incident, it was announced that many rip-offs of this kind of show would be on the air the next season in 1965. The most interesting of these was called *"Hullabaloo."* It would be on NBC-TV and directed by Steve Binder. Gary Smith, the producer, called me up, at Steve's request, and asked me to choreograph the show. It would have a new star host every week, and the guests would also be different every week. It would be a much more expensive show than *"Shindig,"* as well as more interesting and creative, with guest hosts like Sammy Davis Jr., Jack Jones, Paul Anka, Peter Noone of Herman's Hermits, Michael Landon, and Soupy Sales. Gary said he would like me to appear in a dance number on the show every so often and to sing, too, which sounded great to me. The dancers would be called the David Winters *"Hullabaloo"* Dancers. I took the assignment, which included a move to New York City where the show would be taped. I was really looking forward to it. Back to the Big Apple, and this time as a choreographer of a new TV series. Wow! Because of their contracts, my dancers were still on *"Shindig,"* so I went back alone, knowing I'd have to hire a whole new bunch of kids for *"Hullabaloo."*

Back in the Big Apple, I moved into an apartment on Central Park West facing the park close to where John Lennon was tragically shot. I announced auditions immediately and hired my friend Jaime Rogers, who was a brilliant dancer and one of the Sharks in *"West Side Story,"* as my assistant. Every young dancer in town showed up for the audition because this was a very desirable gig and had been heavily advertised.

After a few days of auditions, I paired it down from hundreds to just a few dancers. I only needed nine dancers for the show, and Goldie Hawn, who was a dancer in those days, just missed out, as she was the tenth dancer. She was a great dancer with a fantastic personality even then. I love dancers. They are a breed unto themselves! And I hate turning down dancers, as I myself have gone through the process. It hurts when you dance your heart out only to be rejected, usually in a casual and cold manner, like being told, "Don't call us, we'll call you." God, those are horrible, hurtful words, and of course they never call.

I did make a personal statement with my choices, as this was the first TV show that ever had an African-American dancer as a regular in the chorus. Gary and Steve both stood behind me, and NBC eventually agreed to it. I was always kind of a fighter; must have picked that up from my dad. If I had lost that fight, Goldie would have gotten the job, being next in line. I also fought for and was allowed to hire Patrick Adiarte, who was a great dancer who happened to be Asian—again, a first for American TV.

Michael Bennett, one of my dancers, went on to fame and fortune with eighteen Tony Award nominations, winning seven times. He created, choreographed, and directed many Broadway shows, including the award-winning smash-hit musical *"A Chorus Line."* Ironically, I always thought that Michael was my weakest dancer. That just shows that you don't have to be an exceptional dancer to be a talented choreographer. I've been told that the great Busby Berkeley, who was responsible for so much fantastic film choreography, was also not an exceptional dancer. Sadly, Michael passed away at the young age of forty-four. His talent is greatly missed on Broadway.

I'm happy to report that *"Hullabaloo"* is where Michael first met Donna McKechnie, another of my dancers. They were married for a while. I have personally known Donna since she was fifteen years old, when she ran away from home and took a bus to New York City to become a dancer. My girlfriend at the time, Jennifer Billingsley, knew her and told me to go to the Port Authority Bus Terminal to find her. I told Jennifer she was crazy as hundreds of thousands of people used that terminal every day. Amazingly, I somehow found Donna there, and we have been friends ever since that fateful day.

In addition to hiring Donna for *"Hullabaloo,"* her first TV series, I also took her to Hollywood, where she did her first film, *"Billie,"* starring Patty Duke as the lead dancer. Donna eventually became a top Broadway star, winning a Tony Award for best actress in a musical as Cassie in *"A Chorus Line."* She also won the Drama Desk Award and the Theatre World Award for the same show. Other B'way productions she appeared in include *"Company,"* *"How to Succeed in Business without Really Trying,"* *"On the Town,"* and *"State Fair."* She was also featured in the cult TV series *"Dark Shadows"* and the film *"The Little Prince,"* with the great Bob Fosse. Donna currently tours the world with her one-woman show, *"Same Place, Another Time."* I was fortunate enough to see her in her SRO London engagement, and recently in Florida. Donna is to this day an incredible dancer and singer!

Joey Heatherton was a beautiful, sexy young actress, singer, and dancer. Joey would be a guest star on the opening show hosted by my friend, the incredible Sammy Davis Jr. I had recently worked with Joey on the TV series *"The Breaking Point"*, where she played the lead dancer in a dance company. I choreographed all the dance sequences and a dance concert for the show. We had worked together really well, and we were both looking forward to working together again.

An article from *Dance Magazine* with Joey Heatherton and me, with Patrick Adiarte, who was the first Asian to dance in the chorus of a TV series

Left to right: Jaime Rogers, Joey Heatherton, and me in my Russian Moiseyev dance boots

At the production meeting, it was decided that I should do something sexy with Joey, so I came up with a sexy little movement that anyone could do. I wanted to create a dance craze like the twist had been years before. And what a perfect place to introduce it: during prime time on a major network, with Joey Heatherton. Joey would wear a leotard bottom so that every move would be exaggerated. I worked with her on it, and—wow!—Joey couldn't help being sexy, no matter what. She was born with it.

We rehearsed the number with the other dancers until I felt it was ready to show the executives at NBC. As it turns out, the Coca-Cola people were in town and asked if they could come over to rehearsals, and I said sure. Coca-Cola was one of our main sponsors. They spent over $100 million a year on TV advertising and were one of, if not the biggest spenders on TV at the time, so I wasn't about to say no. Well, I got their attention, but not quite in the way I had planned. After they saw Joey's dance number, they went right back to Atlanta and cancelled their entire sponsorship of *"Hullabaloo."* We are talking about millions and millions of dollars. Ouch!

Well, all hell broke loose. The producers were called in to meetings with the NBC top brass, and I thought for sure that I would be fired, and maybe Joey, too, along with who knew who else. The dreaded call came, but when I went to the meeting, I was told that nothing had changed. NBC was standing behind us and would not be censored or told what to do by any sponsor, no matter how big. The next day, all the New York papers ran stories of the situation with shots of Joey doing my dance. Of course, they were very suggestive pictures. They even made me want to watch the show.

Well, for sure, a lot of people did watch the show, and we received an excellent rating. Joey and the dancers were terrific. I called the dance "the jerk," and sure enough, before too long, people all over the country were doing it in their local discos. It involves a bump with your pelvis while your arms move in and out, with them meeting the pelvis when it's forward. I'm sure you've all seen it at one time or another. Joey cashed in on all the publicity and seemed to be working all the time after the show. Me—I was stupid. I had just created a dance craze that was sweeping the country, yet I never made a cent from it. But the show was a big hit, which was eventually helpful to me and my career.

A shot of me during rehearsals of one of my solo dance numbers

A photo that Lada Edmund Jr., my featured cage dancer, took of me during the show *"Hullabaloo."* Thanks, Lada!

Barbara Alston was the African-American dancer I hired. A very disturbing thing took place during rehearsals one day. The NAACP, the National Association for the Advancement of Colored People, sent a representative down to watch my rehearsals. They were very pleased about me hiring Barbara. But then the rep said to me, "David, if Barbara leaves for some reason, you'll replace her with another African-American dancer, won't you?" I couldn't believe what he had said, and I replied, "I thought you wanted equality? That's what I've been fighting for most of my life. Don't you understand? I hired Barbara because she was the best dancer, not because she was black. And if she does leave, I'll hire the next best dancer whether she's black, white, or purple, I don't care. I didn't think that you wanted me to hire someone just because they're black, as a token. I gave her an equal opportunity, the same as everyone else at my audition, and she stood out as one of the best, so she got the job." I was truly disappointed by this exchange.

The show attracted its fair share of groupies. One of the groupies turned out to be the now famous and terrific actress Nancy Allen (all three *"Robocop"* films, *"Dress to Kill,"* *"Poltergeist,"* etc.). As a young girl, she was always hanging around at the studios where we taped the show every week. I remember her as a very sweet young girl.

We had all the top current English groups appearing each week: The Rolling Stones, The Animals, The Yardbirds, The Hollies, Herman's Hermits, Freddie and the Dreamers, Gerry and the Pacemakers, Lulu, etc. We also had all the top Motown groups: The Supremes, The Miracles, the Four Tops, and The Temptations, to name a few. We even created our own hit group on the show: The Young Rascals. And since big stars like Sammy Davis Jr., Paul Anka, Jack Jones, and Michael Landon hosted the show, it became a ratings success and took a lot of the steam out of *"Shindig."* Obviously, everyone wanted to see and hear all the latest hits by the number-one groups, and you couldn't get this on *"Shindig."*

As I walked into the rehearsal hall one day, someone called out my name: "David, over here." I turned around, and there was Paul Simon. I said, "Hi, Paul. What are you doing here?" and he replied, "I'm on the show." Then I asked him what group he was with. Looking at me incredulously, Paul said, "Simon & Garfunkel," and I stopped in my tracks. Oh my God, I had heard about the act but had never put two and two together. My friends Paul Simon and Art Garfunkel were actually Simon & Garfunkel. I felt pretty embarrassed. Later that day, Paul and Artie and I spent a lot of time catching up. They said that when Paul and I had split up, he had gone to Europe, where Artie was already living, and they had gotten back together again, but this time they were writing from the heart, not trying to be commercial, just writing it as they felt it. They made some recordings, and one of them, "Sound of Silence," was picked up by a German DJ who played it over and over, and the song became a local hit. It spread from there to become a hit all over Europe before coming to the US. And as they say, the rest is history. Paul and Artie went on to become one of the biggest acts ever. They played to a million people in Hyde Park, London, and have sold over 25 million copies of their *Greatest Hits* album. I always liked Artie's lovely voice better than Paul's, although Paul, now that they've split, has been much more commercially successful.

"*Hullabaloo*" was also where I met and choreographed my dear friend Liza Minnelli. She is so talented, just like her mom, the legendary Judy Garland. Liza is unique in that she is a great dancer as well as singer. I think it's in her genes. Even as a young girl, she was so professional. At the time, she was starring on Broadway in "*Flora the Red Menace*," for which she received incredible reviews.

I remember the great Sammy Davis Jr. coming to rehearsals at 9:00 a.m. with his mug filled with "whatever" in his hand, drinking that early in the morning. None of my dancers could believe it either. But it didn't affect his work capacity at all. Sammy could work all day and all night. He was another incredible talent that I had the good fortune to work with. We worked hard, and we played hard. Working with Sammy was a dream because he had his own style and he could do anything. He could play a million instruments as well as sing, dance, and do impersonations. He did it all—the ultimate showman! They called him Mr. Show Business, and, boy, was that appropriate. During rehearsals, I sometimes used to think about how, as a little kid, I had snuck into the Broadway Theatre between acts to see the great Sammy Davis Jr. in the show "*Mr. Wonderful.*" And now, here I was, working with him and giving him steps to dance to, and I could also consider him one of my close friends. How lucky I felt, how blessed. There will never be another Sammy Davis Jr.

Then there was Berry Gordy. And Berry is a whole other story! Berry was the creator and owner of Motown Records, which gave us the Detroit sound, better known as the Motown sound. He had hit after hit, and every group whose records he released wound up in the top-ten record charts. When it came to records, Berry was a genius. He came to the show with his acts, and he really cared about their presentation. He didn't have to since he was already a multimillionaire, but it wasn't about money with Berry. As I got to know him, I saw how he paid attention to small details. The little things were very important to him, whereas other managers let them slide by.

I was honored one day when Berry approached me and asked me to sign with Motown. He had seen me on the show, where I would dance and later sing a song in the same segment. However, I also had an offer from Decca Records. Berry suggested that he would like to bring me to Detroit and let me get a feel of his place, and maybe even fool around and sing a bit with Smokey Robinson and Marvin Gaye since I knew them both very well by this time. I thought that sounded great, so on a day off, I flew to Detroit with my manager, Lynne Russo, and we visited Motown.

When we arrived, I couldn't believe it. There was no office building, no big sound studio—just four little houses where everything happened. Incredibly, these four little houses were responsible for a large percentage of the entire record business at the time. And inside were these little cozy studios and lots of singers, writing and making demos. They were rehearsing harmonies, and everyone chipped in. Motown was like one big, happy family. I then understood Berry's genius. He had created an atmosphere where everyone wanted to participate and help each other; thus, he got the best from all the talent. It was a music workshop that ran all the time as long as there was someone there to sing or write.

Me dancing a solo to a Beatles medley on *"Hullabaloo."*

And there I was, working with Marvin Gaye and Smokey Robinson and others, just like Berry had said. The guys would either sing me something that I would then copy or they would play it on a piano or lay it down on tape, and then I would record it. I wasn't an R&B or a soul singer, so it was difficult for me. We spent all day and night working away. For me, it was like being in a musical fantasy. There were no egos. If you were a star or an unknown didn't matter' it was the work that came first. How different from some of the people I had to work with, where it was all ego and limited talent.

Everyone was being very positive and saying how good it sounded. But it wasn't like the Motown sound that I loved. Well, of course it wasn't. I was white and sang differently than they did. They sang a lot better than I did, that's for sure. At least some of the tracks that we laid down sounded good, but I couldn't really tell if my sound would be right for Motown. This was very different for them, too. I was confused. Was Decca a better place for me? More appropriate for my sound? Would Motown know how to promote their first white artist? I had so many questions; I still didn't know what to do.

After bidding goodbye to Berry, Marvin, and Smokey, Lynne and I returned to New York. We decided to meet with Shelby Singleton, the main man at Decca, to hear what he had to offer. We told Shelby about our Motown visit, but through his connections, he already knew about our trip to Detroit, which surprised us. "They're the best," he said, "but are they the best for you and your sound?" He made an offer, and we decided to go with Decca. We would introduce the A side on *"Hullabaloo,"* and then Decca would release the album, and hopefully we would have a hit. It was called, "The Unprotest Song." I knew right away we'd both made a big mistake, but it was too late. I don't know if I would have become a big recording star if I had gone with Motown, but I often wonder. It's certainly an experience that I will never forget.

It was also during *"Hullabaloo"* that I met two lovely and talented girls. One, Lesley Anne Warren, hadn't yet turned professional. Soon enough, though, she got the coveted part of Cinderella in the TV special of the same name and has been a star ever since. She was a stunningly beautiful young girl, both inside and out, and so natural and unaware of her beauty. The other girl, Andrea Marcovicci, was studying dance with my hero, "Luigi" Eugene Louis Faccuito. Andrea became a star, singing and acting. She has a natural and calming beauty. She knew she'd never be a dancer, but went to class for other reasons. Having control over your body and knowing how to move it is very important. If you're thinking of being an actor or a singer, or just for your health, I recommend taking dance classes, if only for one's posture.

The great dance teacher Luigi is the perfect example. He was in a terrible car accident in 1946, and they said he would never stand again, let alone walk. His entire body was literally broken, but not his mind. He did bar work every day in excruciating pain. He pulled himself up to the bar and forced his body to respond, even though clinically his muscles were dead. After years of this, he was eventually dancing and became an inspiration to all those who might suffer from a disability. The human spirit is an amazing thing. At ninety years of age, he was still teaching his world-famous dance class, and many of his disciples around the world teach the Luigi method, such as Francis J. Roach in New York and myself when I taught and choreographer Walter Painter, who is still teaching today. Whenever I was in New York, the first place I went was Luigi's Dance Studio. Whenever Luigi introduced me to other people, he would always say, "David is the son I never had." What a compliment!

I shared Luigi's class with Liza Minelli, Robert Morse, Elliott Gould, Donna McKechnie, Ben Vereen, Alvin Ailey, Michael Bennett, Bette Midler, Joel Grey, Ann Reinking, Richard Chamberlain, Ron Field, Christopher Walken, Valerie Harper, Barbra Streisand, and anyone and everyone who ever danced in a Broadway musical while he taught. When I attended Luigi's class, he would have me demonstrate the dance routine we would all be learning that day.

Luigi always used to say, "Never stop moving." He was an amazing man who created his very own revolutionary jazz dance technique. His dance was about life, love, freedom, and true artistic expression. Just after he passed away, he was honored at the Tony Awards. I cried as I watched it; I was so happy for him! In this world of glass, Luigi was a diamond.

I am showing Luigi's dance combo to the other students in class.
In this photo taken by Milton Oleaga, Luigi, wearing black tights and a small white rolled-up shirt, is hidden a bit behind my right arm.

"Hullabaloo" was picked up for a second season, and I was asked to return. But I was also scheduled to do a film with Ann-Margret, which was shooting in L.A., so a deal was made. Saturdays and Sundays, I would be in New York with Jaime Rogers rehearsing *"Hullabaloo,"* and then late on Sundays, I would fly to L.A. to shoot Annie's film from Monday to Friday. On Friday evenings, I would fly back to New York again for the next TV show. What a schedule. I did this for sixteen weeks, and it worked out pretty well. *"Hullabaloo"* was cancelled after the second season, so I moved back to L.A.

"The T.A.M.I. Show"

Early September 1964...

The director, and my friend, Steve Binder called to invite me to join him on a project he was planning to direct for Hollywood showman Bill Sargent, named *"The T.A.M.I. Show"* (Teenage Awards Music International). It was to be a recorded concert taped in Electrovision, which was a cutting-edge high-quality videotape process that would allow the production to later be transferred to film. The movie version would then be released in December 1964 in cinemas across the country.

The show line-up included legends like The Rolling Stones, Diana Ross and the Supremes, Marvin Gaye, The Beach Boys, Smokey Robinson and the Miracles, The Temptations, Gerry & the Pacemakers, James Brown and the Famous Flames, Chuck Berry, the Four Tops, Jan and Dean, Lesley Gore, Billy J. Kramer, The Blossoms, and many others. In the band were Glenn Campbell as guitarist and Leon Russell as one of the pianists.

It was scheduled for October 28–29, 1964, at the Santa Monica Civic Auditorium, and once I read the incredible list of performers, I immediately agreed to take the job of staging and choreography. I got started right away rehearsing with my regular dancers that I had recruited: Teri Garr, Toni Basil, and Anita Mann. Other dancers I hired included Melanie Alexander, Debbie Butler, Rita D'Amico, Pam Freeman, Gail Ganley, and Carlton Johnson, to name a few.

On the afternoon of the event, chaos ruled backstage, as many of the scheduled performers threatened not to perform because checks written by Bill Sargent were bouncing and people feared not being paid.

All this to the deafening screams of girls in the audience.

The moment Chuck Berry stepped into view, the atmosphere in the auditorium electrified as music history was playing out before everyone's eyes. They called it an "unplanned miracle" or the Battle of the Bands. In the audience were two soon-to-be-famous young men, John Landis and David Cassidy.

In the show was the little-known James Brown from the southeast of the country, who delivered the most overwhelming performance of the entire production. It has been said that Mick Jagger regretted having to follow the amazing James Brown's performance. To this day, I have never seen anyone dance or work so hard on stage as James. But then again, he had The Rolling Stones watching him from the wings, so he had to deliver, didn't he?

Overall, the entire event, shot with only four cameras, defined popular music for an entire generation and created the template for how concerts became movies. Director Steve Binder did a fantastic job! The *"T.A.M.I."* concert was billed as a groundbreaking show, and in 2006 it was deemed "culturally, historically, or aesthetically significant" by the United States Library of Congress and selected for preservation in the United States National Film Registry.

To create some real rock-and-roll excitement, Binder decided to have all the acts come onstage at the end of the show to dance. Binder told everyone—except the Rolling Stones. "They finished and thought that was it," Binder said. But suddenly the stage was filled with dancers and all the other performers—The Supremes, The Righteous Brothers, The Miracles, etc. What's great is, you see Mick smile and just go with it. It's total mayhem and so rock and roll.

Unlike with most of today's filmed performances, there was no lip-syncing or miming with instruments. Everyone from Marvin Gaye to Gerry and the Pacemakers sang and played live. "I didn't go back and edit or fix a thing," Binder said. "We actually shot over two nights. Half the rehearsals were in the afternoons, and then I shot the acts over a two-day period. But I never did a retake when it was over. If it felt right, I kept it. That's one reason the film is so exciting."

The original poster for the all-star "T.A.M.I. Show."
Look at all the superstar names—amazing!

"Lucy In London"

After successful collaborations on *"Hullabaloo"* and *"The T.A.M.I. Show,"* Steve Binder and I decided to partner up to produce more television shows together. He asked me to join him for a meeting in the flats of Beverly Hills at the home of superstar Lucille Ball. When we met with Lucy, she told us that her current contract with CBS allowed her to do three independent specials and that this particular show was to be called *"Lucy In London."* I was taken by surprise by the warmth and confidence that this great America comedienne showered on us, and she was so down-to-earth. I honestly thought our youth would be a problem, but instead it turned out to be a big plus. What a great meeting we had!

Lucy wanted the special to be "youthful" with a "today" feeling and thought that Steve and I would be the right guys to produce it. Steve and I left very excited. He was to be the producer and director, and I was to be the co-producer and choreographer.

Once our deals were finalized by the William Morris Agency, we immediately launched ourselves into pre-production. It was during this period that we met an Egyptian-born director of photography named Fouad Said. This diminutive man, whom everyone called Fou, started a revolution in the film industry by creating the "Cinemobile," which was a sixteen-foot van equipped with cameras, generator, xenon lamps, dolly and tracks, and an amazing camera platform that raised itself twenty-three feet above the roof of the van—a first in the industry: a self-contained production unit on wheels. It would generate a huge sixty-percent savings on our production costs. It didn't take Steve and me long to buy into the idea that this mobile camera unit would be ideal for *"Lucy In London."* Once we finalized the technical logistics with Fou, we presented the concept to Lucy, who accepted without hesitation. After all, she wanted a "today" feeling, and this innovative production unit was just that: the production technology of the day *and* tomorrow.

Within days, I found myself in London scouting locations and hooking up with my buddy Gary Cockrell, who was in the West End cast of *"West Side Story."* Gary had gone to London with the *"West Side Story"* stage production in 1957 and never returned. Once there, he started the Dance Center with his partner, Valerie Hyman. And that became the base for my auditions and rehearsals.

During the production of her special, Lucy and I became close friends, and we often talked about my personal life. At the time, I was having serious marital problems with my wife Kay Sutton. I was seriously considering a divorce, but Lucy advised against it, and I listened to her, at least through the end of the show. Lucy always took great interest in my career and showed me great warmth and caring despite everything that was going on in her life. I considered myself very fortunate to be her friend for the rest of her life.

Once in London, all our ideas and concepts came alive, and the pace picked up. Steve and I decided to surround Lucy with young men. We hired British heartthrob and multiple award-winner Anthony Newley to be Lucy's London tour guide. He had an Academy Award nomination and won the 1963 Grammy for best song. We also hired the popular group The Dave Clark Five to appear and sing "London Bridge Is Falling Down." I even got to choreograph a mod ballet and include Lucy in it. What fun! And Phil Spector wrote and recorded the lead vocal on the song!

Steve and I really loved working with Lucy as she would try anything. One time she did a scene in the river Thames, and the boat she was in was supposed to sink. Of course, we would normally have gotten a stand-in or stunt person to do that. But not Lucy—she insisted on doing it all herself! And it made all the difference because Steve was able to shoot all the time the boat was sinking and never had to cheat on any shots. Steve and I had a great time making this special.

Lucy and co-star Anthony Newley trying to get dry after their scene

Steve and I in the studio listening to the playback of the recording of "London Bridge
Is Falling Down" with one of the guest stars of *"Lucy in London"*
and one of the top singing groups of the day, The Dave Clark Five, who are also
listening in the background.

Lucy became like my second mother and did so many favors for me later on in my career. So many people helped me through the years—I have been truly blessed. Lucy was always such a doll and a true American institution! She was truly a genius at what she did. All of America loved her. And I can truly say, "I love Lucy!"

The day the show aired, The William Morris Agency, placed this ad in the show-business bible *Variety* announcing my first producing job with Steve for the *"Lucy In London"* TV special.

I was so thankful for the opportunity to meet and actually work alongside the great Lucille Ball as well as the amazingly multi-talented Anthony Newley and The Dave Clark Five. I don't know if I ever thanked you, Steve, as we were always so busy and into the work, so please accept my heartfelt and sincere thanks now. A huge thanks, man!

Sonny & Cher

Sitting in front of the TV one day, I saw an act called Caesar & Cleo on a local music show, lip-syncing to a record. They had an interesting look, and I thought that I must remember them, because they were unique, not your regular singing group. My partner Steve Binder and I were always trying to think of ideas we could sell or looking for shows that were already sold that we could produce. With this in mind, we sold a rock-and-roll music show concept to ABC-TV. It was called "T. J.'s" and was named after the movie *"Tom Jones"* because Steve and I wanted the dancers to dress like they were in England during that time period. We wanted to combine the *"Tom Jones"* concept with the 1960's look and feel; something different for TV, we thought.

The week we made the deal, Caesar & Cleo, who had now changed their name to Sonny & Cher, had their first record, "I Got You Babe," hit the 100 spot on the Billboard top 100 chart with a bullet. The bullet meant it was climbing fast. I had heard the song and knew it would be a number-one hit. I soon found out that they were with the William Morris Agency, and we went to meet with Harvey Kresky, their agent, whose office was in the very back of the building and was about the size of a closet. We made a deal with Harvey for them to host our show, and we wanted The Rolling Stones as the performing act. The concept was that we would dedicate the entire half-hour show to one group, and some of the numbers would be with my dancers and some without.

When Steve and I went to ABC with our choices, they turned down both Sonny & Cher and The Rolling Stones. They said they'd never heard of Sonny & Cher and thought The Stones' image wasn't clean enough to put on their network. We told them that Sonny & Cher would be huge stars by the time the show aired, but they insisted no Stones and no Sonny & Cher. So we wound up with Phil Spector and my friend the actor Sal Mineo as the hosts, and the group was the very clean-cut The Dave Clark Five. Needless to say, the show wasn't what we had envisioned, and it didn't work as well as we had planned and hoped for. But Sonny and I stayed in touch and became closer friends.

Sonny & Cher eventually went to England, where they were once not allowed in a hotel because of the way they dressed. They got a lot of publicity, and "I Got You Babe" became a big hit in London. They became huge, as I knew they would, and I went to see them in concert many times. However, after a couple of years, their popularity began to wane, and they were now playing Vegas. I once took Burt Rosen, my new partner, backstage at their show, but there was nobody there, unlike in the old days when it had been so crowded with all the phonies from Hollywood—the good-time Charlies, as we called them.

Sonny & Cher were both very thankful for my continued support, especially in these lean times. They were down on their luck, and I wanted to help them, so I spoke to Burt about doing a TV show with them, kind of a comedy/music show. He liked my idea, and we set up a meeting at their house in Bel Air—actually, at Tony Curtis's house, which they had rented. At the meeting, we sat with Sonny, Cher, and Chastity, their new little baby, in their bedroom. I told them that I wanted to do a comedy-type show with music and call it *"The Sonny & Cher Nitty Gritty Hour."* I wanted them to insult each other during their act so it would be humorous and funny. I said that Cher could make fun of Sonny's height, and so on. Then Cher said, "But, David, that means I would have to act, and I can't act." That sentence of Cher's stayed with me, and years later, I was watching Cher receive the Oscar for best actress for the film *"Moonstruck."* It made me smile and feel good for her. I had to laugh out loud, flashing back to that moment— "But, David...I can't act." Yeah, Cher, right!

As it turned out, we made the show as a TV special and as a pilot for a series. We had a ball. It was a terrific concept, and Sonny and Cher were great. We almost got it sold as an ABC-TV summer series, but ABC went with the Smothers Brothers instead. CBS, who had seen our special, basically copied our show, hired a couple of producers and writers, and stole Sonny & Cher away from us. I didn't blame Sonny & Cher, as they had to survive. Their series became hugely successful and ran on the CBS network for four years. I watched my own show get stolen by another network. I always wanted to sue CBS, but our agents said not to alienate one of the major networks, so we didn't. I always thought that was a big mistake because their show was an exact copy of ours, and we could prove it.

Meanwhile, Sonny & Cher were reinvented yet again. I got screwed, but at least I had the satisfaction of knowing that I had the idea first and I was right. Nevertheless, Cher and Sonny and I remained friends, and Cher sang a song for my Paul Newman film *"Once Upon a Wheel"* and one for my movie *"Thrashin'."* I even gave Cher my pet bird, a talking macaw named Albert. Cher was so crazy that she had outfits made for him. Albert's response to almost everything was "F*** you! F*** you!"—something he'd heard me say quite often on the phone. So sorry, Cher!

From their TV show, Sonny & Cher became more popular than ever. But once again, their popularity decreased, and their show was dropped. Then they split up. Cher went on to have some solo hits, and Sonny opened up an Italian restaurant and did guest appearances on TV and in some films. I used to hang out with Sonny at his restaurant on Beverly Boulevard and La Cienega. I always supported my friend.

After he and Cher broke up, Sonny was really down on women, and he once said to me, "David, don't forget: they're the enemy!" He then decided he wanted to try his hand at politics. "I know nothing about politics, David," he said, "but these bastards just lie and lie and do nothing for the people. I want to try to change that," to which I answered, "Go for it, Sonny." He ran for and was elected mayor of Palm Springs. He remarried, had two more children, and seemed very happy with his new life.

He called me one day and said they had a film festival every year in Palm Springs, and he'd like to open it that year with *"West Side Story"* and then afterwards have a question-and-answer period with the audience. He asked me to come down and be a part of it along with my buddy Tony Mordente, who was Action in the film; Robert Wise, the director; and Saul Chaplin, film score composer and musical director. I said, "Sure, Son, I'd be happy to."

"I'll take good care of you, and it won't take much of your time," he said.

"No problem," I said. "Count me in."

So Tony Mordente and I went down there, and after the sold-out screening, we got up on stage and answered questions. I am amazed how well that film holds up—even today! Sonny hosted a party afterwards, where he introduced me to some politicians. He thanked Tony and me, and then we went back to L.A.

Many times Cher would show up at Hugh Hefner's house, and we would chat. We never talked about Sonny because at that time she was pissed with him. It was the first time she had ever been alone. She felt that Sonny had been too overbearing, and she said she was happy to be free. One day, just after she had sold the house she had designed and built in Benedict Canyon to the actor Eddie Murphy, Cher and I were buying towels at a department store in Westwood. She told me that Eddie also wanted all of her furniture because he liked what she had done and had no taste of his own, so he insisted that she leave everything as it was, and he would pay her a huge bonus for doing so. We both had a giggle at Murphy's expense, as we were both feeling silly that day.

Sonny went on to be elected to the United States Congress, where he was very well liked and was a respected Representative. Unfortunately, Sonny was killed in a freak skiing accident. Many of his colleagues attended his funeral, and Cher gave a very moving eulogy that was broadcast all over the world. In a very emotional way, she said he would always be the man she truly loved and cherished. I just wish Sonny could have heard that. Sonny's life provides a good lesson for anyone who is feeling insecure about making it. As Cher herself once said to me, "He was a little, short Italian with a bad voice who took a skinny sixteen-year-old and created the top singing duo in the world." She was correct, but I can tell you he sure made a difference here and definitely left his mark on this world. Sonny, you will always be remembered—by me, but more importantly by Cher. Rest in peace, Sonny, my brother.

CHAPTER 19

The Monkees, Jimi Hendrix, and Iron Butterfly

My career was going in top gear, and I was one of the most sought-after choreographers in the business. I had many, many offers but turned down most of them. I now wanted to fulfill my ambition to become a director. I just had to wait for the right moment and the right offer.

I didn't have to wait too long, as I received a call from Columbia Screen Gems, who had a huge hit with a brand-new TV show and recording group called The Monkees. They were the biggest thing next to The Beatles; in fact, they knocked The Beatles off the number-one spot on the top-ten music charts. The producers were two young guys, Bert Schneider and Bob Rafelson. Bob later went on to direct the award-winning film *"Five Easy Pieces,"* starring Jack Nicholson and Karen Black, as well as *"The King of Marvin Gardens"* and *"The Postman Always Rings Twice."* They wanted me to create a stage show for the group, who were going on their first world tour. The problem was, this was a group hired mainly for their acting ability, not their vocal talent or musicianship. In fact, I was told they hadn't played on their own records and didn't sing much on the show. The show's musical director, Don Kirshner, recorded all the material with studio musicians, and each song was a huge hit. Don really knew what he was doing, and he did a remarkable job. This appealed to me because it was a challenge. On the other hand, I also saw it as a way for me to possibly get my Directors Guild of America card and my first directing credit.

I told them I didn't want the job, and they came back with more money. The more I turned it down, the more money they offered me. In fact, they were offering me much more than the job was worth; they really wanted me badly. So here was my chance. "Let me direct just one segment of your TV show," I said, "and if it's a disaster, I'm sure you can piece it together because of the crazy style of your show. And I want a little more money, and then I'll do it." They agreed.

Once this comedy series aired, it received fantastic reviews. Every weekly segment had two "musical romps," as they were then called. These were actually the first music videos as we now know them. No one had ever done this before, and the country loved them. The show had a different, disjointed approach, especially in the editing—lots of handheld shots with lots of camera movement. It was a youthful and energetic show. Plus, The Monkees used the TV show to plug their songs every week and created numerous hits. For the first time, it showed how powerful TV was with younger music-buying audiences.

As they were on a break in filming, it was time to rehearse for the tour. They were nice guys, and two of them, Mickey Dolenz and Davy Jones, had been professional actors before the show. They were a very appealing group, clean cut and full of mischief. Bert and Bob gave me a soundstage at the Columbia Studios lot, and we went to work. It was quite funny to me because the boys had to learn how to play the instruments of their own hit songs as well as learn to sing the vocals. To add insult to injury, they had to mimic the voices of the studio singers who had actually recorded their songs. This was a first for me, and I sure saw the humor in it, as did the boys. The guys got it together, and then we worked on the staging. They were easy to work with and full of energy.

I wanted to let the audience get to know each guy individually, so in the second half of the show, I had each one doing solos; then they all came back at the end as a group. Then I came up with an idea I thought would blow everyone away. At the beginning of the show, I had two huge speakers placed on either side of the stage with the boys preset inside of them. That meant the guys had to be in those speakers for the entire length of the opening act before it was their turn to come on stage, probably thirty-five minutes. These speakers were not comfortable at all, but the boys never complained, not even once. As the audience was seated, they never suspected that the boys were inside because they hadn't seen them get in. Then, at the beginning of The Monkees' part of the show, the boys would literally burst out of these false-fronted speakers, and the audience would go totally mad, just as I knew they would. They had been tricked, and they loved it.

I also used film in the show. I liked to use film as much as I could in my live shows because it added another dimension and was good for costume and set changes without stopping or slowing down the energy of the show. Plus, I always wanted my shows to stand out and be more creative than the other choreographers' shows. Film opened up many possibilities and got you outside the confines of the arena.

The boys were very dedicated and worked extremely hard because they wanted to prove to the world that they were talented singers and musicians in their own right. We were ready to open, and Honolulu, Hawaii was the first stop. When our plane touched down, it was a riot. Every girl in Hawaii must have been at the airport, and they never stopped screaming. At that time, not many big acts had started a tour in Hawaii, and The Monkees were bigger than big. The girls broke through the police barriers and ran towards the plane. Police sirens filled the air, and we decided to make a run for it. It was madness as the girls chased their favorite Monkee around the tarmac. Some were chasing me, and I wasn't even a Monkee. They were actually pulling at me, and I started to get scared. Somehow, we all arrived safely at our limousine, and our driver slowly drove off, trying not to hit or crush anyone in that great pile of souls surrounding us.

When we arrived at the Royal Hawaiian Hotel, a huge, charming old pink palace, there were more girls—many hundreds, if not thousands, of them. We were rushed in and were finally safe. A huge contingent of police guarded us twenty-four hours a day, as the girls were climbing up the outside of the hotel walls, then knocking on our room doors or just running around the hotel in hysteria and crying out the boys' names. I had seen similar footage of The Beatles. It made it difficult to get anything done. The hotel was designed in a beautifully open way, making it easily accessible from the vines growing on the outside walls, and these girls were really good climbers!

Finally, it was time for the show. We checked out the stadium and were ready. The show went as planned, without any hitches, and was a huge hit. We got great reviews; everyone loved the boys. They finally got the recognition they so wanted, and everyone was happy. As it turned out, Hawaii had been a good choice.

Right after Hawaii, the boys took a break before picking up the tour again. Then they toured again in 1967, and this time their opening act was none other than Jimi Hendrix. At the time, he was an unknown in the US, but a star in England. After a few performances, it became very clear that Jimi Hendrix's music was not what The Monkees' fans were into, and it was decided that he would not continue with the tour.

Our 1966–67 tour was a big success, and I'm happy to report that when it ended, the TV series started up again and I got my Director's Guild card and my first directing job. In my episode, I used two friends of mine—Ruth Buzzi, who was a big hit on TV's *"Laugh In,"* and George Furth, who wrote the Broadway hit *"Company"*—as actors in the show. They were comedic character actors, and they helped me a great deal. I was very proud when Bert and Bob asked me to direct more segments of the show, which I said I would be happy to do when I had the time. The show ran for two seasons, and we won Emmy Awards both years as the best TV sitcom. I had finally made the leap to directing. Yes!

My first directing job, *"The Monkees"*
Left to right: Mickey Dolenz, Mike Nesmith, Ruth Buzzi,
George Furth, Mickey Morton, Peter Tork, Davy Jones, and me. Peter Tork is busy
inspecting my ring that I got as a present from Elvis

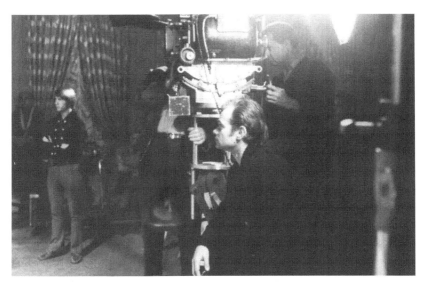

Directing *"The Monkees"* with Peter Tork looking on

Setting up a shot with Mike Nesmith and Davy Jones on stage

During my involvement with The Monkees, I got a call from a girl I knew named Sonny who lived in San Diego. She told me about a local group called Iron Butterfly. She said they were a great new group and were coming to L.A., and she wanted me to hear them and see if there was something I could do with them or for them. So I arranged with my buddy Elmer Valentine, the owner of Whiskey a Go, to have them play for me in the afternoon when the club was closed. Each one of them was an excellent musician, and I thought their sound was terrific. I especially loved one of their songs, "In-A-Gadda-Da-Vida,"

written by Doug Ingle, the keyboard player. At over seventeen minutes long, it was a very long track, but I thought it could be a huge hit, so I signed them to a management contract right away.

I let them stay in my house in Laurel Canyon (something I came to regret because of the condition they left it in). I had Elmer listen to them, and he booked them into his club for one week. When The Byrds first started, they had played the Whiskey for a long time and built up a loyal local following, which really worked out for them when they released their first record. There was a club just down the Sunset Strip called the Galaxy. A new group played in there every night, but they weren't happening. I had the Butterfly play for the owner and told her my idea, and she agreed, but she was hesitant. I told her if it didn't work out, we wouldn't want to stay there anyway.

Night by night, the word of mouth spread, and before you knew it, the club was packed and you couldn't get in. Everyone loved their music, and the girls were all crazy for a couple of the good-looking guys in the group. I was there in the club every night giving the boys notes on their performances.

The word was out on the street, and I got offers from many record labels. I decided to go with my friend Ahmet Urtegan and his ATCO Records. The famous music impresario Bill Graham called me from San Francisco and asked us to play the legendary Filmore West, where they would appear on the same bill as The Chambers Brothers, who had a big hit at the time, "Fire." I thought this was really great, and they loved them in Frisco so much that the boys had to do an encore of "In-A-Gadda-Da-Vida."

The venues they played were getting bigger and bigger, so when the album broke, it went right to the top of the Billboard 100 chart, where it stayed at number one for thirteen weeks and spent eighty-one weeks in the top ten. (Whenever I saw Ahmet, he would ask, "Where's my next group, David?") It stayed on the billboard charts for 140 weeks, setting an all-time record. To date, the album has sold in excess of 30 million copies and remains an undisputed classic in the archives of rock with DJs and audiophiles worldwide! It was the industry's very first platinum album!

In 2009, "In-A-Gadda-Da-Vida" was named the 24th-greatest hard rock song of all time by VH1. On September 12, 2010, Iron Butterfly received the lifetime achievement award at the 20th-annual San Diego Music Foundation Awards. Their theme song is often regarded as an influence on heavy-metal music as well as being one of the firsts of the genre. Iron Butterfly and their psychedelic music became synonymous with the Love Generation, and "In-A-Gadda-Da-Vida" became an anthem for the era.

I eventually became too busy with my own career and didn't have the time to give the proper attention to the group, so we split up. But for years after, whenever I would read the top-100 chart and see "In-A-Gadda-Da-Vida" listed, it always brought a smile to my face. I felt good for whatever small part I played in getting this group started and getting their music out to the world, though I should have sued them for what they did to my house in Laurel Canyon. Needless to say, I never managed another singing group again!

Nancy Sinatra, and My First Emmy Nomination

I had many offers, but when I was asked to guest star on the Nancy Sinatra TV special *"Movin' with Nancy"* in 1967, where I would appear alongside Frank Sinatra, Dean Martin, Sammy Davis Jr., Lee Hazelwood, and Nancy, I accepted the offer without even a blink. I would choreograph the special, as well.

I knew Nancy from years before when I had played cards at her and Tommy Sands's apartment in New York City from time to time, but we had never really spent any time together alone. Jack Haley Jr. was set as the director, which, to be honest, was the job that I really wanted. Nancy was so hot at the time and was one of the top recording artists of the day, so I would happily take whatever job I could get. I loved her music, and I felt I could do it justice with my movements put to it. It was a good vehicle for me, with such huge stars as Frank, Dean, and Sammy. You couldn't get any bigger than that. Little did I know that Jack Haley Jr.; the director of photography, Vilis Lapenieks; and I would all receive Emmy nominations. What can I say? To be at the top of your game and then to be acknowledged by your peers is sheer heaven! It doesn't get much better than that!

I was so thrilled on receiving my first Emmy nomination for
"Movin' With Nancy"

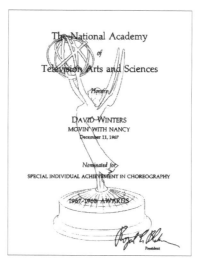

Notification from the National Academy of Television Arts and Sciences
regarding my first Emmy nomination

Nancy and I got along fabulously, as did Jack Haley Jr. and I. It was work, work, and work. I hired some great dancers to work with me, some from before and some new. There were always new kids coming up in the dance world, and I always gave auditions so I could find them. That kept me in touch with what was happening in their world. The entire show was to be shot on location, and I had to figure out my own big dance number and where and how to shoot it.

During the show, Nancy and I started a friendship that lasts still today. This was totally unexpected by me, being that Frank Sinatra was her father and she was his favorite child. He even sang a song about her called, you got it, "Nancy." So how do you grow up sitting on the number-one star in the universe's lap and not be spoiled? Frank was mesmerized by his daughter and let it be well known to the entire world. Everything she wanted was given to her, yet she is as humble as anyone I've ever met. She doesn't have a bad bone in her body. As the show progressed, our relationship did, as well. There were times that she and I felt the stress of the show, so some evenings, we drove up to a lot that her father Frank Sinatra owned in Beverly Hills overlooking Coldwater Canyon, which nobody else knew about. Needless to say, these moments were very special to both of us and always added a certain spark to the next day's filming.

We decided to do a Lionel Bart medley from *"Oliver"* with Nancy singing and me and my dancers dancing. How great was that—dancing to one of my best friend's hit music with the girl of my dreams singing the same number? Talk about a great life. Wow is all I can say! This special had become very personal to me, and it was one of the joys of my life to be a part of it. Forget all the hard work and the long hours; none of that mattered. All that mattered was that the work was good and the company even better.

Receiving my first Emmy nomination was such a big deal to me, as I had been working in TV for so many years, and finally I was being acknowledged for all of those years of hard work. This particular nomination is the most important one in my life for another reason. The year the Academy of Television Arts and Sciences decided to nominate me, there was no category for choreography in existence, so they didn't know where to put me. They decided to place me in an existing category called "Outstanding Individual Achievement on Television." Many different arts and artists were put into this category— acting or choreography, anything. In fact, there were even two star TV actors. So how do you beat actors who are on TV every week for an award? You don't. The Academy realized this, so they decided that they needed a category just for choreography. The next year, they nominated me again for the *"Ann-Margret TV Special,"* and they created a category just for me, "Best Choreography on a TV Show," and that award still stands today.

That is why this award nomination is so special to me. Because of me, there is an award given out every year for best choreographer on TV. Because of me, the art of dance and choreography is recognized along with all the other arts every year. I was able to achieve something special for dancers, and I also got to give back in a little way to a business and an art that I have loved and lived for all my life. Dancing *is* my life, and it will always be! Whenever I'm interviewed, I always say, "No matter what I may accomplish in my life, I will always just be a dancer!" *This* is my motto.

To top it all off, after the show Frank Sinatra sent me a lovely letter, which I cherish. In it, he thanked me for helping Nancy with her special and said lots of flattering things to me, ending with "From Nancy's Dad." How perfect—Frank Sinatra, the ultimate showbiz institution, simply calling himself Nancy's Dad. It doesn't get much classier than that! I was truly touched. I saw where Nancy got it from. What a sweet and humble man. I wish he were with us so I could thank him for his most kind and generous words.

Nancy Sinatra
@NancySinatra

Please light a candle for my friend, David Winters who's having open heart surgery. He choreographed Movin' With Nancy. Won an EMMY for it.

So *"Movin' With Nancy"* was a definite milestone in my life, and I love Nancy today like she is my family. Three years ago, when I was in the hospital, not knowing whether I would live or die, Nancy tweeted the message above for everyone to pray for me. Thank you so much, Nancy! I was so touched by your kindness and your sensitivity. Nancy Sinatra, you are a very special person to me. Thanks for being there and for being my friend when I really needed one. I love you!

Princess Grace Kelly of Monaco

Once upon a time there was an actress named Grace Kelly. The so-called "wealthy" family Grace was born into was actually an immigrant family of bricklayers of Irish and German descent with barely a generation of newfound business success. Grace's father and brother were both Olympic gold-medal scullers. She won the Academy Award for Best Actress for her role in the film *"The Country Girl."* Her leading men were the top stars of their day, such as Cary Grant, Jimmy Stewart, Clark Gable, Bing Crosby, and Gary Cooper. She gave up her acting career at its height to marry Prince Rainier of Monaco and become a real-life princess. MGM even released a Technicolor film of their wedding ceremony. In 1993, the US and Monaco simultaneously released a commemorative postage stamp honoring her, the first actress to be recognized in this manner.

Even though she died in 1982, she is still remembered as a major movie star. Her body of work speaks for itself: *"High Noon," "Dial M*

For Murder," "Rear Window," "To Catch a Thief," "High Society," and "The Country Girl." She was also nominated for an Oscar for "Mogambo" with Clark Gable and Ava Gardner. Her death in an auto accident following a stroke stunned the world and ended what had truly seemed a fairy-tale life.

In 1968, Hollywood master producer David Wolper, who was responsible for hundreds of hours of excellent TV, hired another producer, Roger Gimbel, to do a musical TV special with the most beautiful and elegant woman in the world at that time, Her Highness Princess Grace Kelly of Monaco. Roger called and asked me to participate as a guest star and also to do all the staging and choreography. How exciting, especially since it would be shot in beautiful Monaco, known worldwide as the playground of the rich and famous, and I would get to see my beloved Cannes once more. Most of all, I kept thinking about this divine female creature who gave up Hollywood to become a princess. What a fairy-tale life she had while she was with us, and she certainly left her mark through the many charities she sponsored. She was unlike anyone else, more of an angel than a real person. The idea of actually meeting this face that graced thousands of front pages and newspapers throughout the world was enough for me to immediately say yes.

So I was called in to meet the director and the writers. The director was a German fellow by the name of Michael Phflager, and the writers were two guys I had worked with on "Hullabaloo," Frank Peppiat and John Aylesworth. We met at Wolper's office to discuss the concept of the show, and then they hired Terry Thomas, a brilliant old comedian from the UK; Gilbert Becaud, an incredibly emotional French singer who was the rage of Europe; and Francois Hardy, the top singer in France at the time. I decided to bring along two of my very best dancers, Toni Basil and Anita Mann, and they were thrilled, never having been to Monaco before. They were both about 18 years old. So off we went to France, then on to Monaco. We flew first class on Pan Am, and the flight was filled with such anticipation. I had been there many times before, but never to work. We were all nervous wrecks just thinking and talking about it.

For the next shot, imagine the three of us in a helicopter flying over the harbor of Monaco with all of its incredibly beautiful yachts.

We landed on a helipad between the famous Hotel de Paris and the Monte Carlo Casino. We stayed in the Hotel de Paris, the best hotel in Monaco, right across the street from the Monte Carlo Casino. Since we had a couple of days to get over jet lag, the first thing I did was to become the tour guide and show Toni and Anita all over the place. I explained about the famous race, the Monaco Grand Prix, which takes place there once a year quite close to the Cannes Film Festival. Monaco was the very first city in the world to use its streets as a race track.

After some fun, it was time to get down to creating and rehearsing the dances and choosing the locations I had come up with for my guest-starring appearance. The crew taking care of us were from Germany and France and didn't speak English well, so communication was a problem. Dance is a worldwide language, though, and after they saw some of our moves, we were all on the same page. But I still kept thinking about this legend, and when could I, when would I, meet her? Meanwhile, I had to keep my mind on the job. I decided to do a ballet where the three of us were tourists in this magical kingdom, Monaco. In my number, we would visit all the amazing tourist destinations as so many people do in real life.

In front of the Prince's Palace de Monaco, shooting photos as we dance

Unbeknownst to me, when Anita flew in from St. Louis, she forgot to bring money with her. While we were rehearsing the first section of this number, Anita saw a limousine with a driver standing by the car. She went and asked him if it was possible to loan twenty dollars from him because she felt funny about asking me to loan her money. The driver gave her the money and literally five minutes later, a gentleman came up to the driver and said, "Your Highness, are you ready to leave now?" Anita was obviously in shock because she realized she had just borrowed twenty dollars from his Royal Highness, Prince Albert of Monaco. When she told me this story years later, we both howled with laughter, and she said, "David, I was just a young, innocent eighteen year old and I had never been out of America." Ha ha ha! Anyway, she and I had a great laugh about it.

Rehearsing the dance number I created that began with Toni, Anita, and myself arriving by parachute.

Then the day came, and like a vision, she appeared. I saw her for the first time stepping out of an old, chauffeured Rolls Royce in front of the palace. I was actually nervous and shaking. Why was she having this effect on me? I had grown up with and worked with some of the biggest people in the industry. When we met, her smile was so radiant, her skin so pure, and her face so elegant and angelic that I was stunned into submission. She was unlike any other girl, any Broadway or movie star, I had ever seen. She was like an apparition, like something spiritual, almost religious. I know it sounds dramatic, but she was that special. I immediately thought, I want to marry someone like her—so genteel.

She welcomed me to her country and made me feel as if it were mine. She stayed for a while and seemed impressed with what we were doing. She said she loved the ballet and really admired professional dancers. In a moment of forgetfulness of whom I was speaking to, I said that maybe we could dance together at the gala party. She smiled, winked at me, and said, "Why not?" I loved it. I had, in terms of protocol, just basically insulted the princess of the country I was visiting; and she, with a great sense of humor, had gone along with it and made me feel so wonderful.

Goofing off with a statue of Jacques-Yves Cousteau Monaco
outside the Oceanographic Museum founded by Prince Albert I

I was so glad to be there and to have the honor of meeting her. I saw her a few times after that at functions, at press conferences, and at parties. She was everywhere. This was a TV ad for her country, and as the star of the show, she was doing her utmost to help us.

Our filming went very well, and everyone, including the director and writers, was extremely pleased, which of course made me and the girls very happy. On our final night in Monaco, we were invited to a fantastic fireworks display. I was watching by myself near the water, a bit away from everyone else, going over the trip in my mind. I was stunned when, out of the shadows, none other than Princess Grace, herself, approached me, without bodyguards or handlers or chauffeurs. She was all alone. I was blown away as we proceeded to have a long conversation about so many things—politics, show business, her life, her family, my family, even dancing…and much more!

She opened up to me and told me that she felt like a bird in a cage. She told me that she often felt uncomfortable living a life of such luxury in a world where so many were impoverished. I felt like I was talking to the girl next door. She had left the princess somewhere behind in the palace. This Grace Kelly was just like so many other girls that I have known, although she never lost her elegance, her femininity, or her sincerity. Her straightforward honesty was beguiling. She was the ultimate princess.

I will never forget that conversation, and I often thought about sending her a letter to thank her, but I had second thoughts about it. I thought it would be presumptuous of me, so I left it alone. She opened up and told me so many things that she said she needed to express to another human being, but she had never found herself alone with someone whom she felt so comfortable with. Since that day I have been to Monaco many times and have passed by the palace and the spot where we had our long conversation, and I find myself smiling and very happy. I was one of the most fortunate people in the world to have met and gotten to know her beyond the public persona that she had to maintain. She was a beautiful person inside and out. I know she was troubled by the weight of her world, but one would have never known it. Grace, you were truly a living angel!

Winters/Rosen Productions

I. Two Ann-Margret TV Specials

After *"The Monkees"* and *"Movin' with Nancy,"* I got many offers, but now I was being sought after as a director/choreographer or choreographer/ co-producer. One offer was from executive producer Al Burton, who had two specials he was producing with NBC-TV that he wanted me to direct and choreograph. The producer he had hired, Burt Rosen, and I met and hit it off, so it was a go. They were both youthful shows; this was Al's area of expertise.

Ryan O'Neal, star of the huge hit movie *"Love Story,"* and Noel Harrison, son of Rex Harrison and a popular singer in his own right, would host the shows. A few of the guest stars were to be Goldie Hawn, the star of TV's *"Laugh In"*; Cher; The Association; and Bobbie Gentry. Burt and I hired two young writers, Richard Dreyfuss and Rob Reiner, whom we paid $200 a week. They were just starting out as writing partners, and I recall that this was their first job. Of course, Richard became a superstar film actor, winning both the Academy Award and Golden Globe, and Rob won the Emmy as star of the number-one TV show, *"All in the Family,"* as well as being an award-winning director.

After we finished the shows, Burt asked me to be his partner in a production company that would be called Winters/Rosen Productions, with a 50/50 split. I had already been signed with Steve Binder to co-produce and choreograph *"The Leslie Uggams Special"* by Barry Diller, who was head of programming for ABC-TV at that time, so I had to do that show first. Afterwards, Burt and I met, and I agreed to the partnership. It was understood that I only wanted to paint pretty pictures; I didn't want anything to do with the business end of it. So it was agreed: Burt would handle the business and I would be the creative side. I realized later on that I had been a bit hasty and should have checked things out better.

To announce the company, we took out full-page ads in all the trade magazines because in the first month I had four big TV specials on all three of the major networks: the two shows with Burt and the two I had done with Jack Haley Jr. and Steve Binder—the Nancy Sinatra special *"Movin' With Nancy"* and *"The Leslie Uggams Show."* Plus, since I had just been nominated for my first Emmy for the Nancy Sinatra show, it was the perfect way to announce our company. We started off with a bang. We were the hot, new kids on the block. I was twenty-nine years old and full of pep and vigor. They were exciting times, as everyone wanted to meet with us.

The first show I wanted to do with our new company was a TV version of my Ann-Margret act that I had created, directed, and choreographed for Annie, which had been so successful in the main showroom at the Riviera Hotel in Las Vegas. It was so well received that after it, I became much sought after for other performers' stage productions and wound up doing acts for Connie Stevens, Barbara Eden, and Lynda Carter. I thought this was a good choice for our first TV special, as it had been tried and tested and had worked extremely well. Burt met with Allan Carr and Roger Smith and made a deal with their company, Rogallan Productions, for the show with options for another. Allan was still Ann's manager, and Roger, who had starred in *"77 Sunset Strip,"* was now Annie's co-manager. Annie and I were very excited. We hired Bob Hope, Jack Benny, Danny Thomas, and Carol Burnett, and Burt sold the show to CBS. Winters/Rosen was off and running, and we never looked back.

I also hired all the great boy dancers and singers who had been in the original stage show: Walter Painter, Jimmy Hibbard, Pete Menefee, Gus Trikonis, John Harris, Larry Billman, Roger Minami, and Joe Cassini, and I again used my dear friend Lionel Bart's song "Big Time."

In the Vegas act, I had used ten Harley Davidsons on stage and had Annie change her clothes right on stage, using strobe lights to great effect. The way I did it, you couldn't really see that she was undressing. If I must say so myself, it was pretty clever!

At first, the network fought us on it as being too outrageous. CBS said no one had ever changed their clothes live, right in front of the audience, on family TV. And in *prime time*! They went berserk and threatened to cancel the show right then and there. But after I proved to them that you really couldn't see anything, they said that the strobe lights could somehow affect viewers' brains and might give them epilepsy. Nevertheless, I eventually won that argument, and I went back into creative mode and got on with the work.

Annie and me with script in hand for the Ann-Margret special

In her stage show, Annie used to sing a lovely Swedish ballad her mother had sung to her when she was a little girl in Ostersund, Sweden. It was a truly beautiful song, and I thought, what if we go back to Ann's home town and film there and let the audience see her in a totally different light, not as just the go-go sex queen that she was being portrayed as? I thought that I could reveal her as a sweet, sensitive, simple human being, the girl I knew her to be. I was sure the TV audience would also connect with her and like her as a person as well as a movie star. Annie went crazy about the idea and was jumping around like a kid. I was also excited because I thought it would add a new and different ingredient to the show and would be very entertaining.

Ann sang the song so very well, so sweetly and truly from the heart, that I just knew it would be one of the highlights of the special. I wanted to film it in a very simple way, too, not with a huge Hollywood crew, to capture the essence of Annie in her natural habitat. So Annie and I and my cameraman/director of photography, Stephen Burum, took off to Stockholm. Stephen and I kind of grew up together making these musical specials. Today he is one of the top cinematographers in the world. He has an Academy Award nomination for *"Hoffa,"* starring Jack Nicholson, as well as many other awards including a lifetime achievement award from the American Society of Cinematographers. He is brilliant, and I was extremely lucky to get him early on in his illustrious career. Some of his other credits include *"Apocalypse Now,"*

"Mission: Impossible," "The Untouchables," "Carlito's Way", "Uncommon Valor," "The War of the Roses," and *"St. Elmo's Fire."*

We made a great team, and sometimes Stephen would let me shoot camera as well. I wanted certain things to happen on specific notes of the song. I wanted Ann to leave the frame or come into the frame on particular beats. This was most important to me, as I had pre-edited the sequence in my head before we ever got to Sweden. This was only possible if you were also a choreographer, which Stephen wasn't. So he deferred to me, and I got exactly what I went to Sweden to get—Annie at her very best! It turned out to be a wonderful sequence with a wonderful performer, and it was visually stunning and sensitive, just as I knew it would be. And what was truly great about that Swedish sequence was, I was able to give back to Annie for all she had done for me in the past.

Mike Nichols was directing *"Carnal Knowledge,"* starring Jack Nicholson. When Ann's name came up for the leading role, Nichols said she was like a go-go dancer in the musicals *"Bye Bye Birdie"* and *"Viva Las Vegas,"* and he wanted someone more sensitive. One of his assistants then showed him our Swedish lullaby number, and he immediately changed his mind and hired her for the part. Ann won the Golden Globe Award and was nominated for an Academy Award for her role in the film, and I felt fabulous about being able to repay Ann for her belief in me!

That first TV special was a big success—yes!—and Burt and I decided to follow it up with another show featuring Ann, which I created—*"Ann-Margret: From Hollywood with Love."*

I hired Dean Martin, whom I had worked with before on Nancy Sinatra's special, as one of the guest stars. Dean was so funny. One day he said to me, "Hey, David, let's go for a drink," and I replied, "Dean, you know I don't drink." Then he said, "What a shame. I feel sorry for you," so I asked, "Why is that Dean?" and Dean answered, "Cause when you wake up in the morning, David, that's as good as you're ever going to feel." We laughed and then went back to work. But I thought about Dean's remark years later when Dean and I shared the same doctor, Charles Kivowitz, in Beverly Hills.

While making the film *"Mission: Kill"* in Mexico, I contacted endocarditis, a very serious disease, and I wound up in the hospital for six months. Dean Martin was also in Cedar Sinai Hospital because of a liver problem. Dr. Charlie told me Dean needed to stop drinking; otherwise, it would kill him. Well, Dean never did stop drinking, and one day during my stay, Dr. Charlie told me that Dean had just died of a liver complication, the result of all those years of heavy drinking. This saddened me to no end. Dean was such a wonderful guy; everybody loved him. What a waste, I thought. As for me, I never drank, not even champagne on New Year's Eve, I never smoked, and I always kept my distance from any legal or illegal drugs. In this business, I was a bit of an oddity, but I have always had the need to be in total control of my life. Captain of my own destiny, master of my universe! Yes, I am a control freak, but it has worked for me. And, now back to the show…

My second mother, Lucille Ball, agreed to come on the show as a favor to me, and she worked for **AFTRA** scale, which at the time was a huge $390! Can you imagine? $390 for the number-one TV star in the world! This was the first of many favors Lucy did for me throughout my career. Annie and I were both so thrilled to have Lucy on our special, and the two of them performed a vaudevillian song-and-dance number that I had specifically written for them. Boy, were they great!

For the opening of this special, I shot a scene on the Hollywood Freeway, and it was quite dangerous for both Ann and myself. I honestly didn't realize this before we stepped out onto the highway. The cars were going very fast, of course, but the real problem was that when anyone would look out of their window and see Ann-Margret standing on the highway next to them, they went gaga. They couldn't believe their eyes. There she was—the American sex kitten Ann-Margret live, right in front of them, and dancing on the freeway! Yes, dancing on the freeway. It was pure madness! People slammed on their brakes, others skidded, and still more stopped to take pictures. And then it started to happen on both sides of the freeway. I was afraid the highway patrol would kick us off the freeway, and I would never get this incredible opening scene.

Annie and me on the set of "The Game of Hollywood"

I finally decided that we should get off the freeway for a while and get some rest. I had hired four big cherry pickers to hold the cameras, and it was quite a sight. Don't ask me how we did it, but we eventually got all the shots I had planned, and then Annie and I scurried away as fast as we could. Annie was always such a good sport and never once questioned anything that I wanted to do, no matter how crazy it was! We totally believed in each other.

For this same special, I had a great idea to re-create Monopoly, the game that the world loves, into a story of how you become a star in Hollywood. I called this sequence "The Game of Hollywood." I had a huge Monopoly board built in what was at that time an empty parking lot in Century City. I then had it painted just like the real game, only about the things one goes through to become a star in Hollywood. Annie and I had great fun doing the sequence until the day we almost had a total tragedy.

The Monopoly board was so big that the only way to get the full shot I was looking for was to use a cherry picker on a crane that had to go way up in the sky. A normal movie crane would never be able to go that high to get the shot I wanted. So right before shooting, we strapped the camera to a bucket attached to the front of a cherry picker. Stephen Burum, my director of photography, got in the bucket and went up to check out the shot and make sure that we could see the entire board in our frame. My crew tied Stephen into the bucket for obvious reasons. As it turned out, someone must have had a premonition.

Directing Annie in "The Game of Hollywood" sequence

Satisfied that we could get the wide shot, he told me everything looked good from up there, but he was going to have his three assistants go up one more time to check it out. The cherry picker went so high in the sky that each time it went up, the entire cast and crew watched, fascinated. Then the unthinkable happened. The bucket turned upside down, and the three assistants were thrown into the air. Well, some of us screamed, others cried out, some said nothing; we were all in total and complete shock. We expected all three people to come tumbling down to earth and a sure death. I guess God was watching over us, as, luckily, one guy grabbed the lip of the bucket, another somehow got his feet in the bucket and was hanging upside down like a child on the playground, and the third also somehow hung on when one of his large, muscular arms got caught in the bucket as he fell towards the earth. It seemed like an absolute miracle.

As I screamed out to the man in control of the cherry picker, I heard him crying and actually praying out loud as he tried to slowly and carefully bring the bucket down to street level. He was so scared, he was shaking. I guess he felt responsible for this tragic event. As he was bringing the cherry picker down, unbelievably, it flipped again. Oh my God, I thought, for sure they're dead now. For some reason, at that moment, I looked over to the stills man, and I couldn't believe my eyes. He was snapping away, left and right. Most of us ran under the cherry picker to try to break the falls of those so desperately hanging on for their lives, but not him. He was intent on getting as many shots as he could of this near disaster. I couldn't fathom how, or why, he was doing what he was doing. Was he going to sell his pictures to the newspapers or to a magazine? It boggled my mind.

Luckily, by this time, they were closer to the ground, and one of them tumbled on top of my crew, who were waiting for him to do just that. I saw another literally fly through the air and land on a grassy knoll nearby. The third person managed to hang on to the bucket and arrived safely on the ground, where we all exploded with gratitude and screams of exhilaration. The women on the set were all crying out of happiness, and we all rejoiced at our good fortune. The production manager immediately called three ambulances to come get our three crew members and take them to the closest hospital.

It seemed to last forever when this near tragedy was unfolding, but in reality, it all happened in less than thirty seconds. The guy who was praying out loud collapsed, sobbing and sobbing. I could see there was no sense in continuing, so I closed down the set and sent everyone home. I felt that we all needed time to rest after this scary, almost tragic day. I was thankful that Stephen had not been in the bucket when this took place, although he had been in the bucket only a minute before. I think we all took a minute to thank God. I know I did.

The rest of the show went according to plan and schedule, and to top it off, the National Academy of Television of Arts and Sciences again nominated me for an Emmy Award—my second in as many years. Annie and I had planned to do a third special together, and I don't know what happened, but it never came about. I heard there were disagreements between Burt and her husband and manager, Roger Smith. I just loved Annie and wanted to keep it that way without having to deal with all the business crap. How crazy is life?

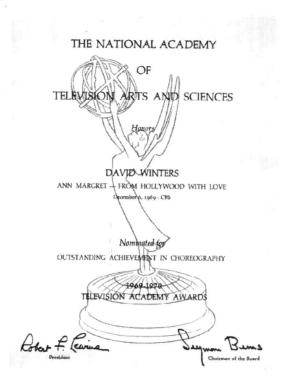

THE NATIONAL ACADEMY

OF

TELEVISION ARTS AND SCIENCES

Honors

DAVID WINTERS
ANN MARGRET — FROM HOLLYWOOD WITH LOVE
December 6, 1969 · CBS

Nominated for
OUTSTANDING ACHIEVEMENT IN CHOREOGRAPHY

1969-1970
TELEVISION ACADEMY AWARDS

II. "THE SPECIAL LONDON BRIDGE SPECIAL"

Establishing wide shot of me driving down Sunset Boulevard in Los Angeles in my Rolls Royce Continental convertible... I come to a stop because of a traffic light. Right next to the traffic light, looming over it, is a huge billboard.

Cut to a medium shot of the billboard that reads, "See the USA in your Chevrolet," in big letters written right across it.

Cut to a close-up of my face reading the billboard. I start to smile like the billboard just gave me an idea.

This billboard was the sales campaign that General Motors used all across America to encourage people to drive their cars at home and see their own country before even thinking about going overseas. At the time, General Motors was the biggest corporation in America and one of the largest advertisers on TV. Since Burt Rosen and I were in the getting-sponsors-for-our-TV-specials business, I thought, hey, how about Chevy or actually General Motors? So I drove to the office and started to create a concept for a TV special that would work into their sales campaign. During my research, I discovered that a guy named C. V. "Woody" Wood, the chairman of McCullouch Oil, was building a new city in Arizona called Lake Havasu. He had bought the London Bridge and was moving it to Arizona as a tourist attraction. I later found out that he had been the master planner for Disneyland. He was a true entrepreneurial type, having been responsible for designing many American amusement parks. I went to see him and told him my idea for the TV special, and by the time I left his office, he and I had come to an understanding that I could shoot my show in Lake Havasu. He agreed to help me in several ways, such as with lodgings, airfares, etc. This would bring my costs down and allow me to shoot on film with a TV budget. This would make all the difference and would make the show much more financially viable.

Back at the office, I had meetings with my writers, and we came up with a fantasy idea for a show that would start in London and then work its way to Lake Havasu, all because of the London Bridge. Everyone in the world had heard of the London Bridge and knew the song about its falling down. My original idea was to star Barbra Streisand and Rex Harrison, the star of *"My Fair Lady"* on Broadway. I knew if I could get the two of them, we'd win an Emmy for sure.

Now that I had the idea, I just needed to get General Motors or Chevy to put up the money, which turned out to be much harder than I thought; the reason being that Chevy had been sponsoring everything that a competitor production company was producing. We found out there was a close relationship between the company and someone very high up at Chevrolet. Burt and I discussed this, and Burt said we must get to the chairman of General Motors and pay him off. Ha, I thought. Well, at least my partner is thinking big.

A man named John DeLorean, yes, the one who made the DeLorean car many years later, was their chairman. As it turned out, an ex-girlfriend of mine was involved with a guy who owned a Chevy dealership on the Sunset Strip. To cut a long story short, we made a deal with him to pay off DeLorean $125,000 for every show that Chevrolet or General Motors sponsored for Winters/Rosen Productions. The money would go to this car dealer, who would make sure that John DeLorean received it. This way, DeLorean was not directly involved in the payoff. I thought DeLorean was nuts. Here he was, the CEO of the largest corporation in America, taking a kickback—crazy, but he did. That's how we broke down the Chevy door and got their business away from our competitors.

They became a very good account for us, as we did four or five specials with them. I am still amazed that DeLorean took the risk. We definitely paid him more than our competitors were paying, and maybe that's what made the deal work. Of course, it may have been that the dealer kept our money and somehow got DeLorean to do the special with us, but that didn't matter to us. What mattered was that Chevy sponsored our specials. To tell you the truth, I didn't care. All I wanted was to get to make my show! I could see an Emmy sitting in our offices, maybe even more than one. Yes, you're right, I was getting carried away, I was dreaming.

I promised DeLorean a fabulous star-studded cast, and I was determined to deliver that, even with my TV budget of just $375,000 after we paid John (or the dealer) his fee. The budget was actually $500,000 before John's fee. This didn't bother me, because I really wanted to secure his ongoing business for our company and deliver what Burt had promised him. I thought we could have a really big future business with an advertiser like Chevrolet in our pocket.

The funny thing is, C. V. Wood made a huge mistake and bought the wrong bridge. He thought he was buying the Tower Bridge, which is the bridge American audiences are accustomed to seeing in photographs. It has two large towers and a drawbridge in the center and is really quite beautiful. The actual London Bridge that Woody bought was just a plain span bridge with nothing interesting about it at all, except for the name. He had paid a fortune for it and another fortune to have it shipped to the US, and it was a huge undertaking to ship it. I felt bad for C. V., but how funny for someone to buy the wrong bridge, especially the wrong London Bridge.

Barbra and Rex Harrison turned down my offers because within this budget, my offers were very low. I was prepared for this, as I had to be realistic about the kind of money they both made and what we had budgeted, especially for a show that was to be built around them and their unique talents. But I was still determined to be true to my word, so I filled *"The Special London Bridge Special"* with an all-star cast, even better than I first thought I could. The final cast included Tom Jones, Jennifer O'Neil, Kirk Douglas, Rudolph Nureyev, the Carpenters, Jonathan Winters, Hermione Gingold, and my dear buddy Elliott Gould, plus cameos by Englebert Humperdinck, Charlton Heston, Chief Dan George, Michael Landon, Lorne Greene, George Kirby, and Terry Thomas—a pretty strong cast, even if I say so myself!

Tom Jones and Jennifer O'Neil in a romantic love story set against the backdrop of the London Bridge in Lake Havasu, Arizona

We filmed both in London and Lake Havasu, Arizona. I liked to shoot on film because I could be more creative with it, so all of our shows were like movies. They took me much longer to make, but I enjoyed it. Also, by doing them on location, we were able to get out of the confines of the soundstage, and it made what we were doing unique and different from what all the other producers in America were doing.

While I was shooting a number with Kirk Douglas and Tom Jones, both of them in top hat and tails, I got an idea. Kirk had this evil look in one of his eyes, and I thought, why don't I do a musical version of *"Dr. Jekyll and Mr. Hyde"* starring Kirk Douglas? I told him the idea, and he loved it. More on this later…

Almost everyone on the show was terrific; my biggest problem turned out to be Rudolph Nureyev. He was a real pain in the ass, although the ballet sequence I did with him is one of the best things I have ever done. It's ballet as you have never seen before, extremely cinematic.

After signing Nureyev to a contract, I went to London to see a performance of *"Romeo and Juliet"* featuring him and Dame Margot

Fonteyn at the Royal Ballet. After the performance, my girlfriend and I went backstage to meet with him, and he was quite charming as he invited us into his dressing room. He was a fantastic dancer, and since ballet was not my strong point, I was questioning how I would choreograph him. After all, he was the most renowned ballet dancer in the world. I told Rudolph that his sequence in the show would be unique and wonderful. He seemed genuinely excited and told me he was looking forward to the challenge. We went out for food and drinks. He seemed a bit insecure, and I liked that about him. I thought it would be a lot of fun, but I was later proven wrong.

Weeks later, when it came time for the shoot, I hired a Russian girl, Olga, who was a good friend of mine, to pick him up at London's Heathrow Airport with flowers, etc. When he got settled, I called him and told him his call time was 9:00 a.m. He told me in no uncertain terms he would not be there that early. I explained that the whole crew would be there as well as one of his partners from the Royal Ballet, Ms. Merle Park, and that we only had the studios for a certain amount of time. "That's your problem," he said in his bitchiest tone of voice, which really got me going. I told him I was paying him $25,000 for one number, and if he didn't show up when I asked him to, I would sue him and stop him from doing any other work in the business. "You better get your f**king ass to the set at 9:00 a.m. or I'll see you in court," I said. "I'll get an injunction and publicize the hell out of it; you'll never work again, man." Obviously, I was furious. I figured that this guy got his own way all the time, so I had to be extra tough with him if I wanted to succeed. I simply had to let him know who the boss was. I didn't wait for his answer; I just hung up the phone. The funny thing was, the whole time I was talking to him, my girlfriend, Susanne Benton, and I were trying to hold down the record button on our tape recorder to have proof of the conversation, but the button wouldn't stay down. I wanted proof just in case it really did come to a lawsuit.

The next morning, he showed up at 9:00 a.m. on the dot. We smiled at each other in a fake manner, and he went to his dressing room. When I called him out to rehearse, he told me he wouldn't dance on the floor of the studio because it was concrete. I told him that if it was good enough for Gene Kelly and Fred Astaire, it was certainly good enough for him. I repeated my threat, and he got the message loud and clear. He gave me an "I don't want to smile" smile and went back to change into rehearsal clothes. I was already tired of this prima donna, and I wanted to belt him, but I cooled my heels in the interest of the show. I hate prima donnas; I don't have time for them. I know so many talented stars and non-stars who are down-to-earth and genuinely nice people. Unfortunately, I couldn't blame anyone else; it had been my idea to hire him.

I bought these shots of me that were taken during *"The Special London Bridge Special"* on eBay for $50. NBC's publicity department took them unbeknownst to me at the time.

We rehearsed, and as I had anticipated, he was simply fabulous. He had an elegance about him and did everything I asked of him and more. Now it was time to shoot, and everyone was ready. We rolled cameras, and I wanted them to go to very high speed so that when it played back, it played back in slow motion. Nureyev stopped and called me over. "David, you can't film me in slow motion. Everyone will see my technique. They'll know that I'm not very good technically," he said dramatically. "I understand, Rudy," I told him, "but when you see this whole idea I have, with the editing and everything, with you coming out of yourself, it will blow your mind." Rudy's response was: "I cannot let you film me in slow motion." I looked at the clock and instead of arguing with him I just said okay, with my fingers figuratively crossed behind my back. We started again, after I told every one of the cameras not to use slow motion. But behind his back, I told everyone to go slow motion once the music had started. This way, he wouldn't hear the cameras revving up, and that is exactly what we did, take after take, until I got what I wanted. I often wondered if he ever saw the sequence. It was beautiful, but he was right: you could see every mistake he made, although nobody cared. Rudy in slow motion, exposed to the world, is still better than any other ballet dancer you will ever see. Absolutely magnificent!

III. *"Raquel!"*—the TV Special

When I was teaching dance in Hollywood, Raquel Welch was just one of the beautiful starlets who studied under me. The next time I saw her, she was a regular on a big network variety show in which she introduced the next guest with a sign. Soon after this, her career took off when she made the film *"One Million Years B.C."* Raquel subsequently became the new sex symbol, replacing Marilyn Monroe, for my generation, and the still picture of her in a fur bikini from that movie was known all over the world.

I had heard negative stories about her attitude on set, but I figured that since I was a contemporary of hers and we already had a good working relationship, whatever anyone else's problems were, they wouldn't affect me. I called Raquel and told her I'd like to meet up about doing a show with her. "Really, what kind of a show, David?" she asked. I quickly improvised and told her, "A show where we follow you as you chase the sun around the world. People have this concept of you being a jet-setter and sex symbol from somewhere mysterious." She liked the concept, and after a meeting, we agreed to work together. But I felt like I needed to protect myself because of all the bad rumors about Raquel and her temperament, so I staged press conferences in every country we shot in so that if she walked out on the show, I could still piece something together to deliver to our sponsor and to CBS. I didn't want to take any chances.

To co-star in the show, I signed John Wayne, Bob Hope, and Tom Jones—three of the biggest stars in the business at the time. It was a terrific cast, and the show got fantastic reviews. We also got a 52-percent share of the TV-watching audience that night and 58 percent in NYC, so the CBS network brass were thrilled.

Our first location was the Teotihuacan pyramids outside of Mexico City. I saw the pyramids as an amazing set and decided to do a number based on our horoscope signs. *"Hair"* was the most popular Broadway show at the time, and its music was simply amazing. It seemed to fit so well for this location. I had stunning costumes made of each horoscope sign and used this city of pyramids as the background for a medley of songs from *"Hair."*

My crew and I, filming at the pyramids

I'm on the crane (lower left) directing Raquel and the cast.

Once I got Raquel to come on the set, the local paparazzi started filming her. I instructed one of my crew, a seventeen-year-old young man, to stand right in front of their lens so they couldn't take shots of her. Then one of the Mexican paparazzi hit my crew member with a lead pipe and injured him. Well, that was all I needed. I picked up my chair and took off my camera battery belt and started slashing out at him with it, kind of like a lion tamer might do in the circus. I could see their cameras shooting me, but I was so furious that it didn't even bother me. When he saw my anger he backed off, and I closed down the set and waited for them to leave. Once they did, we went back to shooting this fabulous number in an even more fabulous set. Nothing would stop me.

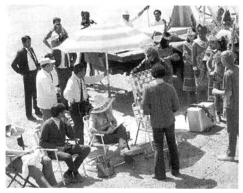

Me confronting the Mexico City press with the actors and crew watching from the sidelines, afraid to move

When the press left, they must have gone straight back to their jobs, for the very next day, it was all over Mexico City's main newspapers, not just the headlines, but two pages of centerfold pictures to boot. They covered it really well, I'll give them that. It became a huge scandal, as they said we had desecrated an historical monument.

Showing the Mayan dancers where I wanted them for the number

Conferring with my DP, Stephen, about the next shot,
which I have decided to shoot camera on myself

Showing my DP, Stephen, that I want to use the crane for this shot

When we left the set that day, it was quite eerie, as all the tourists
had been asked to leave just after our little incident with the press.
There we were, in a three-mile-long city, and it was totally empty
except for us. It was truly creepy, and I started to think about making
a horror film.

It became so crazy during this shoot and things got so out of hand that I had to ask John Wayne to call his friend, the former president of Mexico Miguel Alleman Valdez, to intervene and get some of my crew out of jail and my film out of the country, which he did. John was a real macho type of man and, I must say, a very helpful one, but working with John Wayne was interesting, even kind of strange. He would tell me where I should put the camera and what size lens I should use, etc. I was always respectful of him and never forgot that I was working with a true living legend. I think that he was just so used to being in control for so many years that he couldn't help himself. But with John's help and participation, it turned out to be a beautiful show.

Our next move was to Chapultepec Park, located right in the middle of Mexico City. Fortunately for us, we didn't encounter any problems there at all. Chapultepec is the largest city park in Latin America. It's classed as one of the world's great urban parks, along with Bois de Boulogne in Paris, the Imperial Gardens in Tokyo, and Central Park in NYC. When we wrapped there, we set off to shoot the *"Tom Jones"* segments of the show in London.

My crew and I getting the equipment ready for the next number

Raquel following me as I show her a dance step to the hit song
"Raindrops Keep Falling on My Head"

Scouting locations before the shoot at the majestic Chapultepec Park fountain

On arrival, and now back to more familiar settings, I rented the top club in London, the Revolution, to film a rock-and-roll medley that Tom and Raquel were to sing together. It took many hours to light the set and get it ready for filming. When we were ready, Raquel wasn't, and we had to wait and wait and wait. Eventually, I was told that Raquel didn't want to come out. I was so mad that I told one of my assistants, "Tell her she better get herself out here, or I'm cancelling the whole segment." Within minutes, Raquel came to the set, and we exchanged fake smiles as I instantly had flashbacks to the Nureyev episode. Finally, we started to film. We only had a certain amount of time with Tom, and she had jeopardized the whole segment. God only knows what she was doing in her trailer all that time.

I had many fights with Raquel during the filming, as she never understood what I was trying to accomplish. She was forever pushing her hair out of her face as she was being filmed singing. I told her over and over, "Forget about your hair, and just think about the words you are singing." I even sent her to Seth Riggs, the finest voice production teacher in the world. Michael Jackson and Stevie Wonder went to him, need I say more? Despite six months with Seth, I still had to replace her voice in the special with one of the King Cousins. Raquel was pissed with me, but after sitting in the Denham recording studios in London, for hours and hours, all night long, I had no other choice. She sounded terrible, and there was no way I could have used her voice in the show. Which reminds me of a funny story...

After we finished the show, Roy Gerber, her manager at the time, called me up and asked me for a print of it. He said he wanted to show it to a hotel in Vegas and get her a booking. I said, "Roy, it's not her voice in the show when she sings"; and Roy said, "I know, but they'll never know." And Roy was right; he booked her into Vegas for about $125,000 a week. I couldn't believe it.

Then, another time, I had a huge argument with Raquel in the editing room. She wanted more close-ups, and I told her that if she had listened to me during the shoot and thought about the lyrics during filming instead of always worrying about what she looked like, there would be no problem. But that wasn't the case. She cursed me as she left the room and told me, "You've exploited me all over the world." I told her, in the most polite manner, to f*** off. As I think back, it seems that I was always telling her to f*** off. I told her I had been working on this show for over a year, and I was currently working twenty hours a day with five editors trying to make her look good. I was trying to make the air date and that she was an unappreciative b**ch. The next day, *Newsweek Magazine* interviewed me and asked me how I felt about working with Raquel. What timing, huh? I told them that she was impossible and that I would never again work with someone so untalented. Well, did that cause an uproar! Everyone read it, and it probably helped our ratings go sky high.

After the article hit the streets, I didn't hear from Raquel again until the show aired. In fact, as I was watching it on TV, the phone rang. Susanne, my girlfriend, answered and told me it was Raquel. "Yeah, what about?" I said skeptically. "It's some joker. Just hang up." When the show ended, the phone rang again, and again she said it was Raquel. This time I took the phone, and it was her. "I saw the show and it was fantastic," she said. "I just wanted to tell you that I'm sorry for all the problems. I now understand what you wanted to say creatively." I was truly taken aback by her phone call. I told her, "I appreciate the call, and it is certainly more than I had expected of you."

We went our separate ways, and Raquel was later in a Broadway musical in which she had to sing live. To give her all the credit where credit is due, she received very good reviews from the critics. In fact, they were raves. And she is certainly one of the most beautiful women in the world, even now. After all she and I went through, today we are friends on Facebook. Sometimes, in the heat of battle, you say things you don't really mean, and so I apologize for the foul words I said to her.

Bob Hope and Raquel in the comical Rocky Raccoon number

Funnily enough, I think I did some of my best work on this show. But I couldn't have done it without Stephen Burum, who was my cameraman. He was amazing. We did some of the best work we ever did during our partnership on this show, and we received some of the best reviews I have ever gotten in my life. As William Shakespeare said, "All's well that ends well!"

IV. *"Once Upon a Wheel,"* with Paul Newman

Hang on to your seat! We're on a wide-angle shot inside the cockpit of a racing car and driving around the bend of a race track. It's very confining in the cockpit as there is no extra room because the car is built for speed.

But—wow!—is it ever exciting! A once-in-a-lifetime experience.

At Winters/Rosen Productions, Burt Rosen handled the money and I was the creative partner. One day he told me, shockingly, that we needed $100,000 very fast or we were going to go out of business. After I got over the shock of what he had just laid on me, I thought hard about it.

I had been invited to a celebrity race with Paul Newman and other celebs attending, and so I came up with the idea to do a racing special. Burt said that he could sell it to Coca-Cola, but we would need to have a big star attached, and then we could get $100,000 as a down payment. I said, "What if I got you Paul Newman's name on a deal memo or a contract?" "Great," he said. Aside from Paul, other celebrities who would be attending were James Garner, Dick Smothers, Dino Martin Jr., John Wayne, Cesar Romero, and astronaut Pete Conrad as well as racing stars Mario Andretti, Al Unser, Bobby Unser, and Parnelli Jones, who were all going to be involved in the festivities, as it was the formal opening of the Ontario Motor Speedway.

My director friend from the Nancy special, Jack Haley Jr., was putting on the event, so I got hold of a lot of passes to the pits. He was also shooting a documentary of the event, so I figured that a few extra cameras would not arouse any suspicion. I made up a release form that three of my young female assistants asked the celebrities to sign, and everybody did, thinking, of course, that it was a release form for that particular event. No one had any idea what I was up to. I told the girls to make sure they got Paul Newman's signature on a couple of the releases. The releases weren't specific; in fact, they were deliberately vague so as not to scare away any of the stars or other participants. I was successful!

So with Paul's signature in hand, Burt went to Coca-Cola. Burt did his thing and sold them a TV special starring Paul Newman. It's amazing, the things you'll do when your back is up against the wall. I told Burt that he was crazy because Paul had said many times, both publicly and in print, that he would never do TV. I had some footage on Paul from the Celebrity Race, but that was like a cameo appearance. It certainly wasn't the same as him starring in or hosting the show. I was really concerned because Burt had come back with a check for $100,000 from Coca-Cola, and if we didn't deliver Paul, we would be out of business and in a lawsuit with Coca-Cola and probably finished in the business. God knows, we might even go to jail.

"David, you've got to deliver Paul," Burt said. I certainly didn't sleep that night. The next day I called our agent, Freddie Fields, at the ICM Agency and said, "Freddie, please set up a meet with Paul Newman." It turned out that Paul had the same agent as us. So did Dustin Hoffman, Steve McQueen, Barbra Streisand, and Ryan O'Neal. Obviously, Freddie was the most powerful agent in Hollywood.

"Forget it, David," Freddie said. "Paul will not do TV."

"Freddie, it's real important," I said. "Can you give me his home number? I've known Paul for years."

I told Freddie that I used to play baseball with Paul in the Broadway Show League in New York City. And because of that, Paul and I were actually friends. Freddie gave me his number after making me swear not to tell Paul where I got it.

Paul lived in Connecticut with his wife, the lovely actress Joanne Woodward, and also had a beautiful home just off of Coldwater Canyon in Beverly Hills. I called Paul, and he seemed a little cold on the phone. After a while he said, "David, how did you get my number?" and I said, "I can't tell you Paul, but if you ever need anyone's number, call me." He laughed and that broke the ice. Then he was very friendly, and we talked about old times on Broadway and the Show League. I asked him when he'd be in L.A. and told him I had something I'd like to get together and talk to him about. He gave me a date to meet at his house.

About a week later, the night before our meeting, I came home to find a message on the phone from Paul. I thought, what should I do? I called Freddie, who said, "Don't call him back. He's found out that you want to talk to him about doing TV, and he's going to cancel the meeting. Just show up at his house." So I took Freddie's advice. The next morning as I drove to Paul's house, I was nervous as hell. Paul answered the door, and I could see again why all the women went crazy for him with those big blue eyes. He was truly a beautiful man.

He invited me out to his pool and offered me a seat. I had done my homework on auto racing, and Paul was surprised by the information I gave him about a couple of drivers, and my knowledge about the sport overall. But right away he said he wouldn't appear on TV and wouldn't do this show. I told him he was right, that a show about car racing would get boring to most of the audience who weren't die-hard racing fans. Then I gave him a book that I had that was split up into four sections: the Driver, the Machine, the Spectator, and the Race. As it turned out, by fate, that book was his favorite book on racing. I glanced up at the sky, thanking whoever's up there for my good fortune. That moment opened the door for me. I explained specifically how I saw the show and my ideas for it. My title was *"Once Upon a Wheel."* I told him we would buy a Can-Am racing car; that I would get Freddie Fields and ICM to come in with us, which I did; and that we would go to all the races and have a ball. I would hire a Lear jet and a helicopter to take us right into the pit and out again after the races. Anyhow, I got him going, and by the time I left his house, he had agreed to be my partner in the project, buy two cars with me, and only take a fee of $50,000! Here was the biggest, most expensive film star in the world, only taking fifty grand. I just couldn't believe it. I wanted to kiss him. I called Burt, who wanted to kiss me. I wanted to kiss everyone.

Freddie Fields called me later and said, "I don't believe it, David. I don't know what you said or did, but Paul's instructed me to draft contracts." Freddie couldn't believe it. Man, was that a close one for Burt and me.

Directing Paul Newman in *"Once Upon a Wheel"*

We did the film, and Paul was so easy to work with, a true professional. Like I had said, I rented a Lear jet and helicopters, and we went to the races. We took the Lear from L.A. and I had a helicopter standing by to take us to the pit stop at whatever race track we were at. It was very funny, though, when Paul and I landed in the pit stops: all these macho grease monkeys just stared at him with their mouths open and started pointing at him and whispering to each other, "Hey, that's Paul Newman." They were all like little kids, in awe of Paul. It was hysterical to see.

Burt and I spent about $600,000 on this little car racing fantasy. As planned, we bought two cars and hired Bob Bondurant, who ran the Bob Bondurant Racing School at the Ontario Motor Speedway in Los Angeles, to be one of our drivers and Karl Messerschmidt to be the other.

Well, happily, when I showed him the film, Paul liked it so much that he suggested we blow it up to 35mm. He also suggested that I add about forty minutes to it and that we sell it around the world as a feature, which is exactly what I did. What a great partner Paul turned out to be! In Italy alone, we got a $3 million advance on the longer film and made a 25-percent profit.

Me with one of my drivers, Bob Bondurant

What Burt forgot to tell me was that he had told Coca-Cola that we would deliver life-size blow-ups of Paul holding a Coca-Cola bottle and wearing a Coca-Cola racing jacket. When I discovered this, I said, "Burt you're f**king mad. Paul could get millions for that type of promotion."

Burt said, "But I forgot to tell you, and I've already promised them in Atlanta. They loved the show and Paul so much that they've agreed to spend tens of millions on promoting this event. It will be their biggest promotion of the year."

Shit! Here we go again! I decided just to tell Paul the truth. When I explained about the predicament my partner had created, being a real gentleman and now also a very close friend, he agreed to do it for me. Wow, what a guy! So, all over America, in every 7-Eleven store, there was Paul Newman, selling Coca-Cola. I couldn't believe it, even when I saw it with my own eyes. The Coca-Cola Company went crazy, the biggest star in the world was actually selling their product to America. Because of this promotion, Coca-Cola loved us, and we wound up selling them a thirteen-part series on racing, also called *"Once Upon a Wheel."*

Whenever Paul came to my office, the whole neighborhood went wild. All the girls would hang out of their windows and throw their underwear at him. I'd never seen anything quite like this before with an older guy who was not a rock'n'roller. The girls were sure crazy about him. We got really close and hung out together socially and even went to a special theatre to see the Muhammad Ali boxing championship fight. We also went together to the Directors Guild Theater for the world premiere of Paul's latest film. I felt bad for Paul because we were sitting in the back row, and the audience, who didn't know Paul was there, was leaving in the middle of the film. Paul turned to me and said, "I just don't know what the audience wants to see anymore. David, I've lost it." I didn't know what to say; it was such an honest moment. Those big blue eyes were searching for an answer, but I didn't have one. Later on that evening, I told Paul that everyone makes mistakes, and not to be too hard on himself, which seemed to appease him, and he smiled back. I liked hanging out with Paul. He was simple and unassuming—rare qualities in Hollywood.

Paul and Robert Redford made the film *"Butch Cassidy and the Sundance Kid,"* which was a smash hit. I found out a while back that Sotheby's auction house was going to auction off a lot of the props from the film. Burt Bacharach wrote the number-one hit for that film, "Raindrops Keep Falling on My Head," and in that particular sequence, Paul rides around on a bicycle with his co-star Kathryn Ross.

With Paul's birthday coming up, I made a plan with his wonderful wife, Joanne, to get him out of the house. I would buy the bicycle and deliver it, with a ribbon tied around it, to their place, and when Paul came home the bicycle would already be there. I went to the auction figuring it would be an easy buy. It was a five-dollar bike, so I figured I might drop $500. Was I wrong! At $3,000, I was still going head-to-head with someone in the other auction room. I finally got it for $3,200. The truth is, I would have had to pay whatever it was bid up to because I had promised Joanne that I would buy it.

As I was putting the ribbon around my new acquisition, Burt Bacharach and his wife, actress Angie Dickinson, came up and said they had been bidding in the next room and were curious as to who had gotten it. They had wanted it for their new restaurant, which was filled with props from Burt's movies and TV shows. I quickly explained about Paul, while a truck waited outside to take it away. There were lots of photos in the newspapers of the nut (me) who paid $3,200 for a five-dollar bike.

Paul came home, loved it, and called me the next day to thank me. It was worth every penny and all the time I spent at the auction house.

TV Guide did a big article on the show and also gave us the cover.

I considered Paul Newman a very good friend. He was very humble and sincere and one hell of a guy, a man's man, and a great actor.

V. Marlon Brando and the TV Special that Never Happened

While producing our many shows, I came up with a concept for a TV series called "A Last Look At" that would be about things in our society that were dying like old dinosaurs, such as the circus, long journeys on trains, and so much more.

As an actor, Marlon Brando was in a class all his own, and I had always admired his talent. Years earlier, he had played conga drums for a dance class I was in at Frank Wagner's in Carnegie Hall in NYC. *"On the Waterfront"* is one of my favorite films of all time, and I loved his Mr. Christian in *"Mutiny on the Bounty."* I had also seen pictures of his totally ecological island in Tahiti. He seemed like such an amazing guy. He rarely acted anymore, but when he did, it was looked upon as a great event in cinema. And when he occasionally took a role in a film, he was paid the unthinkable sum of $1 million a day! In spite of that, I approached Marlon about doing *"A Last Look at Paradise"* on his island, Teti'aroa, in the Windward group of the Society Islands of French Polynesia.

My younger brother, Marc, was a very close friend of Marlon's son Christian and his ex-wife Anna Kashfi, and Christian would stay at my mother's house quite often. Through Marlon's agent, we had many meetings about my idea. He would come to my office and show me his home movies that were taken on his island, or I would go to his house, part of a compound he shared with my friend Jack Nicholson on Mulholland Drive just down the road from my house, where everything was run ecologically from some kind of windmill. Marlon was really into the ecological thing with all of his heart. His island was a true paradise, and we all knew that they were disappearing from the face of the earth.

He knew about my deal with Paul Newman and asked me what it was. I told him, and we ended up doing exactly the same deal—$50,000 cash and 50 percent of the profits. Wow, I had struck gold twice in a row!

Then, just when I thought everything was great, I got a call from Marlon saying he wouldn't be coming to my office anymore. He had heard about my and Raquel's scandalous fight at the pyramids in Mexico and was very upset with me, as he thought we had desecrated a holy spiritual location. I logically tried to explain what had actually happened, but he did not want to hear about it from my point of view. He obviously had his mind made up, so that was the end of "A Last Look At."

Soon after that, he did *"The Godfather"* and won the Academy Award for best actor. He is currently listed on IMDb.com as the world's greatest actor ever to have lived. I was always sorry that Marlon and I never had the opportunity to work together. He was one of the greatest actors, and I absolutely admired him.

VI. *"Timex All-star Swing Festival"*

On October 23 and 24, 1972, I made entertainment history.

Burt and I sold a jazz show to the Timex Corporation, which was to be filmed in the Philharmonic Hall of Lincoln Center, New York City. The show would star the greatest jazz singers and musicians alive at the time: Ella Fitzgerald, Count Basie, Duke Ellington, Benny Goodman, Lionel Hampton, Gene Krupa, Dizzy Gillespie, Dave Brubeck, Teddy Wilson, Joe Williams, Earl "Fatha" Hines, etc. And it would be hosted by Doc Severinsen of *"The Tonight Show."* These artists had never been on one stage together, and never would be again after this show.

I took over the Lincoln Center in NYC for two nights, and we had the audiences dancing in the aisles. To cap off the concert, after everyone had performed their acts, they all came on stage and performed a salute to the great Louis Armstrong. To see all of those incredible artists together on one stage was mind boggling! The audience went bonkers. It was wild!

I won the coveted Peabody Award for Excellence on TV for this special as well as the very prestigious Christopher Award. And years later it was inducted into the United States Library of Congress as an American treasure. Since this was a one-time-only event, I had all the artists sign the program for the concert, and I still have a copy of it today. The show has been shown repeatedly on PBS. It was a moment in history that can never be repeated. Most of those great jazz artists have since passed. It was a once-in-a-lifetime show, for sure.

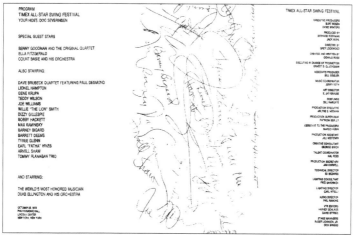

This signed program is a priceless collector's item for jazz fans.

VII. Fred Astaire: A Moment of Magic

Then there was Fred Astaire—my God, quite a difference from Marlon…

I was a Fred Astaire fan for as long as I can remember. Everyone was a Fred Astaire fan. We all grew up watching his magical movements. What a gentleman, what a lovely guy, and what a dancer! Even though I had dreamt for most of my life of meeting him, unfortunately I hadn't had the opportunity…yet. But right after the *"Raquel"* TV special aired, I received a telegram from Fred, and this is what he said: "Your "Raquel" Special was terrific! A wonderful special David. Congratulations on a great show." I have kept this telegram all these years and cherish it with all my heart and soul. It was hard for me to even imagine—Fred Astaire was congratulating me on my work. Oh my God, will wonders never cease?

I came up with the idea—long before *"That's Entertainment"* ever came out—to take all the show-stopping numbers from their old films and have Fred Astaire or Gene Kelly host the show and dance with himself in front of a projected film of the old clips. So I took a chance and contacted Fred, and lo and behold, the guy who had always been my fantasy was now standing right in front of me in my very own office—hard to fathom for a huge Fred Astaire fan like myself. He came to my office many times, and we'd sit on my couch and watch all the old dance numbers and have tea and a biscuit. It was all quite civilized, I must say. But Fred felt negatively about my wanting him to dance in the film. He said he didn't want to dance anymore, that he was too old, and that he wanted his fans to remember him as he had been, in his prime. I understood what he meant and felt, even though I didn't totally agree with him, so we kept watching and watching until Fred could no longer take it anymore.

One day, as we were watching his films, like in some sort of dream sequence, he rose from the couch we were sitting on, and just like the idea I had for the show, he started dancing with himself, in front of the film. It was pure magic! He still had it. God, I wanted to be filming him. This was a dream, a once-in-a-lifetime dream. After a while, he seemed to catch himself and stopped, realizing what he had been doing, and he just stared at me with an astonished look on his face. "I…I'm sorry, David," he said, and then he let out this big nervous laugh and said, "See, I told you," as if he was trying to cover up what he had just done.

Then, embarrassed, he sat down, and after a second or two he said, "Like I said before, I don't want people to remember me like *this*,"—he pointed to himself—"as an old man. I want them to remember me like *that*,"—he pointed to the screen—"like the young man I used to be." With that, he got up again and said, "I'm sorry, David. I can't do your film." Then he walked out of my office, and that was the last time I ever saw Fred Astaire. What he didn't know was, that singular moment was one of the highlights of my life, possibly only matched by my time with Grace Kelly. Thanks, Fred. I will never forget you or that moment!

VIII. WINTERS/ROSEN EXPANDS, PLUS KENNY ROGERS'S FAREWELL TOUR

Things were going really well at Winters/Rosen Productions. We were so hot, *TV Guide* even did a cover story on us. And since it was the best-selling magazine in the US at the time, we started thinking about expanding our operation to other countries. We also decided to go into

TV series production and distribution. So we opened new offices in New York, Toronto, Vancouver, and even London, and we still had our main office in L.A.

We hired some of the best salesmen that we could hire, and we were very instrumental in the creation and implementation of the Prime Time Access Rule (PTAR), the law that made all the networks give back the 7:30 time slot to the local stations. It was a way of breaking the stranglehold the networks had on the TV we watched, while also promoting local and independent productions, which was perfect for us. So we formed a partnership with CTV, a Canadian station owned by the well-known Bassett family, and started to produce many shows for these stations that needed a 7:30 program. Burt made a deal with Murray Cherkover, the president of CTV. For every segment of every series that we produced that CTV aired, we'd pay $3,000 into his wife's account in Atlanta. With all the series and specials that we produced, that must have ended up being a huge amount of cash, but "It's just the cost of doing business, David!" Burt told me.

I got so carried away with our success that reality flew right out the window. I started spending money like there was no tomorrow. I guess it all went to my head, and I lived a life that was over the top and way beyond my means. Even my dog Harlequin enjoyed the luxury of it all. Crazy as it sounds, he and I actually travelled around the country in two separate limousines. How outlandish! Then I figured since I was eating really well, why not him, too? I bought him twelve hamburgers every day for lunch. I must have been mad! I loved him so much that I just wanted to share the wealth with him. He was like family. Looking back, it makes no sense to me at all, but at the time, it seemed like the natural thing to do.

Winters/Rosen produced the music series *"Rollin' on the River,"* starring Kenny Rogers and the First Edition, for two seasons and four or five other series as well as many specials that were pilots for series, such as *"The Sonny & Cher Nitty Gritty Hour."* And we were the first company to feature a black entertainer Barbara McNair in her own syndicated series. By the second year of the show, everyone was calling my TV series with Kenny Rogers "Rollin'." I produced fifty-two shows with such guest stars as Tina Turner, Merle Haggard, B. B. King, Gladys Knight, Jose Feliciano, Cheech & Chong, Jason Robards, Helen Reddy, Roger Miller, Bo Diddley, Paul Revere and the Raiders, Kris Kristofferson, Bill Withers, Jim Croce, Billy Preston, the Edgar Winter Group, Barbara McNair, and B. J. Thomas. The show was a big success, and an album of some of the music was released.

Flash forward many years, and Kenny left the group for a solo career, with numerous number-one hits throughout the years. He became America's top C&W singer and was inducted into the Country and Western Hall of Fame.

In 2016, Kenny started on his two-year Farewell Tour, with a date in Fort Myers, Florida, which was close to where I was living at the time. So Kenny arranged some seats and backstage passes for me to see him perform and meet up after the show. I couldn't wait to see him. It had been way too long!

I took a pal of mine, a big fan of Kenny's, with me, and he loved the show. Afterwards, we went backstage and hung out with Kenny, and he was as sweet and lovely as ever. He and I had both weathered a lot of living. As we hugged each other, we cried tears of joy, with a little sadness mixed in, I think. We were no kids anymore, just two old guys now. And with the passing of Glen Campbell just months before, who was a close friend of ours, we were starting to feel our own mortality.

Earlier, I had thought seeing Kenny again after so many years would be great fun. As it turned out, it was much more. He sang his heart out for two hours to a standing-room-only audience who obviously knew all the lyrics and loved him. While applauding him madly for his effort, I spent much of the time crying to myself. Kenny had named this his Farewell Tour for obvious reasons.

Kenny is one of the bravest people I ever saw. It was very clear to me that he was in failing health. His voice was a sliver of what it used to be, and his memory lapses and yawning on stage were, for me, agonizing. I felt very deeply for my friend of forty-six years, but the audience didn't seem to care and gave him multiple standing ovations. Even with all the problems, he did a super show! Viva, Kenny Rogers! He's a fighter, that's for sure!

Now back to the past and Winters/Rosen…

Selling the *"Barbara McNair Show"* was a difficult task, as in those days the southern stations still had a problem with black stars, and there had never been a syndicated series with a black female singer. So I called up two of the most famous black entertainers in the world, who were friends of mine, Bill Cosby and Sammy Davis Jr., and much to my surprise, each one of them had a reason, or I might call it an excuse, not to show up for the taping, which would have taken them at most two hours to do. What angered me was that I often used to see Cosby at Hugh Hefner's Playboy Mansion hanging out with the Playmates, but he had no time to help me try to break down barriers against his own race. Man, they really let me down, big time. I wound up calling my buddy Bobby Darin. My dear pal Bobby—he had no excuses and was excited about our venture. He showed up as promised with very little up-front notice. Bobby was wonderful.

As we stood there, side by side, in the studio trying our very best to break down racial barriers on American TV, I said to Bobby, "It's funny. These big superstars, they get up on soapboxes in front of all the world and profess to want to help their own people; but as it turns out, you, Bobby, a little short Italian, and me, a little short Jew, are the ones who are actually out there doing it."

"How true your words are, David," Bobby answered.

In spite of their absence, the show did well and we produced fifty-two-and-a-half hours. Some of our guests were Carol Burnett, Frankie Avalon, Bob Hope, B. B. King, Cher, Tony Bennett, Joey Bishop, Zsa Zsa Gabor, Kenny Rogers, Sonny Bono, Little Richard, Leonard Nimoy, and Lou Rawls.

But I felt really betrayed, and from that day forward I never attended another civil rights march. Sadly, I never did anything more to further equality between the races, even though I had been a civil rights advocate all my life and had really gone out of my way trying to help the cause, even at times jeopardizing my own career. Enough said.

IX. DAVID GEFFEN AND A MISSED OPPORTUNITY

I first met David Geffen around 1961 in the mailroom at the William Morris Agency. That mailroom became famous as the breeding ground for the best agents in the business. David progressed rather quickly, becoming a junior agent and then an agent. For a short period, he was my agent, and even afterwards, we kept in touch with each other. We were and are still good friends

He told me he was going to manage Crosby, Stills & Nash, as well as Joanie Mitchell and Neil Young. From my background in the music business, I knew he was on his way to a fortune. David Crosby and Neil Young were friends of mine, and I really respected their talents, and also Graham Nash's, who joined them later on. I told my partner Burt that David and I had talked about becoming partners by bringing him into Winters/Rosen as another partner.

Burt hesitated at first, but eventually I got him to agree. I was excited, and we got on the phone with David. After a long discussion, we had agreed on everything but the name. David suggested that we call the company Winters/Rosen/Geffen, but Burt refused. David insisted, but Burt said, "No way." He didn't want to change the name right away, but might consider it later on. I was trying to sway Burt because I believed in David and his very special talent. I wanted the deal to happen, and I didn't really care what it was called, but Burt would not budge.

According to my deal with Burt, unless we both agreed, one couldn't do anything without the other, so it never happened. Anyway, David and I always stayed in touch, and deep down I always hoped that somehow I could resurrect the partnership. Burt and I, thanks to his financial ineptitude, eventually went bankrupt. Life, huh? And oh, by the way, David became a multi-billionaire from films and music.

David Geffen's *The Rising Sun* anchored in the Mediterranean

From a humanitarian point of view, David also gave back to society in a big way. He funded the David Geffen School of Medicine at UCLA. He also co-founded DreamWorks SKG Studio with Steven Spielberg and Jeffrey Katzenberg. In 2010, David was inducted into the Rock and Roll Hall of Fame. He received the President's Merit Award from the National Academy of Recording Arts and Sciences at the 53rd Grammy Awards, and he funded David Geffen Hall in New York City's Lincoln Center for the Performing Arts, which is home to the New York Philharmonic Orchestra.

I'm very happy for David. Whenever I think of him, I think back to that fateful phone call with Burt Rosen. Just think: I was practically an inch away from splitting billions of dollars.

X. "DR. JEKYLL AND MR. HYDE," STARRING KIRK DOUGLAS

The last production of Winters/Rosen was a musical version of *"Dr. Jekyll and Mr. Hyde"* starring Kirk Douglas, Donald Pleasance, Sir Michael Redgrave, Susan George, Susan Hampshire, Stanley Holloway, and Judy Bowker. I was following up on the idea I first came up with for Kirk on the set of *"The Special London Bridge Special."*

Kirk has been a major movie star almost all of his adult life. Not long ago, he celebrated his 100th birthday. It's fair to say he is a living legend. He's number seventeen on the American Film Institute's list of the greatest male screen legends in American film history, making him the highest-ranked living person on the list. In 1996, he received an honorary Academy Award "for 50 years as a creative and moral force in the motion picture community."

We sold the movie to the Timex Corporation, as they were fascinated with my idea of doing the first musical film of this classic story, *"Dr. Jekyll and Mr. Hyde."* I had my buddy Lionel Bart write the music and lyrics, assisted by two unknown but very talented young writers who had written for the stage in New York, Mel Mandel and Norman Sachs. Lionel was practically incapable of writing much because of his health at the time, so Mel and Norman wrote most of the songs, with Lionel contributing a couple of numbers.

We had a budget of $750,000 to work with, and I arranged to shoot it in a studio in L.A. where they had just filmed *"The Barrets of Wimpole Street,"* from which the sets were still available to me. This would save us a fortune and make it financially feasible for us to produce it within budget. Burt said we had to shoot in London because he had promised Bill Storke, the head of programming at NBC-TV, a free trip to London. I said, "Send Bill to London, but let's do the show over here, or we will go way over budget." Burt said that was impossible and that we would pick up the overages from foreign sales. I wasn't happy about this at all, but I went ahead and made arrangements for us to shoot at Shepperton Studios in England.

KIRK DOUGLAS STARS AS 'DR JEKYLL AND MR HYDE'

Mel, Norman, and I rehearsed with Kirk at his house in Beverly Hills, which proved to be a strange experience. He and his wife Anne never offered us a drink of water, or anything else for that matter; we always had to ask. I had never experienced anything like it before. All the saucers with nuts in them were covered with cellophane, and it looked like no one ever touched them. This created an uneasy and uncomfortable feeling, at the very least. Kirk wanted to rehearse at his house, but we were not made to feel particularly welcome or wanted.

At one point I had to go to Yugoslavia and Germany to rehearse with Kirk, who was in the middle of shooting the film *"Scalawag."* Then I found an apartment I liked in London, so now I was ready. Casting went ahead as planned, and I was waiting for Kirk to arrive. He always stayed at the Grosvenor House on Park Lane, so I got him a suite there. He had only been in the suite for about fifteen minutes when I went to welcome Anne and Kirk to London.

I needed to use a phone, so I went into their bedroom for privacy. I couldn't believe it, but sitting on the top of the dresser by the bed was what must have been a thirty-year-old picture of Kirk. It looked like it was from his hit film *"Champion"* that he had starred in decades before. Kirk had only been in the suite for a few minutes—his bag was there, unpacked—but he had put out this picture of himself in younger times so that when he woke up, that young picture of himself was what he saw. I knew I was in trouble. In fact, he had told me when we worked together on the London Bridge show that he was impossible to handle on set, and that he basically directed himself, but because it was a musical, he was insecure and would have to look to me most of the time as the director. At the time, this actually pleased me, but now I was having second thoughts because of that damn picture of him by his bedside. The weirdest thing of all was, sometimes he would bang his own head with his hand many times on the set for no reason at all. I never asked him what that was all about, and neither did my crew.

At the end of the shoot, he left without saying goodbye or even thank you. Instead, he sent a letter to the crew, which was read out loud on the set. In it, he apologized for not saying goodbye, but if he had, he would have become too emotional and would've broken down and cried. The crew listened in disbelief, claimed it was all bullshit, and some even voiced their opinions of what they thought about working with Kirk. He certainly made no fans in this crew, although he always treated me with the greatest respect. He sure was a complicated guy.

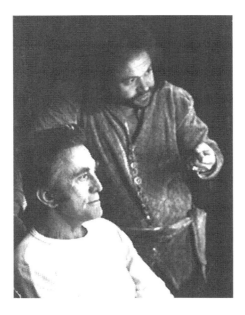

Kirk listens intently as I give him notes about the two characters he is portraying in my film.

Finally we finished the show, and I was told we were a million dollars over budget. The show aired, and we received four Emmy nominations. Our sponsor, Timex, had agreed to rerun the show every year for four years, which would have put the show into profit. But our company had an immediate cash-flow deficit, which Burt never solved. When friends offered to help, he turned them away, saying, "We have no problems." His ego really got the best of him, so we wound up in bankruptcy instead.

The company folded after four years of business. In that time, we produced over 200 hours of programming and had more shows on the air than Universal Studios. We were fifty percent of our agent ICM's entire TV business. And ICM was one of the largest and best TV agencies in Hollywood at the time. So sad!

Alice Cooper, *"Welcome to My Nightmare"*

Alice Cooper and I had met at different clubs around Los Angeles. He and his manager, Shep Gordon, had called me when I had Winters/Rosen Productions and asked me to do a show with him called "Alice at the Palace" at the Palace Theatre in New York City. I had turned it down because I was so busy, but now I had some time. Actually, I had lots of time, so I placed a call to him and said, "Let's do it." He was past that idea, though, and was now into his new album *"Welcome to My Nightmare."* What a great concept for Alice Cooper, I thought.

We met, we talked, and we decided to do it together. Contractually, we would be joined at the hip so that he couldn't make it as a film without me, and likewise, I couldn't do it as a film without him. I wanted to use what I called my Magic Screen, with Alice and the dancers coming off and going back on the screen many times to great effect. Alice loved the idea and was already getting excited about the show.

Shep Gordon rented a huge soundstage at Columbia Studios, and we built our set there. It turned out to be a fantastic place to rehearse. At one time, the set became a huge spider web, another time a huge bed, and another my Magic Screen, which I wound up using a lot during the show. Having just built it, I didn't want it to go to waste, as it was so effective and allowed me to play with the audiences' minds.

I hired eight dancers for the show, including one eighteen-year-old first-timer named Sheryl, who would eventually marry Alice. Funnily enough, she was a preacher's daughter. Over forty years later, he and Sheryl Gail Cooper are still married and have three daughters and just recently became grandparents—amazing. They have become good friends of mine, and I am inspired by their love for one another all these years. They are a wonderful couple! I love to be in their company, as it gives me faith in humanity, love, and relationships again. When I was living in Fort Lauderdale, Florida, Alice performed there, and in Miami, so we got to hang out, and it was truly great! And Sheryl is *still* dancing in the show—unbelievable! And she looks great! Sheryl, Alice, and I are also friends on Facebook, so we keep in touch almost daily.

Alice Cooper, me, and Sheryl Cooper

I took ten of my best friends to see Alice Cooper in concert.
And, boy, was everyone excited to go backstage and meet Alice and his wife, Sheryl!

Sheryl, still dancing in Alice's show. Just look at those legs!

When we were rehearsing "Nightmare," I decided to open up the rehearsals, so I had loads of friends come and experience the show. It was a very theatrical one. The whole "nightmare" concept leant itself perfectly to the show I had in mind and eventually designed for Alice. The rehearsals evolved into a big party when everyone told their friends about it, but there was a method to my madness. I wanted to get an audience's reaction so I could time certain technical features to the split second. Plus, it was good for the band and the dancers, and it let Alice gauge what the reaction to the show would be.

We started the tour of 50,000-seat arenas, with Candice Bergen along as a photographer doing a big layout for *Rolling Stone* magazine. Being on the road was totally crazy! There were girls everywhere. The stench of weed was very noticeable in the hotel halls. It was like Sodom and Gomorrah goes rock and roll.

The funny thing is that Alice himself just likes to play golf or sit in front of the TV drinking beer—so different than his image or what you might imagine. He is actually so average in his likes, no one would ever suspect it. He and his manager, Shep, are very clever people. They're very down-to-earth and know their market well. It was great working with them, as they let me do what I wanted creatively!

We opened our world tour at Madison Square Garden in NYC, where we received rave reviews. No one had ever seen anything quite like it. It was rock 'n' roll, theatre, and film combined. Wherever we played, we got amazing reviews, both Alice and the creative production, some of the best I've ever received!

My ex-wife and daughter, Romé, lived in NYC, and I wanted my daughter to see what her daddy did, but her mother said no. Kay wasn't allowed by the courts to take Romé out of the state, but I didn't want to drag Romé into any court fight, so I let it go. But whenever I called Romé at home, her mom would tell me that Romé didn't want to talk to me. She then told Romé that I never called her, so Romé grew up thinking that her father never wanted to talk to her. How damaging for a child's mind. It's unfair, but it happens a lot, where the wife uses the kid to get back at the husband, or vice versa, and the kids are the ones who get hurt. I don't care what's going on between the parents, keep the kids out of it. But I did at least get to ride with Romé down 7th Avenue in NYC in a hansom cab, which was wonderful. My little girl was growing up, but I wouldn't get to see her for a very long time.

After two weeks on the road, it got too crazy for me and I couldn't take it anymore, so I returned to L.A. to see if I could get the film version of the stage production financed, and I did. I teamed up with Bill Silberkliet, a financier, and made plans to film the London engagement of the European tour at Wembley Arena.

As it turns out, Bill Silberkliet was a relative of the well-known gangster Meyer Lansky, who had casinos in Las Vegas, Cuba, the Bahamas, and London. Lansky, one of the most powerful men in the country, was an associate of Charles "Lucky" Luciano, who created the National Crime Syndicate in the US. Although Lansky was involved in organized crime for almost fifty years, he was never convicted of anything worse than illegal gambling. I was told the funds for our films were coming from Lansky, but I never knew for sure.

Bill had financed a film I had made years ago with my buddy Alan Roberts, called *"Young Lady Chatterley."* It was so successful, he had also financed a sequel, *"Young Lady Chatterle II."* He was a very satisfied, enthusiastic financier and one of the lucky few to have made money on his investment in films, so he was the perfect guy to go to, and that made my job very easy.

Alice with the cyclops monster "Nightmare"

CHAPTER 24

2½ Years with Linda Lovelace

My most publicized romance was with a girl named Linda Lovelace. Before I met her, she became the number-one porn star in the world. Her film *"Deep Throat,"* produced for just $25,000, went on to gross over $600,000,000—still the most successful piece of film in cinema history to this day.

Her real name was Linda Boreman, and she didn't look like a porn star at all. In fact, she looked more like the girl next door; she even had freckles. Unbeknownst to me, I had been recommended to her by two close friends of mine, Sammy Davis Jr. and Hugh Hefner. She needed someone to create and stage an act for her, as she had been booked by her husband at the time into a theatre in Florida for $25,000.

I soon found out that she couldn't sing, dance, or act. But during this time we became romantically involved, and she left her husband Chuck Traynor. After hiding out at the Beverly Hills Hotel for a few weeks, she moved in with me. After many threats on my life from both the Mafia and her husband, I decided to try to help her cross over to the mainstream film business. Her name was extremely marketable, and she was known all over the world because her highly controversial film had been banned pretty much everywhere.

I compared what Marilyn Monroe had done in the '50s with her nude calendar with what Linda did in the '70s, as the morality of the times changed rather dramatically during those different eras. And since Marilyn had become a legend, with people like Elton John writing songs about her, "Candle in the Wind," I thought I could do it again. People were always looking for a new sex symbol.

I started out by booking her at two of the country's top universities, Harvard and Yale, for $4,000 a speech, and that went very well. To write her speech, I brought in two writers, Mel Mandell and Norman Sachs, who had written the TV movie *"Dr. Jekyll and Mr. Hyde"* with Lionel Bart and were now working with me on my film *"Nicholas Jingle."* Their speech asked why violence was acceptable in films, whereas making love was not. The college kids loved it, and at every campus she appeared, they even gave her a parade. This led to a hundred more college bookings. Then I produced a play with her starring in it: *"Pajama Tops."* I planned for her to tour the country, but it never got beyond Philadelphia. It was an unmitigated disaster, mainly because of her inability to act.

The program for the play *"Pajama Tops"* starring Linda Lovelace

Together with an Italian co-producer and 20th Century Fox, I put a deal together in which she would receive $120,000 for a film called *"Laura."* I had a separate salary built in the budget for myself as co-producer. Her co-star in this film was Emmanuele Arsan, famous all over Europe for her books and *"Emmanuele"* soft-porn movies. I also had her next movie, a drama, *"The Bloody Benders,"* all set to go, with her to receive $250,000. Unfortunately, during production, it became necessary to fire her and replace her with a young girl I discovered in a restaurant on the Via Venetta in Rome where I was having dinner with actress Jennifer O'Neill. She was totally unknown at the time but later became a huge European movie star. Her name was Annie Belle. Linda had become impossible to work with because she started to believe the press I was creating for her, trying to change her image. But nothing really worked, as she didn't have any real acting talent or even the charm of Marilyn. It started to become clear to me that, although my idea had merit, the reality of actually pulling it off was quite another thing. With that said, I still decided to take Linda to London and promote her at the world-famous horse races at Ascot.

I did a deal with the BBC to film her, every day, at the same time, in a myriad of outfits I had created for her. They were quite extravagant, with the desired effect that guaranteed us double-truck newspaper coverage every day in all the London rag sheets. By this time, Linda's face was well known to anyone who read a newspaper in or around London.

I eventually sold her life story to *The News of the World* for a record sum at the time of $500,000 and negotiated for them to pay her another $100,000 for a TV commercial advertising the story. The newspaper created a poster that was placed on the back of every double-decker bus in the city, so now she was plastered everywhere, and there was no escaping her image. Everywhere we went, they recognized her, even though no one in London or Europe had ever seen her film.

Thinking of what to do next to further Linda's career, I remembered an Obie Award-winning play, produced by my friend and manager Allan Carr, that had been running in L.A. about Billy the Kid and Jean Harlow meeting in Hell. The play was very controversial because at the final curtain Jean goes down on Billy on stage. Of course, the actress didn't really do it; it just looked that way. The play caused such an uproar that every night the authorities would raid the theatre and close the play down, taking both stars to jail. The next night, the play would be back on, and the authorities would shut them down again. This went on, night after night, for fifteen nights. As a result, they got a bucketload of free publicity in the press, and everybody wanted to see the play. I thought this would be the perfect vehicle for Linda. With that in mind, a friend of mine put me in touch with a lawyer in Las Vegas, and I convinced him to bankroll the production. I arranged for the show to be staged in a hotel in Las Vegas, and Linda and I caught the next plane to sort out the details with our backer.

On arriving in Vegas a limo whisked us to the Dunes Hotel, where we were booked into a beautiful suite overlooking the fountains. That night I took Linda to see my dear friend Liza Minnelli, who was performing in the main showroom at the Riviera Hotel. Linda was ecstatic. Although she had been to Las Vegas several times before, she had never seen a show that didn't revolve around nudity or sex. In a way, I was her Henry Higgins and she my Eliza Doolittle. She wasn't very cultured and had never heard of the likes of George Bernard Shaw, so even a normal stage show was a cultural experience to her. She was absolutely thrilled when Liza spotted me in the crowd, made me stand up, and introduced me to the audience.

After the show, we went backstage to meet with Liza in her dressing room. Liza gave us a warm welcome and introduced us to the other people in the room, among whom were Alice Cooper and Chubby Checker. I had worked with Alice on *"Welcome to My Nightmare"* some time before but hadn't seen him since, so we spent the evening catching up. While we were talking, Alice suddenly broke off and said, "David, man, can you do me a big favor?" Without any hesitation I said, "Sure, Alice, whatever you want." He looked at me hard for a couple of seconds before saying, "You know Elvis real well, right?" and I said yes. "Aww man, he's my hero and idol, and I hear he's in town. Jeez, David, I've got to meet him. Can you fix it?" So I said, "Sure. He should be off stage by now. I'll give him a call."

I picked up the phone and called the Hilton Hotel where Elvis was performing and always stayed when he was in Las Vegas, and sure enough, he was there. When Elvis came on the phone, I explained that I was in town and asked if it would be all right to bring a few friends over to meet him. Elvis was delighted and said, "Of course, David, come on over." Linda couldn't believe it. We'd only been in Vegas for five minutes, and already she'd met Liza Minelli, Alice Cooper, and Chubby Checker, and would soon meet the King himself. I imagined what the press would make of it, if only they knew. The headlines would have read, "The Queen of Porn Meets the King of Rock." We went down to the parking lot, jumped into two waiting limos, and drove the two short blocks to the Las Vegas Hilton.

We arrived at Elvis's suite to find him in great form. As it turned out, he was as delighted to meet Alice as Alice was to meet him. We partied with Elvis until five in the morning, and everybody had a ball. At one point, Elvis, who was a tenth-degree black belt, was entertaining the room by demonstrating his karate skills. Later I was chatting to Alice when El turned to me and said, "Hey, David, do you know what I'd do if someone came at me with a gun?" Alice and I looked at each other with raised eyebrows. "No, El" I said, preparing myself for some kind of mock attack, at which point he got down on one knee, looked up at me with a pleading look, and joined his hands as if to pray. Everybody laughed. He had a great sense of humor, and in the time that I knew him, I was the butt end to many of his practical jokes.

As we were leaving early in the morning, Alice said what a fantastic time he'd had and asked if we could do it again the next night. "Sure," I said. "Why don't we all meet up at Liza's last show, and we'll come back here again tomorrow." Everybody agreed, and we all went off to our respective hotels to get some much-needed sleep.

That night Linda and I were getting ready to go see Frank Sinatra's first show and then meet Liza for dinner. Linda was in the bathroom taking the curlers out of her hair, and I was in the sitting room of our suite meeting with the lawyer about our upcoming production when, all of a sudden, the door burst open and a flood of about seventeen heavy guys, shouting and pointing guns, stormed into our suite. Two of them grabbed me and threw me to the ground, facedown, pressing guns to my temple and screaming, "Don't move and you won't get hurt!" Yeah, like I could move with two fifteen-ton gorillas straddling me.

Being an entertainer, this was not the kind of situation I was familiar with. For the first time, I experienced what pure terror feels like. I couldn't figure out what was going on. They were pulling out drawers and going through the closets, throwing our stuff all over the floor. The only thing I could think was that Chuck Traynor, Linda's ex-husband had hired a hit squad to kill me, something he had threatened in the past.

Meanwhile, Linda, equally terrified, was dragged from the bathroom at gunpoint, and I thought to myself, this is it, they're going to kill us both. I shut my eyes and waited for the gun to go off, but nothing happened. Then I began to think that maybe it was some kind of elaborate practical joke. The night before, we had run into a comedy duo, Marty Allen and Steve Rossi, a younger version of Dean Martin and Jerry Lewis. Marty was a good friend and had a reputation for practical jokes, and this was something he was more than capable of organizing. I so wanted that to be the case.

Then a voice said, "Here it is." Still face down on the floor, I could see, from the corner of my eye, one of the men holding a cellophane bag. "Looks like amphetamines and barbiturates," he continued. At that moment, I knew who they were. By way of confirmation, a police walkie-talkie suddenly crackled into life. They were cops who, for some reason, were trying to set Linda and me up on a drug bust. The drugs didn't belong to Linda, and they certainly didn't belong to me, so someone was setting us up. The whole situation would have been laughable had it not been so terrifying, given that anybody who knows me could have told them that I didn't so much as smoke or drink, let alone do hard drugs. As for Linda, she did a bit of grass, but that was about it. Before we left for Vegas, I'd made a point of making sure that Linda didn't have any grass with her and told her the story of a famous glamour model, called Candy Bar, who'd been working as a stripper in Vegas and got busted with one joint. Candy got seven long years in the state pen. Class A drugs would get you twenty. The ones pulling the strings in Vegas were ostensibly Mormon, and as such, tended to take a holier-than-thou, puritanical view of any kind of drug use.

When they dragged me up off the floor and began to question me about the drugs, I looked around the room for my lawyer friend, hoping to get some help, but the bastard had disappeared. To this day, I don't know what happened to him. I never saw him again. It began to dawn on me that my supposed friend and co-producer was involved in this setup, and that was why he had mysteriously disappeared. He must have planted the drugs.

Meanwhile, the police were waving the packet of drugs in my face and demanding to know where I had gotten them. Of course, I denied all knowledge of them, as did Linda, and suggested that any drugs found in the room must have arrived with them. Feigning outrage at my suggestion, they decided to continue the questioning back at the police station. They cuffed us and dragged us, roughly and humiliatingly, through the hotel and out the front entrance where hordes of press and television news cameras were waiting for us. We were paraded in front of the media, and I overheard a reporter say, "As you can see, these people who deal in pornography also deal in drugs." Not knowing what to say or do, but feeling defiant, I turned to Linda and gave her a lingering kiss for the benefit of the television audience. None too pleased with our performance, the police quickly dragged us to a waiting squad car, unceremoniously threw us in, and whisked us to the station house. Clearly, the whole thing had been staged, but why? I didn't know. At any rate, this was not the kind of exposure I'd had in mind when planning our publicity campaign. It flew in the face of the conventional wisdom "any publicity is good publicity." This was not good.

We arrived at the police station, where Linda was put in a holding cell with about a dozen street prostitutes who had been picked up earlier that evening, and I was taken off for questioning. They sat me down at a table, with the regulation light in the face, and the District Attorney came in and sat down opposite me, glaring menacingly. "OK, Mr. Winters, you know why you're here." He threw the drugs on the table. "These were found in your hotel room. Whatya gotta say about it?" I told him I didn't know anything about it, and if there were any drugs in the room, they must have been planted. I gritted my teeth, awaiting the expected outrage, and was taken by surprise at the calmness of his reply. "I tell you what, Mr. Winters, if you're prepared to tell us that the lawyer gave you those drugs, you'll be free to go." What? I thought. Here was another twist in the tail. Am I stuck in the Twilight Zone or something? Was he trying to trick me? All I could do was tell the truth. "No," I said, "he didn't."

"No, Mr. Winters, I don't think you understand what I said. I said that if you're prepared to say that the gentleman gave you the drugs, you'll be free to go."

"No," I said, "*you* don't understand. I am not about to lie about it. The gentleman did not give me the drugs, and I'm not going to lie for you." The D.A. obviously took the view that people like me, guilty or not, would do anything to get out from under the pressure. I may have been frightened and confused, but I wasn't stupid. If I had taken him up on his offer, I would have automatically incriminated myself, and I wasn't about to do that. "I want to make a phone call," I demanded. He sat there for what seemed like an age and then gestured to one of the other officers, who escorted me to a phone. I called Liza to explain what was going on.

Liza picked up the phone and said, "Hi, David. Are you on your way over?" I explained that I couldn't make it, as I was in jail. She laughed and thought I was joking, but was horrified when she realized I was telling the truth. She told me not to worry, that someone would come bail us out, and that we should head back to her dressing room at the Riviera, and not go back to our hotel. In the meantime, through the grapevine, Elvis had heard about my predicament and had already posted bail. What a guy!

We left the station house and went straight to Liza's, arriving at the Riviera just as Liza was about to go on stage. "Wait in the dressing room until after the show," she said, "and we'll figure our next move then." In fact, Liza locked us in the room so no one else could get in and we would be safe till she returned. She was there for me when I needed her the most, and I'll never forget her for that. I love you, Liza! We sat there waiting for Liza to finish her act, going over and over in our minds what the hell was going on. I picked up the phone and started calling all the people I knew who might be able to help me. I was told that the local sheriff, Ralph Lamb, had an election coming up and was looking to curry favor with the electorate by making an example of Linda and me. Like all politicians looking for re-election, he took the moral high ground, with Linda and I his sacrificial lambs, along with 1,500 streetwalkers he'd arrested in that week alone.

It transpired that Linda's movie *"Deep Throat"* had been playing to packed houses in Las Vegas and had defied all attempts to shut it down, much to the chagrin of the town council and the sheriff's department. Sheriff Lamb saw our arrival as a great opportunity to make a double whammy. For the sake of comparison: the entire population of Las Vegas at that time was 75,000 people; 275,000 people had seen *"Deep Throat."* So he knew the arrest would get a lot of headline space featuring him as a law-and-order man. On one hand, it would provide another opportunity to shut the movie down in Vegas, and on the other, the attendant publicity of a celebrity drug bust would probably go a long way to getting him re-elected. In a strange way, I was kind of relieved. Although we were being set up, at least there was a reason this was happening to us; I wasn't going insane. But the question remained: What were we going to do about it?

As soon as Liza came off stage, she joined us and insisted we spend the night at her house to avoid our hotel until we found out what was going on. Linda and I, still in shock, accepted her hospitality gratefully. When we arrived at her house, she told us to take the master bedroom, and she would sleep in the maid's room. We didn't want to cause her any more trouble than we already had and argued that we would be fine in the maid's room. But she would not hear of it, and we relented. Liza brought out some refreshments, and we sat around and talked as her assistants phoned around town trying to find out, from their local contacts, just what was actually going down.

As the hours passed, our arrest was broadcast on all the TV stations around the world. Many friends of mine, who knew full well that I didn't use drugs of any kind, started calling to offer their support. One of them, Joe DeCarlo, the manager of Sonny & Cher, told me not to go back to the Dunes Hotel for my luggage, as the word on the street was that there was another setup waiting for us. Apparently, they were going to arrest us again in front of a hungry media. Nancy Sinatra called and told me that her father, Frank, suggested I use his attorney, Oscar Goodman, in Vegas. I thanked her for being a good friend, and asked her to thank Frank for me. She told me that everyone in Vegas knew it was a setup and that the local paper, *The Panorama*, was going to print the truth on the front page of their next edition tomorrow morning. My dear friend Lionel Bart even called from London asking what the hell was going on and if he could help me in any way. There was, of course, nothing Lionel could do, but I thanked him for the thought.

Based on the calls, we decided that the smart thing to do was to leave town straight away. We'd been warned not to try to take a scheduled flight, as they would be looking for us, so Liza booked a private jet to fly us out. Her personal assistant would pick up our luggage at the Dunes and meet us at the jet. We sat in Liza's limo at the airport waiting for our bags, with our hearts in our mouths, hoping that the police or press wouldn't follow her assistant. After what seemed like a thousand years, the assistant finally showed up and thankfully had not been followed. It wasn't until we were airborne that I finally let out my breath and slumped back into my seat. I was never so glad to leave a place in my life. As the jet rose high above the city, I looked back down on the bright, sparkling lights of Las Vegas and realized with some irony how true the saying was that "all that glitters is not gold."

The next day, *The Panorama* printed an expose on the powers that be in Vegas, hinting at corruption. That same day, I went to see my attorney and dear friend David Rudich. Being a contract lawyer, he recommended an up-and-coming young criminal attorney from L.A. named Robert Shapiro. David thought he would be the best guy for the job, as he was trustworthy, and we were going to need someone local to work with Frank Sinatra's attorney in Vegas. This fresh-faced young attorney would achieve worldwide fame many years later as the attorney responsible for getting O. J. Simpson acquitted.

When Linda and I first met with him he seemed distant and negative. I told him we were innocent, and he said, "Yeah, they *all* say *that*." After listening to our story the first thing he said was, "Would you take a lie detector test?" Without hesitation we said, "Yes, of course we would," at which point his attitude changed. I guess he thought we were guilty at first, but our lack of hesitation in agreeing to a lie detector test must have convinced him. Then he became more relaxed and friendly. He told us to leave it all to him; he was determined to prove our innocence.

As I took the test, I must say that I got really nervous and began sweating profusely. Oddly, as I answered the questions, even though I was telling the truth, I felt like I was lying—even when they just asked me my name! It was a weird sensation. For some reason, I was sure that I would fail. I didn't, of course, and neither did Linda.

Robert Shapiro assured us we had a strong case and was extremely confident of a positive conclusion. I wasn't so sure because lie detector tests were not admissible as evidence in court. What followed was a series of hearings in Las Vegas with just the lawyers and the judge in attendance along with Linda and myself. We always flew in by private jet to avoid the media who would hound us wherever we went.

At one court appearance, the judge put the fear of God into me when he said that it was true that, during the course of their research, they had indeed discovered that I was not known to take drugs. He went on to say that if I wasn't taking them, I must have been selling them. He told me it was a crime punishable by up to fifteen years in jail. When he implied I might go to prison for fifteen years, I felt the blood drain from my face. Was it possible that they could put an innocent man in prison? They had me convinced. I'd never felt so helpless and out of control. I was at the mercy of the system and its slippery machinery, and there was nothing I could do about it. Luckily for me, Robert thought otherwise, and after each court hearing, he calmed me down by saying things like "the truth is on our side" and "the prosecution's case is full of contradictions—we've got them beat." It felt to me like it was Linda and I who were getting the beating.

Eventually, without any hard evidence to bring the case to trial, the charges were summarily dropped. Shapiro had won his first of many celebrity cases. I couldn't help thinking how many innocent people were languishing in prison so that some cowboy sheriff somewhere could get re-elected. I guess, on second thought, we were very, very lucky.

Next I did a deal for Linda for a book called *The Intimate Diary of Linda Lovelace* that sold pretty well, and I produced a crazy R-rated comedy film called *"Linda Lovelace for President,"* co-starring my buddy Mickey Dolenz of The Monkees, Scatman Crothers, Marty Ingels, Vaughn Meader, Joey Forman, Joe E. Ross, and Chuck McCann. The film actually received rave reviews in London, where it played in the same cinema for six months. They likened it to Monty Python. Hef gave me ten pages in *Playboy* magazine to promote the film. In those days, each page cost $50,000, so he gave me the equivalent of $500,000 worth of free publicity. Now that's what you call a real friend. I will always be indebted to Hef for that lovely gesture.

The poster from the R-rated comedy I produced *"Linda Lovelace for President"*

Soon after the opening, I had to leave, as I had a film to make with Alice Cooper of my hugely successful stage show called *"Welcome to My Nightmare,"* which I had planned to film in London at Wembley Stadium. So we split up, and Linda never did another film. She was a sweet, unassuming girl who looked like a country college kid. During our time together, we fell in love. Things might have been different if I hadn't tried to mix business with our personal life.

She died on April 22, 2002, at the age of fifty-three in Denver, Colorado, from injuries she sustained in a tragic car accident on April 3rd. After she passed, I read some of her interviews, in which she said nice things about me and our relationship together. I also read a book she had written, *Ordeal*, in which she dedicated a chapter to me. She closed the chapter by saying, "Living with David was like living in a bubble, but sometimes even bubbles burst." We lived with each other just over two and a half years, which is quite a long time in anyone's life, and we had many warm and lovely moments. As I read the many articles and mentions about me, I felt bad about how our relationship had ended. But she was now gone, and there was nothing I could do or say anymore to at least keep a friendship going. Remembering the good times is not always easy. She really was a sweet thing, and I will always remember the good times we had together. Sleep, my princess. You are now in peace.

Linda and Hef at the Playboy Mansion

Linda and I on the Red Carpet at the Academy Awards ceremony in Los Angeles

Linda and I happily entering the Academy Awards presentation for the Oscars
at the Dorothy Chandler Pavillion

Left: Arriving at the Cannes Film Festival in FranceR
Right: Directors' Guild of America Governor's Ball

Left: Publicity shots in Hyde Park, London, with two rented Rolls Royces.
Note the license plate.
Right: Hanging out backstage at Liza's with friends Keith Moon of The Who and
Mickey Dolenz of the Monkees

Barbra Streisand, *"A Star Is Born"*

It was while doing postproduction in London on *"Welcome to My Nightmare"* that I received a hello call from Lynn Russo, my manager and psychic, in New York. Since she had called me, I asked her if she could do a reading for me over the phone. Although, she said it would be difficult, she agreed to try. I concentrated very hard on my thoughts, and she did also. Much to my surprise, she told me that I would soon get a phone call from Barbra Streisand asking me to join her in a musical film project. I thought that sounded crazy, especially after my ex-partner, Burt Rosen, had screwed up a TV special that Barbra and I had planned to make together, but Lynn said that I would be doing more musical projects in the future. I really couldn't believe my ears when she said Barbra would be calling me. So I said thanks, and that was that.

Three days later, there was a message for me from, you guessed it, Barbra Streisand and Jon Peters, who said they were co-producing the remake of the old Judy Garland film *"A Star Is Born,"* which, by the way, was being made as a musical. It floored me, and I had to call Lynn right away and tell her. "I told you, David," she said.

By this time, Barbra and Elliott Gould had divorced, and Barbra was going with my friend from the past, Beverly Hills hairdresser Jon Peters, known as hair dresser to the stars. Jon had given up hairdressing, as well as his wife Leslie Ann Warren, and he and Barbra were the hot item in Hollywood. This would be their first project produced together.

I called Barbra and Jon back, and they said they wanted me to stage and choreograph the film and also to work closely with Barbra as a consultant on the entire film. Barbra wanted to make sure all the ideas in the script and their execution were au courant. Jon promised me a single-card opening-title credit and a good cash deal, so I agreed and went back to editing *"Welcome to My Nightmare."* I completed it ahead of the US cinema release and took the film back with me. As soon as I got back to L.A., it was just about time to start rehearsals on Barbra's film.

Originally, the studio wanted Barbra to co-star with Elvis, which would have been incredible, but the good old Colonel was fighting them on billing. It's sad because it would have been a great vehicle for Elvis to showcase his talent, and he had never made a film with a major star like Barbra. Knowing both of them as I did, I am sure the chemistry would have been fabulous. And it would have been great to have worked with my buddy Elvis again. What a missed chance, and all because of egos.

Rehearsals began and I heard they needed a location, so I recommended my friend Bernie Cornfeld's Beverly Hills mansion, Greyhall. Greyhall was an amazing house that had been built by a railroad baron and was later owned by the movie star Douglas Fairbanks Jr. and the first mayor of Beverly Hills. There is supposedly a tunnel from Greyhall to Pickfair, which was the home of silent-screen movie star Mary Pickford. It was said that she and Douglas Fairbanks Jr. had a secret love affair, so they built this tunnel between their homes and used it when they wanted to see one another.

Needless to say, everyone loved the house and agreed to use it in the film. When I started meeting with Barbra about the film, she gave me the latest script and asked me to read it and look for anything that I didn't like. She asked me not to let anyone know that I had her script and was reading it, especially the director. I came back the next day with loads of notes and told Barbra of some things in the script that I thought were outdated. In fact, I had done this kind of stuff with Ann-Margret years before. Barbra sat me down and explained that I should share any comments I had with her and no one else, as people on the film, especially the director, were somewhat insecure. She said that the director, Frank Pierson, had made some terrific films, like *"Hud"* with Paul Newman, but had never made a musical before. My being a director of musicals had upset certain people at the studio. She also said that she and I would work very closely together every day, but Jon Peters then changed my deal, giving me less money. However, I stayed with the production because I had wanted to work with Barbra for a long time, and I wasn't going to let money stand in the way.

Barbra Streisand and I rehearsing the "Queen Bee" number for *"A Star Is Born"*

Barbra works twenty-four hours a day, and so do I. The only reason some people in Hollywood resent her is because she cares so much about the work. She is a perfectionist, and I respect that. She wants it to be right. She pushes and pushes to get what she believes in. She makes waves, and in Hollywood they don't like that. They want you to play by their rules. Just look how the great talents Charlie Chaplin, Orson Welles, and numerous others were treated. Some days Barbra would say to me, "David, how come you and I are the only ones working right now? Everyone else is at lunch." Because she and I hadn't thought about eating. We were into the work, New York-style.

Sometimes Barbra would call me in the middle of the night with a great idea. I would say, "Barbra, are you aware it's 2:30 a.m.? I'm sleeping." And she would say, "David, I'm so sorry. I didn't realize how late it was. Sorry for bothering you." Then, without even a blink, like I had never mentioned the time, she would say, "But I've got this great idea," and proceed to tell me her idea. To tell you the truth, I've done the same thing to other people because when you are really into the work and passionate about it, you are not even aware of the time.

I love her—her voice, her passion, and her endless amount of energy, even after all these years. Lots of men in Hollywood seemed threatened by her, which was crazy. She only wanted the film to be great. Working with her was a dream come true.

Every day, to rehearse, I would go to her home in Beverly Hills and she would sing for me, and me only. Barbra also wrote some of the songs in the film. So I was her guinea pig—she tried them out on me first. I would sit in this huge white chair in her white living room, and she would stand at her white piano and sing to me and ask for my comments. I used to think to myself, you are the luckiest man alive right now. Barbra Streisand does a private concert for you every day and pays you a lot of money to sit there and listen to her. Wow! What a job! I love her voice so much. She has been gifted with the most incredible instrument. To this day, I still get goose bumps when she sings. She is a gift from God!

Barbra and I rehearsing for the Academy Award-winning film *"A Star Is Born."* Here, I am showing her some moves that I'd like her to do during one of the songs

When it came time to rehearse the movements, we would also do it right there in the living room. But it was all work, no chitchat, no small talk. Almost all our conversations were about the project. I used to thank God out loud for allowing me to be doing this. Sometimes while we were rehearsing, they'd have a guy shooting film and video of us. Damn, I never got to see it, but I sure wish I could have.

Once we began shooting, it was apparent who was in charge. I must say that Barbra really directed the film, even though Frank Pierson got the credit. We would shoot a section of a number, then walk right past Frank to a TV with video playback. After watching it and deciding whether it was satisfactory or if Barbra or I wished to shoot it again, we would walk right past Frank again and do another take, without ever talking to him. Honestly, I felt sorry for Frank. Barbra is so strong and knew exactly what she wanted. I think the director's only contribution was saying "action." He was in way above his head and out of his league with Barbra. She is so caring; I couldn't see her letting anyone else control her baby. And this film was definitely her baby.

Eventually, Jon only gave me credit in the closing credits, when I was supposed to have a single-card credit in the opening credits. But I don't really care, as I finally got to work with Barbra, and it sure was a gas. In fact, I'd work with her anytime…and for no pay! That's how much I love her and respect her talent! Barbra Streisand, you are the best of the best! I guess all our hard work paid off, as the film won an Academy Award. Also, *A Star Is Born* won five Golden Globe Awards and was nominated for a Grammy.

CHAPTER 26

Johnny Hallyday, the French Elvis; and J'len, My Second Wife

Johnny Hallyday, adoringly known as the Elvis of France, was the biggest French singing star of all time. He sold over 110 million albums with thirty-three number-one hit singles, and President Jacques Chirac awarded him the French Legion of Honour. He was a superstar for over fifty years. Later on in his career, he also became a huge movie star and made thirty films with wonderfully talented directors such as Jean Luc Godard and Costa Gavras. It was my pleasure to meet him years ago when he was just twenty-one years old. We remained friends for all these decades until he passed away December 6, 2017.

I first met Johnny when his wife, the gorgeous young French superstar Sylvie Vartan, came to the US and guest starred on *"Hullabaloo."* We hit it off, and she asked me to come to France to work with her husband. Johnny and Sylvie flew me to Paris, and I stayed with them at their place. But I could never get my schedule to work out, so Johnny and I never actually got an opportunity to work together, which I am most unhappy about. He was such a lovely, fun guy that I know it would have been a great experience for both of us, but instead we struck up a friendship that lasted a lifetime. I have so many memories of Johnny through the years. I used to go to Paris practically every year, so I saw him quite often, as I normally stayed at their house.

Johnny and I used to ride bicycles in the streets of Paris. We rode to singer/movie star Maurice Chevalier's and singer Charles Aznavour's homes, where Johnny introduced me to both of them, and

I was totally thrilled to bits. They both seemed very gentle, and they loved Johnny and were proud of him and his amazing success. On our bike rides, Johnny and I started out alone, but when people saw Johnny they would start to applaud and cry and scream, and many followed us on bikes. Before you knew it, there were dozens of people behind us, then hundreds, and then literally thousands. And when people saw us coming, they would make a long line and wait for Johnny along the streets, and some would run alongside us, as far as they could, in full adoration of this son of France. I recall mentioning to Johnny that I felt like the pied piper of Hamlin! The people on bikes behind us would say, "We love you, Johnny" or "You're the best, Johnny." Some even started singing his songs. Johnny smiled through all of this and took it all in stride. It was a wonderful experience for me, and I realized how much the entire country adored this guy.

Johnny Hallyday (lower left), J'len, and me (lower right) at lunch in Cannes during the making of *"The Last Horror Film"*

During the Paris filming of the *"Raquel!"* TV special, when I had Raquel on a large boat on the River Seine, which cuts right through the center of Paris, I was shooting her singing a song when all of a sudden this crazy person started chasing the boat, running alongside of it on the riverbank. He was waving his arms madly, trying to get our attention. I ignored it for quite a while thinking it was a mad fan of Raquel's, that this nut would soon tire out, but he didn't. About thirty minutes later, I glanced over, I saw that it was Johnny Hallyday waving at me, screaming my name, and desperately trying to say hello. Unbelievable! Johnny wanted to say hi to me so badly that he ran over half a mile to do it. He was yelling to me, "David! David! It's Johnny! Johnny!" We yelled hello to each other, he on shore and I on the boat.

People nearby were in awe to see their idol doing this. They started applauding him and pointing him out to their friends. It was their Johnny Hallyday. Johnny was too cool! He was so down-to-earth. Elvis and Michael Jackson were just two of my many singer friends who were adored by millions of fans, but I have never seen such a love for anyone as that shown by the average Frenchman towards Johnny— never before or after.

Coincidentally, Johnny passed away Tuesday, December 6, 2017. Just the day before, on December 5, in a *Watch and Listen* magazine poll, Johnny Hallyday's 1985 hit "Quelque chose de Tennessee" was voted the greatest song in the history of music. Once every decade, the world-renowned music magazine conducts a global poll of music producers and critics from eighty different countries, translated into twenty languages. According to their poll, here are the five best songs ever written (followed by their percentage of votes):

1. "Quelque chose de Tennessee" (Johnny Hallyday, 1985): 45%
2. "Imagine" (John Lennon, 1971): 22%
3. "Like a Rolling Stone" (Bob Dylan, 1965): 11%
4. "La Tortura" (Shakira, 2005): 8%
5. "Stand by Your Man" (Tammy Wynette, 1968): 7%

Most people would think that "Quelque chose de Tennessee" was a song about the American state of Tennessee, but in fact, that is not so. It is a very deep and sensitive song about an American writer named Tennessee Williams, and Johnny sang it beautifully. The lyric of the song reminds me of Johnny:

We all have something of Tennessee in us
This will to prolong the night
This crazy desire to live another life
This dream in us with his words to him
Something of Tennessee

This force which pushes us toward infinity
There is not much love with such want
So little love with such sound
Something in us of Tennessee

Thus lived Tennessee
The fevered heart, and the demolished body
With this formidable desire for life
This dream in us, it was his cry

Something of Tennessee
Like a star which fades in the night
In the hour when other are madly in love
Without a shout and without sound
Without a single love, without a single friend

Thus disappeared Tennessee
In certain hours of the night
When the heart of the city slept
He floated a sentiment
This dream in us with his words
Something of Tennessee

When Johnny was laid to rest, France came to a halt as it said goodbye to its native son. President Emmanuel Macron gave the eulogy, and former French presidents Nicolas Sarkozy and Francois Hollande joined in. The Champs Elysees, which is rarely closed, was totally shut down as the funeral made its way past the Arc de Triomphe to the Place de la Madeliene. Even the Eiffel Tower said goodbye to

Johnny, with a huge neon sign that read, "Merci Johnny." In 2000, Johnny did a concert there for over 600,000 fans and a TV audience of 9.5 million—about one-fifth of the entire French population. The crowds at his funeral procession were in the tens of millions. Bon voyage and au revoir, Johnny, my dear, dear friend!

Singer Celine Dion tweeted, "I'm very sad to hear the news that Johnny Hallyday passed away. He was a giant in show business...a true icon! My thoughts go out to his family, his loved ones and to the millions of fans who adored him for many decades. He will be sadly missed, but never forgotten. —Céline xx" RIP, Johnny. You are with your maker, and I know you are singing up there with the angels.

His funeral brought to mind how years ago as a young man Johnny had tried to kill himself, distraught over his relationship with Sylvie. I was so glad he had failed. Speaking of attempting to kill yourself, that's how I met my second wife, J'len…

I came home one night to find that a female friend of mine had brought a young lady named J'len to my house. She was depressed and had tried to slit her wrist. A great way to start a relationship, right? J'len was half Danish and half Cherokee Indian—boy, what a combination. She was a knockout! She was a model and a Las Vegas dancer. I fed her milk and cookies, while checking on her wrist. Girls in Hollywood seem to do this or threaten to do this frequently. I gave her one of my bedrooms and put her to bed. In a few days, she had recuperated and was on her way home. We talked on the phone a few times, and I learned that she was engaged to be married and had to go back east to meet her fiancée's family and send out invitations to the wedding. I was about to go to St. Croix in the Virgin Islands to shoot a film, *"The Island of Doctor Moreau,"* starring Burt Lancaster and Michael York, and she jokingly said, "Can I stow away in your luggage?" Then she offered to come visit me on her way back from the east coast. I gave her my numbers in St. Croix, never expecting to hear from her again, but lo and behold, she called me and told me she was on the island and on her way over to stay with me. And stay with me she did. In fact, she didn't leave, from that moment on, until we separated years later.

She had sent out the invites but was obviously not planning to show up for her wedding to her now ex-boyfriend. I told her she couldn't do this, but she did. As soon as she came over, she prepared me a bath with rose petals and candles and basically seduced me, not that I was fighting it. She was lovely and had this incredible figure, standing at 5'9" to my 5'6" The island of St. Croix served as a romantic backdrop for the relationship that soon blossomed. She and I got along really well, and we fell in love. There were many wild animals on the set, and J'len just loved them. She loved to go swimming in the ocean with the trained Bengal tigers and got me to do the same, then with the dolphins as well. She had such good energy. It was a beautiful sight to see. A bit scary, too.

By the time we got back to L.A., J'len was telling all my closest friends that she and I were going to get married. They all told her she was crazy, as did I, but before I knew it, we were standing in my living room vowing to love, honor, and cherish each other till death do us part. The entire wedding party then celebrated in my Jacuzzi. What fun! I'm still not sure how she did it, but in her own way, she was a pretty amazing young lady. The best thing about J'len was, she was on my side one hundred percent. It was she and I against the world. For the first time in my life, I felt like I had a real partner, someone who truly cared.

She was also into other women, and that was great with me. I never had to worry; she would pull them for me in all the clubs we went to. She had a wonderful personality, very positive, very up. Everyone liked her. We filled the house with animals of all sorts. We even bought a mountain lion that was really beautiful and playful. I took her to Cannes where she was very helpful in promotion. And I wrote a part for her in a film I shot there, *"The Last Horror Film."* Even Johnny Hallyday was charmed by J'len and complimented me on my fine taste. J'len could be a charmer when she wanted to.

I didn't realize it then, but she was schizophrenic, and she also couldn't hold her liquor. But I found out soon enough. One day I came home to find an older couple waiting at my house. They told me they were J'len's parents, Mr. and Mrs. Splawn. I could easily see the family resemblance. When J'len came home, she denied that they were her parents; her parents were dead. I didn't understand, but I could certainly see the hurt in their faces and felt bad for them. I asked her what she was doing; they were obviously her folks. She denied it over and over, and eventually they went away heartbroken. I felt terrible, but I had done all I could.

J'len also talked about a son she had, whom I never saw, and I started to question her about her past. She wouldn't go into it, and I didn't want to push her. I told her any problem she had was also my problem, but she closed right up. From then on, she would drink wine in the pool until she passed out, and I would have to pick up this heavy dead weight and carry her out of the pool, then call emergency at UCLA Medical Center. They would send over an ambulance and take her to hospital. I did this so many times that the hospital staff and I were on a first-name basis. Once, she vomited all over the nurses in the ambulance. That was it for me. As terrific as she was when she was sober, she was impossible when she drank, and I couldn't take it anymore. I'd had enough, so I divorced her.

After our breakup, she somehow seemed to know every time there was a girl with me in my house, and she would invariably show up and ruin my night. She had these female instincts that we men will never have, or even understand, for that matter. She tried to get us back together again many times, but to no avail. I had closed that chapter of my life and was moving on.

CHAPTER 27

The Great Diana Ross

I first met Diana Ross when we did *"The T.A.M.I. Show"* together. This was the only rock-and-roll show that was a filmed concert of so many top bands of the time on one stage. After *"The T.A.M.I. Show,"* I crossed paths with many of the performers again on other shows. For instance, Diana appeared on NBC's *"Hullabaloo,"* and as we worked together, we became closer to one another. We were very relaxed at rehearsals, and it felt like I was with a friend.

Ever since doing that first Ann-Margret Vegas show, acts would frequently call to ask me to do their Vegas shows or their tours. Most of the time, I turned them down, as my career was moving more into directing and co-producing films and TV specials and shows. But when my new manager, Roy Gerber, got a phone call from Shelly Berger of Motown asking me to meet with Diana Ross regarding her new act, that was different, very different. First of all, she had been discovered by and worked with Berry Gordy all her career, and Berry was and is to this day a very good friend of mine. Berry was the owner and creator of Motown Records, and he has an uncanny sense of what will sell on records. And secondly because I was such a big fan of hers and loved her voice and her personality. So I met with Diana, and it was like old home week.

When we started to talk about the show, she told me she wanted to do something different. I suggested opening her act with my special Magic Screen. It was a hard thing to grasp, but Diana said, "I believe in you and your talent, David, and I'm sure what you're talking about will be fabulous. Just do it." That's one of the greatest things about Diana: she lets you do your thing and you feel totally free to be creative. We agreed to work together on several engagements. She had a date at Universal's Amphitheatre coming up as well as a Vegas date, a New York date, and a world tour.

Understanding the creative spirit, and to put me in a relaxed and comfortable workspace, she set me up in a two-bedroom bungalow at the Beverly Hills Hotel for eight weeks—so expensive!—but nothing was too much for Diana. She wanted my total attention so that she and I could create her new act together and make it special. And special it certainly was.

I took Diana to a club in L.A. to see some of the street dancers I had been working with. Although she had seen all the latest street kids, when she saw mine, she agreed with me that she hadn't seen anything like them and immediately said I could use them in her show. As it turned out, the number she did with them stopped her show every night. She has very good instincts.

For the next eight weeks, we did nothing but work on Diana's act. As we further discussed the opening act, and wanting to make use of my Magic Screen concept, I said, "What if we start the show with a film of you coming down a staircase and we continue the staircase live so that when you walk down the staircase, it appears as if you walk right into the arena from the film? It will freak out the audience. Nobody will quite understand what they have just seen, and they won't be able to figure out how you did it. And you'll still be wearing the same long-trained coat from the film. During this opening, you'll be singing 'Ain't No Mountain High Enough.'" I knew it would be incredible. And she screamed and jumped around excitedly, like a little kid, yelling "yes, yes, yes!" She could see it. Here I was, watching the diva, one of the most sophisticated ladies in the world, acting like a child, and I loved it. In fact, it was always the child in Diana that I loved the most as we got closer to one another during these creative get-togethers.

After many such sessions, we decided that the act would be a sort of striptease, without being obvious about it. At first, Diana would be in this huge coat; then, little by little, as the show progressed, Diana would subtly be wearing less and less; until, at the end of the show, four of the best-looking male dancers would pick her up above their heads and walk back into the film. By this time, Diana would be dressed in only a one-piece bathing suit. We would finish the show with Diana back on film. In my concept, it would be like a fantasy where Diana came and visited the audience and then went back to her world, that world being film, as she was also a big movie star at this time.

That was it, Diana was thrilled, and she gave me the go-ahead to put everything into motion. It would be an expensive and complicated production. We now had to start rehearsals and shoot the film sequences upfront. She arranged for the amazing cinematographer Vilmos Zsigmond, winner of the Academy Award, Emmy Award, and the Lifetime Achievement Award, to shoot the film sequences. Amongst his many films, he had shot *"Lady Sings the Blues,"* Diana's first film, produced by Berry Gordy, for which she had received an Oscar nomination for best actress. He was one of the top-five cinematographers in the world. Like I said, everything was first class with Diana.

She was really into the show, but we did have one argument: Diana didn't want to sing all the old Supremes songs. She wanted the act to be all new except for a couple of familiar songs. I told her that her audience loved her, but they still wanted to hear those great old songs they grew up listening to. Well, she went to Mr. Gordy, whose opinion she obviously had listened to for many years. Berry told her I was right, and from then on, we never disagreed about anything.

Opening night at Universal Studios Amphitheatre, and we were all very nervous. Because of the film and other effects we were using, it was an extremely hard show to do, technically. Everything had to be timed to the second; otherwise, it would be a disaster. Plus, I had a surprise for Diana. Secretly, I had arranged with a local helicopter company for them to fly over the Universal Studios open-air theatre one minute before the show started. Underneath the chopper, in a bank of lights, a large champagne bottle would appear to pour champagne into a glass, and then the lights would spell out, "THANKS FOR BEING A PART OF MY LIFE. HAVE A GOOD TIME. LOVE, DIANA ROSS."

The audience as well as Diana all looked overhead as the helicopter hovered over them. At first, she had no idea what was going on, but when she saw what I had done, she loved it and came up to me and said, "You're crazy. Can we have it every night?" I could see she was energized, and she hugged me. And we did have it every night—because I had already booked it for the week. It became a part of the act for the entire engagement at Universal. I felt it was a way for Diana to personally say hello to each and every one of her fans in a unique, theatrical way.

Then, without Diana's knowledge, I had taken a copy of her signature and had a large laser beam project it onto the screen on stage, going round and round, until you could see that it was Diana's handwriting. From that, we went to the film of Diana singing the opening song. Then, as she went through the huge screen, I blasted all the lights right onto the audience's faces, blinding them for a second. And a split second after that, there was Diana live on stage, still singing the same song and walking down the same stairs. The audience rose to their feet immediately and gave Diana a long standing ovation. They loved it, and I could see by the look on Diana's face that she was loving it, too. She was sailing.

Diana conquered L.A. with the act and then went on to conquer New York, Las Vegas, and the world. I stood backstage making sure everything went right. We sometimes had a few technical problems, but the audience never knew. At the end of that first show, when Diana was taking her bows and introducing her cast and musicians, I heard her say, "And there's this little guy backstage, who never sleeps, who's responsible for all of this, my director and producer, Mr. David Winters!" She brought me out on stage, and I took a bow. She did that from then on, after every show. I just couldn't believe her; she was so appreciative and caring. And I was so proud of what we achieved together. The show received absolute rave reviews.

I loved working with Diana. She's so open and talented, and she cares about the work. No wonder she's a living legend. And she's like a child, too. Once, in Las Vegas, I went out to a friend's store to buy a hat for J'len, and when I came back to Diana's dressing room, she asked to try it on. I said sure and gave it to her. She put it on and said, "I love it. Thanks." I told her, "Diana, it's for J'len, and she knows I went to buy it for her," at which point Diana ran into the second area of her dressing room and closed and locked the door. I tried everything I could to get that hat back, but she wouldn't part with it. Just like a kid, she said, "Go buy another one." I was pissed at the time, but laughed about it later. She's such a kid, you have to love her!

I got back at Diana, but unless she reads this book, she'll never know. I saw a fabulous painting of her and bought it for her. Once I got it home, I put it up on the wall, and it was so beautiful that I decided to keep it. I felt bad, but then I always thought to myself, that's something that Diana would do, and then I felt better. I still have the painting on my wall over the fire place. Sorry, Diana.

After J'len and I divorced, Diana and I went out a couple of times. In 1979, when I was in New York, we went to see my buddy Mickey Rooney, one of the most underrated actors in the world, in the Broadway show *"Sugar Babies."* It was most uncomfortable. We came in late, and as soon as the audience realized that Diana was there, they were staring and pointing and talking to such a degree that it started to interfere with the show. Intermission was a nightmare; although Diana handled it very well, she really needed at least one bodyguard. She was mobbed, so we left a bit early, as it wasn't fair for the actors on stage, who were working very hard.

Then, in L.A., my friend Don Grenough invited me to hear Billy Preston at a club in Beverly Hills. I thought, no problems here, since we were in Tinsel Town and it would be a small, trendy crowd who had seen it all. Boy, was I wrong. As soon as they saw us come in, we were swamped. Don tried his best to hold back Diana's fans, as did some of the bouncers. We finally got to hear some of the music, but again, once the music stopped, they were pushing and trying to get autographs and pictures. Everyone had been drinking and was feeling friendly, especially towards Diana. She just smiled through it all.

Billy Preston, Diana Ross, a backup singer, me, and Don Grenough

Diana was set to do a TV special, and she and Steve Binder, my pal who was directing, asked me to work on it with her. I would be the creative consultant and choreographer. Michael Jackson and Muhammad Ali were to be guest stars, and when Michael turned up for rehearsals, Diana introduced me to him. "I know you, David" he said. "I don't think so, Michael. If I had met Michael Jackson before, I would certainly remember it," I replied. With that, he picked up his hand and snapped his fingers and smiled. I understood. He was snapping his fingers just like we had in *"West Side Story."* That was it—we clicked!

Right away, Michael said, "I watch you almost every week. You know, *"West Side Story,"* it's my favorite film, and I have loads of questions I'd like to ask you about it, if that's alright." Michael was very polite and respectful, even a little shy and withdrawn. He was a sweetheart, and I certainly loved his work. I see a lot of *"West Side Story"* in his movements. Certainly, the video for the song "Beat It" was a complimentary tribute to *"West Side Story"* in spirit, right down to the knife fight. I also recognize a lot of Bob Fosse and Fred Astaire in his dancing. Well, I always say, "If you're gonna steal, steal from the best," and Michael certainly did, not to take anything away from Michael's talent. Obviously, he didn't steal the moonwalk from either of them. But you can't help being influenced by the great ones, even if you're a great one yourself, and he certainly was. From that day forward, Michael and I became close friends until Michael's death. And indeed, he did have a million questions about *"West Side Story."* In fact, every time I saw him after that first introduction, he asked about the film. I know he would have loved to have been in it. In fact, he whispered that to me once.

Michael and Diana dancing on the TV special *"Diana"* that I staged and choreographed

Then I met Muhammad Ali, and what a thrill that was. You may remember that my father was a boxer when he was a young man but finally had to quit because of pressure from his family. I myself am a big boxing fan and have been to quite a few heavyweight championship bouts in Vegas. My dad taught me to box at a very young age, and it has stayed with me to this day. I love it. I know it's violent, but what can I say? It's in my blood.

Also guesting on that special was the Robert Joffrey Ballet. We came up with the idea to have Diana sing a medley of her hits, and then I thought it would be great to have my street dancers and the Robert Joffrey Ballet dancing together around and with Diana. When I first mentioned the idea to Diana and Mr. Joffrey, they thought I was crazy, but I always liked the idea of the raw street kids and their kind of spasmodic movement juxtaposed with the polished ballet dancers and their fluid movement. It was different, it was exciting, it was today, and as usual Diana said, "Go for it."

When we first started rehearsing, just having the two groups together was weird. They looked each other over like they were going to fight. It was like two gangs; it was definitely a clash of two different cultures. But they all agreed on one thing: that it wouldn't work. Yet as they started to dance together and began to see what I had planned, they really got into it and had a great time. It did work, and it was very interesting to watch. I was very proud of what I had accomplished. Both Diana and Robert Joffrey complimented me over and over about it. The show was nominated for both an Emmy and a Golden Globe.

Next we opened Diana's act at the world-famous Radio City Music Hall in the Big Apple. It had been many years since I had been in New York, but what a great way to return. In the past, I'd had offers to choreograph and direct Broadway musicals, but I always turned them down because I never liked any of the scripts. But now a show that I had created with Diana Ross was opening, and I just knew the audiences and especially the dancers would love it. The approval of and recognition from the Broadway dancers, or gypsies as we're known, was the most important thing to me. They came, they loved it, and at every show Diana would bring me out onto that humongous stage for my acknowledgment and bows. Wow, what a trip!

One day, when the theatre was empty and the curtains where open and you could look way into the back of that 5,000-seat theatre, I sat by myself, feet hanging over the lip of the stage and thanked God for making all this possible and for sending Diana into my life. I thanked Diana for making it all possible and said a little prayer for her. I've never told anyone about this before, not even Diana. It was a quiet and reflective moment, and I felt very spiritual. The empty theatre added to that ambiance, that's for sure.

During our run there, President Ronald Reagan heard about Diana's TV show and my unique match-up of street and ballet. He asked Diana to do a command performance at the Metropolitan Opera House for himself and First Lady Nancy as well as all of New York's royalty, so to speak. What an honor for Diana, and she again asked me to help. She wanted to know if I could rework the Joffrey Ballet and street kids dance for a live show. I said sure, and we went into rehearsals. It was incredible. We had to have special badges to get anywhere we wanted to go and special clearance and approval from the FBI and the Secret Service. And there were all these dogs wandering around with their handlers, smelling everything in sight. They even checked the orchestra's instruments and cases.

Wide shot of an SRO audience on their feet applauding madly and screaming bravo. We cut to an extreme close-up of President Reagan leading the applause. What security, what excitement! What a great audience!

They were absolutely mad for her and gave her a standing ovation, even the President. And then he invited us to a party in the mezzanine. More and more security checks, more sniffing dogs, and even more security men. We were tired by the time we finally reached the party, but it was a wonderful experience and one I shall never forget. We were toasted and applauded, and I tell you, man, Reagan was sure a great guy.

The program for the command performance for President Reagan

After this incredible experience, and with the applause still ringing in my head, I left Diana and went to Mexico to produce and direct an action film, *"Mission: Kill."* It was such a complete change, to go from the music and dancing to guns firing and stunts and blowing things up. I kept thinking about Diana all through that shoot, and when I finally returned to Los Angeles, there was a message waiting for me from her. I called her right away, apologizing for not getting the message sooner. She said, "David, let's make magic again." Well, I tell you, even now I get chills just thinking about it because no one else in my whole life ever said anything like that to me, but that's what I always thought it was—MAGIC! It was such a beautiful way to refer to our work, I just wanted to hug and kiss her. Everyone else just called it work, but Diana called it magic! I was, for once in my life, speechless.

Diana talked to me about her new album and this incredible place in Brazil where we could shoot the video. I was so excited and asked when we could meet, and she said, "Come to my place in Malibu right away." I got there as fast as I could, and we discussed the video and the shoot, but sadly, it never got made. I really wanted to work with Diana again. She is truly such a special person. Over a three-year period, we had worked together a lot, and I had really come to cherish that diva/ sometimes little girl who came from the humble Brewster Projects in Detroit.

To all you young girls that think life is tough, take heed from this great woman. She overcame unbelievable obstacles and is now considered one of the all-time greatest artists to have ever lived! *Never* give up your dreams! Everything starts with a dream, so go and make your own kind of personal magic. You can do it—she did!

For me, working with Diana Ross was truly one of the great pleasures of my life. She is a remarkable woman and a one-off. When Diana was born, they threw away the mold! I love you, baby! I am so proud to be your friend! And to steal a phrase from Bob Hope, "Thanks for the memories."

The stunning Diana Ross at the Hard Rock Casino & Hotel, 2016

With Diana at the Hard Rock Casino

CHAPTER 28

"Racquet"

Cut to a close-up of a tennis racquet hitting a ball. Hear the sound of the ball go swishhh.

Cut to a wide shot: the ball goes over the net and drops in the perfect place on the other side as the opposing player tries without luck to retrieve it.

As I was in the business of getting films made, I was always trying to come up with commercial ideas for films. Warren Beatty, a friend of mine, had done a film about a hair dresser who slept with the stars and the rich ladies of Beverly Hills. It was called *"Shampoo"* and, as we all know, it was a huge success. All these rich ladies had their own special hair person, and they also had their own special tennis trainer, so I thought that this might be fertile ground for a film about a young, good-looking tennis coach who beds all these rich and beautiful women. I came up with a title that I thought was really cool—*"Racquet."* I called my buddy Alan Roberts, whom I had done *"Young Lady Chatterley"* with, as I enjoyed working with him. This time I would also direct the film, with a plan for Alan and I to produce it.

    I had met a young girl, as one does, around Hollywood who wanted to be an actress, but also had ambitions to be involved in the production end. She had a rich boyfriend, who she said was financing films. Oh yeah, I thought, another one of those men who entice these young Hollywood starlets, but who rarely deliver. She told me he had a big tax-shelter company and that his company also owned coal mines. Well, I thought, it's always worth a try—you never know. Maybe for once this one is real. So she introduced me to Ken Fisher at dinner one night. He was a young, good-looking, and friendly guy, and we hit it off. The very next day, I was in his office, where he expressed interest in my film. Haven't I heard all this before? I thought to myself. But we had numerous meetings, and he seemed to love the idea. He played tennis and thought it was good timing for this kind of a film. As it turns out, he was actually financing a couple of other films then. I remember *"The Toolbox Murders"* was one of them only because it was remade in 2005.

He introduced me to his in-house attorney, whose name was John E. Crooks. At the time, I thought, what a strange name for an attorney. Surely he must have been tired of all of the jokes that came his way from such a handle. Anyway, with as straight a face as I could muster up, we went into negotiations on the financing for my film.

Ken just seemed enamored with the film business, especially all the young, beautiful models and actresses he was meeting now, being a financier of films. Surprisingly, he turned out to be for real, and we signed contracts after he agreed to fund my film. When he deposited funds into my film company account, I knew for sure he was for real.

So I begin to cast. There was a part that I wanted Sid Caesar for, as he was the granddaddy of all the comics, and since this was a comedy, having him in the film would be the *Good Housekeeping* stamp of approval. I knew it would attract a lot of incredible comic actors to the film. His agent turned it down very quickly, almost too quickly, I thought. Years later I bumped into Sid at a film event. When I brought up *"Racquet,"* he told me he had never read it, was not told about it, and was pissed because he would have liked to have done it since he had not been getting that many film offers. Sometimes these agents in Hollywood decide for themselves whether an actor should do a film or not, and many times it's a mistake.

I remember a story Martin Landau told me: Woody Allen had called Martin's agent to get his home number to talk to him about a part in one of Woody's films. The agent immediately declined, saying it was not one of their, the agency's, packages, so they didn't want him to do it. Can you imagine turning down Woody Allen? Eventually,

Woody got Martin's number from another source, and of course Martin was thrilled to do the film. And guess what? He received an Academy Award nomination for his performance in that film.

I often wonder how many other situations like this have happened, where the agent makes the wrong decision on the actor's behalf. I had the very same situation happen to me, with Martin Landau's agent turning me down. Fortunately for me, I already had Martin's number since he was a good friend of mine, so I just called him directly. I told him what his agent had said, but he said not to worry, he would do my film for sure, and he did. Martin kept his word to me like the true gentleman that he is. I have been blessed through the years with many friends in the business who have helped me many times when I was in need. I've tried to repay those kindnesses by helping others, but there's no way to measure them and keep score.

Anyway, back to *"Racquet"*... So having been turned down by Sid Caesar's agent, I went to Phil Silvers of TV's *"Bilko"* fame. Phil said yes, as it was a fabulous part for an older comic, and he knew he could shine and stand out in the film. I then cast Edie Adams, who was a wonderful comedienne, as his wife. I also cast Bert Convy as the lead and the beautiful Lynda Day George as the leading lady. I even got the tennis superstar Bjorn Borg to appear in the film and pretend to lose a game to Bert Convy.

Here I am, directing the incredible six-time Wimbledon champion Bjorn Borg and Bert Convy on the tennis court for *"Racquet"*

This became a newspaper and magazine's dream, so we got lots of press on the film. Bjorn was a charming guy, and he and I hit it off so well that he came to the Cannes Film Festival without charging me and made an appearance when I was selling the film. What a lovely and humble man he was, and what a tennis player! Certainly one of the all-time best!

But now here came Hollywood in the shape of a telephone call from my friend Robert Evans. Bob was the head of Paramount Studios and had announced a tennis film called *"Balls."* Bob said to me, "David, I want you to cancel your film as Paramount has a huge amount of money invested in my film, and my film stars Ali McGraw (star of *"Love Story"*) and Dean Paul Martin (son of Dean Martin) as well as Maximillian Schell and Steve Guttenberg. I also have tennis greats John McEnroe, Pancho Gonzales, and Vijay Amritraj, and it is written by Arnold Schuman (two-time Oscar nominee and award winner) and directed by Anthony Harvey (Oscar and Golden Globe winner), so you can see it's a major film."

I told him that I couldn't, that I needed to make films and money, as well. I said I could only cancel if I had a production deal with Paramount for a lot of money; otherwise, I had to go on and make my film. He then asked me to delay my film, just so his could be the first tennis movie released. He said it would take the bloom out of his production, otherwise. I told him to start production earlier and beat me out, but he said that was impossible. He offered me no incentive to delay, so I declined. It was a friendly conversation, but it ended with no agreement or understanding between us.

I continued on casting, hiring such people as Tanya Roberts (of *"Charlie's Angels,"* the TV series *"Sheba,"* and a James Bond film) and Susan Tyrrell (nominated for an Academy Award for *"Fat City"*) as well as Bobby Riggs (a famous tennis player), Bruce Kimmel, Kitty Ruth, Ilie Nastase, and Monti Rock III.

Then another call came in from Bob Evans. I liked Bob very much, but this time he had seen the poster for my film, so the conversation was not quite so friendly. Bob threatened me with litigation if I went on and said to me, and I love this quote, "You'll never work again in this town if you make this film." And that, coming from a guy who knows how hard it is to get a film financed and made independently? The funny thing is, he hired me years later when he was to direct *"The Cotton Club"* with Richard Gere. (Not many know this, but Sylvester Stallone was originally hired for *"The Cotton Club."*) My job on that film would have been to choreograph it and to direct the musical sequences. I guess he forgot what he had said to me all those years before. As I think back and laugh, that's Hollywood, folks. Anything can happen, and it usually does. As it turns out, Francis Ford Coppola took over the reins in directing *"The Cotton Club,"* and I was sent a nice letter from Dysen Lovell, the executive producer, saying that they didn't need my services any longer. I had already had several meetings with Gregory Hines about how we would do the dance sequences. Oh well, all in a day's work.

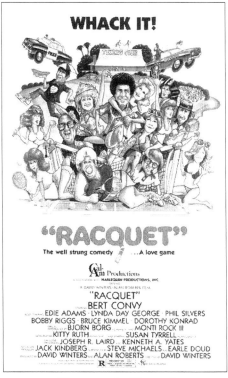

The poster for *"Racquet"*

So I went ahead with the production of *"Racquet"* and never heard from Bob again until years later when he was seeing this gorgeous actress, Merete Van Kamp, who starred as *"Princess Daisy"* on TV. He called me numerous times pushing her and telling me I would be smart to hire her, that she was going to be a big star. Smiling as I talked to Bob, I remembered his clichéd line to me: "You'll never work again in this town." I told him Merete had a very good chance, but that many other actresses had auditioned and also wanted the part. If she got it, it would be because I thought she was the best actress for it, not because of his phone call. As it turns out, she did get the part, as her readings and video tests were the best of all the girls. Knowing she was going with Bob, I cautioned her, as I knew both of them loved to party and I did not want her going away for weekends while we were shooting in Mexico. I knew it would cause her to get back to the set late. Well, of course she did just the opposite and went missing in Acapulco for a few days. I was furious, so I cut her part dramatically and gave all of her lines at the end of the film to another actor. To her credit, she apologized to me numerous times through the years and would tell me she was now a serious actress. To this day, Merete and I are good friends, and in fact, she is currently teaching an acting class in Paris and producing a TV pilot at the same time. So you can see, she became very serious about her craft, and I give her all of the credit in the world for doing so. Good luck Merete!

Back in production on *"Racquet"*... I had hired a helicopter to fly over Beverly Hills to take shots of all the residents playing on their tennis courts on a Sunday morning. Amazingly, there was no one out on any of the courts. No one was playing tennis, and very few were swimming in their pools. You had this huge area called Beverly Hills, home to all the film and TV stars, where almost every home had a swimming pool and many had tennis courts. They must have cost a fortune to build, and just a few people were out in their pools, and nobody was playing tennis. Unbelievable!

So I told the helicopter pilot to fly over some public courts, and we got some shots there. It wasn't what I had wanted, but it would have to do. I then looked for a unique car to use in the film and wound up renting a car from my friend Keith Moon, the drummer in the famous rock and roll band, The Who. The car was an Excalibur, of which they only made 250 a year. This one was a one-off that had been built for Liberace, who had used it for his stage entrance in his Vegas act. It was so beautiful that I bought it for myself when the film was finished.

With many difficulties, I finally finished the filming and started postproduction. Then it turned out that the company Ken Fisher (my financier) was with had big problems with the Securities and Exchange Commission and the IRS. Apparently, their "coal mine" was nothing but a small hole in the ground with an old man sitting in a tent guarding it. They had raised something like $70 million from the public and were summarily closed down. The lawyer, Crooks, ironically wound up being involved and went to the slammer. I think some of Ken's partners also went to prison, but miraculously Ken never had to do any time. Obviously, this was not good news for me, but we managed to finish the film and took it to Cannes for sales.

These company problems altered everything, as the money to promote the film just wasn't there, and I had to make do with a small fraction of what had originally been allotted. Also, the funds to promote the film in the US cinemas just totally disappeared. As it turned out, Bob Evans finished his film *"Balls"* (I think they changed the title to *"Players"*) and released it ahead of me in the cinemas, but it was a flop anyway. All those phone calls, pressures, and anxieties were for nothing. Sorry, Bob.

"The Last Horror Film"

While I was in New York City for the Diana Ross TV special and the command performance for President Ronald Reagan, I bumped into a friend of mine, the beautiful English movie star Caroline Munro. She and an actor named Joe Spinell (of *"Rocky"* and *"The Godfather"* fame) had made a film, *"Maniac,"* together. It was a big hit, and now they wanted to team up for another film project.

Caroline was really hot now, after starring in a couple of Hammer horror films and in the Harryhausen special-effects film *"Sinbad."* She was also the Bond girl in the James Bond film *"The Spy Who Loved Me."* I first met her when I flew to Yugoslavia to rehearse *"Dr. Jekyll and Mr.*

Hyde" with Kirk Douglas. She was starring with Kirk in a film shooting there called *"Scalawag."* Caroline and I had hit it off, and we became friends. She had introduced me to her husband, Judd Hamilton, an American whose brother was a singer in the well-known rock and roll group Hamilton, Joe Frank & Reynolds.

With Caroline and Joe in New York was a writer named Sean Casey, an Englishman. Later over drinks Judd told me of a film they wanted to make and had the funding for, but they needed a director. He asked me if I would be interested and told me the story. I agreed, and he said they'd call me when the funding was definitely in place. In this business, everyone you meet is a producer or financier with a project, but almost all of them never see the light of day. But defying all odds, they called me about a week later, and we talked some more about this film idea that they wanted to shoot in Cannes during the film festival. Ever since I first went to the Cannes Film Festival when I was eighteen, I had always wanted to shoot a film there. There is this incredible, infectious energy in Cannes.

Judd was happy that I knew Cannes so well, and I was happy they had called, but I thought they were nuts. They didn't even have a finished screenplay, and the festival was to start in about a month, so obviously there was no time for pre-production. I also knew that the massive crowds in Cannes would be uncontrollable and, with so many police around, would make it totally restrictive. Furthermore, there was no time to go through all the red tape that the French authorities impose on anyone wanting to film there. And without a script yet, it was just suicidal.

They told me they were going to do it anyway, and after a couple of phone calls, surprisingly, they showed up in L.A. Sean and his co-writer, David Jones, were working on some sci-fi film idea, but Judd and I had a meeting and, together, came up with an idea for a horror film that would take place in Cannes. We all sat down and quickly came up with a script. They rushed back to London and sent me a ticket to come over immediately. I couldn't believe it. They were actually going ahead. I thought, how can they get it together so fast? But lo and behold, a couple of days after I arrived they were already in pre-production. I should hope so, as the festival started in just two weeks.

They had magically put together a terrific crew in just a few days and made arrangements to rent a chateau that sat on 125 acres just outside Cannes in a town called Valbonne. The property had a vineyard, so a deal was done for fifty cents a bottle of wine, much to the delight of the English crew. The property had twenty-three bedrooms, a huge swimming pool with a bridge over it, a tennis court, and horses for riding on the grounds. It also came with cooks and a handyman.

They had made arrangements for me to stay at the magnificent Carlton Hotel right on the beach in the center of Cannes, one of the finest hotels in the world and very expensive. During the film festival, they charge a small fortune to stay there. I couldn't figure out how we were paying for this on a low-budget film. Joe Spinell, who had been signed to co-star in the film, would be in the adjoining room to me, and Judd and Caroline would also stay there. There went the budget!

A Shot of the magnificent Carlton Hotel, on the beach in Cannes. This hotel is the center of the Cannes Film Festival.

A girl named Tara, whom I had met in L.A., made her way over to Cannes and stayed with me. After some time, I told her that she would have to go; my wife, J'len, would be arriving soon to act in the film. I also hired my ex-girlfriend Susanne Benton to be in the film. Susanne had just done a nine-page layout in *Playboy* magazine. She also starred in *"Catch-22"* with Jon Voight, Martin Sheen, and Orson Welles; *"A Boy and his Dog"* with Don Johnson and Jason Robards; and Robert Altman's film *"That Cold Day in the Park"* with Sandy Dennis.

Susanne Benton and me in a scene from *"The Last Horror Film"*

And I hired another ex-girlfriend, Victoria Pearman, to be one of my assistants. Victoria eventually went on to became the producer of *"The Rise of James Brown," "The Women," "Enigma," "Shine a Light,"* and *"Get On Up,"* and co-producer with Martin Scorsese on the TV series *"Vinyl."* Today, Victoria has been partners with Mick Jagger in their production company, Jagged Films, for over twenty-five years. Victoria is such a lovely person, and very successful I might add. We are still very good friends to this day.

Additionally, I hired a little French girl, who was yet another girlfriend of mine. The only problem was, she didn't speak English and I didn't speak French, so we just said ça va ("okay" in French) all the time to each other and smiled affirmatively. What can I say? I do love women!

So there I was, with five women on my hands, about to direct a film that had no real script, during the Cannes Film Festival. I know, I'm nuts! Everyone I knew said I was crazy, that it would all end up a disaster, that probably one of the girls would shoot me, and that the film would more than likely never get finished. I agreed with them. Anyway, we were off and running. The equipment was driven in from London. I don't know how they ever got it through customs, and I never asked.

The production of this film required lots of improvising as we went along. All during the filming, scenes were rewritten on the spot and locations had to be changed because no arrangements had been made in advance. It was generally a nightmare. Except that the footage we were getting looked very good, and that's what drove us on.

The production value was incredible, with thousands of extras in the film. And what we had thought would be a negative turned into a positive. There were so many cameramen from all over the world shooting, and when they saw us with our big crew, everyone assumed that we had gotten permits to shoot there. So the police would stop traffic for us, do anything we wanted, thinking that no one would be doing what we were doing without first having set it up with the officials. Boy, were they wrong. Right in front of the Palais du Festival, with their help, we built a very large scaffolding to shoot from. The police let us drive a limo up to the front of the Palais and let my actors get out to be photographed by about a hundred photographers. Then the same policemen stopped all the stars from coming into the Palais, just so I could get a shot of the photographers. It was amazing! I even got shots of Isabell Adjani, Kris Kristofferson, Cathy Lee Crosby, Marcello Mastrianni, and other stars that I used in the finished film. If we had asked for permits to do this, the answer for sure would have been a resounding "*non, pas possible.*"

But while we were shooting, I was definitely having my own personal problems, which I had created for myself. When my wife J'len arrived, my girlfriend Tara had to leave in a hurry. As J'len was unpacking, she found a pair of Tara's underpants in the closet. I knew Tara was pissed because she didn't want to leave, so I'm sure she left them there on purpose. J'len started screaming at me and crying at the same time, and threatened to jump off our fourth-floor balcony. She obviously meant it, as she tried to. I grabbed hold of her arms and legs, and anything I could grab hold of, to stop her from jumping over the edge of our balcony. She was actually hanging over the edge. I could see that I was going to lose this kind of tug-of-war. She was determined to jump. I screamed for Joe Spinell to help me, as our adjoining doors were open. He did, and after a couple of minutes, we finally brought her back into the room and got her to settle down to a mild scream. I think she must have woken up the entire hotel. My God, I never heard the end of that one. But back to the shoot…

Without any proper pre-production, it's almost impossible—in fact it is impossible—to stay on budget. And regarding the schedule: we didn't have one most of the time, so we had no choice but to improvise over and over again. It was madness. Almost every day there was a new crew member flown in from London. And just as I was starting to recognize them, they were replaced by someone else. One particular young girl who joined us had been on vacation in the French Riviera with her mother, and only God knows how she somehow wound up on our crew. Her name was Stephanie LaMotta, and she was the daughter of the world-champion heavyweight boxer Jake LaMotta. They made a great film about him, starring Robert De Niro, called *"Raging Bull,"* which won the Academy Award for best picture. Stephanie was a sweet girl.

Joe Spinell was really off the wall and quite bizarre. For instance, one night, while I was shooting without Joe, he showed up on the set with Luke Walters, a member of the crew. He sure looked crazy. He had marked up his face with black paint and divided it up into small sections, like a map or something. He was carrying a kid's pinwheel that kept spinning around, and he had on a big black coat. He opened his coat to reveal that he was completely naked underneath except for a woman's bra and underpants. This apparition was one of the strangest sights I have ever seen. Joe was definitely not gay, but he sure was out there! He and Luke wound up in the Circus, a famous disco in Cannes, later in the evening, and Joe got up on stage and started rolling around doing a striptease. I saw the film Luke shot of this madness, and it was great, so I figured out a way to build a scene around it in the film. Joe's character in the film, Vinny, fantasizes all the time, so I made it fit, and it turned out to be a terrific scene. It's funny how things work out sometimes, but that's really the fun and excitement of low-budget independent filmmaking. You could never have the freedom in a studio film to improvise this way, and there's a lot to be said for that.

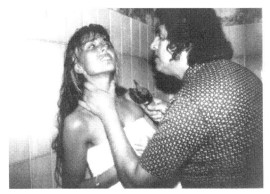

Caroline Munro threatened by Joe Spinell in a scene from *"The Last Horror Film"*

Joe Spinell in his wonderfully mad makeup

Then there was an incident with Adnan Kashoggi's daughter Nabilla and Joe Spinell. I wasn't there, but word got back to me that Joe had insulted Nabilla and punched her. What the hell else could happen? Adnan Kashoggi, in case you don't know, was one of the richest and most powerful men in the world back then. He had introduced Lockheed Aircraft to the Saudi government and received something like a $250 million finder's fee.

From left to right: Devin Goldenberg, (my co-writer) myself, cinematographer Tom Denove, and a local crew member filming a scene inside the Carlton Hotel

I was honestly anxious to finish filming and get the hell out of Cannes. But there was a wonderful surprise awaiting us. There was a music bar in town called La Chunga that was open all night. After the discos closed, everyone went to La Chunga. One night Stevie Wonder unexpectedly came in, went right up to the piano, and sang for hours. What an incredible surprise and treat. He was fabulous and such a warm person. It was our going-away gift.

At the end of the shoot in Cannes, we were going to go to my good friend, financier Bernie Cornfeld's castle just outside of Geneva near a village called Desingy in the Auvergne-Rhône-Alpes region in southeastern France. Based on our friendship, he was happy to let me shoot there for nothing, so we planned on filming there for about five days. When I was ready to check out of the hotel in Cannes, I went downstairs to the lobby and asked the cashier for my bill. I was stunned. It said that I owed $80,000. I gulped, as I didn't understand. There was no way I had spent that much since I was rarely in the hotel, only to sleep. I looked over the bill and saw all these charges for jewelry from the gift shop, loads of flowers, and huge dinners and lunches, and every bill had a signature—David Winters. They had been signed, only it was not my signature. Someone had gone crazy with spending and had signed my name. I was feeling a bit frantic as my mind jumped about trying to figure out what to do.

It could only be the madman Joe Spinell. Who else would have the balls? I smiled at the cashier, like there was absolutely no problem, told him "I'll be right back," and went upstairs to my room. I wanted to ring Joe's neck, but what was the point? I just had to get out of there and on to our next location, Bernie's castle.

I had J'len go downstairs to the hotel's garage and bring the car around and had her stop right underneath our window. When she did, I took our bags and threw them down, from the fourth floor, into the convertible parked below. Some of the bags fell into the car, and some hit the street with a thud, their contents falling all over the place. J'len thought I was nuts, but quickly recovered the bags and clothes that were sprawled all over the street and threw them in the car.

I went downstairs and pretended to be going out for a walk, smiling at the cashier as I walked by. He gave me a sheepish smile back, and I hoped he wouldn't call me over as I nonchalantly mouthed the words "I'll be right back" again. Thank goodness he didn't, and I was out of there. Once outside, I ran and jumped in the car, and with my heart pounding, we took off. It was a long drive to Bernie's castle, and I cursed Joe Spinell all the way there.

I'm gonna fire him—no, can't do that. I'm gonna report him to the Screen Actors' Guild—no, I can't do that. I'm gonna kill him—no, I can't do that. But what am I going to do? Both Mr. Marret and Mr. Bonnet, the co-managers of the Carlton Hotel, are old friends of mine since I was eighteen. What will they think of me? How embarrassing. Will they sue me? Will they send the police after me?—my mind was racing—I'll write the two managers a letter with the truth and explain to them exactly what has happened. I'll tell them that I'm sorry, but I don't have $80,000 on me, and I'll send them $20,000 right away. I'll tell them I will send them something every few months until I pay off the bill. That'll hold them off for a while and keep them happy… I hope!

Fortunately, they were very understanding and agreed to my terms, and as promised, I eventually paid off the bill.

Me relaxing on the camera during a break in all the craziness

Bernie's castle, Chateau de Pelly, is something else. It sits on over 200 acres of beautiful rolling hills. You have to take a long drive through his property until you arrive at a moat and drawbridge. Once over the drawbridge, you come into the courtyard of an 11th-century castle.

It's magnificent, with turrets, domed chapels, huge stone fireplaces, stained glass everywhere, and spectacular views of the countryside with not another property in sight. And it's so quiet and peaceful that you feel like you've travelled back in time. It's like a fairy-tale, and your imagination starts to work overtime. It's absolutely amazing!

Thinking about the wonderful production value this location would bring to the film, I was very thankful to have friends like Bernie. He never asked me for a cent, and a bunch of us stayed there, while the crew stayed in a lovely hotel next to a river in a village nearby. Chateau de Pelly turned out to be just the bit of sanity on this picture that I needed. It was so easy to shoot there, as we didn't have to fight any crowds. There was no one else there but us.

Finally, we all went back to London to shoot some gory special-effects scenes. While in London, Judd came up with the idea to go back to Cannes since the festival was now over and do some pickups and new scenes that we could add to the film. I had no problem with this as long as the money didn't run out.

Arriving back in Cannes, Judd took me to Sainte Marguerite Island, which sits directly in front of the Carlton Hotel, about a quarter mile out to sea. This beautiful island attracts many tourists, who come to see the prison and the actual cell that housed the real "man in the iron mask." Walking into the cell, you can imagine that poor man looking out through the bars of the one small window years ago. You can feel the energy there; it's very strong. The island also has some wonderful restaurants, and many yachts anchor there.

So we came up with a scene and filmed it there, after which we went back to London, where Sean and Judd had words, and Sean left the production. In London, I started editing and moved into the Royal Garden Hotel on a permanent basis. It was recommended to me by Dustin Hoffman, who had lived there while making a film in London. Dusty was right. It's a very nice hotel, and my view looked right out at Kensington Palace. This was years before Princess Diana lived there.

I was peacefully editing away when Judd showed up and said, "David, we need to go back to Cannes one more time!" I didn't believe my ears, but Judd said, "This will be the last time, I promise." As I picked myself up off the floor, Judd said he wanted to shoot something new there. I was starting to wonder, who's really picking up this tab, and why haven't they put an end to it? But off we went yet again to Cannes, and back to shooting.

While we were there, the Cannes Lions would be holding their awards ceremony for the best commercials in the world in the main Palais. There would be over 1,500 people in tuxedos and gowns in the auditorium. Judd said that he had a great idea, if we could get in there. One scene in our film was supposed to take place at the Cannes Film Festival awards show, in which Caroline's character wins the best actress prize. Judd's idea was that during the Lions' event, he and Caroline would walk down the aisle, in character, and wave at everyone. I would be on stage filming, and everyone in the audience would join in when they saw that they were being filmed. We'd pay someone to save two seats in the front row. He and Caroline would keep doing it, over and over, until I signaled that we had the shot. I must admit that this was one of Judd's best ideas for the film. The biggest problem was: How do we get on stage facing the audience with a camera and camera assistants; Tom Denove, my director of photography; a script girl; and myself? You get the idea.

On the night of the ceremony, we all entered the backstage area, and a policeman came up to me and asked to see our permits. I shrugged, did some doubletalk, and pointed nonchalantly to one of the crew in the back, and we proceeded to go on stage with the camera and Tommy and his crew. The audience started to get excited when they realized we were going to film them. As we're setting the camera up, my so-called production manager was searching through one of his large carrier bags, pretending to be upset that he couldn't find our permit.

We were ready. I cued Caroline, and she entered the theatre. Immediately, much of the audience recognized her and began applauding and waving back at her. I was over the moon. It was perfect; I couldn't have staged it any better. After the first take, Caroline and Judd returned to the back of the auditorium and did it again, and again the audience obliged, applauding wildly.

Meanwhile, I kept glancing at the policeman, who was getting jittery. He didn't know whether to kick us out or keep waiting for my production manager to find our permit. My guy told the policeman he now thought it was in his second bag that was filled with all sorts of papers. I started to chuckle, under my breath of course. We were getting away with it—amazing!

On the fifth take, our welcome was starting to wear thin. In fact, the audience was starting to turn on us. They wanted to see the award-winning commercials, and we were holding up the show. I heard a few boos, clearly a good clue that it's time to leave. So I gave Judd the thumbs-up, and they left from the front of the auditorium, as we exited from the back, passing by the policeman and my production manager, now arguing that he had the permit for sure, he just couldn't find it. The policeman, in frustration, motioned for him to follow us out the backstage door, which he did obligingly, and we couldn't believe it; we pulled it off and wound up with the scene just like we had discussed. What a triumph. We got many different angles and close-ups on the actors as well as the audience. It would be very easy to edit.

When we all met up, it was hugs and kisses all around, like little kids who just got away with something naughty—and we certainly did. Later, I figured out how much that scene would have cost us if we'd had to pay for it. With 1,500 extras at $100 per day, gowns at $100 a day, rental of the auditorium, permits, taxes, food and beverages, lights, night shooting and overtime, it's a total of $403,000 (US)—more than a bit out of reach for a low-budget production. I would say that was a good day's (or night's) work. Now it was back to London for, I hoped, the final time.

I was in the middle of editing—again—with Judd continuously interfering by putting his two cents in. It seemed he now wanted to be the director. So I did a Sean and left for Los Angeles. Upon arriving home, I faced another problem. Everything in the house, except for my seven-foot TV and two antique hand-carved chairs had been stolen. I found out that Tara had come back from Cannes very upset and emptied out my entire home. She didn't even leave me a bed.

One day our backer, Mr. Harrison, called me and said he was concerned about the spiraling costs. "It's about time, isn't it?" I said. In our conversation, it came to my attention that Judd was blaming me and Sean for the extravagances and overages of the production. In fact, I had never seen the actual budget, but I certainly knew that we had spent way more than the original $500,000. By this time, even Mr. Harrison was getting suspicious and wanted some form of proof from Judd where the money had gone.

I don't exactly know what happened, being in L.A., but I received a call from Mr. Harrison telling me that he had relieved Judd of his position, which he had the right to do under their agreement. He asked me if I would come back to London and take over the reins of the film and get it finished. Can you believe this? I was off to London again. It's a good thing I love London as I do. Plus, with no furniture in my house, it was an easy decision to make.

On my arrival, I went to the editing room where I discovered that Judd had taken all of the film with him. I thought he'd gone mad or he had a death wish, as the film's backers were very substantial people and could cause him problems. Mr. Harrison tried talking to Judd, but that got him nowhere. Mr. Harrison then took Sean and me as witnesses, we met up with his attorney, and we all trotted down to the West End Central Police Station in Saville Row where Mr. Harrison filled out a criminal complaint against Judd, who still insisted that the law was on his side. So Mr. Harrison had him arrested, and when Judd was brought before the magistrate, he said he had forgotten where the film was. The judge told Judd that he was going to sit in a jail cell until he could remember.

I just couldn't believe it had gotten to this. I told Judd he was crazy, to just walk away from it. He still had his profit percentage. But it became an ego situation, and Judd refused to budge. He was being his own worst enemy. The judge kept his promise, and Judd was sent to jail. After five days in jail, his memory seemed to return, and we were told where the film was. It was returned to Mr. Harrison, and Judd was let out of jail.

After returning to L.A. to finish the film, I found that it was very short. Sean and I came up with some great ideas that we figured we could shoot with a small crew of only four people. We brought Joe Spinell to L.A. and shot some amazing stuff. The scenes we shot with that tiny four-man crew wound up being about twenty percent of the entire film and really made all the difference. I entered *"The Last Horror Film"* in a few festivals, and these are the awards we won:

Best Actor and Actress—Paris Film Festival

Best Cinematography—Sitges Film Festival, Spain

Golden Scroll Award for Best Director—Academy of Science Fiction, Fantasy and Horror Films, USA

Best International Film Nominee—Academy of Science Fiction, Fantasy and Horror Films (We lost to Mel Gibson's *Road Warrior*.)

ACADEMY OF SCIENCE FICTION
FANTASY and HORROR FILMS

Honors

Best International Film Nominee
The Last Horror Film

Dr. Donald A. Reed
President

Somehow, through all the insanity, we finished with a product that a lot of distributors around the world bought and that won many awards.

Whip pan to one year later. The film is ready for its world premiere where it was filmed–in Cannes at the Cannes Film Festival.

We booked cinemas; we also booked a sit-down dinner for over 200 buyers and friends after the screening. I hired a group of lovely young French girls to walk all around Cannes wearing t-shirts advertising my film, and we took full-page ads in all the trade magazines.

The premiere screening was packed to capacity, and we had to quickly organize another screening. We sold lots of important territories. The next day, everyone was talking about the film that was shot in Cannes. They said I was an absolute nutcase and my crew were all mad, but at the same time they admired us for getting it done and now screening it. What a relief we felt. It was all worthwhile, and we celebrated. I felt sorry for Judd, that he wasn't there to get some of the glory, but he had created the situation all himself. He just wouldn't listen.

From the screenings, US distributor Twin Continental bought it for theatrical release. They released it as *"The Fanatic"* in the cinemas. They also bought DVD rights as *"The Last Horror Film"* for video.

In reality, we were all nuts, and had we known what was lurking before us, we probably would have never gotten out of bed. I can't help but think that a film about the madness of making this film would have been a much better film than the film itself. Personally, I'm very happy with the outcome of *"The Last Horror Film,"* as the film has become a cult classic with a great following. I received some terrific reviews and a wonderful award as best director from the Academy of Science Fiction, Fantasy and Horror Films. Thank you to everyone who helped me make this film! You done good, buddy boys!

CHAPTER 30

St. Tropez and the Thief

After the screenings for *"The Last Horror Film,"* I hired a 125-ft. yacht and took it to St. Tropez to relax and party. David Blake, another of my good friends, decided he'd like to come along, so he and I split the costs. We invited ten friends to join us, and it's all aboard, we're off.

The boat was a charter from Cannes named *"Don Juan."* It had an extra-large living room with a fireplace in it. On either side of the fireplace were two huge ivory elephant tusks. It was beautiful and quite unique, and it came with a crew of three, so we didn't have to lift a finger. The crew took care of everything.

We parked right in the middle of the trendy area of St. Tropez, and we were designated "the party boat" by all the other people who had also come down from the festival. *"Don Juan"* was ringed with little lights all over, so it had a very festive feeling about it. Every night, I would have a party on board, and every day, we would go to the special beaches for lunch, swimming, fashion shows, music and dancing, and of course people watching. Lunch was usually a very French three-hour affair, followed by dinner on the boat and then party time.

My friend, actress Joan Collins came on the boat often, as did Harold Robbins and numerous other celebs from both sides of the camera. One night, producer Ilya Salkind came on the boat and was introduced to me as the producer of the films *"Superman"* and *"The Four Musketeers,"* two expensive big-studio blockbusters that had huge theatrical releases in the US. He congratulated me on my film, which he had just seen at one of our screenings, and said it was a great concept to film during the festival. I told him I had another fabulous concept and proceeded to tell him of my idea to do a film about Santa Claus. He seemed very interested. "The three most famous—or in one case, infamous—people in the world are Jesus Christ, Hitler, and Santa Claus, and the first two have already been done. But no one has ever done Santa Claus," I told him. "I have a film that explains who he is, why he gives away toys to the children, why he wears a beard and a red suit, why he lives at the North Pole, why he flies around with reindeer, etc." Then I added, "It's a musical, a cross between *The Wizard of OZ*" and *"Mary Poppins."* Gene Kelly, Robert Wise, Tom Laughlin, and others were all involved with me with this project at one time or another." He flipped and said, "That sounds incredible. Do you have a script?" I said I did, and he asked me to send it to him right away. As soon as I got back, I sent him the script, the music, and ideas for the sets. I waited to hear from him, and I waited, and I waited. Nothing, not a word, so I figured he didn't like it but couldn't be bothered to call me. But I thought, that's still rude and he should have the decency to at least call.

Then, about six weeks later, I was reading through *Variety* (the showbiz bible) and there was an eight-page ad for *"The Story of Santa Claus,"* a new movie to be produced by the Salkinds. In those days, he and his father worked together, but since then they have sued each other, and I don't think they talk to one another anymore. Can you imagine suing your own father, or him suing you?

I called Salkinds' office in London right away, but he wouldn't take my call. I called several more times, and each time he ignored me. I had a friend, a big producer in London, Elliott Kastner, who knew the whole world. I called Elliott up, told him the story, and asked him to call this jerk and find out what he was up to. Elliott reported back that they were not stealing anything from my script. They were doing a contemporary version, totally unlike mine. I asked Elliott, if so, why didn't he pick up my calls? And didn't they feel some obligation to talk to me, seeing that I gave him my idea? Elliott had been told that they had bought a finished script and were signing Dudley Moore to star in it. I thanked Elliott for his time and for helping me. But a couple of weeks later, there was a press release in *Variety* announcing that the Salkinds had just signed two writers to write *Santa Claus*, with Dudley Moore to star. Obviously, they had lied to Elliott. It was also announced that Columbia Tri-Star had bought North American rights for the film.

I waited for a while and then, through a friend at Tri-Star, I got hold of their script. The first eight pages were an exact copy of my script, with many other similarities throughout the film. So I went to see my attorney, David Rudich, and asked him what we should do about this theft of my property. David said that we should wait for the film to come out to see if the finished film did plagiarize my script, and if it did and was successful, then we would sue for damages. That's what is so wonderful about David: he is always so clear and precise, non-emotional and correct. That's why I've been his client for many decades. He said I could sue them right away, but if their finished film didn't plagiarize my script, that could needlessly cause me great expense, and that French law, which wasn't very favorable, might well apply since France was where we had met and discussed it. An American in a French court applying French law probably wouldn't have the best chance of winning, and it would cost me a lot of money for a French lawyer. So he advised waiting till the film was determined to have plagiarized my script, was successful, and opened in America. I was steaming. This bastard was getting away with stealing my creativity and work. David calmed me down, as he always does, and I now had to wait. Other lawyers would have had me suing this bastard just to get their fees from me, but not David. Thank God for you, David, for all these years we've been together, and all the miracles you have pulled off for me.

As it turned out, their film was a disaster and lost all of its money. So according to David, there was considerably less to sue for, if anything, and I still had my original project and still hoped to make it one day. But I have never forgotten that thief. Remember this name! Ilya Salkind Dominguez.

CHAPTER 31

"Thrashin'"

Alan Sachs was a friend of mine who produced the TV series *"Welcome Back, Kotter,"* which got a lot of press because John Travolta was discovered in it. Alan hung around with alternative music groups and knew a lot of talented writers and singers in L.A. He had developed a skateboarding film with a young writer, Paul Brown, and got it to Chuck Fries of Fries Entertainment, who had produced hundreds of TV movies and was looking to break out of this mold. He wanted to do something exciting, like making an indie film that appealed to young people.

Alan called me up about this idea he had called *"Thrashin'"* and asked me to read the script and take a meet with Chuck Fries and him about it. I had met Chuck years earlier when he was the financial controller at Screen Gems when I directed some of the *"The Monkees"* TV series. At the meeting with Alan and Chuck, we agreed to a deal for me to direct the film. Part of the deal was that Chuck would have final approval of the casting for the film. He had heard about what I had done with *"The Last Horror Film"* and wanted to do something similar. He wanted to take *"Thrashin'"* to the Cannes Film Festival and do some pre-sales on it, so we got some artwork done, and off he went.

When Chuck returned from Cannes, Alan told me we were a go, so I began casting the film. Hundreds of young actors and actresses read for me, and I was particularly interested in one of them. He had this great look and reminded me of a young James Dean. I thought he was very special; he really stood out. His name was Johnny Depp.

Although he was an unknown, I saw a certain star quality about Johnny, so I called him in a few more times to read for me. I liked his readings and thought I could even improve them a bit, when and if we got to work together. I decided I wanted to hire him for the leading role in the film, so I called Chuck and brought Johnny in to read for him. But Chuck didn't like Johnny's reading and told me so. I told him to imagine Johnny's face on a huge sixty-foot screen and said, "The girls will *all* go nuts and pee in their panties. Chuck, as far as his reading goes, when I work with him and direct him, it will get much better." But Chuck was firm. "David, go find another actor for the role." I was pissed, but Chuck had final say, so I agreed to go back to the search.

I spent the next two months combing the country for a replacement. I must have seen thousands of actors. After two months, I called Chuck up and told him I wanted to bring in the latest guy I'd just found, who would be great in the film. Chuck sounded pleased, so we set up a time for the audition. When the day came and I walked in with Johnny Depp again, Chuck went ballistic, screaming, "I told you, David, I do not want this actor. He's not good enough! This kid will never make it." He was screaming this right in front of Johnny. It was embarrassing. I told him Johnny would be a huge star and to just let me cast my own film; he should just stick to the sales and the financing. That got him even crazier, and he stormed off, still saying I needed to get another actor for the film. I felt terrible for Johnny and apologized to him for Chuck's rudeness, and he seemed to understand. I went back to the grindstone looking for another actor.

Fortune was smiling down on me, as a young actor named Josh Brolin came to read for the part. I liked his look and reading very much, and this time I was successful in having Chuck agree as well. This was Josh's first adult role, having been just a young kid in *"The Goonies."* Since *"Thrashin'"* Josh has starred in the Academy Award-winning *"No Country for Old Men,"* and he was nominated for an Oscar for best supporting actor for the film *"Milk"* with Sean Penn. He has also starred in numerous other films and currently is one of the most in-demand actors. Having signed Josh, I also signed Robert Rusler, Sherilyn Fenn, Pamela Gidley, and my old buddy Chuck McCann. I also hired the very best skateboarders in America: Tony Hawk, Tony

Alva, Mark Munski, Christian Hosoi, Steve Caballero, Mike McGill, Lester Kasai, Tony Magnusson, Per Welinder, and Stacy Peralta.

One of my young crew was Catherine Hardwicke. I hired Catherine right out of school for her first professional job as a production designer. She went on to become a top director, directing the highly successful *"Twilight"* films as well as the award-winning films *"Thirteen"* and *"Lords of Dogtown."*

For the *"Thrashin'"* soundtrack, we discovered several unknown musical groups, who all later became major recording stars with worldwide hits: The Bangles, Fine Young Cannibals, Meatloaf, Devo—and the Red Hot Chili Peppers went on to superstardom.

"Thrashin'" is the favorite cult film of skateboarders today. Recently, I was honored with a special screening at Munich's biggest, most prestigious International Film Festival.

I used to get the biggest kick by calling up Chuck Fries's office and leaving a message that David Winters and Johnny Depp had called. I just wanted to rub it in Chuck's face. His words, "This kid will never make it," were still ringing in my ears.

Theatrical poster for *"Thrashin'"* starring Josh Brolin

CHAPTER 32

Bernie Cornfeld

On the party circuit in Hollywood, Bernie Cornfeld was right up there with the crème de la crème. But unlike Hugh Hefner, he didn't like big parties where thousands were invited. He preferred to be able to converse with his guests and get to know them better in a more intimate fashion.

Bernie was well known all over the world. He had a massive mutual fund company, named Investors Overseas Services (IOS), which was based in Europe with at one time 25,000 salesmen and loads of airplanes. Many of his salesmen became multi-millionaires themselves. He was on the cover of *Fortune* magazine a couple of times and was worth approximately $6 billion—that's right, billions in the 1960s and '70s. He had the best homes money could buy in London, Paris, New York, Los Angeles, and Geneva. His home in Geneva was situated right on the lake and was the house that Napoleon Bonaparte had built for Josephine. In Desingy, France, he had an 11th-century castle nestled in the middle of over 200 wooded acres, where we shot part of *"The Last Horror Film."* His home in London, No. 1 Halkin Street, was seven stories high with a professional disco in the basement, and his L.A. home, Greyhall, was a 22,000-sq.-ft. chateau with a 23-bedroom dormitory for girls. Plus, it had a Jacuzzi that could easily accommodate at least thirty people. He bought the home from actor George Hamilton and then proceeded to spend millions and millions on it, making it a match for his lifestyle, sort of like a European palace. I stayed in every one of his homes. Bernie was one of my best friends. He always travelled with an entourage of beauties by his side. In fact, when I first met the actress Victoria Principal, of *"Dallas"* fame, she was one of Bernie's girls. He had three of his own private Boeing 727s. He was the real jet-setter that everyone else only pretends to be. In other words, he had it all—and he is probably one of the only Jewish people to ever have a private audience with the Pope.

In his early years, Bernie started out as a social worker. Through his brilliance and the people he hired, he built up his business to such a degree that he could affect the financial stability of a country by how he moved his money and stocks around. Kings, queens, prime ministers, bankers, and government leaders from all over the world would come to meet Bernie just to get on his good side, this way keeping him in check, so to speak. He could play with their financial markets just by what he did. He was one of the most powerful people in the world in terms of money, and also one of the biggest players.

Bernie Cornfeld and one of his toys, his *Excalibur*

In 1977, when I was producing *"Young Lady Chatterley,"* Bernie said, "Use the house," so I did. Greyhall really increased the production value of the film. Then, when I was doing *"A Star Is Born"* with Barbra Streisand, I recommended the house to Barbra and Jon Peters, and it was used in that film also. I used it one more time years later for a video I did with Universal Studios called *"Love Skills,"* an educational show featuring several couples making love.

Every night at Bernie's, there would be approximately ten to twenty men and about twenty to forty girls. You could always bump into movie stars there, such as Jack Nicholson; Warren Beatty; United States Supreme Court Justice Douglas; a prince or two; the governor of California at the time, Jerry Brown; and anyone else who was anyone—and for sure, some of the most beautiful girls in the world. Some were models, actresses, or centerfold girls. The girls were not generally picked for their intelligence, although some were in fact very bright. The girls were there to meet and go out with or even marry a rich, powerful man. The guys were there to get laid, although many relationships did start off at some of Bernie's wonderfully enlightening evenings.

Bernie's place was different than Hef's, in that Hef's was very informal and Bernie's was much more formal. Everyone sat at long tables, and it was like a normal dinner party with interesting conversation. Bernie's style was more European than Hef's. But Hef would be a guest at Bernie's, and Bernie would be a guest at Hef's. Bernie also liked to have his guests express themselves, thus exposing themselves to all the other guests. He tried to mix it up. His dinner guests didn't only talk small talk; they got into some heated discussions as well. Intellectually, it was a lot more stimulating that Hef's, although Hef himself was an intellectual, for sure, and he had many interesting discussions with a select number of his guests. Bernie was also in the business of financing films, so that always crept into the evening's conversation, one way or another.

Every night, the program was pretty much the same. In the early evening, everyone met in the lounge, where a couple of Bernie's young girls served drinks and hors d'oeuvres from his massive bar. Then on to dinner, where everyone was seated at one of the two main tables. Of course, the places of honor were directly on either side of Bernie. I had my own special place, but occasionally, I might give it up for a king or queen or a head of state. There were always some extra plates on a third table for the girls who would invariably show up later. After dessert, it was downstairs to his luxurious theatre for a new film. Then it was Jacuzzi time or do-as-you-want time. By now, many couples paired off, some going to bedrooms in the main house or the pool house, which had four bedrooms itself. Some would go back to the bar lounge or the magnificent living room, which was the size of a ballroom, and some to the billiard room.

I enjoyed Bernie's hospitality for many years. In fact, I lived in his home Greyhall for a while. I met many girls there, but one stands out the most. Her name was Patricia McLaine, and she was a *Playboy* centerfold. When I first met her, she was staying in Bernie's dorm, and after a while, she moved in with me. At the time, I was living in a small castle in West Hollywood. You had to climb fifty-two steps to get to the castle, and the master bedroom was a circular room. Patty was a great party girl, as were so many of them. They were fun and open, and I don't think times like these will ever exist again. I feel lucky and happy to have enjoyed its pleasures.

My girlfriend, centerfold Patricia McLaine, playing one of Bernie's Pinball machines

Bernie introduced me to many young girls, both in the US and overseas. For instance, I met Heidi Fleiss, the Hollywood madam, at Bernie's house when she was a young girl just looking for a job. David Stein, a mad friend of ours had found her. He was forever finding girls, usually on Hollywood Boulevard. She was broke and needed a job, so Bernie hired her as one of his secretaries or assistants. Through Bernie, she met the Beverly Hills madam of the day, Alex, and saw how much money Alex was making. So later on, when Alex got busted by the police, she just took over Alex's business. I think she may have started with Alex's book of celebrity names. Through the years, Bernie and I introduced each other to many girls. It was just one big party that went on for years, interrupted only by work and our family responsibilities.

One day, Bernie's empire came crashing down on him as President Richard Nixon's friend Robert Vesco maneuvered him out of IOS, and Vesco eventually fled the United States and became the FBI's most wanted criminal. Robert Vesco had stolen $800 million in cash, securities, and gold out of the IOS vault, and had taken his mercenary army and a few planes and fled to Costa Rica where he did a deal with the government to allow him to stay there. He also supplied them with American girls and became the biggest financier of drug smugglers and wholesalers in the world. Eventually, it got too hot, as the FBI never stopped pursuing him, so he was politely told to leave the country, at which point he made a deal with Fidel Castro and was allowed to stay in Cuba.

Meanwhile, Bernie tried to regain control of IOS, but he failed. This was a crushing blow to him, from which he never fully recovered. Bernie always spoke about IOS as if it were a country and he had been deposed. He compared himself to Haile Selassie of Ethiopia, who in fact was on IOS' board of directors along with retired Supreme Court Justice Douglas, US Representative James Roosevelt (the president's nephew), and other such luminaries.

Bernie went through money like it was water, and it took a lot of water to support his lifestyle. The BBC did a couple of documentaries on Bernie that were very negative, as a lot of IOS investors had, by this time, lost their life savings in the company. Some of them interviewed expressed a lot of anger towards Bernie. I and some of his other friends, fearing for his safety, suggested he lock his doors and tone down his lifestyle a bit. Bernie didn't listen. In fact, he didn't seem fazed at all by the threats. Instead, he kept up his lifestyle and threw it in their face. His front door at Greyhall was always left open. To teach him a lesson, I snuck into the house one day with some friends. We carefully emptied his living room of all his expensive art work and certain pieces of rare furniture. When he discovered it all gone, I had made my point. My guys put it all back, and he said he would lock his door from then on. But he never did.

When he was called to Switzerland to answer some legal questions, both Hef and I told him not to go. He insisted and wound up waiting in jail for a year until he faced a criminal trial. His jailing was big news all over the world, but with his money, he was able to buy himself a very comfortable jail cell/apartment. He paid off some authorities and was allowed certain privileges not allowed other inmates. For instance, his mother was allowed to stay with him. Bernie loved his mom so much. Like all good Jewish boys, Bernie was extremely close to his mother. He even had a special apartment in Greyhall for her. Ultimately, Bernie was acquitted of all charges, and upon his release he immediately flew back to America. Bernie had gone through untold millions in cash and was now having to sell some of his magnificent properties to support his lifestyle. This started a trend that never ended until his death.

Everything that Bernie touched seemed to fail. Eventually, he was arrested and put in prison in Lompoc, California, for owning and using one of those black boxes for making long-distance telephone calls without paying for them. I had told him that it wasn't worth it to save a couple of thousand a month, or even a week, but Bernie never listened. I would drive up to see him in the Federal Correctional Institution in Lompoc, where he spent about eleven months. Amazingly, everyone at this penal facility had lawyers there and were doing business deals and signing contracts. It was so weird. It didn't feel like a prison at all. Kids were running around and playing, and everyone was eating food they had brought with them. It felt more like a Sunday family picnic. Bernie told me he had organized all the inmates to strike for extra pay for the license plates they made in prison. Only Bernie could think of that one—hysterical. What a character he was.

It struck me as sad that none of the people who were at his house all the time and at his dinner parties came, even once, to see him. Those "good-time Charlies," who are there when it's good, but aren't when it's bad—they make me sick! I tell you, Hollywood is a hard town to find a real friend in. Most relationships are out of convenience. Bernie would ask me or Skye, who was always there for Bernie, how so-and-so was, and we would have to lie and say they were shooting or out of the country so as not to hurt his feelings. The very same people who admired him for going to jail for stock fraud were now turning their backs on him because telephone black boxes weren't so glamorous. Before his conviction, discussions about Dustin Hoffman playing Bernie in a film based on a book about him had taken place. Now they were cancelled. I thought, what's the big deal? He made a mistake, that's all.

Bernie himself seemed to change once he got out of Lompoc. He called me one day and said, "David, it's my birthday today, and I'm all alone with nothing to do." Feeling sad for him, I said, "I'll take you out to a birthday dinner. I'll be over at eight with David Rudich." Bernie's spirit seemed to rise then. I had introduced him to David, and he had hired him as his attorney. When David and I arrived at his house, three of Bernie's limos were waiting in the driveway. Bernie said, "I was lonely so I invited a couple of girls," at which point twenty of them came out of his house and piled into the limos. As we sat inside the limo, Bernie had this sheepish half smile on his face waiting for my approval, which I of course immediately gave. Then we all sped off to the Chinese restaurant I had booked. I was glad to see Bernie back to his old tricks. Needless to say, it was a wonderful evening with Bernie, David, me, and twenty girls.

As I mentioned earlier, Christopher Walken and I were in the same dance class when we were thirteen years of age. He was now in Manila in the Philippines shooting a film called *"McBain"* with a couple of my buddies, director James Glickenhaus and actress Maria Conchita Alonso. Bernie and I flew to Manila to hang out with them on the set. I thought it would be great to see Chris after all these years. While we were hanging out, *"West Side Story"* came up, and Chris told me he had toured in the show early in his career and met his wife while in the show. I mentioned that I always travelled with my *"West Side Story"* jacket. Chris asked me if he could borrow it, just for old times' sake. Well, would you believe it? To this day, he has yet to return it to me. Chris, don't you think that forty-plus years is a bit much, even between friends? *Please*, Chris, return my *"West Side Story"* jacket, even if it's just a rag at this point. It has sentimental value to me.

Bernie had financed many films, such as *"Hitler: The Last Ten Days"* with Alec Guinness and a film with Peter Sellers called *"Ghost in the*

Noonday Sun". Bernie told me the Sellers film was a piece of shit pirate movie and was sitting unreleased on a shelf at Columbia. I arranged for us to see it and came up with an idea to save it, but it would take shooting a couple more days with Peter Sellers. Bernie and I flew to London and had dinner with Peter at San Lorenzo's, and Peter said, "No problem, I'll do whatever you want." I told Bernie we could make a bundle if he could get it released from the studio. An unreleased film with Sellers was worth a lot of money in those days. Every time I brought it up, he promised me that he would try to get it, but he never did. He didn't seem to care about business anymore. I tried and tried to inspire him, but his heart just wasn't into it. To this day, that film still sits on the shelf of the studio, unfinished.

One afternoon, as we were partying at Chateau de Pelly in France, there was a knock on the main door, and a man and woman announced themselves as being from the IRS. We all quickly got dressed and went downstairs to see what the hell was going on. They were for real and had found Bernie to tell him that he owed Uncle Sam $3.6 billion for unlicensed trading in gold. Bernie said that the USA was full of shit, he didn't owe them a cent. So Bernie, believing in himself, went back to fight it, like he had a death wish, or maybe he just enjoyed a good fight.

He hired the best (and most expensive) lawyers money could buy, including retired Supreme Court Justice Douglas and the mammoth Dewey Ballantine New York law firm, and started to defend the charges.

As the case proceeded, it became increasingly clear that he was going to lose. He had spent many millions of dollars fighting the case, but he eventually fired his lawyers. He then asked David Rudich to sue the US government for persecuting him because he was Jewish. To his shock and mine—in fact, to everyone's surprise—David found a flaw in the government's case that none of the other hotshot lawyers had found. It was some old case law in a Supreme Court case more than 130 years old. And so David got the charges dismissed. Bernie gave David a Maserati Ghibli and a half-million-dollar bonus, even though money was much dearer to Bernie by then.

As Bernie grew older, he spent a lot of time in Israel. He was there when he became very sick, with no one who could help him. He had run out of cash. No one called me, and I only found out about it after he passed away. I was very upset about this, to say the least. Skye was with him and accompanied him to London where he died. When he died, he was virtually broke. I guess that when we all die, it doesn't matter how much money we have or have had. Bernie lived a life like very few other men do. He was one of a kind and very generous to his friends. I miss him dearly. I cherish all the wonderful memories of our days together. L'Chaim, Bernie. You were such a mensch!

Lynda Carter—My Very Own Wonder Woman

My lawyer and dear friend, David Rudich, told me about this girl he was seeing named Lynda Carter. She had been a contestant in the Miss World USA contest, which meant she had to be beautiful with a shapely figure and probably quite bright. One day, he and I went to his amazing house in Benedict Canyon in Beverly Hills, which had belonged to Carole Lombard, where he introduced me to Lynda, and my God, she beat all of my expectations in every area. Not only was she all of the above, she was also elegant, feminine, classy, and had a great sense of humor, to boot. She was absolutely stunning!

A professional picture of Lynda Carter

So one day David invited me for a weekend at a country house with him and some of his other friends. He said he was bringing Lynda. I graciously accepted and decided to take Patricia with me, even though our relationship was coming to an end. It wasn't her fault. That's just one of the major problems in my life, staying interested in one girl for very long. When we all met at the house, it was quite obvious to me that David and Lynda were not emotionally involved with each other. And after two nights, Patricia and I were hardly speaking. Hey, I got it. I was never even interested in committing to eating only one flavor of ice cream for the rest of my life, although David was. He's far more the monogamous type than I.

Then the conversation in the house turned to the stars in the sky, and everyone was talking about how clear and bright they were. Lynda asked me if I would like to look at them with her, and I said yes. So we went outside and stood side by side looking at the stars. Lynda said some very pretty things about our view, and ever so slightly, she touched my fingers and my hand, until, before you know it, we're holding hands in a most romantic way. This, I must say, was the most subtle seduction I had ever experienced, and I was quite enjoying it. But I was also feeling very nervous, not knowing what was going on between David and Lynda for sure. Lynda reassured me that David and she were just friends, there was no romance at all. I told her that before we went any further, I had to talk to David because he was very close to me and I would not want to do anything that would upset him. To tell you the truth, I was not expecting this, and it took me totally by surprise, as Lynda had never let on in any way that she was interested in me. But I was certainly attracted to her. She is absolutely stunning, intelligent, and feminine. So with that in mind, we all said goodbye to each other and headed back for the city.

A couple of days later, I talked to David, and he said not to worry, he and Lynda were not seeing each other, and he hoped that I would have a great relationship with Lynda as she was a wonderful girl. Ironically, years later David married my ex-girlfriend actress Susanne Benton. As the saying goes, "All is fair in love and war." Being only mortal and of the flesh we met, and Lynda was everything a man dreams of in his lonely hours. I was definitely stricken with her. Now my problem was what to do about Patricia, as I saw our relationship going absolutely nowhere.

I was at home one day with Patricia when Lynda stopped by. As I came down the stairs, she was like a spring vision to me, and I couldn't stop myself from hugging her. I was thinking, I must be nuts, and at the same time, what an incredible life you have, Winters. You have a Miss World USA contestant in your arms and a centerfold upstairs waiting for you. Soon Patricia came downstairs, and I said a rather quick goodbye to Lynda, although I was wishing that she could stay there with me. I knew then that I had to split up with Patricia, so I asked Bernie Cornfeld if she could move back in with him, and he of course said yes. So Patricia moved out to Bernie's. This left me with lots of time for Lynda, who was a much more independent girl than most of the ones I had been with before. The next few weeks were wonderful, and I felt like I wanted to marry this girl. I was absolutely fascinated with her. I also found out that Lynda was extremely talented and had a terrific voice, so we spent hours fantasizing an act for her when she became famous.

Lynda was working every so often as an actress, and one day she told me about an audition she was going to go on for this TV series—"Wonder Woman." This didn't impress me at all, as it wasn't a very creative job. In fact, it was a joke to serious actors, so I didn't give it much thought. After a few auditions, she called to tell me they wanted her for the starring role, and aren't I excited? I think Lynda was expecting a very different reaction from "That's nice." I tried to explain to her that all those discussions we'd had about her becoming a star and a great actress would not materialize if she accepted this part. I was sorry to burst her bubble, but that was what I truly thought. It reminded me of the "Superman" TV series, whose star, George Reeves, could never get a job after the series ended because no one took him seriously as an actor anymore. I explained that this TV show could be the kiss of death for her.

In fact, George Reeves eventually committed suicide by jumping out of a window, it became such a problem for him. I told this to Lynda, but she was so ecstatic about getting the part—and rightly so, I guess—I don't know if she ever really heard what I was saying. I told her she would make lots of money, but we had discussed that money was not the reason we were both in this industry. It was our love of acting, music, and dancing that drew us both into the business and also what made us such good friends. We had always talked about doing excellent work and hopefully winning awards, like the Academy Award, the Emmy, etc.

When she accepted the part, I thought, her dreams will never come true now, she has sold out. Of course, what a tough thing I was asking her to do. An unknown new girl in town beating out all the competition and getting the lead on a TV series and probably being set for life, and I am telling her to go on being a struggling actress in a city of thousands of them, mostly out of work. So, in a way, I understood her, and I probably would have done the same thing at the time, given the opportunity. It's a lot easier telling someone else not to sell out than it is not to do it yourself. But still I felt she would one day regret her decision. I wonder if she ever did? Probably not. She overcame the Wonder Woman image and went on to do lots of TV films as well as an act in Vegas and on tour. As it turns out, I wound up doing her act for her, although, unbelievably to me, I was not her first choice.

So we whip pan to a few years later.

Lynda became a star with *"Wonder Woman,"* and she and I drifted apart. She married Ron Samuels, a producer in town, and seemed quite happy, although who really knows about the true depth of other people's happiness. Ron also became her manager, and he booked some club dates for her in Denver and other cities, ending up in Vegas. I couldn't believe that after all the hours we spent talking about her act, when she finally got to do it, I was never called upon. This hurt me very much, to say the least. Instead, I was told she was using somebody else. I was surprised that Lynda hadn't called on me. I loved her as a person and would have bent over backwards to help her, and I thought she knew this. Anyway...

I was driving down Santa Monica Boulevard in Beverly Hills one day, and out of the corner of my eye, I saw Lynda driving next to me, trying to get my attention. So I slid down my window, and she said hi. I felt a bit put out but didn't let on, and I said hi back to her. She said she had been trying to reach me about doing her act but hadn't been able to. I knew this was bullshit, because I hadn't changed my number, it was the same as it was before. She yelled that she would call me later because she had something she wanted to talk to me about. We smiled at each other with a fake smile, blew some phony Hollywood kisses to each other, and drove away.

A day passed before the phone rang and it was Lynda. She apologized and said it had been Ron's idea to hire someone else, which kind of makes sense. Why would you want on old male friend staging an act for your new wife? He also seemed very insecure to me, even though he put on a show to look otherwise. Hollywood is full of men who prey on successful women. So I just said to her, "You know I would do anything for you, Lynda. You are my friend, no matter what happened."

She went on to tell me that she was opening in five weeks and had no act prepared at all. She said, "I am really scared, David. Please help me." So I asked what the problem was, and she said, "the person doing my act is very busy, and talked a lot of great ideas with me, but they never showed up, and there is no schedule set, and I am feeling very insecure and can't continue this way."

"What do you want me to do, Lynda?" I asked.

"Let's meet and you do my act, just like you and I dreamed and talked about years ago," she replied.

"Fine," I said, "I can do that for you, but since you didn't call me as a friend, you need to pay me just like any other job, and I am expensive."

This she knew so she said, "No problem, Ron will work that out with you."

We made an appointment for the next day, and off I went to meet Ron Samuels in his office in Beverly Hills. I was all prepared to give him a hard time, but he was charming and made me feel needed. And he knew how I felt about Lynda. Ron was good. Like most people I meet in the business, he knew my past and acted like we had met before, which I don't think we had. He had been an agent and a manager as well as now being a film producer. Ron was very smooth, and since this meeting was for his superstar wife, he was extra good.

I explained to Ron that every act I had done before had become a TV special, so that was how I thought when I put these shows together.

He knew what I had done with previous acts and said that was exactly the kind of act he wanted so he could use it to get Lynda her own TV special. He assured me that I would be involved in the TV special if and when it happened. Ron and I made a deal, and I was paid $25,000 to create and stage an act for Lynda.

We met every day, and I created and staged the act for her. When we opened in Denver, everyone was so surprised by how well Lynda sang. The show went over very well, and she did SRO business. Lynda actually is a terrific entertainer, one of the best, and I was more than pleased with the results. Ron and Lynda both expressed their appreciation to me and said I had saved the day. We wound up in Las Vegas as planned, and the show received great reviews.

It's funny how people in Hollywood forget so easily. When Ron did sell the TV special, using my creation, he and Lynda forgot to call me to be a part of it. That left me with a bad taste in my mouth, to say the least. I was more than hurt by it. I had saved their asses when when the person before me didn't deliver and left Lynda with no act only a few weeks before her opening. She not only had a very successful act that I created but also a series of musical TV specials, just like we had dreamed of together, and I was given the brush off by her husband. After this experience, I started to think about leaving Los Angeles.

I felt bad for Lynda, being married to this lying, insecure creep who broke all his promises. Lynda and Ron eventually broke up. And of course she had to pay him loads of money in settlement. I guess the marriage wasn't convenient for him anymore.

Lynda and I recently re-established our friendship, and I still have great affection for her. Fame is fleeting at best, but friendship should be there forever! At least, I thought so. I have a love for Lynda, no matter what. I know she is a good person inside, so I will always remember the good times and the dreams we shared together, and she will always be my very own Wonder Woman.

Donnie & Marie

Sid and Marty Krofft, who were famous for their puppet shows, were to produce the *"Donny & Marie Show"* and asked me to join them, which I did. The Osmonds were a very large family with seven sons and a daughter and were practicing Mormons from Utah. When I first met Donny and Marie, we hit it off really well. I liked their positive energy and personalities, and they were very talented, so it made my job as choreographer and musical consultant on the series easy and fun.

Olive, the mother of the family, seemed to be the boss. She was a real prude. She once had a producer tell me that I should not wear tights to dance rehearsals. *What?* Yes. But I complied, and I must say, she seemed somewhat more comfortable after I did.

I'm showing Marie and Donny some dance moves

Donny once asked me to join him at the imposing Mormon temple on Sunset Boulevard in Los Angeles. He was hinting that it would be great if I, too, were a Mormon; then we would all be one big, happy family. No way, Jose. Although I believe in God, I am not religious, I am just spiritual. Donny was not pushy in any way and never made me feel uncomfortable, even though I rejected his suggestion. He was a lovely guy and quite low-key for having such a successful career at his young age, as was Marie. They were both so easy to work with.

Me and my assistant Casey Cole rehearsing with Donny and Marie as Mae West and W. C. Fields

The Osmond Brothers, who were now taking a back seat to *"Donny & Marie,"* would appear from time to time throughout the series. Years later, I had my own record company, Winro Records, and had a big hit with the youngest member of the family, Jimmy Osmond. Even though he was just a kid, Jimmy had split from the family and gone out as a single artist. His song "Long-haired Lover from Liverpool" became number one in the UK—kind of a novelty song, very cute and catchy. It was written by Christopher Kingsley, a guy I had given a lift to when he was hitchhiking on Sunset Boulevard. He was standing on the street with a guitar in hand and his thumb out, and after I gave him a lift, he told me he was an aspiring writer/singer. So about a year later, I had him come by my office and eventually signed him to a recording/writing contract with my record company. Years later, I directed Jimmy in a Disney Channel show filmed in Utah. My buddy

Jim Rich was producing and knew I had a history with the family and Jimmy specifically.

But after twenty-two segments of *"Donny & Marie,"* I grew tired of the show and needed something more challenging, so I gave my notice to Sid and Marty, who were very understanding, being creative artists themselves.

Me and Donny during rehearsals

David choreographing Latin Singer Charo

"The Star Wars Holiday Special"

I received a call from Gary Smith, who, with his partner, Dwight Hemion, has won seven Emmy Awards. He was producing *"The Star Wars Holiday Special"* with George Lucas. He told me my buddy Steve Binder would be directing with George, and he wanted me to stage and choreograph the TV special. It had been about a year since the original film had taken the world by storm.

Gary told me the TV special would have an all-star cast in addition to all the actors from the *"Star Wars"* film: Harrison Ford, Mark Hamill,

Carrie Fisher, Alec Guinness as Obi-Wan Kenobi, even Chewbacca, R2-D2, and Anthony Daniels as C-3PO. The guest stars would be Art Carney, Diahann Carroll, Bea Arthur, James Earl Jones, Harvey Korman, The Band, and Jefferson Starship. Wow! This sounded like a great challenge to me.

The show would air on CBS-TV from 8:00 p.m. to 10:00 p.m. That in itself was quite amazing, as usually TV specials are one hour at most, and this was to be two hours straight, even longer than the original film. He said it would become a collector's item, which it certainly is today, especially for fans of the Star Wars film series.

I had enjoyed working for Gary before when he was the producer of the NBC-TV series *"Hullabaloo,"* and I loved Steve. Gary said Bob Mackie was doing costumes, and Bruce Vilanch was writing it. Steve and I had done many shows together, so I immediately said yes.

My first rehearsals were with Diahann Carroll and Art Carney, and they went very well. During those rehearsals, though, I heard that George Lucas had actually paid for the network time himself. This was amazing to me, and I didn't understand why he would do that, knowing it was truly expensive. So when I met George, I asked him. He told me that the first *"Star Wars"* movie had been released one year ago, and the second one was to be released in about another year. Then he asked me, "David, do you know how much the first *"Star Wars"* made at the box office?" I said, "No, George, how much?" "$300 million," he said. "Do you know how much the merchandising from the film has made?" I again said no. "$1.2 billion, and I own that one hundred percent myself," Lucas said. Wow, I thought, amazing! He continued: "I don't want the audiences to maybe forget about the second *"Star Wars"* film by the time it comes out, probably a year from now. So I decided to buy the network time myself and produce this TV special so that the film stays fresh in the audience's mind when we release the second installment of the film next year." I thought, shit, George, you are brilliant, what a great idea!

Well, to date, the merchandising alone on all of the *"Star Wars"* films has reached around $33 billion. Can you imagine? Who said creative artists are not so smart? George Lucas certainly is, and he had the last laugh all the way to the bank! Need some help with all that cash, George? Good for you, George, and thanks for the job!

The special was broadcast in its entirety only once in the United States, on Friday, November 17, 1978 (the week before Thanksgiving), on CBS from 8:00 p.m. to 10:00 p.m. (EST), pre-empting *"Wonder Woman"* and *"The Incredible Hulk."* It soon became a cult classic among *"Star Wars"* fans. In fact, in a 2008 online poll on Christmas specials by the Paley Center for Media, the *"Star Wars Holiday Special"* was selected to be shown at the Center by fifty-nine percent of the voters, who selected five titles each. It beat *"A Charlie Brown Christmas," "How the Grinch Stole Christmas,"* and *"Rudolph the Red-Nosed Reindeer,"* among others.

A Race Horse Named
David's Winter

In the mid-1980s, I created a film called *"Mission: Kill"* and decided the best place to shoot it would be in Mexico. While I was at home preparing the film, a most interesting letter arrived in my mailbox from a Miss Cynthia Elliot. The letter explained that she had seen me in *"West Side Story"* on Broadway when she was just twelve years old, and as a young girl, she had fallen in love with me. Now she was thirty-eight years old and a well-known race horse trainer and owner, living in Miramar, Florida. In the letter, she said her whole house was an homage to me, with pictures of me on every wall. She mentioned shows that I had done as an actor many years ago, some so old that I had even forgotten them myself. She said she owned every album that I had ever sung on. She told me I was her Elvis Presley! She went on to say that dancing was one of her loves, but she was not particularly good at it, so she had turned to horses, as she was a very accomplished rider. She wrote about the mane of a horse in very poetic terms, comparing it to the beauty of dance. I could see from her letter that she was an artistic, aware, and sensitive person.

She had just paid $1.5 million for a race horse that was sired by Nijinsky, a world-famous champion race horse that had recently been syndicated for £40 million, the equivalent of over $60 million. She said she wanted to rename this horse and call him David's Winter in honor of me and the joy I had given her as a twelve-year-old seeing her first Broadway show. If nothing else, her letter was a big ego booster. In her letter she said that she wanted to come to L.A. and meet me. It was most intriguing, I must admit, but when I showed it to my girlfriend, Simone Overman, she got a bit upset. It even seemed as if she was kind of jealous and threatened by this unknown person. Simone had nothing to fear. I was very happy with her, and Simone had no reason to be insecure. Not only was she a great companion, she had been Miss Philippines and was still exceptionally pretty. I wrote Cynthia back thanking her for her lovely remarks and said she could certainly change the name of her horse to my name, and that I was very flattered by her numerous compliments. When Simone read my letter, she seemed even more threatened.

A couple of days later, I got a phone call from Cynthia saying she was coming to Los Angeles and that she had decided to also make me a partner in the ownership of David's Winter. I told her that was crazy, there was no reason for me to own a piece of her horse, and that changing its name was kind enough, but she insisted and said that her mind was made up. She had already booked a flight to come see me.

The day arrived, and the doorbell rang, and of course it was Cynthia. We had a meeting about David's Winter, and I tried again to talk her out of it, but she was not having it. She showed me pictures of the horse, and I must say, he was a beautiful animal. She told me that she thought our horse, as she put it, could be a great champion just like his sire, Nijinsky. She had all the legal documents written up, officially giving me part ownership of David's Winter for the amazing sum of one dollar. She was being generous to a fault, and I told her so, but she didn't care. She insisted, and that was it. I asked her if David's Winter could win the Kentucky Derby, and she said yes, she thought he could. I said, "Cynthia, let's just say he does win the Kentucky Derby, I should not be on the cover of *American Turf* magazine. I don't deserve to be." But she said, "David, you are my partner, and I can see this horse going all the way. If it does, I want you to be a part of it. Your dancing changed my life, and I will never forget it. We're partners and that's it. Conversation closed." Well, she certainly was forceful and stubborn, so who was I to fight it? We both signed the agreement, and I was now part owner of a champion-to-be race horse. And for only one dollar. Can you imagine?

Cynthia would come over every day to discuss her plans for David's Winter. She was gung ho about it and truly believed in the horse. In her mind, he was already a champion because of his bloodlines. His mother was Northern Dancer, also a champion. And to tell you the truth, I was hoping she was right! She taught me all sorts of things about the business of horse racing. For instance, she explained to me that you don't pay for a horse until he fully stands up on all four legs. When a horse stands up, everyone knows that the horse will be able to run, and so the purchase money is then paid.

It was now time to cast *"Mission: Kill"* and get down to Mexico to make it. As I was the director, producer, and writer of the film, I got to do all the casting myself. I hired a young rising star, Robert Ginty, who had just starred in a big Warner Brothers hit, *"The Exterminator."* Other stars in the film were the gorgeous and talented Merete Van Kamp, star of TV's all-star miniseries *"Princess Daisy"*; Cameron Mitchell, star of the TV show *"High Chaparral,"* who was also amazing in Arthur Miller's classic film *"Death of a Salesman,"*and the very beautiful Olivia d'Abo, star of *"Conan,"* opposite Arnold Schwarzenegger.

I said my goodbyes to Simone and flew down to Mexico City to begin pre-production. Two days into the film, I received a call from Cynthia telling me she was coming down to discuss some business about the horse. She told me we'd already had a very substantial offer for it from an Arab sheik, and we needed to figure out what we wanted to do. It seemed like I'd just hung up the phone and she was there. She told me that a certain sheik from the royal family of Bahrain had seen her at the track one day shoveling horse manure into the back of her pickup truck, which was all in a normal day's work for her. The next day, as she was doing the same thing, he came up to her and presented her with the keys to a Mercedes car. He said she was lovely and should be driving something better than the pickup truck, and he insisted that she take the keys. After that, it seemed like he was always around, hitting on Cynthia and expressing interest in David's Winter. He seemed really interested in him. This sheik was well known in the business to spend fortunes buying many foals of champions, but for some reason, his horses never won.

Elliott - Winters Stable
King Loomis, 2nd
Overdeposited, 3rd
5 Furlongs - 1:01 3/5

David's Winter

C. Lopez, up
Trained by
Cynthia Elliott

David's Winter ran at Belmont and won.

I suggested that she negotiate for a higher price with the sheik, but she had other ideas. She felt that she had struck gold, and she wanted to go for the ride and gain fame along the way. So she returned to Florida to train the horse, full of positive energy about his future and ours.

Because of her generosity towards me, I decided to buy a few more horses and made Cynthia my 50/50 partner in all of the acquisitions. I still remember a couple of their names. One was Curtain Puller, and another Pick the Flower.

I got back to business and starting shooting my film. The problem was, it never stopped raining for days and days at a time. I then found out that it was the rainy season, and when I asked my production manager why he hadn't told me this before the shoot, he calmly said, "Senor Winters, if I had told you that before, you would have never come here to shoot." Mexican film logic, I guess, but nevertheless, I was truly pissed.

Meanwhile, back in the US, Cynthia and the sheik were getting very serious. She called me one day and said his father had sent his brothers to Florida with a check for her for $12 million with the understanding that she would stop seeing his son. She asked me what I thought she should do. I told her to take the money and, if she truly cared for him, to keep on seeing the sheik anyway. We laughed about it, but she said she was just going to turn them down. And, unbelievably, that's what she did. It seems that she was starting to care for the sheik and wanted to continue their relationship.

He travelled around the world doing business and buying horses in his own private jet. He had diplomatic status, so wherever he landed, his stretch Rolls Royce would be unloaded from the back of the plane, and he was driven wherever he needed to go without even going through customs or immigration. He was what one could legitimately call a real jet-setter. The strange thing was that, with all of his money and status, he could have had the most beautiful girls in the world, but he was obsessed with Cynthia, who was not a beauty at all. I never knew what made him want her so badly. Was it all about the horse that he couldn't get?

Now back in L.A., I was giving another one of my Hollywood parties. Some of my friends and I thought it would be fun to cook some chickens ourselves with the help of my buddy Bruce Lewin, who was the top caterer in all of NYC. So I invited Cynthia to join us, and she gladly did. Under Bruce's tutelage, it was great fun plucking the chicken feathers, something most of my friends and I had never done before. Cynthia told me she had a blast. We all joked around and kind of had an informal party before the party in the kitchen. Well, when Cynthia went back to the sheik after the party, he gave her such a hard time and made her very unhappy. He also sent me a very nasty letter chastising me, which I still have just in case I should ever need it.

In time, they got married and had two kids. Periodically, she would contact me regarding our horses. She once told me that David's Winter was so horny that in one race he tried to mount one of the other horses as they came out of the gate. I kind of laughed inwardly as I thought, how appropriate. She said they had to geld him, which is a nice way of saying they removed his testicles. Ouch! He was never the same when he ran after that, so she put him out to pasture in Kentucky. The startling thing was that, even after that, her husband was still trying to buy him, and to my eternal dismay, she still refused to sell him.

She eventually did sell him her percentage of David's Winter for $900,000, so now he and I were partners. This was definitely not someone I wanted for a partner. I kept hoping he would offer to buy my percentage as well, but unfortunately that never happened. All I ever got from him were nasty letters and bills, like one for $80K for insurance on the horse for one year, which I told him to shove.

World-champion jockey Willie Shoemaker and Eddie Delahoussaye visiting me at my home in Beverly Hills

My last two calls from Cynthia were one telling me she had made a deal to go back to Bahrain with her children, as the Sheik's father wanted the children to be brought up as royalty and had given each of them $25 million dollars. In another call, she told me that she was going into the dog breeding business, as she was getting too old to take care of and train horses. I worried about her safety and expressed my concern, but she had already made up her mind, saying this was best for her kids. Who was I to argue?

Years before, she had told me she kept a daily diary of all the events in her life. Eventually, she sent it to me. I read it and thought her story was incredible and even toyed with the idea of doing a miniseries on it. In one of her by now ex-husband's nicer letters to me, he mentioned it and asked me to send it back to him. I procrastinated for a while, but then I sent it back to him. Now I wish I hadn't.

All in all, my venture into the world of horse racing was a total loss financially. I never recouped a cent. And I never even had the time to go to the track to see any of my horses run, and some won their races. I have some lovely videos and photos, courtesy of Cynthia, of David's Winter winning some races and a few pictures of my other racing acquisitions, but that's all.

Not long ago, I tried to contact Cynthia, but to no avail. I even hired a detective agency to track her down, but with no luck. It seems like she just disappeared. I hope she is alive and well. Who knows? Maybe she is still in Bahrain. As they say, "Truth is sometimes stranger than fiction." Ain't it the truth?

The Creation of AIP Productions, and My Third Marriage

During an eight-year period, I produced, financed, and distributed forty-eight films, and I directed a few of them as well. That is a hell of a lot of films in eight years, more than most people make in a lifetime. This is the story of the beginnings of the company I called AIP, Action International Pictures, later named West Side Studios.

In 1986, I sat back and took a hard look at the film industry and realized that the power in my business was in the ownership of intellectual properties and the marketing of them. I looked at all the major studios who controlled the industry and their assets. They all owned real estate in the form of a movie lot, which of course had intrinsic value, and a huge library of films. I soon realized that the film library was truly the real basis and value of their businesses. The high-priced executives were bought and sold, always available, as was the talent to make the films. Every few years, the studios would either fire their executives or rotate them with other studios or give them an independent producer deal as a way of getting rid of them. The absolute key was ownership of film negatives.

As I looked at the libraries that the studios owned, I began to see that each studio only had a small group of blockbusters and a slightly larger group of successful films, but most of their libraries consisted of low-budget or unsuccessful films. The ratio of hit films made by the studios then and today is one out of ten, but the big one usually pays for all the flops. And of course the big one is publicized so much that you forget about all of the others. When all these films are sold in a package to TV, the big hit becomes the locomotive that pulls all the others along. The studios can ask for huge sums because they know that the TV station must buy that blockbuster film.

Having thought this through pretty thoroughly, I decided that I would open a film production and distribution company and would produce as many films as I could and build up a big library. Then I would either make a big film or buy one from someone else, thus giving me my locomotive. I also planned on buying some real estate in the near future and housing my company there. I knew that directing and producing a film myself would take me a year, so I decided to get some young filmmakers who could make two or three films a year, allowing me to spend most of my time marketing the films and building up the company. I would take an executive producer or producer credit and maybe also make a picture or two as director/producer.

I found a young guy named David A. Prior, who had just finished a very good little indie film for $80,000. I met with David and explained my plan. He loved it, and we decided to become partners. David seemed a bit afraid of me, and so he suggested that we also team up with Peter Yuval, a young producer he had worked with in the past. I think he felt that, in the event of a disagreement, it would be the two of them against one—me.

Well, I thought about it. Here I was with 100 percent of my idea, but if I did this I would wind up with only 33 percent of my idea, and I was also responsible for funding it. Then again, I could have them making ten films a year, which would get me to my goal sooner. Plus, without me funding them, what would they do? As long as I had my hands on the purse strings, they were under my control, so to speak. I was basically their boss, and we all knew it, so we agreed on a deal.

I rented offices on the Sunset Strip in West Hollywood, and we were ready to go! I put up the office sign—"Action International Pictures"—and gave my partners all of $210,000 to make two films with. That's not even the catering budget on most studio films, but I knew that our films would look like we spent much more on them. I put up half, and my buddy Bruce Lewin, in the catering business in New

York, put up the other half. It was now late 1986, and my girlfriend at the time, Chris Hall, became pregnant.

I found out on the phone one day when she bowed out of coming to a screening of *"Thrashin','"* as she was feeling nauseous. She was crying but wouldn't say what the problem was. I pushed her for half an hour until she finally told me that she was going to have an abortion. I pleaded with her not to be so hasty, that we should talk further, and I promised to be there with her when she had the child, unlike her last boyfriend who wasn't with her when she had her son James. After a long conversation, she eventually agreed not to do anything, and I remember thinking that I really loved this girl because she wasn't trying to force me to marry her or anything. In fact, had I not prodded her, she would have handled it all by herself and I would have never known.

Chris was making much more money than I was then, selling illegally imported exotic birds. She would sometimes make as much as $25,000 in a single day. I had no idea what a huge demand there was for these kinds of birds. She would pick up them up in San Diego, then drive them to L.A., where she would take ads in the local papers, and they would sell like hotcakes. The highway patrol, who were on the lookout for illegal aliens coming over from Mexico, and who had roadblocks along the 405 freeway, never once stopped her, as she was a gorgeous white female. They never suspected her of any wrongdoing.

Since I had convinced her not to have an abortion, I thought to myself, the gentlemanly thing to do would be to marry her. So one Sunday, while we were driving out of town, I bought Chris some flowers and a card and proposed to her right then and there. She cried many happy tears and said yes, so we went back to L.A. to work out our future. This would be my third marriage. And for someone who never wanted to get married, I thought. Oh well. When it comes to women, I'm just a little bit nuts. We're all a bit nuts in one way or another.

We decided to have a traditional Jewish wedding, so we went to see a rabbi and arranged for the wedding to take place in the grand ballroom at the Beverly Hills Hotel. It was a fabulous affair, and she looked stunning. Well, she was a model, even if she was five months pregnant. And there was her son, cute little James, seeing his mom getting married for the first time. There were candles everywhere. It was beautiful and so romantic. We agreed to play one of my favorite pieces of music, Pachelbel's "Canon," as we walked down the aisle. We broke the glass, as in all orthodox Jewish weddings, and the rabbi surrounded us with a cloth, and I felt that this was the real thing and would last forever. Boy, was I wrong!

All of my friends were there, and it seemed like we danced all night long. Of course, Chris and I started the dancing—like a true professional, I had rehearsed this with Chris for many hours. Then my mom and dad took to the dance floor, and boy, was he smooth. They looked like Fred Astaire and Ginger Rogers. They just glided across the floor doing one dance step after another, each one more complex than the last. He was leading her around the floor like they were skating on ice. They were incredible! I knew that they had met dancing, but I had never realized what a wonderful and elegant dancer my dad was. I thought, *that's* where it all comes from, David. You've inherited the best from both of them. They received a standing ovation, and deservedly so. I was proud of them both.

That evening, I had rented a suite at the Beverly Hills Hotel, and I carried my wife, who was 5'9½" to my 5'6", over the threshold as you're supposed to. I almost broke my back doing it, though. As I think back on it now, these are the moments to cherish in one's life—the oh-so-special moments, pictures that never fade with age.

And as we hear the Jewish wedding music cross-fading with the sound of African music, we dissolve to...

Hollywood in South Africa

Hope Holiday is a friend of mine to this day whom I met in 1957 when we took jazz dance classes together at Frank Wagner's in Carnegie Hall. Hope was appearing on Broadway in the musical *"Li'l Abner,"* and I was in the original production of *"West Side Story"* at the time. We both went to Hollywood to appear in those same shows, and Hope, like me, also went on to have an acting career in some great films like the Academy Award-winning *"The Apartment,"* starring Jack Lemmon and Shirley MacLaine, directed by Billy Wilder; *"The Rounders."* starring Glenn Ford and Henry Fonda; and *"The Ladies Man,"* starring Jerry Lewis as well as numerous other films and TV series.

While shooting *"Mission: Kill"* in Mexico, Hope and I met up again. It turned out that she was good friends with Cameron Mitchell, who was part of the cast, so we hung out together during the making of the film. Hope told me that she knew we could raise some money to make films in South Africa because of a tax shelter there. I checked it out and found that it was true. My friend, producer Menahem Golan of Cannon Films was over there making films as we spoke. I got to work right away creating and writing three concepts and films.

When I completed them, I gave them to Hope, and soon after, she informed me that a law firm she had spoken to already had the funds waiting in Johannesburg, South Africa, for us. I couldn't believe it, but when I called the law office they said yes, they were waiting for us to come to South Africa. They had the cash ready to finance our films.

Talk about timing! With all the rejoicing of the wedding still ringing in our ears, my new wife and I boarded the plane to a new adventure awaiting us in a foreign country, one that neither of us had ever been to before.

In South Africa, the investors were given a 2½:1 write-off on their investment in any film shot in their country. The government was getting filmmakers to shoot there, and boosting up their economy at the same time. Because of this, many filmmakers were going there. The law firm took a big chunk from the money raised, but it still left us with plenty to make the film.

I decided my first film in South Africa would be *"Codename: Vengeance."* I used Robert Ginty again as the leading man because we had gotten along really well on *"Mission: Kill,"* and that film had sold very well around the world. I also used Cameron Mitchell again as he was a great actor, and needless to say, Hope was really glad that I did. I hired a *Playboy* magazine centerfold, Shannon Tweed, as the female lead opposite Robert Ginty, and cast James Ryan as the bad guy. James had just starred in *"Kill or be Killed,"* which was a world-wide hit, and he lived in Johannesburg, so it was very convenient for him. He was a wonderful actor and seemed excited to be part of our production.

A group cast shot from *"Codename: Vengeance"* that includes Robert Ginty, Shannon Tweed, Cameron Mitchell, James Ryan, and myself.

Chris, James, and I checked into the Sandton Sun, a terrific five-star hotel in a very nice section of Johannesburg, South Africa.

Attached to a huge mall with many restaurants, both in the hotel and in the mall, it was the most convenient place you could ever imagine, with everything and anything right at your fingertips. Hope got there before me, so she facilitated setting up the offices and preparing for production prior to my arrival. By now, I had a completed screenplay, and after meeting with the law firm and signing all the contracts, we finally got down to work.

My first job was to scout locations for the film in a helicopter. What a joy, as I adore helicopters as a means of transportation. Honestly, one of my all-time favorite things to do is to hang out of a helicopter with a film camera, shooting scenes for a film. I don't know what it is, but I get such a rush. It is like nothing else I have ever done in my life. It's also a bit scary, which probably adds to the excitement.

Me in my directors chair during shooting.

My crew was wonderful, right down to the guy who used to do nothing but follow me around with my director's chair. His only job was to make sure that when I went to sit down, my chair would always be there ready for me. He was so good that it got to where I didn't even have to look behind me to make sure my chair was there. Without thinking about it, I could just sit down and I would always land in my chair. He was an amazing piece of manpower. He came from an African tribe and spoke Swahili with some of our other crew members.

He was very sweet. In fact, much to my surprise, the entire crew that Hope and our production manager, Barrie Saint Clair, hired for me was truly wonderful! My only problem was, as time went by, I began to realize that many in the crew were carrying guns, even the girls. They kept them in their purses, which they seemed to carry at all times. This made me kind of nervous.

I did have one serious altercation during the shoot, which I remember very well. Jonathan Vanger, the seventeen-year-old son of the owner of the completion bond company that I used on the film, began working for me on this picture. Lawrence Vanger, his father, was a very close friend of mine, so as part of the deal, I agreed to hire his son Jonathan and give him his first job in show business as an associate producer on the film.

One evening Barrie Saint Clair's wife, Sheilagh Saint Clair, got drunk on the set. Jonathan fired her on the spot, as those were his orders from me in case an incident such as that happened. The next day, my set was visited by a bunch of brown-shirt Afrikaners, armed with rifles and shot guns and attack dogs. Afrikaners were similar to Nazis. In fact, their flag was a three-sided swastika, they had these meetings at night where everyone held burning torches, and they all wore brown shirts and pants—just like in Hitler's Germany.

They proceeded to tell me that Jonathan had insulted a local and that they were closing up my set. They informed me that if any actor or crew were to step over a certain line past the set, they would be shot dead. To tell you the truth, this sent me into a state of shock, never having experienced *anything* like this before in my life. I didn't know what to do because they were holding all the aces, and they seemed very serious as they instructed their men to stand guard in different places throughout my set with their nasty dogs growling at us.

They closed down my set for the rest of the day and evening and the entire next day. This was unbelievable and frustrating as hell. All I could do was think to myself, and I have two more movies to make here after this one? Shit. I was ready to get on the plane and go back to America right then and there. Fortunately, we eventually got everyone to cool down and come to their senses. So the production went ahead, and from that day forward, the rest of the shoot went ahead without any more dramatic incidents.

During the shooting, my first son, Jonathan, was born. I checked my wife Chris into a local Johannesburg hospital, and I remember flying there by helicopter one day after filming when I received a call that our son had been born. From the fuss they all made on my arrival, it seemed like the first time the hospital staff had ever seen anyone fly in by helicopter. You would have thought I was a visiting head of state! Well, it certainly was great for the ego, and it was really exciting, too!

Me kissing my newborn son

Left to right: Cameron Mitchell, Hope Holiday, and David Winters.

When the shoot was completed, I started the usual editing process. While I was editing, I started to prepare for our next production, which was *"Space Mutiny."* Because of the bad situation during *"Codename: Vengeance"* involving Barry Saint Clair's wife, I decided not to hire him ever again. Debi Nethersole, whom Hope knew, was hired as the production manager for the new film. Her husband, Vincent Cox, was hired to be the cameraman, and the rest of the crew I already knew.

There was a hot young actor named Reb Brown who had starred in a very successful Australian movie. He had received great personal reviews, so I thought he would be a good choice for the lead in my next film. When I contacted Reb, he asked me if I would also hire his wife, actress Cisse Cameron, to be in the film. As it turned out, I had a good role for a young female in the film, so I agreed.

I also cast Cameron Mitchell and James Ryan again, as they were talented, easy to work with, and already in South Africa. And for extra marquee value, I added the Golden Globe nominee John Phillip Law. I remembered him as Jane Fonda's co-star in the sci-fi blockbuster hit *"Barbarella."*

On the first day of shooting, I got up very early, all excited about the new film I was directing. Strangely enough, the phone rang, and I thought to myself, who could be calling me this early in the morning? When I answered the phone, it was a family member, who apologized profusely for disturbing me so early, but it was an emergency.

I still get chills when I think of this moment. I knew what he was going to tell me, and unfortunately I was right. He went on to tell me that my father had just passed away. He was only seventy-one, but he had been struggling with heart problems for a couple of years. In fact, the doctors would not let him travel by airplane anymore. My father had been sitting in his living room watching television while my mother was in the kitchen cooking. When my mother came back with their food, she discovered his body. I guess he died quietly and hopefully without any pain.

Even though I knew what my relative was telling me, it was still a shock when he did. I didn't know what to say, as words at this point were meaningless. Everything was meaningless. I was numb, and my mind just stopped thinking. I felt hopeless. I was halfway around the world, and there was nothing I could do. I had to get off the phone right away as I was about to burst out in tears. My cousin understood, and after giving me his condolences, he hung up the phone.

I felt so alone and empty. I knew I had to get myself together and go to America. I had to be there for my dad's funeral and to support my mom. I called my mom and asked her to please hold off the funeral so that I had time to fly back to Los Angeles for the memorial service and the burial. She was a wreck but she agreed, and now I had to deal with the problems I was facing in South Africa.

I woke up my wife and told her the news. I also told her that she and I and the kids had to go back to America immediately for the funeral. Next, I had to deal with the film. This was supposed to be the first happy day of filming. I can tell you, it was anything but.

With great hesitation, I went to the set and sat with my assistant director, Neal Sundstrom. I explained my situation to him and told him that he would be directing this production. I was going to bury my father in Los Angeles and did not know when I would return to South Africa, if ever. Neal was obviously shocked, but wished me luck. In a strange way, my problem was actually a good thing for Neal because he was promoted from an assistant director to a full-fledged director. Life is so strange, isn't it? One man's tragedy is another man's opportunity.

In the back of my mind somewhere, I remembered that I had another film to make after this one, but I guess I just refused to deal with it. All I could think about was getting my family and myself out of there.

I went back to the Sandton Sun Hotel and called my travel agent, Andrea Gilbert, who booked us on a flight back to L.A. as soon as possible. It was the most depressing flight I have ever taken in my life. The entire time, my life was flashing before me—all the wonderful moments I had shared with my dad, beginning with seeing him for the first time when I was just seven years old. The flight was an absolute nightmare for me as I cried much of the time. I knew I needed to be strong for Chris and the kids' sake, but it was so difficult. On landing, we went directly to my mom's place, and she and I just hugged each other and cried. It was all we could do, as words did not suffice for this terrible tragedy.

Dad had reserved a grave next to Grandma and Grandpa at Mount Sinai Memorial Park in the Hollywood Hills. At the memorial service, everyone in the family got up and spoke about Dad. When it was time for my mom to speak, she got up and walked to the coffin, but as she started to speak, she collapsed. A few of us ran to her and successfully stopped her from falling on the floor. She regained her composure and gave her last goodbye to dad. She then collapsed again and hugged the coffin as her knees buckled. It was like she was holding on to Dad for dear life, and she didn't want to let him go. They had been married for over fifty years. Mom was in a terrible state, and I felt so sorry for her. She was eventually comforted and everyone made their way to the burial site.

In Jewish tradition, when someone dies, the youngest member of the family takes a spadeful of dirt and throws it on top of the coffin just after it has been lowered into the grave; then the next youngest does the same, and so on until the oldest person in the immediate family throws his spade of dirt on the coffin. This supposedly helps those who are still living to realize that their relative has passed away. Being Jewish, I had to do it, and being the oldest, I was the last one to go. In some ways, I understand it, but in other ways, it seems kind of barbaric to me. I know that this is part of my religious tradition, and so I accept it as such. But as I threw that spadeful of dirt on my father's coffin, it all seemed so crazy and strange, and I didn't feel comfortable doing it at all.

The memorial took a lot out of me, especially with my mother fainting in grief all the time. There was no way I could go back to South Africa as I had planned. I needed to stay and comfort my mom, who was in dire straits. A week had passed, and I was getting calls from the law firm in South Africa asking me when I was coming back. Although I explained my situation, they insisted. They explained to me that as part of their presentation to the investors, my name and my film credits had been featured prominently. They were afraid they would get into trouble if any of the investors found out I was not in fact directing *"Space Mutiny."*

I spoke with my partner, Hope, about it, and she was also worried about getting sued by the investors. She even said it might destroy our careers in Hollywood when the news got out. Millions of dollars had been invested, and it was a very serious situation, one that might land us in jail if it ever got out.

They pleaded with me to come back, but I refused. I told them there was no way I was capable of directing a film right then. I told them I had Neal Sundstrom replace me, and it was now his film. They sounded desperate on the phone, going so far as to say that if I could just come back to Johannesburg and check in to my hotel, that would be okay with them.

I wouldn't have to show up on the set at all, not even for a day. It was enough that if an investor asked about me, they could say I was there in J'burg and give the investor my hotel room if need be.

This sounded like a good compromise to me, and I agreed. I didn't want to drag my family all over the planet, so I suggested to my wife that she and the kids stay in America, and as soon as I was finished in South Africa, I would come back and join them. We both agreed to this arrangement, so off I went again, back to South Africa. And I did exactly what the lawyers had suggested. I checked in to the Sandston Sun Hotel again and never left it. I didn't need to because it was attached to this incredible mall with everything I needed readily available. I never told Neal Sundstrom or any of the stars of the film that I was even in Johannesburg. In other words, during the entire filming of the movie *"Space Mutiny,"* I was never once on the set. The movie proceeded just fine without my presence, and my secret was just between me, the law firm, and Hope. Fortunately for us, no investor ever visited the set, so our plan worked out perfectly.

I have seen many bad reviews on this film, and it makes me laugh because they always mention my name as one of the directors. Nothing could be further from the truth. This was Neal's baby, and his baby alone. I'm always billed as the director, or one of the two directors, when in fact Neal Sundstrom was the real director, the *only* director. Sorry about that, Neal. But the truth always eventually surfaces, doesn't it?

CHAPTER 39

Bigger Stars and Pamela Anderson

After *"Space Mutiny"* was completed as I previously mentioned by Neal Sundstrum, I started to become myself again and began to feel strong and capable of directing my next film, which was to be *"Rage to Kill."* I had been trying for a long time to hire award-winning superstar actor Oliver Reed. I really admired this guy's talent, but he was always busy working on one film or another. While in South Africa, I filmed a promo for *"Rage to Kill"* without Oliver Reed, as he had turned me down two times already.

At my desk in my office at AIP Distribution (Action International Pictures Distribution)

I flew back to L.A. for the American Film Market in February/March and announced my new company, AIP Distribution, to the buyers from all over the world who had gathered there to buy films. With two films in the can, one film in post-production, and another one in pre-production, we were looking like a serious company. I took a big chance when, even though Oliver Reed had turned me down, I still sold *"Rage to Kill"* with him listed as the star. I knew the buyers wanted a name actor. I just had to get him, or someone just as big.

In four days at the market, I did $2.5 million in sales, and my partners, David and Peter, and I celebrated. We were the hit of the market—the new kids on the block! There wasn't much time for celebrating, as I had to get back to South Africa to start re-writing, directing, and producing *"Rage to Kill."* So back on the plane for another thirty-hour journey.

Being an Aries, and because I had already sold the film with him in it, I kept trying for Oliver Reed. And then, thank God, by some miracle via his brother David Reed, I was able to secure his services for my film. Again I signed Cameron Mitchell and James Ryan, and also Henry Cele, who had starred in the highly successful miniseries *"Shaka Zulu."* And again, timing was my friend. The buyers were all very happy, and we were on our way.

Left to right: Henry Cele, Cameron Mitchell and me

Oliver was one of those rare English actors who can believably do an American accent. Most English actors find it very difficult to accomplish this, as likewise do most American actors. I myself can always hear the difference and tell where they are really from.

I had heard about Oliver's drinking habits from my dear friend Keith Moon of The Who, and they were legendary! But Oliver had another special talent. He could drink all night long and still come in to work early the next morning as if nothing had happened. It was amazing! One evening, he had been drinking with young Jonathan Vanger when he got so drunk that he grabbed Jonathan by the shirt and pulled him right across the table. This was a bit of a shock to Jonathan. Yet a few hours later, there was Oliver on the set, all ready to go.

I don't know how he did it. He knew all of his lines perfectly, and you had no idea that he had been drinking a couple of hours ago. I must say, working with and directing Oliver Reed was a dream come true. What a great actor he was. He was also very humble on the set and took direction perfectly.

Cameron Mitchell and James Ryan were also terrific to work with and were very professional as well. Working in South Africa was generally a wonderful experience for me, and I was pleasantly surprised at the quality of the crews there.

Years later, young Jonathan Vanger produced his first film, *"The Revenger,"* which was also shot in South Africa and also starred Oliver Reed. He asked AIP to handle all of the sales for it. Jonathan has since gone on to produce many films and is a major figure in the industry, and, we are still very close friends, in fact more like family.

After *"Rage to Kill"* finished shooting in South Africa, I went straight back to my family in L.A. By this time, my partners and I had completed many new movies for our company, AIP Distribution. These were the first of forty-eight films we would make over the next eight years at AIP. More than a dozen of them were filmed in Mobile, Alabama, with the help of the local film commissioner, Eva Golson, and mayor of the city at the time, Mike Dow. For their generosity, I reciprocated with a $10,000 scholarship to the local University of Mobile, presented by Martin Landau in my company's name.

I eventually bought out both of my partners, bought a studio on a property to house my company, opened a video company and a domestic theatrical distribution division, and set up my own in-house art department and sound and editing facility. Basically, I was a self-contained mini-studio. Before I knew it, I employed thirteen people working full time, with an overhead that was growing by the day. I upgraded the budgets on the films and signed my ex-partner David A. Prior to a multiple-picture contract. I started a new company, West Side Studios, and promised my buyers bigger and better films. I was doing everything according to plan, just like the big boys.

Many of these new films won awards, such as *"Night Trap,"* starring Robert Davi, Michael Ironside, Lesley-Anne Down, Lydie Denier, John Amos, and Margaret Avery, who was nominated for an Oscar for her performance in Steven Spielberg's *"The Color Purple." "Night Trap"* won the Gold Award at the WorldFest Houston Film Festival.

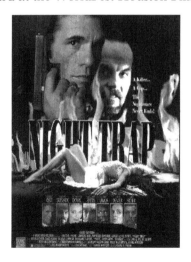

"Good Cop Bad Cop," winner of the Bronze Award at the WorldFest Charleston, starred Pamela Anderson, Robert Hays, David Keith, Stacy Keach, and Ted Prior. It was later released on Paramount DVD as *"Raw Justice."*

Another of my films released by Paramount, *"Double Threat,"* starred Sally Kirkland and Anthony Franciosa, both winners of Golden Globe Awards and Oscar nominations, she for best actress in *"Anna."*

"Firehead" starred three-time Academy Award-winner Martin Landau and 2012 Academy Award-winner Christopher Plummer.

"Raw Nerve" starred Glenn Ford, winner of the Golden Globe and six other awards and nine nominations. Co-starring were Jan Michael Vincent, Sandahl Bergman, Traci Lords, Randall "Tex" Cobb, and Ted Prior.

"*Center of the Web*" won the Best Drama Award at the Charleston Film Festival and stars legend Tony Curtis. Tony won the Golden Globe and was nominated for the Academy Award and nineteen other awards

"*The Dangerous*" starred John Savage, Elliott Gould, Joel Grey, Michael Pare, Robert Davi, and Cary-Hiroyuki Tagawa. The first three stars of the film are Academy Award nominees with one winner, Joel Grey as best actor for the film "*Cabaret.*"

"*Codename: The Silencer*" starred Steven Bauer, Robert Davi, Brigitte Nielson, and Jan-Michael Vincent, who was a two-time Golden Globe nominee and winner of numerous other awards.

...And three films with my dear friend David Carradine, winner of nine awards and nominated for another thirteen and star of the "*Kill Bill*" series of films.

Forty-eight films in eight years—life was good and life was fun.

I remember doing "*Good Cop Bad Cop*" with Pamela Anderson. We were shooting the film in New Orleans and Mobile, and I took Pammy out for dinner at a great seafood place, which she loved and made me promise to bring her back to. We had a fun evening and talked about doing other films together. I had auditioned 400 girls for the part, but I had seen something special in Pamela, so I went with her. She was starring in *"Baywatch"* at the time and getting a huge amount of publicity, but she told me she wanted to get into the movies where she could do some real acting. If I'm not mistaken, this was her first film role.

When I hired her, her agent told me that Pamela was concerned about one particular scene where the script said she made love with David Keith in a warehouse while the two of them were hiding from the bad guys. Pamela requested a shot list from me and wanted it signed by me and the director to make sure that we weren't going to exploit her. I met with the director, and we came up with a list that had no frontal nudity shots, or any shots of any kind, for that matter, that were of dubious taste. I wanted her to feel totally at ease and comfortable. We said it would be lit in such a way that you wouldn't be able to see anything, other than two topless shots filmed from the side in dark shadows. Pamela seemed very pleased indeed. In fact, I had no intention of exploiting Pamela in a sexual way. That was not what my films were about. My films were geared more for the young action audience, with lots of fights and stunts and car crashes and explosions, but not much if any nudity at all.

The funny thing is that I had complained for a long time to my directors that they never gave me any nudity, even when it was appropriate, and I had given up on it, so this certainly was not on my or the director's mind. Also, for TV sales at the time, it was better not to have any nudity so that it didn't have to be censored out, which involved extra costs and time in editing.

So now it was the big day and time for the big scene. My director and I were very specific about his shot list, so we meticulously went over every angle and every shot with the cameraman and the rest of the crew so that there were no misunderstandings. I told the crew that it would be a closed set and that only the director, two cameramen, the script girl, and I would be allowed to watch the shooting of this particular scene. Everyone understood.

So I went on the set, and there were Pamela and David, and Pam said to me in her sexiest voice, "David, sweetheart,"—she knew just how to get me—"David Keith and I rehearsed this scene last night, and we'd like to show you what we'd like to do with it, if that's okay with you?" I thought, great, that will simplify everything, but then I thought it would probably be a boring, nothing-happening scene. But okay, we have more than enough action in this film, so I said, "Sure, Pam, let's see it." Well, to tell you the truth, I couldn't believe my eyes.

It started out tamely with them kissing, and then David proceeded to take Pam's breasts out of her shirt and start kissing them. Things only got steamier from there, with Pamela sighing sexually the whole time. Then he slowly turned her around, aggressively pulled down her pants, and then pressed up against her as if he were having sex with her from behind.

I was in complete shock. The director looked over at me with a big shit-ass—excuse the expression—grin on his face, nodding his approval. It was so funny to me that this was the same girl who was worried about the way I would handle the scene. And she was approaching it like it was just another scene in the film. It was much more than I would have ever done.

After what seemed like an awfully long time, they broke and Pam said, "Well, David, what do you think?" I said, "Yeah, that'll work fine. Good work, guys," and with that I took hold of the director and walked him away from the set, not wanting to change a thing. As soon as we got out of sight, we both let out a huge roar of laughter and tore up all the storyboards we had taken so much time to get just right. Women, huh?

She was a game girl, Pammy was, but also one heck of a sweet girl!

CHAPTER 40

My Adventures
in Moscow

Having my own sales distribution company meant that I was heavily involved in the American Film Market Association and attended many meetings to keep up to date on what was happening and what was new in the field of foreign territorial sales. At one of our many meetings, it was announced that the American Film Market Association, or AFMA, would be sending a small contingent to that year's Moscow Film Festival in Russia. I immediately signed up, along with just seven other companies. I was anxious to visit Moscow and to see what, exactly, was happening over there. In the back of my mind, I also thought that just maybe I would get an opportunity to see the Bolshoi Ballet and the Moiseyev Dance Company, who were my two favorite dance companies in the world. The tall dancing boots I always wore were, in fact, the same boots that the Moiseyev dancers wore for all their performances. So I was very excited about the prospect of this trip.

But more importantly, my grandfather Abraham had been born in Russia, and I had photos of him when he was an officer in the Tsar's army. He looked so dashing in the photos, all dressed up in his army regalia with many medals on his chest, quite impressive, to say the least. He had told me some amazing stories about himself and about the rest of our family, who originally came from that part of the world. He and I had talked about them many times through the years, and it fascinated me. I still have some photos of them, and I especially love one where Abraham was a very young child with his mom and dad.

I hold these pictures as priceless treasures. We had a lot of family in Belarus, Russia, Lithuania, and Ukraine. Abraham was actually born in Lvov, in Ukraine, close to the main city of Kiev.

When the revolution happened in 1918, he had to hide in a basement as the population was looking for soldiers to execute them. My grandfather had been a champion wrestler and swimmer, so after hiding in a huge trunk in a friend's basement for a year, only coming out to eat and go to the bathroom, one day he came out of the basement and made his way to a river. He swam across the entire river and escaped into another country, then another, until he eventually made it to England. There he met my grandma Jenny, and they fell in love and married. They were a lovely couple, and I have many wonderful memories of them as a child. Grandpa also told me that Hitler had killed eleven of our Lipshitz family members in Lithuania. During World War II, Hitler killed over twenty-eight million people from that part of the world, but Prime Minister Mikhail Gorbachev, who had been elected general secretary in 1985, had given a new sense of freedom to this Communist country. It seemed as though there was a breath of fresh air in the USSR, a new sense of excitement about the future. Gorbachev became the first president of the Soviet Union in 1990 and won the Nobel Peace Prize that same year. It seemed as though things were rapidly changing.

For me, this trip was a once-in-a-lifetime opportunity to explore my roots. Grandpa and I had talked many times about the two of us going back to the old country and seeing his sister. He had written to his sister for over fifty years, until she passed away. Sadly, Abraham wasn't alive to take this trip with me.

The day finally came, and we all flew to Moscow, Russia. My friend and sometimes partner Bruce Lewin also accompanied me on the trip. The Moscow Film Festival had arranged lodgings for us at the five-star Mezhdunarodnaya Hotel, recently renamed the Crowne Plaza Moscow World Trade Centre Hotel, a grand 575-room hotel that sits on the north bank of the Moskva River, which runs right through the center of Moscow.

Before we knew it, we were at our sales booth in the market section of the Moscow Film Festival, where a separate area had been designated for US companies. We immediately put our promo reels on the monitors that had been supplied by the film festival. Much to my surprise, no sooner had I put my promo reel in and started showing it than a huge crowd convened in front of my booth, almost surrounding it. The crowds got bigger, until they were soon standing five deep watching my promo reels in awe.

I had never seen anything quite like this before, but I soon realized that these buyers never got to see Western productions. Many of them came up to me after viewing the reel and wanted to buy it. I tried as well as I could to explain that what they had just watched was only the promo for a film, not an entire film itself, but they didn't care and made me offer after offer for my promo reels. This was incredible and hard to believe. A long line developed of people all asking to buy the promo reel. I have a gold mine here, I thought. I had my assistant take all of their contact details and explained that we would be back in touch with them just as soon as we got ourselves organized properly.

That evening, I turned on the local television in my room just to get an idea of what these people were seeing. I was blown away. Every station showed basically the same kind of thing. There would be shots of waves crashing against rocks, and over this would be a Russian flag flying in the wind; then the picture would dissolve to shots of marching soldiers and men and women breaking up rocks with axes. Accompanying all of these scenes was the Russian national anthem. I began to understand the buyers' reaction. When they saw my action film promos that were filled with stunts, fights, beautiful young girls and guys, people shooting each other, people tastefully making love, and all the rest, they just couldn't get enough of it. They wanted it badly and would pay me outrageous amounts to get the rights for their territory.

It seemed like my booth was getting all the attention, as these buyers were starved for action films and knew that their customers would also love the kind of films I was specializing in. And oh yes, the name of my company was Action International Pictures. Taking a page from our American concept of supply and demand, I started selling my movies for much more than I had thought I would be able to sell them for. In fact, I made $30 Million dollars selling my films in Russia. Russia had never been much of a market for us before. I had only been in Moscow for a day and a half, and boy, was I loving it. I didn't let on to the other American companies participating in the market what we were raking in. I thought about setting up a Russian company after the film festival and coming back to Moscow on a regular basis to conduct this amazing new business I had just discovered. And that's exactly what I did.

They had some wonderful private clubs in Moscow that were mainly for politicians, celebrities, and visiting celebrities. One night, at one of these clubs, there was a beautiful young girl in a local modern dance company performing on stage. When she came off stage, I saw a photographer taking pictures of her. I got close to him and made sure that he heard me speaking in English; I was quite sure that would get his attention since there were very few English-speaking guys in the club. Sure enough, he came over to me and introduced himself as Vladimir Kirusha. He spoke some English, so we talked for a bit, and when I pointed out the girl dancer to him, he told me her name was Tatyana. He asked me if I would like to meet her, and of course my answer was yes!

Tatyana and I hit it off really well, and she spoke some English, which made it easier for both of us. Vladimir and I exchanged contact details and made plans to hook up the next day. Tatyana came back to the hotel with me, and all I can remember about that beautiful night was looking up and seeing the moon shining on her naked back and face.

The next day, my friend and co-financier Bruce Lewin, my newfound friend Vladimir, and I arranged to fly to Saint Petersburg for a few days. Lovely Tatyana, who had left my hotel early that day, showed up at the local airport, much to my surprise, to see me off with a large bouquet of flowers. This really touched my heart, especially when she teared up. I thought, wow, this girl has developed a crush on me, and after only one night together. She seemed truly sorry that I was leaving, even though she knew I was only going for a couple of days. It made me wonder, is this the way all Russian girls are? Do they fall in love so quickly? Are they really this sensitive? Her tears certainly seemed real. I told her I would see her as soon as I returned. She gave me a smile and a sweet kiss, and then Bruce, Vladimir, and I were on our way.

Because Vladimir was with us and we had decided to go at the last minute, we hadn't even booked a hotel. Upon arriving, Vladimir suggested a lovely hotel next to some amazing statues right in the middle of the city. Surprisingly, when we went to the front desk to check in, they already knew who we were and everything about us. How could they? They even knew our passport numbers. We hadn't told anyone else we were going because we hadn't decided till the last moment, but they had our airline flights and everything else about us. Unreal! I thought, welcome to communism! It was the weirdest feeling—Big Brother looking over us! Bruce and I didn't get over it for days. How could they possibly have known our movements? We were strangers in a strange country—a huge country, too. Incredible!

To begin our short visit to Saint Petersburg, we went to see the famous Peterhof Palace and fountains, known as the "Russian Versailles," and they were stunning and surely worth the visit. Anyone traveling to this part of the world should definitely not miss them. They are beautiful eye candy, to say the very least, and you will thank me for recommending them. As our cultural tour continued, we also went to the L'Hermitage Museum. I remember seeing a huge diamond there that they told us had sat on the head of the main horse of Catherine the Great. It was a diamond bigger than my head, the biggest one I had ever seen. I couldn't believe it! Saint Petersburg was one of the most beautiful cities I have ever seen, with its canals, many statues, and gorgeous architecture.

Here I am taking in the different sights of beautiful St. Petersburg.
Bottom right: picture is Vladimir Kirusha, me, and my partner Bruce Lewin in front of the famous L'Hermitage museum in St. Petersburg, Russia

We returned to Moscow and landed at the Sharapova Airport. Tatyana was waiting at the airport with yet another bouquet of flowers. With her was a friend of Vladimir's, Igor Medvedev. Igor picked us up in this amazing Zil 111D convertible. It was great to be back in Moscow. After Vladimir introduced me to his friend, who looked like a mac truck, he suggested that Igor could be one of my bodyguards. I had heard many stories about foreigners who came to Moscow to do business and were thrown out of moving cars or who supposedly jumped off the roofs of high buildings. So I thought I needed to surround myself with people I trusted, if I could find such people.

Tatyana waves at Andrei our photographer and Igor pick us up in the only Zil 111D convertible in all of Russia

I got down to business the next day and met with Vladimir and a few of his friends and associates to see how comfortable I felt with them. He introduced me to Andrei Chsherbakov, who became our photographer, and a few of his other friends. They hung out with me for a few days, and I became more comfortable with them with each passing day. I told Vladimir of my plan for my Russian company, and I hired him and his friends to work for me as my bodyguards and to take care of me, in general. After hearing all these horror stories about the deaths of foreign businessmen in Moscow, I decided I would only do deals with Vladimir or his guys' families or people that their families had known for more than five years. I did not want to do any deals with anyone involved with the Russian government or the Communist Party.

Andrei with me in a rare photo of himself taken by another photographer

I made a deal with the Mezhdunarodnaya Hotel to lease their presidential suite. It was two floors with four bedrooms upstairs and many rooms downstairs, separated by a grand "Gone with the Wind" Southern plantation-style staircase. Downstairs were a full kitchen, a large dining room, a huge den, and two extra living rooms as well as quite a few bathrooms. It was mind boggling, to say the least! And you will not believe what I paid for all of this. Are you ready? A grand total of $400 a night. Today that suite would probably cost somewhere between $20,000 and $30,000 a night, maybe more. I was told James Baker, the US Secretary of State, also stayed in this suite. It seems that Mr. Baker liked this suite as much as I did. The funny thing was that our schedules seemed to work out perfectly. As he was leaving, sometimes on the same day or at most a few days later, I would check in. And the same thing when I left. He would check in the very same day or a couple of days later. It started to feel like I was sharing an apartment with the United States Secretary of State. In fact, a couple of times we actually passed each other while checking in or out, and we would acknowledge one another with a slight smile and a nod of the head. We never really had any conversation between us, so I have no State Department secrets to tell you.

Next, I needed to hire a car and driver. Igor suggested the car he had used at the airport to pick me up. As it turned out, it was the only Zil 111D convertible diplomatic car in all of Russia. So I made a deal to have three drivers work eight-hour shifts a day, each and every day. This way, I had a limousine at my disposal twenty-four hours every day of the week. I paid each driver ten dollars a day, so my total cost was thirty dollars a day, or $210 a week, for the limo and the drivers—really cheap!

A shot of Leonid Brezhnev in his car, the only Zil convertible in Russia during a parade

I later found out that this one-of-a-kind car had been owned by Leonid Brezhnev, the ex-president of the Soviet Union, and everyone knew it had belonged to Brezhnev, so whenever we drove down the streets, soldiers would salute the car. In those days, there were soldiers on every street corner. Another great thing about this car was that my drivers would always drive in the middle of those huge Moscow roads, built so that the government could bring tanks right into the middle of the city if there was a revolution or a serious protest. We didn't stop for red lights or anything. Everybody made way for us, and other cars would stop as they saw us approaching. Little did they know that little ol' me, not Leonid Brezhnev, was in the car. I had more fun in that car!

Having set up my office, I hired two lawyers as my legal representation and had them set up my company as a legal Russian entity. They told me that I was the only American entertainment company that was registered in Russia as a legal Russian company as well.

Now to get down to the business of selling films. I had Vladimir and his buddies bring in their friends and friends of their families to meet with me regarding marketing my films in Russia. At the same time, I was trying to learn as much Russian as I could, and as fast as I could. I hoped this business would turn out to be very successful, and it was. I concluded many deals for a lot of my films. Sometimes Vladimir and the other guys' friends and family would buy the films directly from me, and other times they would bring in buyers and businessmen who would buy my films, and they would get a small percentage for arranging the deals. My films played in lots of major cinemas in the Moscow area and always pulled a full house with an enthusiastic crowd.

I was the first person to ever advertise films on television in Russia. When I first mentioned it, everyone thought I was crazy, but when they saw the business my films were generating, there was nothing else for them to say. For instance, one of my films, *"Future Force,"* starring my pal David Carradine, played at the premier location for films to be presented in Moscow, the Rossiya Theatre, located in the center of Moscow on Pushkin Square. It was built by architect Y. Sheverdyaev on the site of the demolished Strastnoy Monastery. At the time, it was Europe's biggest cinema and the main cinema in the USSR with a capacity of over 2,500. The Moscow International Film Festival is held there every other year. Downstairs, and on either side of the Rossiya Theatre, were two smaller cinemas. I took one as my new office, and my address was now the very prestigious Rossiya Theatre, 2 Pushkin Square, Moscow, USSR.

A picture of the Rossiya Theatre and my offices on the entire lower left hand side

As it turned out, very close to my office was the latest and the largest McDonald's hamburger joint in the world. There were 150 young people serving customers. Seventy-five of them would take your order, and the other seventy-five would prepare the food. It became so popular that at times there was a waiting line of over three hours just to buy a hamburger. They even had to have special guards and barricades to control the customers in line. Can you imagine waiting three hours to buy a hamburger? The rich people who came in droves would hire others who were hanging around to stand in line for them.

To many, this operation represented a modernizing of the old Russia. Luckily for me, it was right next door to my offices. After grabbing a burger one day, Tatyana took me to see Lenin's Tomb on Red Square. The guards there were most impressive! Then, spontaneously, we started dancing together in front of St. Basil's Church. What fun! And because Tatyana was a dancer, we were improvising real ballet steps. Neither of us cared what anyone passing by thought or said, as we were having one great time!

Tatyana and I dancing in Red Square in front of St. Basil's Church and Lenin's Tomb.

One Tuesday night, at 9:30 p.m., I wanted to check on the capacity for my film *"Future Force,"* so I went to the Rossiya to check on the sales. As I walked up and down the aisles, every seat was occupied by a paying customer. I couldn't believe my eyes. In America, or any other country for that matter, there would have been loads of empty seats, but here in Moscow, my films were sold out to capacity. I went many times to many different theatres to check on my films, and the results were always the same. So I started to think, what if I also owned the cinemas?

In those days in Russia, when you purchased a cinema ticket, you had to sit in the exact seat that you had bought, just like in a live show. There was no popcorn, candy, or sodas for sale. The best you could get in those days was an apple or an orange at the food counter. So I decided I would buy thirty-six cinemas in Moscow and eighteen cinemas in St. Petersburg, and create a movie experience just like we had in America. I would call the chain Hollywood Movie Cinemas and sell popcorn, sodas, and candy, and when you bought your ticket, you could sit anywhere in the cinema you wanted, just like in America.

I thought, this is a multi-billion-dollar idea, and I went about making it happen. For any film to be shown in Russia, it had to first be approved by the government agency Goskino, so I got in touch with the head man, Yuri Mishkin, whose title was Chief Deputy Chairman of Goskino. I put him under contract to my company for the express purpose of finding cinemas in Russia that I could buy. Because of his position, he knew every cinema in Russia and took me around to many of them. Some of them I thought would be great business opportunities.

For instance, he took me to a cinema called Hanoi, which was actually three separate cinemas in one building, built right in the middle of an area where the government had just completed construction of many apartment buildings that would hold over 250,000 soldiers who had come back from active duty and were retiring from the armed forces. The plan was for these soldiers and their families to live in these high-rise buildings with shops, restaurants, cinemas, etc., all very near to their residences. This would mean that my three cinemas would have a built-in audience, and I would make a hell of a lot of money. Mr. Mishkin showed me many such deals and was worth his weight in gold.

The only problem was, and it was a huge problem, because the government was a Communist one, when we tried to find who the actual owners of the cinemas were, we kept ending up on a dead-end street. The mayor of the city said the city owned it, the local governor said that his office owned it, the Communist party said that they owned it, the workers in the cinema said that they owned it, and so on and so forth. It seemed as though there was no way to buy the property legally without having someone chasing you and telling you that they actually owned the property, not the party you had bought it from. After a while it became so frustrating that I gave up the idea of my Hollywood chain of cinemas. Such a shame, as it was a great idea that just couldn't be implemented, basically because of the Communist system of government.

The actor Jon Voight is a very good friend of mine and was chosen to play the leading role of Dr. Robert Gale in the movie *"Chernobyl: The Final Warning,"* the true story about the tragic nuclear power plant accident in Chernobyl, Ukraine. He was coming to Russia to prepare for shooting the film. He called me when he arrived, and Jon and I hung out together. I turned him on to some great restaurants that I was frequenting, like Café Pushkin and Arlekino. One night, we were having dinner with Katya, one of my girlfriends, in this wonderful Italian restaurant, Arlekino. Every day, Arlekino had a truck come from Italy with authentic Italian food, so I used to eat there quite often because the food was always fresh and delicious.

In those days, if a Russian citizen wanted to travel from one city to another, they had to have an internal visa. Katya didn't believe me when I told her that in America we didn't need such a visa, that we could go from city to city without any interference from the governmental authorities. She asked Jon over and over if this was true. She was only eighteen years old, and she had known nothing but Russian law, which prevented her from traveling outside of Moscow. She couldn't fathom how such a thing was possible in the United States, that no visa was needed for going from city to city. Jon assured her that this was the way it was in America, as well as almost all of the other countries in the world. Jon, himself, was shocked when he heard that this was the law for the Russian population.

Also in those days, Moscow had special grocery stores for foreigners. Russian people were not allowed to use them. You could buy things like Swiss cheeses and chocolates and all sorts of foreign foods imported from Germany, Switzerland, etc. There was always a line outside these stores, and you had to show a foreign passport before you were allowed to enter. By contrast, the Russian people didn't have such stores with such a wide variety of foods. They had to stand in line for bread at a bakery. They had to stand in line for meat at a butcher shop. In fact, for anything they wanted, they had to stand in line at shop after shop. This made shopping for one's food a very long and tedious event. And many times, by the time one got into a shop, it would be sold out of whatever item it specialized in. Living in Russia in those days was a very hard life for its citizens.

I had my office in Moscow for over five years, and ultimately everyone in the industry knew I was working between Hollywood and Moscow. The *Los Angeles Times* wrote an article about me called "Czar Winters." Then *The Hollywood Reporter* followed with another article about me and my business in Moscow, so all my friends who belonged to the American Film Market Association started calling me "Czar Winters."

People in my industry who wanted to do business in Russia started calling me, asking me either to represent them or to help them. For instance, ABC Films, a division of the ABC-TV network, called me one day and told me they had many movies with big stars that they would like me to sell for them in Russia. They mentioned a film starring Jack Nicholson and another one starring Meryl Streep. I told them that I had about fifty films myself and since I had only sold twenty-three of them to date, I could not sell their films unless they could wait until I sold the rest of my own. I couldn't believe it. Here was ABC Films, this huge company, with all these high-priced sales execs, asking me to sell their films—totally amazing!

During those five years, I would fly to Moscow at least twice a year and sometimes stay for as long as six months. I really loved it, as I got to see my favorite ballet companies on a regular basis. We are all aware that some of the greatest ballerinas in the world came from Russia, as well as some of the greatest male dancers. In my career, I was fortunate enough to work with Rudolph Nureyev and Alexander Godunov, as well as the master—George Balanchine.

I eventually moved from the Mez to the Hotel Metropol, which first opened its doors in 1901. The Metropol is essentially a cross between a five-star hotel and a world-class museum, oozing history from top to bottom. It is also famous for its stained glass ceiling in its main dining room. What a stunning room! I had another amazing presidential suite at this hotel. It even came with a huge antique grandfather clock, and I could look out my bay window and see the Bolshoi Ballet right across the street. Other celebrities who loved this suite were Queen Sofia of Spain, Julio Iglesias, Michael Jackson, Giorgio Armani, Marcello Mastroianni, Prince Philippe of Belgium, and Pierre Cardin, as well as many, many more.

The amazing dining room at the Metropol Hotel

Every day during the Bolshoi season, Igor would purchase a fabulous seat for me from a scalper on the steps in front of the ballet. My seat would be so close, I could almost reach out and touch the royal box. Every night, I would sit there and imagine that Catherine the Great, the Czarina of Russia, was sitting right next to me. I would think about my grandfather and speak to him, telling him that I was sorry we never made it there together, but at least I was there for both of us, just like we had talked about so many times in the past. Having these conversations with my departed grandfather was very sad for me, but in another way, I felt like I had accomplished something that he and I had talked about so many times: visiting his Motherland.

As the years went by, I continued to do amazing sales of my films, but politically, things were changing rather rapidly. Leonid Gorbachev stepped down and was replaced by Boris Yeltsin. This didn't come easily to a country that had been Communist for so many decades. There were three attempts on Yeltsin's life—supposed car accidents where, fortunately, he escaped unharmed. There were many protests and actual street fights using tanks and all kinds of armaments. It got to the point where the word *revolution* was on everyone's lips.

Following the constitutional crisis of 1993, a ten-day stand-off between President Yeltsin and the Russian parliament where the Russian Parliament was actually blown up by Russian tanks, in which hundreds of people were either killed or injured in this attempt to take over the government. I took a two-page ad in *The Hollywood Reporter*. It read, "A.I.P. Studios U.S.S.R. is proud of its employees, Vladimir Kirusha, Igor Medvedev, and Alexander Posukh, who stood for freedom in the streets of Moscow for three days and nights, side by side with Boris Yeltsin."

After this mini-revolution, my two lawyers visited the Kremlin daily to keep up with all the new laws that Boris Yeltsin and his parliament put into place. Being a legal Russian entity, I certainly didn't want to do anything that was illegal in any way. I wanted to make sure that my company and I were following all the new laws as they were presented to parliament. I went to great lengths to comply with all that was expected, as I was a guest in this wonderful country, something I never let myself forget.

Years passed and I found myself in Bangkok, Thailand, producing *"The King Maker."* After our fifty-one-day shoot, I had made plans to record the music in Moscow. Having spent so much time there in the past, I was aware of how much money I could save by doing this. First of all, Russian musicians and singers are terrific, as they come from a history filled with creative geniuses. Plus, in Russia you do not have to pay royalties to either the musicians or singers, which is also a huge savings later on down the line when you sell your film around the world. Most filmmakers don't realize this.

Through a friend of mine, I found a young English composer named Ian Livingstone who had yet to do a film. Ian sent me an audition tape with his music composed to scenes from my film. Well, he blew me away, so I made the deal with him right then and there. For about a month, he and I spoke many times daily as he was composing my score. We made a schedule, and I told him that we would be going to Moscow to record the film, which he was very excited about. Now I had to find an orchestra, a conductor, and a recording studio in Moscow.

Through Igor Medvedev, I contacted Marina Dubovskova whose company, A&M Producers Group, worked out of Mosfilm Studios. Mosfilm is one of the largest and oldest film studios in the Russian Federation and in Europe. It also has the latest in recording studios, their biggest being large enough for a symphony orchestra of 150 musicians together with a choir of a hundred singers. This sounded perfect to me. To top it off, the great Soviet directors Tarkovsky and Eisenstein had recorded there, as well as the famous Japanese director Akira Kurosawa. Some of the films recorded there are *"War and Peace,"* *"Moscow Doesn't Believe in Tears,"* and *"Burnt by the Sun,"* which received an Oscar for best foreign film in 1994. Wow! This was sounding really great.

Marina suggested Sergei Skripka as my conductor. He had conducted recording sessions for 600 films and was the artistic director and chief conductor of the Russian State Symphony Cinema Orchestra. He won the very prestigious National Artist of Russia Award, the highest title awarded in the performing arts, and he was also a professor at the Russian Academy of Music. So I made a deal with Marina, who made a deal for me with Sergei, a deal for the Russian State Symphony plus a choir of 100. She arranged all of our hotels and transport and of course the deal with the Mosfilm Recording Studio. Ian and I then flew to Moscow.

Amazingly, as Marina had promised, both the orchestra and the singers never needed more than one rehearsal of the material before recording it. And Ian had written a very complicated score, similar to the very popular and beloved cantata "Carmina Burana." Sergei, impressed with Ian, asked where I had found this incredibly talented young man. Sergei said, "He will go very far in our business, David." And he was right. To date Ian has hundreds of credits to his name, including *"My Big Fat American Gypsy Wedding"* and *"Harry Potter and the Half-Blood Prince."* Coincidentally, Ian works at the same place my all-time-favorite group, The Beatles, recorded at—Abbey Road Studios in London.

Ian Livingstone, Sergei Skripka, and me at Mosfilm Studios

The time I spent in Russia was very fulfilling, both professionally and personally. I am so proud of my roots. Many parts of Russian culture appeal to me. To this day, I think that Russian women are the most beautiful in the world. What separates them from other women is that they are extremely cultured and intelligent; they read a lot and go to museums, the ballet, and the opera. Their culture values knowledge.

The soundtrack from the motion picture *"The King Maker"*

Russian contributions to the world of literature and music include such incredible writers as Tchaikovsky, Rimsky-Korsakov, Rachmaninoff, Stravinsky, Shostakovich, Prokofiev, Tolstoy, Borodin, Pushkin, Dostoyevsky, Nabokov, Solzhenitsyn, and Anton Chekov. Russia has certainly given the world its share of creative geniuses! I am so impressed when I see, hear, and read the works of these amazing human beings. They are artists of the highest order, and I am truly humbled.

CHAPTER 41

Trouble at Home and Work

Things began to fall apart. I didn't have the bank financing that some other companies had, and I was producing so many films and reinvesting all of my profits back into the business and expanding it. Not only that but my lovely wife, who at the start of our relationship would not let me spend a dime on her, began spending money on clothes and accessories like she had won the lottery. I used to cringe every time my credit card bills arrived. I had to keep refinancing my house just to be able to keep up the lifestyle we now were living.

We had a big mansion and guest house on Mulholland Drive in Beverly Hills. We had the Rolls Royce, a Range Rover, an Excalibur, and a van that I had fitted out with cassettes and monitors for the kids. We also had two nannies who lived in our 1,000-sq.-ft. pool house with their families. We travelled first class all over the world, stayed at the most expensive hotels and in their best suites, and hosted many lavish parties, as well. When I would rent a yacht or go to Vegas, we would take everyone with us, including the nannies and their kids.

You could say I got caught up in the Hollywood lifestyle. I approached a bank for a loan and was successful in getting a $2 million loan from Imperial Bank in Beverly Hills. When they looked at my numbers, they could see that every film I had made was profitable, some of them very profitable, and this they liked. My percentages were much better than the studios', that was for sure, so they gave me enough money to allow me to make four extra pictures a year and continue to grow.

At this precise time, I wanted to open my own video company. Eric Parkinson was sent to me regarding this venture, and he assured me that for $150,000 he could open AIP Home Video and we could release at least two videos a month. That sounded fine, so I went for the deal. In fact, I made him a partner on the video side.

Well, a million and a half later, I was still pouring money into the video company, so that extra money from the bank loan to make films was never really there, and I was getting deeper and deeper into debt. Through Diane Daiou, an employee of AIP Home Video, I found out later that the company was giving our tapes to Handleman, a big buyer, on consignment. When the tapes came back to us six months later, I wasn't told about it. I eventually learned that my warehouse had over one million tapes just sitting there, which had cost me $3 million to duplicate. I also discovered that someone had been selling tapes out the back door for less than it was costing me to duplicate them. I received a call from a gentleman wanting to continue this arrangement, and I obliged, just so that I could have a copy of his check for proof.

I slowly closed down the operation because we had a lot of receivables that would never have been paid if the customers thought we were getting out of the video business. And so, little by little, I let AIP Home Video fade into oblivion. There were a lot of fun times during the AIP/West Side Studios era, and that is what I prefer to remember.

I woke up one morning and thought to myself, you've become one of them, those whose lives are filled with trying to please everyone else but yourself. And for what? You're not happy here, even with all the toys. So go somewhere else. But where? Then I thought about England and Europe, about how I felt when I was over there, what good films they made, and the fact that I had a few good friends living in the UK. I decided that's where I wanted to live. I was tiring of making the same old action films, and I felt my creative juices bubbling with thoughts of making some commercial, but more interesting, films.

Since my life was not going as well as I had hoped for, I decided to move my entire family to the UK. Filmmakers in London always seemed to make more interesting and intelligent films. Maybe some of this would rub off on me, I thought. I told my wife, who had sworn earlier in our relationship that she would stay with me through thick and thin and would follow me to the ends of the Earth, that we were moving to England. She must have forgotten those earlier love bites, or else England was beyond the ends of the Earth, as she said she and the kids were not going to pick up and move to the UK. I was really pissed, and from then on, our relationship soured and was never the same again. I recall her swearing to "love me till I died," but to my surprise, she said, "No way." She wanted to keep the children, James, Jonathan, and Alexander, in Los Angeles. She also said that she wanted to stay near her family. I tried to persuade her many times, but she was not moving, and that was that. In some ways, I understood her position, but I always thought it was most important for kids to have a whole family with both a mom and a dad figure nearby all the time. Okay, I thought to myself, I'll have them visit me a few times a year. This I knew she would accept, and even like.

Me and my family in happier times

When I came home from work one day, to my surprise, she asked me to move out. I thought, this is crazy. I bought this house way before she and I had a relationship, and now she is asking me to leave my own house and kids? That's California law, or at least a California marriage, for you. Not wanting to create a problem, though, I agreed and moved into a hotel on Beverly Boulevard in Beverly Hills.

At this hotel, I met a guy by the last name of Armani. While I was very unhappy and missed my wife and children terribly, he was always trying to get me to go out with him to all the hot spots in town. But I stayed in my suite most of the time, and he would bring me food and try to cheer me up. He would go into Emporio Armani in Beverly Hills almost every day and get a bunch of clothes, and when I was with him, I never saw him pay for anything. He told me he was a member of the Armani family. A couple of times, he tried to buy me something, but I declined. He and I hung out together a lot, and he told me that he wanted to invest about $8 million with me in films. Boy, that was what I needed. Then I could make some really good films with bigger budgets.

At West Side Studios, I had a film I was supposed to make with Robert Davi and a Japanese investor, and so I took Robert with me to Japan to meet with the investor. We checked into the Peninsula Hotel near the Ginza after a very long ride from Narita Airport. The Peninsula cost me $800 a room per night, which at the time was very expensive, but I had to stay at a five-star hotel suite because the investor would be coming to see me, and of course Robert had to stay in the same quality accommodations.

Having just arrived in Tokyo, I went down to the Rappongi area, where all the nice restaurants and clubs are, and I was standing on a street corner thinking to myself, so many people here and I don't seem to know any of them, when a voice called out to me in a Japanese accent, "Mr. David… Mr. David Winters?" I turned around, and there were one of my buyers and his assistant. We exchanged niceties, and they expressed their pleasure at seeing me in their city. Just as they started to leave, another voice, this time American, called out, "David, is it you?" I quickly turned around and there, right behind me in a limo, was a friend of mine, Richard, and his model girlfriend. Years before, she had been my girlfriend, Simone's, best friend. They asked me to jump in the car with them. I couldn't believe my luck. Just a minute before, I had felt kind of lonely in this big city of millions of Japanese, and in that short time, I had bumped into four people I knew. It was a very nice feeling and made me realize that I did have friends all over the world, in any country I might visit. That's one of the nicest things about my business. You can never be lonely for long.

Well, Richard and I went out clubbing, and he obviously knew where all the foreign models hung out. We had a blast. He introduced me to a bunch of his friends on my first night in Tokyo, so I was all sorted out with the opposite sex. The girls were from everywhere but Japan. I wound up with Irena from Czechoslovakia, and she was everything they say about Czech women. She was in Japan on a six-month work visa and was having the time of her life. I was more than happy to be one of her new experiences.

The next day was business, and Japanese legend Shin'ichi "Sonny" Chiba took us to dinner with the investor. Sonny had just starred in a film for me with Robert and Brigitte Nielsen— *"Codename: The Silencer."* In Japan, Sonny was a household name as a movie star, singer, producer, director, and a martial artist, of course. He had a school of 600 ninjas. Some of the stunts they did were mind-boggling. It seemed that he and the investor were very close friends. In fact, Sonny showed us a watch the investor had given him that cost $500,000. I had never seen a watch before that cost that kind of money. We had a traditional Kobe beef shabu-shabu dinner, which is where the lucky Japanese cows are force-fed beer and massaged. After an amazing feast, that cost the Japanese Investor $5,000, we all shook hands on a deal, and I thought that was it. Japanese people are very concerned about honor, and when they say yes it usually means yes, or so I thought. We had agreed to a $3 million budget, so then Robert and I went out together to celebrate.

A friend of mine, who has lived in Japan most of his life and has many businesses there, joined us and took us to a geisha house. He knew all of them, and this facility was his favorite. I mean, you can't go to Japan and not visit a geisha house at least once. The girl assigned to me was from Thailand, and that surprised me. She spoke a little English, so I could make out that she was making a lot more money in Tokyo than in Thailand. It was my very first experience with a Thai girl, and one that I will never forget. She was so gentle, so feminine, and so careful with me that I just wanted to melt into her. Her skin was so smooth and her eyes so telling. She was really good at her chosen profession. She made you believe that this was a love affair, and you did not want it to ever end. She was very spiritual, and the odor of her incense permeated the air. I let my senses float into the most wonderful fantasy, and she bathed me like one would a child. Then came the sensual side of the traditional Thai bathing ritual and then the soothing massage and so on… It was the memory of this magical experience that drew me to Thailand years later, and I've never looked back. Well, as all good things must end, so did this, but I can tell you I sure slept well that night. So did Robert, who thanked me profusely for the experience.

Between Irena and my geisha, I didn't want to ever leave Japan, but we had to get back to reality. On my last day in Japan, Irena took me around to see some of the sights, and then we said goodbye. We both knew it was a spur-of-the-moment thing and that nothing would become of it, and we both enjoyed it for what it was. I have never seen or spoken with Irena again. I hope she is well and happy, wherever she is.

So as the sun sets in the west, Robert and I get on a plane back to Los Angeles and, unbeknownst to me at the time, London, England.

Back to London

After many questioning and sleepless nights, in September of 1995, I packed my bags and all the masters of the fifty films that I owned. I shipped all the films, as well as my Rolls Royce, and took off for London myself. Back to my roots. Many people thought I was crazy, and to tell you the truth, so did I. I was no kid anymore, and here I was, uprooting my entire life to start all over again in a country I hadn't lived in for decades. Well, I guess the gypsy in me was at work.

I knew many people in and around London, including close friends Patrick and Jill Meehan, whom I had known for many years. They offered to let me live with them, but since I had brought my Israeli bodyguard, Elan, with me, I thought it would be better to rent a mews house right in the center of London, which I immediately did. Elan and I waited patiently for the container with all my film negatives, prints and video masters, all of my office files, and the artwork from all of my fifty films to arrive by ship in the UK. The mews house I rented was in Knightsbridge, but after about a month and a robbery, where the robbers had the nerve to enter the house while Elan and I were sleeping, I moved to a house in Chelsea, in Swan Place. It was right around the corner from a pub that was also a famous restaurant because Prince William used to go there to hang out because nobody bothered him there.

For the first six months, I was really the man about town. With a Rolls Royce that had a California license plate that read "MUVIES" and a bodyguard, everyone I met seemed to be intrigued with me and wanted to get to know me and hang with me. Almost every night, I went to the discos, usually taking an entourage of young models and actresses with me. They all piled into the back of the Rolls, with Elan next to me and a girl on his lap. In retrospect, I guess we were quite a sight as we pulled up and entered the clubs, and of course we were always seated in the VIP section. When we went to the clubs, I on occasion smoked Cuban cigars. So, with the girls and I all seated together and Elan standing right next to me, cross-armed and looking quite obviously the part of a bodyguard, we had lots of curious visitors. Elan always looked to me for a signal before allowing anyone to sit next to me. I know a lot of people asked Elan if I was the American Mafia. Hilarious—how far from the truth that was—but I understood that I looked the part with the cigar, the bodyguard, and the lovelies. Every night when we left the clubs, there would always be a crowd around us, fascinated by the California license plate and our whole entourage and persona. It was great in a way, as I never had to approach a girl I wanted to meet. They would always come over to say hi or join us.

I was spending a lot of money, but aside from the girls, this scene was also taking its toll, and I was slowly getting bored, especially since I don't drink at all. So it was time to settle down and get back to what I love…the work.

I was also missing my kids—Alexander, Jonathan, and James—a lot and thinking about them all the time. I arranged to have Chris and the kids come over, and we went to Blackpool because it has a beach and an amusement park. We also went to Thorpe Park in Surrey, near London, and the largest amusement park in the UK, Alton Towers, and the boys had an incredible time, as I knew they would. They loved the roller coasters and scary rides—the scarier the better—especially Alexander. We had a wonderful time, and we were a family again. It felt so good.

I showed Chris a wonderful house in the country that I wanted to buy. It was a huge Tudor-style house, but she wasn't interested. Later, I showed her a beautiful castle with loads of land, right near the ocean, but nothing could persuade her to change her mind. I really wanted to buy that castle, but not without my family to fill it with laughter and joy. I also thought that it would be terrific for the boys to study in the UK as the schools there are sensational, much more advanced than American schools. But Chris dashed any hopes I had of them joining me on a permanent basis.

I introduced Chris to Patrick and Jill, and we would often visit them at their amazing country home in Penshurst, right up the street from Penshurst Castle. Their home was 1,100 years old. It had a music gallery built into the living room and amazing fireplaces so big you could sit in them and warm yourself. It was like a set in a film. And the gardens were ever so lovely, with the obligatory tennis court and swimming pool, of course. There was also a moat around half of the house stocked with fish. The expansive property actually had its own train stop. There were sheep grazing on it, and it used to house many horses, mostly owned by members of the royal household, who went on fox hunts, just as the gentry has done for hundreds of years. Across the street from the property was a pub the Meehans had bought so that on the weekends they and their friends could use it as they wished.

Patrick and Jill were close friends with an Italian man named Pucci, and he was always around at the weekends in their country home. He was a real character, a very colorful guy. He owned a pizza parlor and Italian restaurant on King's Road, simply called Pucci's, which was the most popular and trendy hangout for every celeb who lived in and around Chelsea. Georgie Best, the living legend of a football player, was always there, as were many other celebrities, actors, and models. Pucci's got crazy around midnight when all the girls would get up on the tables and dance. The place had a great energy. It was so alive with music and dance, and everyone was your friend. It was a blast. Pucci made sure that only the people he wanted got a table, so it was kind of a private club that wasn't really private. Situated right on the street, a passersby could also join in and dance, even if they couldn't get inside. No matter what the night of the week, Pucci's was always packed and jumping. Pucci's son Rufus, a lovely lad, not anywhere near as crazy or colorful as his dad, now runs it.

Patrick had been a shareholder in Hemdale, an English film and distribution company run by John Daly, a friend of mine, which produced such hits as *"Platoon," "The Terminator,"* and *"The Last*

Emperor." His films garnered thirteen Oscar nominations for best film, and he is the only independent producer who ever won two Academy Awards for best film consecutively. Patrick had been involved in this company as it started out as a music company managing many top UK singing groups, and then John moved it into the film business. So I thought that maybe Patrick would like to get back into the film business with me, considering I already had a large library of films that I was selling all the time.

At first, Patrick was cool to the idea. Then one day he got really excited about it and called me in to discuss it. It was funny to me because I had been trying to sell him on it, and now he was selling me. He said we would take it public and raise a lot of cash for new films, just like Hemdale had done. I would run the company and could make some of the films I wanted to make. It all sounded great to me. As majority shareholders, Patrick and I would have equal ownership of the largest portion of stock in the company, and I would have total freedom to run the company.

I was now beginning to think that returning to England was definitely the right move. The boys were on summer vacation from school, so their trip to see me in London was a long and interesting one. I took them to Glasgow in Scotland during the month of the Arts Festival, where all the streets are filled with actors vying for one's attention as they advertise the plays or musicals they are appearing in. During that month, any place in Glasgow that has more than twenty seats is turned into a theatre—sometimes even garages. They have parades every day in the streets of the city, so it is a very interesting time to be there.

From there, we drove up to Loch Ness Lake to hunt for the infamous Loch Ness Monster. We also took a train ride to Paris and then on to Switzerland, where they could view the beautiful Swiss countryside from the comfort of the train. They were broadening their senses and discovering the world through their own eyes, and this made me very happy. They were experiencing things that most American kids never get to see.

Then I discovered that Alexander, in particular, liked to watch dancing and see musicals. So in London, I took him to meet Jerry

Lewis, the famous comedic actor and a good friend of mine, who was starring in the West End in the show *"Damn Yankees,"* and Alexander loved it. I also took him to see *"The Nutcracker"* ballet, and I remember standing in line for hours to see *"The Phantom of the Opera,"* which was playing at Her Majesty's Theatre, coincidentally the very same theatre where the English company of *"West Side Story"* had played many years before. I also took him to see the rock opera *"Tommy"* by The Who, as I saw his delight every time we went to the theatre together. Then we went to see *"Cats,"* a fantastic show, which he told me he loved because all of the characters in the play came into the audience, so Alexander got to see the actors up close.

All in all, in an eight-day period, we went to see seven shows—a record for me. His favorite was *"Tommy."* Jonathan, on the other hand, had no desire whatsoever to see any of this. Shortly thereafter, Alexander could sing the entire score of *Phantom* by memory, a feat that blew me away! Even at such a young age, I could see Alexander following in my footsteps, which of course gave me much pleasure.

When Chris and the boys went back to America, I missed them more than I ever had before. The time I had spent with Alexander, going to all the shows, was so special to me, it made me miss him terribly. For months on end, I would think about those wonderful times we had shared together and how special was the bond we had formed between us.

With Christmas around the bend, the mews house was freezing, and I had to sit in front of a heater in the living room to stay warm. So I decided that I needed some warm and comfortable weather. Patrick mentioned that he owned a Hotel Carlisle Bay Resort in Antigua in the Caribbean right on the beach. He said it was glorious, with no TVs or telephones. He treated the hotel as kind of a family resort, only inviting his friends to buy the bungalows he was selling, or they could rent one at Christmas time and New Year's. He asked me if I would like to go with my family for the holidays. I immediately said yes and then hurriedly called Chris and the boys and told them of our next adventure. Needless to say, Chris and the boys were filled with excitement. I knew that Chris would like the idea of no TVs or phones, but I thought the kids would get bored. Boy, was I wrong. They were in the water from early morning till late afternoon and never wanted to come out. They didn't ask about a TV the whole time we were there. The bungalows were literally five steps from the water.

Carlisle Bay Resort sits directly on the beach on the Caribbean Island of Antigua.

Patrick was right, Carlisle Bay was a dream. He'd had this incredible wooden roof for the lobby built in Canada at a cost of $1.5 million and had it shipped to the Caribbean for God knows how much. Everyone there seemed to know each other, and they were all very posh. It was like someone had cast an Agatha Christie movie; they were all such characters.

For instance, there was the wonderful Dai Llewellyn, the Welsh socialite who was subsequently knighted to Sir David St. Vincent "Dai" Llewellyn. Unfortunately, he passed away in 2009. I knew Dai from the past. He was a friend of mine, and that made me feel very comfortable, as Dai was a fabulous, personable guy. His younger brother Roddy was romantically involved with Princess Margaret, and Dai himself was known as the leading playboy of London in the 1970s and '80s. His late father won a gold medal at the 1952 Olympics for show jumping and was later also knighted by the Queen. Dai could talk to you about any subject with great assurance. He even surprised me with his knowledge of old Broadway show tunes. He and I would sing and talk for hours, sometimes all night long. I was amazed at how he remembered all the lyrics to even the most unknown songs. But Dai was a big drinker, and I think in the end that's what got him. He was such a joyous personality, and I miss him and his always smiling face. Dai was as posh as you could get, but so down-to-earth, too. He was a true gentleman.

Then there were Derek Dawson and his wife. Derek was one of the owners of the original Hemdale Company and was a very wealthy man. He reportedly gave both of his daughters somewhere around $25 million pounds on their 25th birthdays. He had been living in California and was about to move back to London where he had bought a two-bedroom apartment on the same block as the current prime minister of England, Maggie Thatcher, in Belgravia, which had now become the most expensive block in all of London. At that time, he reportedly paid over £5 million for a 2,000 square foot two-bedroom apartment and had two interior decorators, one from the UK and one from the US, design the interior. Derek, whom I also already knew, was a charming person, as was his wife, whom I met for the first time.

Also vacationing on the island were David Bond and his wife and kids, one whose name was James. You got it—James Bond. James and my boys hit it off really well and spent a lot of time together during this vacation. I think his wife was probably used to being the most fashionable, best-looking one in any group, but now, with my wife on the scene, boy, did her feathers rear up. She was smiley but disdainful, as she saw her position as queen of the coop usurped. She wasn't even in the same league as my wife. Chris was extremely beautiful and really sweet, and did not have any idea of how to be catty. But I always caught a sneer or two when I would look out of the corner of my eye at Mrs. Bond. She tried in a very subtle way to make us feel not wanted, and she succeeded. On the other hand, everyone else was very welcoming to us.

And there was Terry Shand, who started a record company called Eagle Rock Entertainment in Patrick's garage, and who had gone on to build a huge video and record company worth multi-millions that was a listed company on the London Stock Exchange.

The cast of characters also included Roger Meyers and his wife Lee. Roger used to work for Patrick and had driven me around town, here and there. Co-founder of Punch Taverns, he had built a chain of 150 restaurants in five years and had just sold his company to Whitbread for £143 million. He was the hottest thing on Fleet Street, the flavor of the month as far as the stock market was concerned.

Roger's chain of restaurants, which were all over England, included Le Dome. I remember Roger telling me that a certain company paid him £25 million just to show up for three meetings when they were trying to launch their new company.

Another woman, Janet, was always popping pills. In fact, twice while we were there, she had to be rushed to hospital. I wound up being one of the guys who picked her up, carried her to a car, and drove her to the hospital in a coma, fearing she would die, after Patrick's wife, Jill, had done mouth-to-mouth on her as she almost swallowed her own tongue. I also picked her up at the hospital and took her back to the hotel, where she proceeded to swallow another bottle of pills the very next day and again had to be rushed, this time by ambulance, to the hospital. Her father owned most of North London, and she was extremely rich, being the only child in the family. Her insurance company eventually sent a nurse to bring her back to England, and there she was, on our plane going back. What a character.

Then there was Nicky Kerman, whose father was the king of the big divorce lawyers of movie stars and famous people in the 1950s. Nicky himself was a restaurateur and owned some of the most successful and trendy restaurants in London, like Sheekey's and Drone's as well as Scots, where all the ministers from Parliament went for lunch. A target of the IRA, it was blown up on three occasions. One time, unfortunately, there were a few people killed in the restaurant. Nicky and his wife and their children were quite close to Patrick and Jill and made us feel very much at home. I had known Nicky a long time through Patrick and really liked him.

Then of course there was my friend and host, Patrick, who was a bigger-than-life character who had made most of his money by ripping off rock and roll groups in the 1960s and '70s before they had lawyers. He is famous for this and has been written about in books and TV shows by some of the old rock bands that he managed, such as Ozzy Osbourne, Black Sabbath, Deep Purple, and Dire Straits. Patrick had owned NEMS, the biggest agency in London, and at one time managed over 400 groups, such as Elton John, Rod Stewart and Faces, and Cilla Black. Ozzy Osbourne actually wrote a song about Patrick and about the group's bills never being paid. It seems that Patrick had a habit of disappearing when it came time to pay bills. In fact, just recently, the expose magazine *Private Eye* did a very negative article about him, as did *The Times* of London even more recently. He was also a large stockholder in Hemdale.

And there was Patrick's lovely wife, Jill. I loved Jill, but there were times that Jill was so drunk that she would just fall over from her seat into the sand. It was so comical that it was hard to keep from laughing. Jill didn't have a mean bone in her body, but I think that all the years with Patrick and his running around with other women took its toll on her, and she found refuge in the bottle. Jill was always upbeat, but her arguments with Patrick were so legendary that people would eventually beg off from coming to their country home for the weekend because they were embarrassed to hear their disagreements. At one point, even their own children told me they didn't want to go.

Years later, as Jill was dying of cancer, Patrick was dating my ex-wife. Jill called me, upset, and asked if I knew about it. I said I did, but I really didn't care since I was no longer with Chris. It was poetic justice as far as I was concerned—they deserved each other. But I must say, it was an awkward phone call, and I felt very sorry for Jill.

Also staying at the resort were Lord Michael and his two children. It was all kind of like a Jacques Tati film, funny but at times dangerous, like Agatha Christie. It was much worse than Peyton Place, with everyone gossiping about each other behind each other's backs. Then, on the beach the very next day, you would think they were the best of friends.

Well, needless to say, we overstayed our intended vacation, as Alexander and Jonathan just did not want to go back home. They were having the time of their lives exploring the island and living on the beach. They didn't seem to miss their TVs at all. But eventually, all good things end, and the kids and Chris returned to our house in Beverly Hills, and I went back to London, which, in the middle of January, is dead cold and windy. Boy, did I ever miss our beach house then.

I trusted Patrick, but I would find out later that this was a huge mistake. I had met a guy named Peter Parkinson through Patrick many years before, and this gentleman, who is a lovely guy, had warned me before I went into partnership with Patrick, that all his business deals ended up in tears, problems, and lawsuits. Peter had this love/hate relationship with Patrick, even though he had been working with him for over thirty years. Peter saw who Patrick really was, and was kind enough to warn me about him. My relationship with Patrick, also over thirty years old, had only been a social one, not a business one, and so I took what Peter said to be a case of possible jealousy. Now, I wish I had listened to him.

He told me that Patrick had signed his dad's signature to a contract, even though his dad had recently passed away. This sent chills down my spine and made me think twice about going ahead with Patrick, but I thought that I could handle him since I would be in control. The problem was that he knew all about public companies and I didn't. I had no idea what I was getting into.

Patrick had been accused of stealing millions and millions of dollars from his singing groups. When he managed these singers, they didn't hire lawyers in those days, so he signed everything. Later on, he even bragged to me that *he* actually owned all of the houses purchased by the members of Black Sabbath. He was maniacal in his dealings with these groups.

I was promised the same number of shares as he would receive, plus a nice salary, and also £750,000 for a deposit on a house as soon as the float loan took place. Well, he didn't get the float to happen for over two years, and meanwhile I was spending my money, thinking that this deal would put everything back to normal.

I was sending $11,000 a month back to Chris to pay for all her and the children's bills, and I was also paying for my overhead in the UK. I was now paying for two households in two different countries, and it was stressing me out, to say the least. My cash was going very quickly. Eventually, I had to let my bodyguard go and move into one of Patrick's apartments, which made me crazy as he was a drama queen and loved chaos in his personal life. This is not my style at all, but I was now in a trap that I had willingly entered into. I had no one to blame but myself. Peter Parkinson's words were coming back to haunt me. I now knew I should have listened to him, but it was too late.

On one of my trips to the Cannes Film Festival, I met a fellow named Addy Pinter, who was in Cannes with a film, and his girlfriend

Grace, from Poland. They were a lovely couple, and I was told that Addy was a superstar football player in his home country of Austria. He was also a painter and lived in a beautiful city named Gratz. He and I hit it off, and he invited me to visit them whenever I wanted. As it turned out, I had a couple of days before I planned to meet my family in Thailand, so I decided to drive the Rolls to see Addie and Grace first, cutting it very close. I got to Gratz, and the drive was stunning, although I had to pay a fine of $400 for supposedly speeding. Then we all drove to Vienna, and Addie showed me around the city and the wonderful buildings there, especially the magnificent opera house. We ate a bite and then took off for Poland via Czechoslovakia. As we were driving, a motorcycle cop pulled up alongside me. All dressed up and shiny, he looked just like the Gestapo. He smiled at me and then pulled me over and said I didn't have some sticker that I needed to legally drive my car in Austria. Although I had bought every sticker the authorities at the border said I had to have, he insisted I was driving illegally. He wanted to immediately impound my car and take me to jail. When Addie got out of the car to see what was going on, the cop recognized him and the conversation changed immediately. He wanted a free poster, watch, and other Addie fan items, but still said that if he saw me driving again in the city, he would take me to jail and take away my car. I assured him that I was going straight to Czechoslovakia without stopping and he would never see me again. Was I happy to see the back of him! So we drove all the way to Katowice, Poland, where Grace was from. What a simple place, and yet we went to the Egyptian, the most incredible disco I have ever been to in my life. Designed like a pyramid, with incredible architecture, it is situated in the middle of a forest. I couldn't believe my eyes. What an amazing place! Like a wonderful movie set.

Later that night, I had to hire Grace's brother to sleep in my car; otherwise, she said it would not have been there in the morning. We parked it right outside my room at the hotel so I could keep tabs on it. In the morning, there was a huge crowd around the Rolls. Although they had heard of a Rolls Royce, they had never seen one in person before. With my car safe, we all went to see Grace's mom. I put her in the front seat and drove her all over the neighborhood with loads of flowers on her lap, which I had purchased for her. She was in hog heaven as all the neighbors stared and waved at her in the car as she waved back at them, just like the Queen of England. This must have been one of the highlights of her life. She was so sweet and such a gracious host when we visited her in her tiny one-room apartment, such a lovely and giving person, I just had to reciprocate.

Addie then suggested we go to Warsaw and stop by the German concentration camp, Auschwitz, on the way. He and Grace would drive separately in their car because afterwards I had to go directly back to London, but Addie had arranged for three lovelies to accompany me in my car, which they were all happy to do. I was thinking that this was going to be very tough for me. I had seen Auschwitz so many times on film, but now I would actually see the ovens in person. Nevertheless, I agreed, and off we went.

Auschwitz is in a beautiful countryside, and while driving there, you hear loads of birds singing and chattering, but as soon as you arrive, there are no birds and no sounds of them at all. It is dead quiet, empty of sound, like even the birds know what happened there. The parking lot was filled with busses of tourists. To enter, you must go under the famous sign that says, "Work will free you." I got goose bumps when I saw the sign for the first time in real life.

When the Jews were brought there in World War II, the Germans had a string quartet playing just inside the gate so that everyone would think this was a wonderful workplace, and nobody had any idea what was about to happen to them. They all walked in happily. I could feel tears coming as I walked into the camp and saw so many pictures of those killed there. And then I was at the ovens and I lost it. It became impossible to hold back the tears. To think that so many of my people were gassed and then cremated was sickening. I was living it all over again. I got weak and could not stand it anymore. I rushed to the exit, but there were still more and more pictures of all those poor unfortunate people looking back at me.

The tears were now streaming, and I was out of it and needed to leave right away. Addie understood, so we were off to Warsaw. But I was still in a daze. Along the way, Addie suggested we stop for pizza. After stopping to eat, about 120 kilometers down the road, I realized that my bag was missing. I must have left it at the pizza place. In my small tote were my American passport, $7,500 cash and all my credit cards, as well as my diamond-studded Monte Blanc pen, worth about $5,000, and numerous other documents. Addie told me to go ahead, that he would drive back to the restaurant to get my bag. I had planned to pay for everyone's lodgings with my credit card, but now I was unable to do so and felt a bit embarrassed. Addie told me to meet him in Warsaw Square at a certain hotel, so the girls and I went ahead and waited for Addie and Grace.

A guy sitting at another table started talking to me in English. He seemed nice, so I invited him to join us. He accepted, and as we talked, he asked me if I knew a guy named Pucci in London. I told him Pucci was a very good friend of mine, and after I told him what had happened to me he asked if I had a checkbook with me. I said yes, and he proceeded to give me $600 cash and asked me to write him out a check for it. I asked him if he was sure he wanted to do this, although I was truly thankful. He said any friend of Pucci's was a friend of his and gave me the cash. I was startled. The coincidence of us both having Pucci as a friend blew my mind in a most grateful way. So when Addie returned, I related this story to him, and he also couldn't believe it. What an amazing circumstance! Addie had been unable to retrieve my bag. It must have been picked up by a customer who came in after we left. This did not dampen my spirits as there was nothing I could do about it, so in a positive frame of mind, I decided I was still going to have a wonderful evening. And in spite of my loss, we all did have a wonderful evening in Warsaw. Downtown Warsaw is truly lovely with its cobbled streets.

The next day, I had to go to the police station to report the loss of my passport and to get a letter to use as proof for the border guards, as I would be driving through many countries to get back to London. If all went well, I would be just in time to catch my plane to Thailand to meet my family. The police were most understanding and took care of me very quickly. I bid adieu to Addie and friends and started my lonely trek back to London. I would have to drive all night if I wanted to make the plane, so I called Chris and she talked to me all through the night to keep me awake. I was really tired from all the driving and all the emotions from the experiences of this trip.

I eventually got back to London in time to catch the plane to Thailand and had a well-deserved sleep on the long flight. All I could think about was seeing my wife and my boys again. I sure love them to pieces. We had an incredible vacation together, and the boys really loved Thailand. There was so much for them to do there that when it was time to go, they really didn't want to.

Afterwards, Chris took the boys back to L.A., and a short while later, I had to cut down what I was sending her because I was totally running out of cash. All I could do was hope for the better days that Patrick promised me were to come. Eventually, Patrick did float the company by backing into a company that was already afloat on the AIM market, what's called a reverse merger. This company was a real estate company, and we changed the publicly listed name to Equator Films. This way, Equator, which represented my library as its agent, got all the money, from which it paid all its overhead, its rent and salaries. For instance, I did a TV syndication deal with some friends of mine for $3 million, to be paid out over a three-year period. Equator would get $1.5 million, which would have been fine for me personally, but instead, all the money went to pay for Equator's overhead, and I received a salary, which after taxes were taken out was very little.

It became increasingly difficult for me to send Chris much money, and I think this was Patrick's idea. I didn't know it then, but he liked Chris, and when things got bad, he started to pursue her in a romantic way. She told me she wanted nothing to do with him, and I believed her. But when she had almost no money, I guess she started to see him—he was the only one around with lots of cash. Ever since Chris was a young girl, there had always been a rich guy around to pay for everything, and so Patrick made himself conveniently available without my knowledge. Despicable! I could never imagine going out with one's partner's wife. Although I was separated from her, he was still married, and to top it off, his wife Jill was dying of cancer. I didn't know what was going on for quite some time. What an asshole and lowlife, but wait—things got worse later.

The Public Company eventually did issue me my stock, which I was told I couldn't sell for at least two years. I never got the £750,000 I was promised. Also, the $8 million we were supposed to get for producing films never showed up—I was told to please be patient and wait. What else could I do? I had no choice. So we continued to sell my films at all the markets.

Always on the lookout for deals, Peter Parkinson, who was now working for Equator Films, and I found out that the Handmade Film Library was available for purchase, with Price Waterhouse representing it. I thought it was a great deal since it was in bankruptcy and could be bought for a very low sum. After calling them, I thought it was a terrific acquisition for Equator. So I told Patrick about it, and he contacted them and set up a meeting to discuss the deal. Then he bought it for himself, not for Equator.

Peter Parkinson's warning was now ringing loudly in my ears, and I was totally pissed. Patrick's excuse was that Equator didn't have the funds to buy it—except he never told anyone this until the deal was done between himself and Price Waterhouse. Then, I think out of guilt, he gave Equator the rights to distribute the Handmade Library for a very good fee, the same as they were doing with my library. We wound up buying the original Hemdale library of twenty-three films as well as a film studio, Isleworth Film Studios, where the Academy Award-winning movie *"The African Queen"* was filmed. I was told that money would be coming in to make a new series of Edgar Allen Poe horror films there at our new film studio. Of course, this never came about. By this time, I was sick of Patrick, so I decided to try Asia, as according to all reports, Asia would be the growth market for the next fifty to one hundred years.

I went to Bangkok this time and met with many Thai people in the business. We talked about lots of different kinds of movie and TV deals. I got call after call telling me to come back to London and stop wasting my time in Bangkok. So I went back and basically told everyone I was not a kid; I was in Bangkok trying to drum up some future business for the company. In one of our board meetings, I exchanged some unpleasantries with a guy I had installed as the managing director of the public vehicle. The situation was absolutely unreal to me and infuriated me.

At the same time, I was struggling to send Chris as much money as I could, so I moved into the film studio and set up a couch/bed in my office. This was not comfortable for me at all, especially since the bathroom where I had to shower was freezing in the morning. When Jonathan came to visit, we stayed together in this room, which in reality was also my office. After Jonathan left, I got a letter from the board of directors stating that my sleeping in the office was not acceptable. They wanted me to resign and take a monthly fee for one year as a consultant, a golden parachute of sorts. I was utterly stunned. I was still the largest shareholder in the company, along with Patrick, but there was really nothing I could do about this situation.

I resigned, hoping that the stock would be worth a lot of money someday. I knew that Patrick was buying and selling the stock, trying to manipulate it, but I honestly didn't understand his game. I felt like I needed to leave London, so I decided to go to back to Bangkok and see if I could get something together there for the future.

Shortly after my arrival in Bangkok, my mom came to visit me. We were having a bite to eat in the restaurant of a synagogue when a husky Caucasian man wearing sunglasses came up to our table and asked, "Are you David Winters?" Puzzled, I looked at him but said nothing. He told me not to be scared, he couldn't stand my partner, Patrick, either. He asked if he could join us, and I reluctantly agreed. Then he told me that he had been hired by Patrick and his associate William Marrone to kill me!

Shocked and naturally concerned for myself, I was even more alarmed for my mom. She was in her 80s—this could have given her a heart attack. God bless her, Mom continued her meal and feigned unaffectedness by anything that was said. Speechless, I offered my would-be assassin some cabbage soup as we made small talk, always keeping an eye on my mom. He told me his name was Daniel Weiss and that he did not do "this type of thing" anymore, as he was now giving English lessons to young Thai children. To my relief, he left.

And my mom sprang into action. "David, am I hallucinating?"

"No, Mom."

"David, is this a dream?"

"No, Mom—eat your soup, it's hot. Soup in dreams is not hot!"

"David, have I lost my mind?"

"No, Mom, you are fine!"

"Then, this is real? You brought me to a Jewish restaurant in a Bangkok synagogue and offered a retired Jewish hit man a bowl of cabbage soup after he told you that your partners wanted to hire him to kill you—did I get it right?"

"Yes, Mom. Your soup is getting cold."

Mom was right—my life was a *mess*!

My Wonderful Moments with Michael Jackson

Before leaving London for Thailand, one of the most meaningful interactions of my lifetime had occurred by chance, resulting in a wonderful friendship with one of the most misunderstood of all celebrities…

I had been in London for a while when I met a stunning young girl from Russia—Irina. We met in Mona Lisa, a popular restaurant on the trendy King's Road, with an eclectic customer base. On any given day, you might see a pensioner sitting near a rock star such as Eric Clapton, who's a regular customer there. It's still one of my favorite places to eat when I'm in London.

As for Irina, I liked her very much, and we started seeing each other every day, and then almost every night. We would just sit in my apartment talking for hours and hours. Eventually, as it usually does, it led to more than talking. She was very young, but so well read. She knew more about politics than most older women that I knew. She fascinated me, and we got along famously. We had great times together, just the two of us. We had a lot of laughs, and she made me feel young again.

During this time, I was putting a deal together to film a pilot for a TV series, *"Star School,"* in Bucharest, Romania. I was also trying to sell the TV stations there some of the films from my library, so I invited Irina to accompany me. Michael Boadica, my rep in Romania, had sold three of my films, and they were released theatrically, but I never got any money from the local distributor. So Irina and I went to check it out and to shoot my pilot.

While in Bucharest, I met a very nice guy, Marcel Avram, who owned an agency in Germany called Mama Concerts, which was the international promoter for Michael Jackson's tour as well as many other superstar recording artists. We got to talking, and I told him that I had worked with Michael. He told me he was actually on his way to meet Michael, and he then excused himself and left. After a few minutes, he came back and said that Michael would like to see me and was inviting Irina and me to accompany him to the show. Avram gave me some VIP passes and said that Michael wanted us to have the best seats in the house.

The stadium held 109,000 people, and we went there with Michael in his limousine, part of a huge convoy of limousines that were guarded by hundreds of soldiers. Michael loved uniforms and the feeling of being a dignitary. When we arrived, there were hundreds of additional military personnel watching over us. We were first served food and drinks; then, when it was time for Michael's entrance, we said goodbye, and Irina and I were led out into the middle of the stadium to an area that was also protected by many soldiers with all their gear on—kind of a cross between a soldier and a riot policeman. We were in a little oasis in this huge stadium, and there was a ring of these special forces of police and army surrounding us for the entire show.

It was an incredible stage show, and Irina was in heaven as she watched Michael perform, having just been with him in the limousine. In all, we saw four or five of his shows that week, every one of them sold out, and every one better than the last. Michael worked so hard to please his fans. He gave it his all. And boy, did they ever love Michael. The only time I had ever seen this kind of adulation before was with Elvis Presley.

After the show, I was sitting in the hotel's coffee shop when one of Michael's people came up to me and told me that Michael wanted to talk to me in his hotel suite alone. Poor Irina. She had wanted to see Michael again, just to tell him how much she loved his show. As it turned out, I also wanted to talk to Michael about a musical film project that I had, called *"Nicholas Jingle,"* the story of how Santa Claus came to be. I wanted Michael to play Oliver J. Twinkleberry, an elf and the spirit of Christmas in the film. So with Irina and Michael Boadica waiting in the coffee shop, I was taken up to Michael's suite.

Obviously, we are all aware of the charges that were levelled at Michael, but I never thought much about it because I know that Roman Polanski was set up with a young girl—even I had my own utterly groundless problems with the law—and I know of many other cases where innocent people have been preyed upon and set up to look guilty. It has killed some careers and ruined numerous lives. Out of frustration and humiliation, some actors have even taken their own lives.

I was being led into Michael's presidential suite when a little boy walked past me. I must say, for that split second even I thought, my God, is it true? Then, as we turned into the living room, there was a little girl playing in the corner. I wondered just what was going on, but then I was introduced to the children's mother, who was on the couch in the living room. She was well off, that's for sure. And then I met her husband. I had seen him filming the show on video throughout the performance. They were close friends of Michael's and had just come to say goodbye to him. It shows you how fast one can jump to the wrong conclusion. Even me, who had never believed what the press said about Michael. I felt really stupid, but I never mentioned it to anyone.

Just then Michael came out and said, "Hi, David. Why don't we sit in the dining room?" I told him what a fabulous show he had put on, and we exchanged pleasantries. I told him that I was very friendly with his dad, Joe, and that his sweet mother, Katherine had on occasion cooked me dinner at their house in Encino, L.A. But all the time I kept thinking to myself, wow, how white he is; his skin is just like mine. When I first met Michael on Diana Ross's show, his skin was a light black, but now it was a totally different color. I guess all those shots he was getting were really having an effect.

He then started in with his questions regarding, you guessed it, *"West Side Story."* As he was talking, he put on these crazy glasses that had Slinkies for eyes. You know the kind—big eyes and these silly round metal things falling from each eye. Michael looked so silly, but his questions were very serious. We sat there for about forty-five minutes talking, oblivious to anyone else in the room. Marcel Avram, the promoter, was also in the room, but Michael never said a word to him; he didn't even acknowledge him. It was terrific. It was the first time I'd had such a long conversation with him, and I realized how well he knew *"West Side Story."* I also talked about my new film, and he seemed quite interested in it. He told me to get him the script, and he'd get back to me quickly. My heart was beating rapidly at the prospect of having Michael in my new film.

We said goodnight to each other, and I left feeling very happy, personally, and very satisfied, professionally, about our time together. Stunned, Marcel went down in the elevator with me. He told me that as long as he had known Michael, he had never seen him talk to someone for so long and so animatedly. In fact, he said, Michael rarely talked to anyone at all. He told me they had a game they played called "Michael Says" that went like this: Every day, one of his people would go to Michael's suite and pass a piece of paper under Michael's door, asking him what he needed. Then Michael slid another piece of paper under the door, and written on it was "Michael Says" at the top of the page, followed by what he needed or wanted for the rest of the day and evening. This was the only interaction between Michael and Marcel's crew. Pretty weird, I thought, but whatever.

I felt truly honored, as Michael had invited me to come to see him again the next day. As Irina and I retired to our hotel, all I could think about was what a lovely, sweet human being Michael was, as well as one of the greatest entertainers in the world! In that way, he reminded me of my friend Sammy Davis Jr.

When Michael moved to Amsterdam with his show, I decided to go and take some friends with me. My friend Skye (ex-stuntwoman), Ciro Orsini (restaurant owner of numerous Pizza Pomodoro restaurants around the world), Gary Stretch (actor and ex-Light Middleweight Boxing Champion of the World), and Rossi Barbarossa (men's clothing designer) all came along. We drove in two cars, Skye and I in one and the rest in another. With the train through the Chunnel, it's an easy drive.

We were met there by my friend Arthur Lodder and his friend George, who owned the local hotspot Heaven for Sinners. There were also two beautiful blondes from Sweden, who were students studying in Holland. I had met them on a previous trip to Amsterdam, and the three of us had had a great time, so I invited them to come along and see the show and meet Michael. Needless to say, they were really excited. Wherever Michael appeared, he was the hot ticket, and in Amsterdam, they sold out in forty-five minutes for all six shows—amazing! He was truly a phenomenon.

At the hotel, hundreds of screaming kids were being held back by the police as they waited for Michael. They screamed even louder when I pulled up in my cream-colored Rolls Royce. They all tried to look in the back, thinking that I was smuggling Michael into the hotel. Security let us through, we picked up our tickets, and just as we were about to go, Michael came in the front door of the hotel lobby.

There was madness outside—lights flashing everywhere, fans screaming even louder than before, and all the handlers trying to rush Michael through the lobby to his suite. Michael stopped when he saw me.

"Hi, David," he said in that hushed tone, barely audible above the din of the fans.

"Hi, Michael," I said. "This is my friend Skye."

"I've just come from the hospital, where I saw a lot of sick kids," he said.

"You must be exhausted," I said. "Go rest and we'll see you backstage tomorrow at the stadium."

He nodded in appreciation and was swooped up and almost carried to the elevator by his entourage. I turned and watched him disappear, and I thought, what a giving person. He just arrived in town, and even before he checks into the hotel, he goes straight to the hospital to visit the seriously sick children in the cancer ward. He really loved children, and I loved the child in Michael!

I accompanied him on many such trips. We would visit two hospitals a day, unannounced. Of course, when we showed up, the hospital went crazy as word spread like wildfire that Michael Jackson was there. He always visited the children with incurable diseases first.

He took photos with the kids and signed autographs for them. They were ecstatic! Then, after leaving the ward, he would meet privately with a nurse and his secretary, where he would ask the nurse what kind of equipment they were most in need of and what might help the children, either to cure them or to at least make their lives easier. His secretary wrote down everything that the nurse told him.

Tirelessly, he would visit these children, just to brighten up their lives. Then we would do the same thing all over again at another hospital. Already about 2:00 p.m., he hadn't even checked into his hotel yet, and he had to leave from the hotel at about 4:30 or 5:00 for the arena. Once he got to the hotel, he would make a call and tell the party on the other end to take down all the secretary's information and to buy all of it and have it sent to the hospital anonymously. In one week, I saw Michael give at least $10 million to different hospitals this way, anonymously. I also know for a fact that he gave tens of millions of dollars to many other children's charities anonymously. Why don't the papers write about these things? The goodness that he took time out to do and his unselfishness in his love for all the children on this planet—he was a very generous person, in every way.

Frank Sinatra also gave tens of millions of dollars to charity, also anonymously, yet no one ever wrote about Frank's generosity either. In an odd way, for a moment, they seemed the same to me, Michael and Frank. They were both singing stars as kids, and both became institutions. And the only press they ever got was negative, yet they were both such good people. They were both misunderstood and were both hounded by the press. And both were bigger than life.

Well, it was show time, and it was arranged that Kenny Ortega, who was Michael's director on this show and a good friend of mine, would drive with me to the stadium. (Kenny has gone on to huge success as the director of the incredibly popular Disney *"High School Musical"* films.) All my friends piled into my car, and off we went to see Michael. Having a special Michael VIP pass made it easy for me to get to the backstage area where the trucks had unloaded Michael's sets, props, and costumes. Michael's show traveled with 250 people. It took four of the largest Russian cargo planes and numerous trucks to move the show from country to country and from city to city.

I parked and we went to the hospitality area before going back to Michael's dressing room, where he saw more sick children before the show. In a way, his whole life was dedicated to sick children. These kids adored Michael, and during one of the numbers in the show, he had about forty of them come on stage, and a little girl would give a flower to a soldier who was coming out of a tank. It was a very touching moment. And yes, he travelled with the tank! He shipped it in one of those huge cargo planes from country to country.

All my friends were thrilled to meet Michael. Skye and I went to see every show that week, and I brought my two Swedish girlfriends to two of them. My friend Arthur, as I mentioned earlier, was part owner with George in a fabulous disco in Amsterdam called Heaven for Sinners, so we all went there after the show. A bunch of the dancers from Michael's show joined us, and we took over the place and danced all night long. We did the same thing at a few other clubs during that week. It was party, party, party! So much fun.

One day, as I was waiting in the hotel lobby for Michael, a bunch of his super fans came over and spoke to me. They had seen me with Michael and wanted to pick my brain. These kids followed him all over the world. They came from Germany, America, South Africa, everywhere. If they could afford it, they followed his tour, even to Hawaii and the Far East. Some of the girls and boys talked about nothing other than Michael, and some of the girls dreamed of marrying him. They were all very friendly with each other. They tried to find out where he would be every day, and then they would wait there, just hoping to catch a glimpse of him. He knew them all, so they were allowed to get closer to him, like in his lobby, and they camped out, all day, all night, for their hero. A couple of these kids later called me, asking me for information about Michael's whereabouts, and I tried to explain to them that I had my own life and didn't spend all my time keeping track of Michael Jackson, which seemed hard for them to understand. There was even a group who waited outside the hotel all night long hoping he'd come to his window for a second. Sometimes Michael sent out food and drinks or soup for these fans. He was very thoughtful and truly appreciated his fans.

During our week together, Michael and I spent the days visiting kids in hospitals or orphanages, and then in the evenings he did the show. He expended a huge amount of energy in his shows. I don't know how he did it, but I can tell you for sure, this man was truly dedicated to helping children all over the world. He was one of the most beautiful souls I've ever met.

"Welcome 2 Ibiza"

Ibiza, the magic island… I don't think there is one person on the island of England or, for that matter, the entire continent of Europe who does not know the name Ibiza. To all of them, the name conjures up images of sunny beaches, huge discos, wild parties, the newest clothing styles, water sports, great restaurants, the latest music, crazy foam parties, and sex, sex, and sex.

The famous, amazing foam parties of Ibiza

During my time in London, one of my best friends, Marco Dehry, introduced me to a gentleman by the name of Andre Bakhtiari. He was in the property business and had about 300 apartments in Los

Angeles as well as homes in London, Cannes, Marbella, Germany, Ibiza, and God knows where else, and thirty health spas and clinics all over Germany. He was a most gracious host, as he came from a very good family, which included his aunt, who was Queen Saroya, the last queen of Iran before the Ayatollah took over; his father, who was the last prime minister of Iran; and his grandfather, who was the last minister of defense for Iran. We became good friends and spent a lot of time together. My only problem with Andre was that he would never let anyone else pay for anything. He was generous almost to a fault.

Soon after our time together, he moved from London to L.A., and I didn't hear from him for a long time, until I got a call from Marco saying that Andre was interested in going into the film business and wondered if I had any projects. Sure, I had lots! Because of the popularity of Ibiza, I was toying with the idea of shooting a youthful comedy there, an updated version of the Marilyn Monroe film *"How to Marry a Millionaire."* When Andre heard about this, he went crazy because he, too, was thinking about a film in Ibiza. He had been going there every summer for the last twenty years and was aware of its worldwide popularity. He also owned a lot of property on the island, including nine discos at one time.

The population of Ibiza is about 130,000 people, but in the season (July–early September) three to four million people visit the island on vacation. It's the most popular tourist destination in all of Europe. It's a very expensive place and attracts the jet set with the biggest yachts and sailboats you will ever see. Some have crews of ninety aboard— basically floating cities that cost hundreds of millions of dollars. Of course, Ibiza attracts loads of celebrities as well. When I told Andre my idea, he loved it because, like me, he loved beautiful women.

He sent over a gentleman from Germany to check me out. Lars came to my movie studio, and I took him to lunch in my Rolls Royce. I must have passed the test, for Andre and I were soon in heated discussions about what direction the film would take. I worked on a few ideas with Sean Casey and also with a young writer/cinematographer in London, James Shanks. The plan was for Andre to come to London and spend a week with me to see if we could work together.

It was then that I decided to go to Thailand, and I suggested to Andre that we meet there. We could work but also have some fun together. He agreed, and we had a terrific time and got along famously. Andre thought my ideas were very commercial and wanted my writers to begin working on the script right away, but he insisted that I actually go to Ibiza with my writers so that we could get the feel of the island, see the locations, and choose where to shoot the film.

The project was a go, and it seemed that Andre was financing it personally. It would be a very low-budget film, but Andre assured me that if we were successful, we would do films with much bigger budgets in the future. We agreed to form a company and be partners in this and other ventures. Andre would finance or bring in funds, and I would be the creative end.

June 27th, my writers and I set off for the island of Ibiza, just off the coast of Spain. When we arrived, the season was beginning to take shape, and every day, or should I say every night, planes would land at fifteen-minute intervals, filled with holiday-makers and partygoers. One would leave London at about midnight and arrive in Ibiza at 3:00 a.m. Most people went to their hotel, dropped off their bags, and went right to one of the main discos, which didn't really get going till 2:30 a.m.

The clubs in Ibiza were like nowhere else in the world. They were filled with literally thousands of people dancing, with many of them on ecstasy. Privilege, the largest disco in the world, had a capacity of 10,000, but sometimes as many as 14,000 people, at a cost of $50 a head, got in. From 2:30 a.m. until 9:00 a.m. the clubs rocked, and the parking lots were abuzz with crazily attired clubbers coming and going. It was a hedonist's paradise. The club Space opened at 8:00 a.m., so if you didn't want to go home to sleep, you didn't have to. The DJs in the Ibiza clubs were the best and most expensive in the world. They included such stars as Paul Oakenfeld and Roger Sanchez, who got as much as $130,000 for a four-hour set, just to play someone else's records! It boggled the mind. Clubbing in Ibiza was a very big business, and the drinks were outrageously expensive. Whenever Andre went out to the clubs, which was almost every night, he dropped $3,000 a night. Now that's clubbing—Ibiza-style.

We arrived at 11:00 a.m. all ready to work. We stayed at one of Andre's apartments, a beautiful five-bedroom condo in Ibiza Town overlooking the harbor, the old walled city, and the castle on the top of the hill. We were blown away by the view.

That night, we went into town, and it was packed with people from all over the world—and some of the most beautiful girls I had ever seen. We couldn't believe there were so many of them on such a small island (ten miles by twenty miles). While we were sitting in an outdoor cafe, a parade of people on stilts, all made up very theatrically, walked by, advertising a disco. There were drummers and dancers, with beautiful girls and guys taking up the rear of the parade. It was outrageous. None of us had ever seen anything quite like it before, especially for a disco. We were told that at midnight, every night, all the discos had similar parades and that they changed the themes and costumes of the parades every night. What a fabulous introduction to this extraordinary wonderland. Sure enough, two minutes had not gone by when there was another parade and then another for Privilege, Pasha, Amnesia, and El Divino, the biggest and probably the most expensive clubs on the planet. It was truly amazing. The outfits were fabulous and highly creative. The parades became street performances, and the whole place was buzzing with excitement. We knew we had to capture this in our film.

For the next couple of days, we were driven around the island and shown most of the beaches. We got to know our way about pretty well. We went to a lot of places off the beaten track, unknown even to some of the local residents. A few days later Andre joined us, and all of a sudden everyone wanted to help us. Andre knew everyone who was anyone on the island, and we were offered everything but their firstborn. We had chosen many locations to shoot in, so Sean and James went off to write the script, while I continued to scout and began to get a crew together for the filming.

Andre was totally right about Ibiza being a one-off and that we had to experience it to write about it. I had never done a film this way before. In the past, I always had the script and then went to the location to shoot. Here, we went to the location and created the script there, where we were to shoot.

I had Patricia Rose, my casting lady in Los Angeles, put ads in all the usual places, and the response was overwhelming. She received 800 applications for the three girl's parts alone. Of course, what a job! Getting paid to go to Ibiza for eight weeks—truly a dream acting assignment! Marco helped her with the auditions, and they paired it down to forty girls. They had the girls read on video and then sent me the tapes so I could choose whom I wanted or request more auditions.

Megan Gray, Athena Cansino, and Sami Reed
in my buddy Rossi Barbarossa's designer swimwear

Athena Cansino in one of the comedy scenes with Mackenzie Astin.

Fortunately, we had some very good actresses the first time around, and I chose Megan Gray, a semi-regular on the TV series *"Buffy the Vampire Slayer";* Athena Cansino, grandniece of movie legend Rita Hayworth; and Sami Reed, who had just finished the film *"Rock Star,"* where she co-starred with Mark Wahlberg. Athena had exactly the right comical attitude and positive exuberance that I wanted for the leading lady. And, boy, was she ever beautiful. Sami and Megan, although young in age, were seasoned pros with a lot of professional jobs under their belts.

As for the men… We had many actors and agents submit pictures and tapes, but I had seen a home movie of an actor named Mackenzie Astin. Although I had never heard of Mackenzie, or Mack as he likes to be called, his mother is Patty Duke (whom I had worked with in the film *"Billie"*), his father is John Astin (whom I worked with in *"West Side Story,"*) and it turned out that his brother is Sean Astin (one of the stars of *"Lord of the Rings"*), so one thing was for sure: he had a good pedigree.

Then Mariano Alameda, a Spanish actor, was recommended for the part of Angelito, who was supposed to be a native of Ibiza and who represented the spirit of Ibiza. Mariano was a big Spanish TV star and the number-one heartthrob of all the young girls in Spain. I must say that he was a beautiful man—kind of a younger Antonio Banderas, only better looking. He had never done an English film before, so I was naturally concerned—first, about his ability to speak English, and secondly, whether or not one could understand what he was saying. This was an area that we worked on during the film. I even went as far as hiring an acting and speech teacher from London, my close friend Alexander Holt, to work with Mariano as well as with the three girls on their motivations for each scene.

Athena Cansino and Mariano Alameda in a scene from the film

This was a unique situation, and I could see that, with all the production problems which were mounting daily, I would not have the usual time a director needs to work with the actors. Alexander was a godsend, as my scenic designer showed up for one day and immediately told me he had to go back to the UK because of a problem with his girlfriend. I never knew why he showed up at all. Alexander and an actor/writer friend of mine, Marc Underwood, who worked with Alex a lot at the Gate Theatre in London, stepped in, and they did a terrific job. They brought the film in on budget with only a week's prep. Thanks, guys.

Actor Gary Busey sporting a black eye in the film *"Welcome to Ibiza"*

I wrote a great part in the film for my mother, Sadie. I called the character "Disco Granny." She was great in the film, and what an absolute thrill for both of us to be able to work together. I also gave myself a small part. But I needed a Hollywood name to play the gangster Cortez, so I hired Gary Busey, who had been nominated for an Academy Award for best actor for the film *"The Buddy Holly Story"* and was a friend of mine.

Then twelve crew members didn't show up for various reasons and were replaced. But finally we were ready to shoot. Ready, except for one thing: I was not totally happy with the script. Although it was quite good, I felt it still needed some polishing. Andre was on my case about the fact that the season in Ibiza is very short, so all those wild people I wanted would soon be gone and places I wanted would be shut. Also, that summer Ibiza suffered the worst weather they'd had in over thirty-one years. I insisted and said that I would have to take my chances, so Sean and James kept working on the rewrites. The film got funnier, and Mack's part grew, until what had begun as a much smaller role was now the main comedy-relief character, making him the main actor in the film.

Once we started shooting, sure enough, as Andre had predicted, pretty much everyone had left and most of the places were closed. Plus, we got hit by lots of storms and rain until we had to close down twice. But the scenes were looking good, and everyone on the set was laughing. Even with the weather, we just somehow kept shooting. I really don't know how we did it, but we finished only one day over schedule, and on budget.

But there were other monumental problems, on and off the set, mostly because of the overindulgence of most of my crew with drugs. In Ibiza one can get anything that one wants, and I guess they wanted it all. Andre, who is the most gracious host in the world, allowed some of the actors and crew to stay in two of his apartments. That was our biggest mistake. They misused his property, left it in a mess, broke things, stole things, and left lots of drugs lying around when they departed. On a few occasions, Andre invited the whole crew and cast on his 150-ft. yacht for the day and entertained them royally. Even so, there were many problems. For instance, Sebastian, a soundman, ran off with the sound tapes for seven days because he and his girlfriend had a fight. And he was usually so stoned that half the time he didn't even record sound at all, and he took absolutely no notes of sixty hours of filming. What a nightmare, and I didn't find out about it until I began to work on postproduction sound in Thailand. I tried to ignore the problem as well as work on post-production. I could and just get my pages every day. To this day, I would like to kill him!

Then I had a UK stuntman who beat up a Spaniard in a bar because of the Spanish fellow's girlfriend, whom my stuntman was obviously interested in. It turned out that the Spanish fellow was a cop. Can you believe this big, strapping, idiotic stuntman actually beat up a little guy in a bar? What a bully. He was drunk, of course, but so what? That was just his way of trying to justify his uncalled-for aggressiveness. Well, he was arrested and carted off, and if not for Andre asserting his influence, that jerk would probably still be rotting in a Spanish jail. Needless to say, we hurriedly got him off the island and fired him from our film. Who needs aggressive bullies like that around?

These were just a couple of the incidents that occurred during the filming. There were so many mad things going on that I could write a book about just this experience. It's a wonder we ever finished the shoot. In spite of all this craziness, we did finish, and incredibly, Andre and I were quite happy with our work. Now it was up to Sean and me to finish the post-production work on the film.

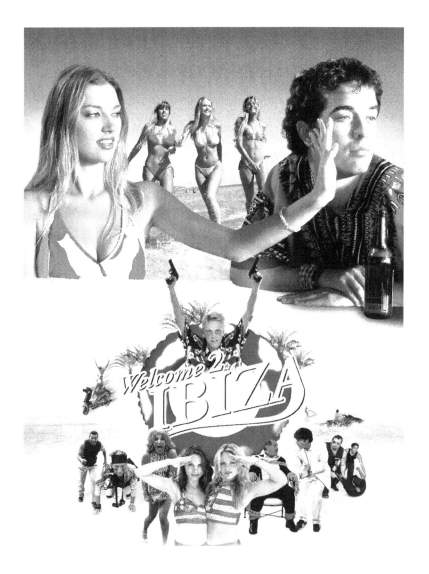

Art work for the poster of the film *"Welcome 2 Ibiza"*

We stopped in London for a few days before flying to Bangkok. I checked in at Equator and saw my friend Peter Parkinson, only to find out that the stock had dropped even further. My stock, which had been worth £5 million, was now worth about £1.28 million. What a disaster. Oh well. Thailand, here we come.

We arrived on November 7, 2001 to more problems. Some of our boxes had been lost. They showed up three weeks later, all except one box that contained the script girl's notes. I thought to myself, this film must be jinxed. After a lot of screaming, lots of fights, and additional wasted time, DHL found the box in their own office in Bangkok, which is where I had told them to look weeks ago. So now we had everything, but that's when I found out about that imbecile Sebastian, the soundman.

Bill *"Oliver,"* my sound designer for the film, had done the sound for fifteen of my previous films in L.A. and five films with Steven Spielberg, as well as numerous others. He was now married to a Thai girl, Lek, and was living and working in Thailand. After listening to all the material and trying to sync it up, he gave me the incredibly bad news, which topped all the other bad news. Man, what did I do in my last life? He told me that we needed to re-record the entire film. Oh my God, that's impossible! I said. "Well, it's either that or we have a silent movie," Bill said. He played me some of the sixty hours of tapes, and I was in utter shock. We would have to bring all the actors to Bangkok and spend six weeks prepping it and at least three or four weeks re-recording every line. The cost was certainly nothing we had planned for, and I had to go back to Andre. Fortunately, he was very supportive and understanding, and luckily, we were under budget at that time. But some of the actors had scheduled obligations that conflicted with our plans. So we wound up re-recording the film in Sony Studios in L.A., Cinecolour Lab Sound in Bangkok, Sound in London, and in Madrid. Can you imagine, a little film like this, and we did looping in four countries? And then it had to be synchronized with the actors on screen? This entailed a huge amount of work from different people in all of these countries. And the cost? Don't ask. And all because of this one soundman in Ibiza. I wish I had never seen him in my life. Anyway, we lived through it and lived to fight another day. We finished the film just in time to screen it for the buyers at the Cannes Film Festival. The show business magazine *Moving Pictures* did a spread on our adventures and how we made it in the nick of time, arriving at the festival on its first day.

The road to Cannes

David Winters and
Andre Bachtiari are
debuting their new
LA/London-based
company Alpha Beta
International in
Cannes, as well as
premiering *Welcome
2 Ibiza*, the first
film of their three-
picture slate

There's nothing like cutting it tight. En route to Cannes, producer/director David Winters
filed the following diary pages to *Moving Pictures*. We *think* he made it in the end...

Saturday, 10 May –
Bangkok, Thailand

PUSHING through final sound mix on *Welcome 2 Ibiza* at Cinecolor Labs. Reels two, three and four done. Film looks fabulous. Buyers will love it. Nervous about finishing on time. Three screenings scheduled in Cannes beginning with a 6.00 17 May at the Star Cinema. I'm booked on an EVA Airlines flight out tomorrow. Couldn't reach my partner Andre on his cellphone. Must have set off already from Ibiza on the *Andre VII*, his 90-foot yacht with all those girls on board. Andre knows how to party! Plan is to meet up in Cannes where the *Andre VII* has a berth reserved at the Old Port. I'll be staying aboard, selling *Welcome 2 Ibiza*. Also *The Warrior King*, for which I've shot a big action scene here with 60,000 extras. Where else but Thailand can you shoot an independent feature with 60,000 extras? But it's a long way to Cannes and I still have to mix reels one and five. And where are the damn sales brochures?

Sunday, 11 May – Bangkok

Disaster. Machines in the lab broke down, absolutely zilch done in the mix. Started up again finally at 6pm but missed my flight. End of season here so airlines booked solid. Everybody's flying out except me! Got Sean Casey, the screenwriter with me,

along with my old friend Lorraine Dexter, the former stuntwoman who has also done ADR on *Welcome 2*. At least misery has company. Meanwhile, brochures arrived at last and look terrific.

Called Andre. Boat docked in Barcelona. Could barely hear him – sounded like a helluva party going on there.

Checking off on my must-bring list for Cannes. 2000 eight-page color brochures; 150 promo VHS cassettes; five beta SP cassettes; three 8x5 blow-ups; two regular-sized posters; a big Alpha Beta International flag for the boat (with white metallic eagle logo); 25ft canvas banner to hang on the back of the boat; 10 Alpha Beta hats (done at last minute); set of business cards. Hauling all this plus our bags. Oh, and 10 reels of film if I can finish the damn thing!

Monday, 12 May –
still in Bangkok

Just finishing reel five. Going to look at the whole thing at 02.00 tonight. Telecine at 08.00, then hopefully out of here and in Cannes in time to make the screening. My wonderful lead actress Athena Cansino (Rita Hayworth's grand niece) is arriving in Cannes tomorrow. Talked with DDA people in Cannes – they've scheduled a photo call on the pier with Athena in her bikini for Thursday morning at 10.30

Tried for a flight out on the following: Swissair (no), Air France (ditto), British Airways (only through Dubai), Thai Airways (not until Thursday – too late!). Called Andre and got some girl who said he was "occupied".

Tuesday, 13 May – Dubai

Quick stopover here. Called DDA. Athena arrived but the boat hasn't.

Where will Athena stay? DDA wants to know. I said get her a room and Andre will take care of it when he pulls into port. Called Andre and whoever answered said there was a storm last night, boat put in at some harbor up the coast. Loud music in background. Must be a party!

In an hour we take off for Berlin. From Berlin to Rome and from

Rome to Cannes. Looks like we'll just make it for Thursday screening if weather holds and all flights are on time.

Wednesday, 13 May – Dubai

A little engine trouble kept us overnight. Sean timed it out. Says if all goes well and drive rental car from Nice about 100 mph we'll get to the

Star Theater with 15 minutes to spare before screening. Well, that's showbiz.

Called Andre – the Old Port closed for the night and he was forced to drop anchor for the night on the high seas. Now he's docked just behind the registration office – a prime spot. My partner says to hurry up – "the party is just getting good!" Cannes here we come!

CHAPTER 45

The Kingdom of Siam
and *"The King Maker"*

The Cannes Film Festival in the South of France was just one of the many film festivals and markets that I attended around the world to sell my films and to meet with buyers. Although it is the biggest and most glamorous, there are many others, such as MIFED in Milan, the AFM in L.A., Sundance in Utah, the European Film Market in Berlin, and TIFF in Toronto. Since I had a lot of action films, I thought I should also go to the Hong Kong Film Festival and Market, as they like action films in Asia.

My old friend Skye was now living in Phuket, Thailand, where she had bought a house and was renting out Harley Davidsons to tourists. I was only a two-hour flight away, so I thought I'd visit her after the film market in Hong Kong and stop in Phuket for a bit of R&R.

Within hours of landing, I was lounging on a stunning sandy beach on the beautiful island of Phuket in Thailand. It's naturally lush with tropical vegetation, and young girls wander past with metronomic regularity. And it's oh-so-very far away from the only worlds I've ever really known: the glamorous world of "smoke and mirrors," known to all as Hollywood, and more recently London, the city of fog and smog, where there's sometimes no sunlight for three months at a time. Life on this island jewel couldn't be more enjoyable. It's certainly different than the unpredictable streets of America and Europe, especially these days. Here, the women smile at you in a shy but respectful manner just because their culture has raised them to be polite and friendly, not because they have an agenda or want to get into the movies or show business. Although I have always enjoyed living in big cities such as London, New York, Los Angeles, and Miami, I was enjoying this little piece of Asian paradise, a world away from the fast and furious life I was used to. It was visually stunning, and now I wanted to actually experience life in what looked like paradise!

Skye introduced me to a beautiful young girlfriend of hers, Nuree, who also rented out motorcycles and scooters for a living. She was twenty-one, and she and I wound up at dinner together when something came up for Skye at the last minute one day. Nuree amazed me by the way she served me first, before taking care of herself. She placed each plate and cup for me and even unwrapped my straw. I certainly wasn't used to such service and care. She was meticulous, very gentle, and ultra-feminine. My downfall is femininity, as I consider it a lost art. Needless to say, I was overwhelmed by her grace and immediately fell under the spell of her charm. One thing led to another, and before I knew it, she and I were back in my hotel room where she continued her subservient care of me. I must say, I was in heaven.

Later that evening, she received a phone call and started crying. Her mother had been killed in a motorcycle accident in the northern city of Khon Kaen in the province of Isaan. I consoled her, and it seemed as if she never wanted to let go of me. Her body was shaking so much from this tragedy. I truly felt terribly sorry for her, to lose her mother at such a young age. She was so sweet and vulnerable at that moment, and she started to capture my heart. Then she informed me that she had to leave the next day to go to her mom's funeral. What a crazy introduction to Nuree, I thought to myself. I later found out that there are approximately 12,000 such motorcycle accidents yearly in Thailand.

She was in a state of shock, and not knowing Thai custom or how to handle this situation, I called Skye and asked for her advice. She said, "If you don't care about her and she is just a one-night stand, then you have no obligation at all, but if you care about Nuree and you go to Khon Kaen, she will never forget you for what you have done." Those were strong words to me, and I decided that not only would I go with her but I would also pay for all the costs of the funeral.

She repeatedly said that I didn't need to do that, but I knew her family had no money—her father worked as a laborer in the fields for fifty cents, yes fifty cents, a day. Over and over, Nuree said she was so sorry for ruining my vacation and that I didn't have to go with her. I kept thinking to myself, what a selfless person. Her mother has just died, and she is worried about ruining my vacation. The more she said it, the more I felt like I wanted to help. So we went to Khon Kaen, and I experienced a Thai funeral.

First I met her father, who was very sweet but did not speak English at all. He was a kind and gentle man, and we hit it off quite well using hand signs and eye contact. His skin was like dark rubber from working the fields every day. He was so grateful for my help.

A Thai funeral is like an Irish one, in that the family sits in front of the casket and photos of the deceased for a week, and other family members and friends come to pay their respects and eat and drink and burn incense by the casket. There was a big photo of Nuree's mom on an easel right next to the casket with a string of running lights around it, much like a cinema marquee. It seemed so incongruous to me, but everyone else in attendance seemed accustomed to this type of display. I joined in every day, seated right between Papa and Nuree. All the visitors were introduced to me as they came to pay their respects. It was quite an experience, and one that I'll never forget.

From then on, whenever I had some free time, I made my way from London to Phuket, where people were always smiling and happy. Many times, I arranged for my wife and kids to meet me there. The boys loved it there. They got to swim underwater with sharks, with supervision, of course, and I took them to see a cobra snake show. They also got to shoot .457 Magnums at a shooting range—all things that kids cannot do in the States. I videoed everything so they could show off to their friends back in the US.

I took so many trips to Thailand that it eventually became my second home. In 2002, I was told about the upcoming Bangkok Film Festival. For fun, I decided to enter my latest film *"Welcome 2 Ibiza"*—any excuse to go to Thailand. Well, my film won the audience award at the festival, so I decided to stay around for a while longer to see if I could put together any future film deals.

Although I had only gone to Thailand for two weeks, I would wind up staying for over twenty years. Oddly enough, I've met many Western guys who have done likewise. The place is like a magnet to us. I amazed myself by eventually resigning from my post at Equator Films and moving to Thailand.

Years before, I had met Lek Kittiparaporn in L.A. through my friend Alan Roberts. At the time, Lek was the hot young director from Thailand who had won numerous local awards. He heard from Alan that I was in Bangkok, contacted me, and took me to lunch at a lovely country club. Lek was from a very wealthy and influential family. His father was the Thai distributor for Disney and was also a cinema owner. Lek had built a successful chain of department stores in Bangkok named Jusco. He and his family owned many amusement parks in Thailand. Lek had gone to school in Switzerland with the then royal prince of Thailand, now the current new king of the country, Rama X.

Lek gave me a book he wanted to make into a film and asked me to read it. It was written in 1547 by a Portuguese soldier of fortune whose travels and adventures took him to Siam, the name of Thailand at the time. At our next meeting, when I asked him where the money would come from for the film, he told me not to worry about that at all.

He told me he wanted to do the film in the Thai language, but I told him I was not interested in doing any film unless it was in English. He understood and said he would get a script written in English for me. About a month later, Lek sent me a screenplay, which I didn't like at all, so I brought Sean Casey over from England to do a rewrite of it. Business-wise, he and I agreed that he would direct and I would produce the film, and I would take care of the worldwide distribution.

I started to work with Sean on the script and changed the title of the film to *"The King Maker."* Lek repeatedly asked if it was ready to shoot, but I put him off until I felt the screenplay was good enough. Meanwhile, I proceeded to cast the film with John Rhys-Davies, the star of all three *"Lord of the Rings"* films and the Indiana Jones film *"Raiders of the Lost Ark."*

John Rhys-Davies on horseback in the award-winning film *"The King Maker"*

I cast Cindy Burbridge, a former Miss Thailand, as the leading lady and hired a lot of major Thai film stars and some local Caucasian actors, as well. Almost all of the Thai actors had never made an English language film before, so I had Sean work with many of them every day on their diction.

I needed a good younger actor to play alongside John Rhys-Davies, who was a brilliant Shakespearean actor, to say the least. For the leading man, I cast Gary Stretch, a friend who had just completed co-starring in Academy Award-winner Oliver Stone's *"Alexander"* and had acted in a few other English films. He is also a former WBC lightweight boxing champion. At a party one night at a friend's house, Oliver told me he thought that Gary Stretch was a shoo-in to be nominated for the

Academy Award for *"Alexander"* as best supporting actor. Coming from Oliver's mouth, that was good enough for me, as he certainly knows his stuff.

Former "Miss Thailand" Cindy Burbridge and John Rhys-Davies
in a scene from *"The King Maker"*

I scheduled fifty-one shooting days and nights for the film. The locations were simply gorgeous—castles, temples, more castles, and more temples. We had more choices than we really needed. I covered the walls of our offices with photos of the clothes and the swords and breast plates that Portuguese soldiers of fortune wore in 1547, and also handed out videos of the period films *"Elizabeth"* and *"Shakespeare in Love"* for the wardrobe, art, and prop departments to get ideas and to copy from. These creative Thais were amazing and picked up the styles right away. They're undoubtedly the best and finest copiers in the world. In fact, what they built was even more beautiful than what I had shown them to reproduce. Lek had told me this before and, boy, was he right on. Since there were no costume or prop rental houses in Thailand, we had to build everything from scratch.

Below are 2 of the many story boards that were used in making the film.

42. EXT - BATTLE FILED - DAY
THE JAPANESE TROOPS LINE UP NEXT TO THE PORTUGUESE

42. EXT - BATTLE FIELD - DAY
THE PADRE GIVES THE PORTUGUESE TROOP'S HIS BLESSING

We had literally thousands of fighting soldiers in the battle scenes and hundreds of extras elsewhere in the film, so it was a massive undertaking. During production, I needed to give Gary Stretch some direction, as Lek was great with the visuals but had not made an international film in over twenty years, so I put on the headset myself and helped Gary with his motivation as an actor as much as I could.

We completed filming, and it certainly looked epic. I cannot fathom the money we saved by producing this film in Thailand. The budget wound up being $3.25 million, but the quality of the film looks tenfold. My friend award-winning writer and director John Milius, nominated for the Academy Award for *"Apocalypse Now,"* thought I was joking, but when he saw the film, he said it had to have cost at least $25 million, probably more. When I told him the real cost, he didn't believe it. From then on, I told everyone that I made it for $15 million, and so far, no one has ever called me a liar.

So now, on to post-production… I asked Lek to let me edit the film, as I knew what the buyers were looking for. Lek agreed and didn't join me or see the film until the final mixing session. I finished the editing and the sound recording, which I did in Moscow, and returned to Bangkok for the final mix. And it turned out spectacularly!

Upon completion, Sony Studios bought all rights for the US, and Universal Studios bought most of the other available territories. *"The King Maker"* sold in thirty-six other countries, making it the most successful Thai film ever made in the history of Thai cinema. And to top it off, we were nominated for and won some artistic awards. The film was nominated for four Thai "Academy Awards" and won the Star Entertainment Award in Thailand. This very prestigious award is voted on by all the Thai newspapers. It also won the Mumbai International Film Festival in Mumbai, India, and the film played in cinemas throughout China for over a month. That's longer than most major Hollywood studios' releases.

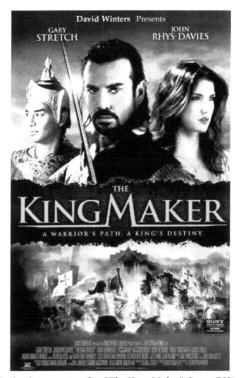

Theatrical-release poster for *"The King Maker"*, Sony (US) version

Thai version of the poster, used by Sahamongkol Films, the #1 distributor in the country. Notice that Yoe Hassadeevichit, the Thai star who played the Queen of Siam in the film but who wasn't even pictured on the US Sony poster, has top billing to satisfy Thai audiences.

The Mysterious Death of David Carradine

David Carradine, star of the original television series *"Kung Fu"* and the *"Kill Bill"* movie franchise, was one of my best friends. David starred in three successful action movies for me—*"Future Force," "Future Zone,"* and *"That's Action."*

Our entire contract was written on a paper napkin in a French restaurant in Cannes. Today, with lawyers (other than David Rudich) being what they are, it would be impossible to have a contract with fewer than at least forty pages. David and I had a wonderful relationship, which allowed for the shortcut. I merely wrote on the napkin the names of the movies, how much I was going to pay him, and he and I both signed it. Can you imagine doing something like that today?

Appearing in over a hundred feature films, David had been a widely recognized and much acclaimed star for decades. He was a fabulous actor who was nominated for sixteen major awards, including four Golden Globes.

David called me out of the blue one day, in May 2009, and wanted to know what it was like living in Bangkok. I told David that I was really enjoying living there and wondered why he was asking. He said he had been offered to do a French film, *"Stretch,"* and the film was to be shot in Bangkok, and he was just wondering about my experiences in the city. So after reassuring him, we said goodbye to one another, and that was that. I didn't think anything of it afterwards.

Six weeks later, in June, and after several missed calls from each other, I woke up and saw that the top CNN breaking news story was about the death of David Carradine. I was in a state of total shock and disbelief. The report claimed that he had committed suicide in Bangkok the night before. It said that he had hung himself in the closet of a hotel room. I was stunned, to say the least.

I immediately went on the internet to get as much information as I could, not wanting to believe it was true. I just knew someone had made a mistake! Unfortunately, the stories all matched, and I felt a real coldness. I just didn't understand it. David had been so full of life during our phone calls since *"Kill Bill,"* a hot Tarantino film, had resurrected his career, and he was back to making millions of dollars a film.

That evening, and for the next three nights in a row, I called Chuck Binder, his manager, in Los Angeles, and had long conversations with him, trying to figure out exactly what had happened, not believing the press releases or the news reports that went on for days about the incident. Chuck agreed and confirmed that David couldn't have been happier about the success of *"Kill Bill"* and its sequel. He was riding high, and there was no way he would have taken a flight from the States to Bangkok just to commit suicide. He could've done that just as easily in Los Angeles if he had so wished. The *Bangkok Post* suicide report was simply ludicrous, and both Chuck and I knew it was not true, as David had been on a huge relaunch of his film career. Chuck told me he had a slew of offers coming in for David's services and had already booked him for a few more films after *"Stretch."*

Being David's close friend, I received calls from ABC-TV, CBS-TV, and NBC-TV, asking me if I would do interviews for them regarding David's death if they flew to Bangkok. I agreed. The English-speaking *Bangkok Post* also asked for an interview, which I accepted as well.

I listened to every report I could and read every newspaper and magazine article about the tragedy, not believing any of them. I knew deep in my heart that a cover-up was going on, but I didn't know the reason. It was driving me crazy, and I was obsessed about figuring it out.

Because it was the nearest to my home, the *Bangkok Post* was the first news company to interview me. A strange thing happened during the interview. After turning off the recording device, the editor said, "This is off the record, David. Our newspaper has people working for us all over the city, in every hotel, in the police force, in all the clubs—people who give us leads and information on big stories like this. And for some reason, nobody here will talk to us about this case. Not one person in the entire city. I don't understand what's going on, as I have never come across this before in my entire career." Then he pushed down the record button and concluded the interview with more mundane questions before leaving my Bangkok apartment.

Through friends of mine in Bangkok, I was able to see a gruesome picture of David's dead body in the Thai morgue report, which was never released. The picture clearly showed a bloody string around his neck. The string, I later read, had come from the hotel room curtains. The story that was being reported in Bangkok was that David had hung himself in the closet and died of asphyxiation. Well, to begin with, the morgue picture disproved that theory.

When interviewed, hotel staff reported that David had been in the bar of the Swiss hotel, Nai Lert Park Hotel, the afternoon before he died. He'd been at the bar drinking with one or two lady-boys, then went to the lobby of the hotel where he played the piano around 4:00 p.m. A very good pianist, he played show tunes, as witnessed by guests of the hotel. Now, does that sound like a guy who's about to kill himself? According to the hotel staff, David subsequently got up and went to the elevator and waved back at the same guests he had been playing the piano for, with a smile on his face as if saying goodnight to them. This was definitely *not* someone who's about to kill himself.

It seems that when the investigators went to get the hotel security videotapes from the police department, they were informed that they didn't exist. I also found out that the room David died in does not exist anymore. The hotel renovated the entire second floor and changed the room numbers so that no one will ever know which room David died in.

Additionally, I learned that there were drinks in his room and footprints on the bed and around where he might have been sitting. There was never a mention of any money found on him, and I know for a fact that all of us expats, myself included, always carried cash with us for an emergency, if nothing else, and we usually all wore watches. There was also no mention of a watch being found on his body.

So detective Winters (that's me), decided that this is what happened: David met two girls, or lady-boys, in his room after he left the lobby. They were drinking in his room, and his two guests decided to either rob him or kill him *and* rob him. It may have even started out in a playful, sexual way and just got out of hand; this we don't know. But David was a big guy, and it probably would've taken at least two people to carry him from the bed to the closet and hang him up in it.

The hotel he was staying at was owned by one of the wealthiest families in Thailand, who owned hundreds, if not thousands, of acres in downtown Bangkok, including the land that the British embassy sits on, which is worth millions of dollars. This family was very powerful to say the least.

A few days after my interview, one of the Thai princesses from the royal family, HRE Mom Luang Rajadarasri Jayankura (known to me simply as Mom Luang), who is a very close friend of mine, invited me to an event where the prime minister would be speaking. As I waited with my good friend Todd Moore for the prime minister to arrive, a lady came up to me and asked, "You're David Winters, aren't you?" I said, "Yes. Do I know you?" "No," she replied with a smile, "but I just wanted to introduce myself to you," and proceeded to hand me her business card before walking away. The card read, "Public Relations, Nia Lert Park Hotel," which instantly sent shivers down my spine. In short, this hotel was watching me and sending me a message to shut up and stop talking about David Carradine.

The threat was very clear and very loud. Otherwise, why would this woman I didn't know just arrive out of nowhere, give me her business card, and then leave right away? My theory was that if there was a lot of publicity about David Carradine being "killed" at one of their hotels, it might hurt and/or kill future business, and it was a very popular hotel. I told the Carradine family of my theory, and they subsequently hired a retired FBI agent to investigate the case. The agent announced that his findings were that the theory of David Winters was correct as far as he could see.

After this horrible incident, I eventually pulled myself together. I had to. I felt compelled to post my thoughts on multiple blogs, as I needed to get it off my chest and also to let the world know that someone had stolen a very close friend of mine. My guilt for encouraging David to come to Bangkok weighs on me still to this day.

Back to Acting

So life in Thailand went on and was back to being wonderful again. I was living a stress-free life and loving it. My son Alexander decided to move there, which made me even happier. I lived in Bangkok, Pattaya, and sometimes Phuket.

Soon after David's death, I was cast as Silas Bridges in the TV miniseries *"Blackbeard"* on the Hallmark Channel. I got to work with my old buddies Richard Chamberlain and Stacy Keach, who co-starred in the miniseries. It was so great to be just acting again that I decided I'd like to do some more of it.

Soon, I got a call about co-starring in a Thai film *"Hanuman: The White Monkey Warrior,"* which was to star the Thai idol Sornram Teppitak, who was all the rage with the young ladies. I took the job, and again it was pretty easy and fun. Sornram and I got to do our scenes together, and we got along very well. I played a Mafia boss, and I was third star billed in the opening credits. Then I was cast in *"Dragonwolf,"* again as a Mafia boss. On this film, they offered me fourth-star billing in the opening credits. Hey, I was starting to get typecast over here in Thailand, but it was easy and I loved being in front of the cameras and just acting again. There was certainly much less stress. And even though a couple of the films were shot in the Thai language, I never had to speak anything but English, so I was thrilled. I was having a ball!

Me as a mafia boss in the film *"Dragonwolf"*

Then the agent Walter van Kalken called me about a casting call for a new Danish film that would be shooting soon in Thailand, based on a nineteen-minute award-winning dramatic short called *"Teddy Bear"* that had been liked by over 5 million people on YouTube, which is quite amazing. It would star Danish actor Kim Kold, a huge bodybuilder in real life, who had won many tournaments for his physique. The first-time director was Mads Matthiesen. After winning many awards with his short film, he went to the Danish government and got them to fund his long-form version of the film. Pretty cool, I thought.

So I was sent the pages for my part, and after studying them, I went to see Mads. Mads was a very young guy and seemed really nice. I read a dramatic scene for him, and he liked my reading and said I had the part. I would get fourth-star billing in the opening credits.

Kim Kold and me in a scene from the award-winning film *"Teddy Bear"*

I play an owner of a bar in Pattaya where I fix Kim Kold's character up with local girls. I also got to insult Kim in a very dramatic scene that we filmed at the bar location. I felt great about that scene, as everyone on the set, including all the extras, applauded me after I finished it, so I knew I had done good, buddy boy!

The rest of the filming went well and without incident. Because it turned out to be a very sensitive piece, Mads entered it into many film festivals. We won seven festivals as best film, including the very prestigious Sundance Film Festival in the US, which has been run by Robert Redford for years. With 46,732 attendees in 2012, Sundance is the largest independent film festival in the United States. It is held in January in Park City and Salt Lake City, Utah. Mads won best director for our film *"Teddy Bear,"* and we were over the moon about it. Best director for his first feature film? Incredible!

I was asked to attend a special screening of the film at Sundance. After the screening, there would be a question-and-answer period and Mads, Kim Kold, and I would be on stage to answer questions from the audience. This sounded great to me as I was interested in the young audience's reaction to our film. I agreed to go, and my friend at the time Gary Stretch drove us there. I had no idea it was over 8,000 feet above sea level. I started to feel a little dizzy when we arrived, but I made it through the screening and the Q&A okay, except I was very disappointed to see that my dramatic scene where I insulted Kim Kold had been cut from the film. We attended the usual celebration party and then checked into the hotel that they had booked for us. I was tired so I fell asleep.

Around 5:00 a.m., I felt Gary trying to wake me up, and he sounded really scared. He was worried about me and my heart. He said that I had been breathing very heavily, but at other times, I had been trying to catch my breath in my sleep. He suggested that we leave right away and drive down to a lower elevation, possibly Las Vegas, which we did. I didn't have an opportunity to tell the others what was happening until later in the day when everyone was awake. But in Vegas I felt better and was breathing better.

After the successful screening, the film got a US distributor. It opened in NYC for the one-week run needed to qualify for the Academy Awards and then played around the world. It got some great reviews, and Kim and I celebrated. He got a terrific part in the next couple of *"Fast and Furious"* films. And me, I went back to my paradise, Thailand, ready for my next adventure.

CHAPTER 48

"Dancin'–It's On!" Back to My Roots

With my mind like a highway interchange, I make a directional note of where I am before embarking on my next mile towards personal production. This mile seems endless, with many a curve to be travelled. I sit back and wander through my thoughts. It takes time and energy, and that inner force within me just won't let up. And neither would my dancin' feet, at least in deep thought, as the sound of finger snapping filters into my consciousness...

I started to think about creating a dance musical that I could shoot in Thailand, the place that I now called home. The title *"East Side Story"* quickly came to mind because it was the original title for *"West Side Story."* And because of my association with *"West Side Story,"* I thought it would be a good idea, commercially speaking. This time, however, the storyline would be about a poor orphan boy, a dishwasher, from Southeast Asia, and a rich girl from Beverly Hills who meet when she comes to Thailand on a summer holiday while staying at a vacation hotel, owned by her father. Being from different backgrounds and cultures, the one thing that bonds them together would be their mutual love of dance.

Alexander, my son, my third-born, was now living in Bangkok and working as an actor/stuntman and model, and his professional name is Alex Winters. There's a special bond that we share that can't be denied. We've always been close, even while separated. Alex always loved the arts, and his thirst for knowledge began at a very young age. He loved music; he loved dancing. He loved going to the theatre, something Jonathan never cared to do. So it was Alex and me all the way. Unfortunately, somewhere along the way, that special connection was lost with Jonathan, Alex's older brother, and my daughter, whom I barely know. How sad not to be able to relate.

Alex, on the other hand, could sing the entire score of *"The Phantom of the Opera"* when he was five years old. Imagine that—at the age of five! Wonder where he got his knowledge and stamina from! He loved the ballet, but I never taught him to dance. Today, he is coming out on his own; a major actor, stuntman, and model in his own right. I'm so proud of him, and he did it all on his own!

I often look back to see what went wrong, in a misty-eyed re-evaluation. I am angered by the silence and betrayal of some; and here, beside me, to comfort me, is my Alex in my later years.

So I began to work on the screenplay. Alexander helped me by doing research on the internet, searching to find new singers and new music that I thought would work for the film. He and I listened to approximately 100–150 songs a day, every day, for an entire year. I did find some wonderful talent: a terrific writer, singer, and DJ named Ray Isaac from Australia who seemed to be quite popular there. I thought his songs and his singing were fabulous and would be great for a few different sequences in my film. Ray was very happy when I contacted him and told him that I wanted at least four of his songs. I also found a few singers in Canada and elsewhere, such as Frankie Vinci, a very talented writer and singer in Massachusetts. My assistant at the time, Guillaume Ellis, who was from Canada, turned me on to a great writer and singer, Jean-Mary John Levi Simon, from Montreal, Quebec, and a couple of other people that he knew up there. Then I found a professional named Ian Prince who had won the Grammy Award with my friend Quincy Jones. Quincy has won dozens of them and is one of the most accomplished people in the music industry. Quincy also worked with my buddy Michael Jackson and with Diana Ross and so many others.

My mind continued to spin, so I spent the next six months writing the synopsis for the screenplay, with Alexander on occasion correcting some of the old-fashioned dialogue so that it was up to date for today's youth.

What fun! I got to act and dance in my own film.

Being in his early 20s, he knew the current jargon. Then I gave it to David A. Prior to do a first draft, and then I rewrote that version again, and then more Alexander corrections. This process went on for over a year. While I was shooting the flim, I wound up writing forty-two screenplays. Imagine—forty-two versions of the film. Forty-two versions? Unheard of, David! You are NUTS!

Me in a dramatic scene with Chehon Wespi-Tschopp

Laura Fillipi making me up before I act in a scene

Poster for the award-winning film *"Dancin'–It's On!"*

I decided to finance the film myself so that I had total control and didn't have to answer to anyone else. In the past, I had worked for many people, but I preferred to work for myself. You wasted less time listening to other people's opinions, and sometimes, with other people, you wound up with a project that was less than you wanted it to be.

Then I decided to invite my buddy Bruce Lewin to co-finance it with me. He'd invested in eighteen of my films before and always let me make them the way I wanted to, without any interference or opinions, and he agreed to do it.

I decided to change the title to *"Dancin'–It's On!"* And bit by bit, my screenplay and my music were coming together. However, there were still many scenes in the movie where I had no suitable song, so I had to have them written specially for that scene.

Finally, with all that behind me, I was ready for the task of auditioning dancers and actors. I had been watching *"So You Think You Can Dance"* and some other shows that had the best up-and-coming dancers in the industry, and if there's one thing I hopefully know by now, it is dance. I looked at hundreds of hours of dancing from these shows on YouTube, as well as watching the live shows weekly whenever I could in Thailand. The quality of the dancing was great. It was very energetic and athletic. The question was, could these kids act? They were fantastic dancers, but none of them had acted before. As it was a low-budget movie, I thought I'd first audition all the local kids in Thailand who were great dancers. Unfortunately, I was grossly disappointed as not one of the dancers who auditioned for me in Thailand stood up to the dance requirements I had in mind for this film. I decided right after that audition to change the entire location of the film to America and get myself the best dancers in the world.

"Dancing with the Stars" Grand Prize winner Witney Carson, with "SYTYCD" Winner Chehon Wespi-Tschopp, holding her

I contacted Nigel Lythgoe, who was the producer, owner, and judge of *"So You Think You Can Dance"* as well as *"American Idol,"* another top-ten-rated TV talent show from the US. I told Nigel about my idea, and it turned out that Nigel's favorite movie was *"West Side Story"* and his favorite performer was Elvis Presley. He already knew about the four films I had choreographed with Elvis; he even told me he was a fan of mine! Perfect!

Nigel, with these two shows on the air, was probably one of the most powerful men in television at the time. We exchanged emails, and then I flew to L.A. to meet with him. His offices were in the old *Playboy* magazine building on the Sunset Strip, and as he walked me into his office he locked the door and took his phone off the hook. I thought, wow, he's really serious about helping me. He asked me what he could do for me. I told him I watched his show and was totally impressed with it and the new dancers he had hired. We had a wonderful meeting that lasted about two and a half hours. He gave me contacts to call if I needed any help, and as we were leaving the office, he asked me, "David, would you do me a favor?" I said, "Yes, sure, what is it?" And he said, "Would you take a picture with me?" He really was a fan! I must say, it sure made me feel good and was great for my ego.

Chehon Wespi-Tschopp and Witney Carson dancing their number
in the finale of *"Dancin'–It's On!"*

After the meeting with Nigel, I called my buddy Grover Dale, who shared a dressing room with me during the Broadway production of *"West Side Story."* Grover and I met, and he turned me on to a lot of dancers he knew or had heard of. His company, Answers4Dancers, helps up-and-coming young dancers. Grover, you are so amazing! Then I returned to Thailand, reassured that my film would have some of the best dancers in the world and some of the best dancing in it.

Comfort Fedoke and Tadd Gadduang dancing in their finale number

I thought the natural place to film was Florida, with lots of beaches, hotels, and sunny weather all year long. I placed an ad on Craigslist, looking for a line producer. Many people answered the ad, but I liked two young girls from Florida State University. Their names were Christina Marie Austin and Jennifer George Hall. Jenni had actually been a dancer before. They told me that Panama City Beach is the number-one destination in the US for students during spring break. Millions of them descend upon the city during that time period, and there would be loads of extras for free, or if not, very cheap. With my low budget, I liked their thinking and hired them and arranged to fly to America. I flew to Panama City Beach, and they picked me up me at the airport. They had arranged lodgings for all of us with the local Panama City film commissioner, Julie Ann Gordon. I met Julie, and she's a ball of fire. She recommended a dance club to me, La Vela, which is located on the beach with fourteen different rooms and is the largest dance club in America—perfect because I had three different clubs that I needed in the film, so I could shoot them all in one place. That alone would be a big help with my production schedule. We checked out La Vela and other locations and then drove down the coast, all the way to Miami Beach.

On the set of *"Dancin' - It's On!"*

As I thought about all the places we had seen, the one that stuck in my mind the most was Panama City Beach for two reasons. One was the club La Vela. They had offered me the club for no money, while a club like that in L.A. would usually charge $25,000 a night. I had scheduled ten days of shooting days there, so that would be a huge savings to me. The second reason was, Julie is a real go-getter and had worked out a deal for us to stay right on the beach in a beautiful hotel—music to my ears! So that was it. We found our location because Julie came through when nobody else had. And Julie seemed to really care, which made a huge difference to me, personally. I love people who are passionate, no matter what their job is.

I returned to Bangkok to get my personal life in order so that I could return to Florida for twelve to sixteen weeks to make my film. Little did I know then that I would wind up staying in Florida for over five years! It's funny how life works out. You just never know…

So I returned to Panama City Beach to lock in my main cast. I first cast Witney Carson, winner of *"Dancing with the Stars,"* and Chehon Wespi-Tschopp, winner of *"So You Think You Can Dance"* as the two leads in the picture.

I also hired Gary Daniels, an ex-PKA world-champion martial artist and accomplished actor (*"The Expendables"*), to play Witney's father.

Next I added Russell Ferguson, an amazing dancer who had won *"So You Think You Can Dance"* in 2010 and also won "World's Best Dancer" at the MGM Hotel in Las Vegas, competing against China in the finals.

For the remaining young dance cast, I choose nine winners and runners-up from *"So You Think You Can Dance,"* including Matt Marr, Pauline Mata, Comfort Fedoke, and Tadd Gadduang, all incredible dancers in their own right.

Then I remembered that I had seen this fantastic dancer, a red-headed beauty—Jordan Clark—who won the grand prize in Canada's version of *"So You Think You Can Dance."* I toyed with the idea of Jordan playing the lead in the film but decided to give her the femme fatale role instead.

Jordan Clark dancing in *"Dancin' - It's On!"*

I reached into Nigel Lythgoe's world again by signing Brandon Bryant a second-runner-up from *"So You Think You Can Dance"* to be my choreographer. Oh yes, I almost forgot—I hired myself as an actor as I had written a part for myself in the film. You didn't have enough to do, David, huh?

Meanwhile, Christina and Jenni arranged numerous auditions for local dancers in Panama City Beach, Panama City, Tallahassee, and Destin.

Wide angle shot... We are now filming at one of these auditions from the back of a very large studio, as hundreds of dancers are auditioning for the film.

Witney Carson was in the front row with Brandon helping to show the dancers the audition steps. I must say, I was pleasantly surprised at the quality of a lot of the local dancers who showed up to audition.

I then asked my dear friend Alan Roberts to be both cinematographer and editor, and he agreed. Either one of these is a full-time job on a film. I felt so comfortable with Alan after all these years, and I knew he would do a great job. I'm happy to say, my belief in Alan was confirmed when he won the best editing award at AMC's WideScreen Film Festival. I'd known Alan since we did *"Gypsy"* on

Broadway, which was over fifty-four years ago. Alan recommended writer Misha Segal, an Emmy-winner, to do the score. He had also won the Israeli Grammy Award and was nominated for the Israeli Oscar, as well as numerous other awards. Taking Alan's word, I hired Misha immediately.

Alan and I crewed up for the shoot. Thirteen was my lucky number, so I decided to start my film on January 13, 2013. But, boy, was I wrong. As it turned out, it was freezing cold in Panama City Beach the whole first day. Of course, my opening scene was poolside with everyone in bathing suits! Amazingly, everyone on the set was so happy to be in a film that it didn't bother them at all. The wind was howling and made it difficult to record any understandable sound. I was wearing a heavy suede coat that was lined in sheepskin, like it was the middle of winter. I was told that this kind of weather never happened this early in the year in Panama City Beach. I felt sorry for all the actors and the extras. They had to sit by and in the pool in their swimwear in this horrible weather. I cursed myself for starting on what I thought was my lucky number. How could I have been so wrong? That day was a nightmare. The weather was horrible throughout the shoot, and it eventually put us behind schedule.

What I thought was going to be a blessing—the free extras there for spring break—turned out to be quite the opposite. These spring breakers ran wild all over the town. They were drunk, and some were on weed, and to my disgust, some even urinated in the elevator of our hotel. They were away from home and out of control. One day, I counted sixty-five people in the hotel Jacuzzi that should've held twelve or thirteen at most. Fortunately, my cast and dancers were professional and stayed well clear of all the carousing around them. Also, the traffic was a nightmare. You couldn't get anywhere without a long, crawling drive.

Hundreds of spring breakers partying in a jacuzzi that should hold fifteen people at the most

First day on the set, and it's freezing cold, and windy to boot.

One day the surf was so bad that it leapt from the sea and wound up all over us. That was it! I called a meeting with the actors and crew, explaining that we would have to come back in June when spring break was finished, as it was impossible to go on under these circumstances. I closed down the production, and Alan and I moved to Tallahassee and proceeded to do some editing.

Meanwhile, I was finding it harder and harder to catch my breath. One day, it was so difficult that Jenni and Christina had to take me to the emergency room at the Capital Regional Medical Center in Tallahassee. I was admitted into the hospital because it looked like there was a problem with my heart. Over the next couple of days, many tests were done, and they found out that I have congestive heart failure.

The cardiologist at the hospital wanted to do surgery on my heart. I told him I had to get back to Panama City Beach to finish my film, which he said was impossible. I explained that I had no choice at the moment, I had to return to at least finish the shoot, and that then I would come back. I knew at the time that I was lying, that I would never go back to that hospital again. I didn't feel comfortable there, with the doctors or the help, because I saw a lot of mistakes being made during my stay. So I signed myself out since they insisted on it and wouldn't let me out any other way.

Fortunately, as far as the actors where concerned, I only needed the two leads and Gary Daniels to come back. Throughout the shoot, the weather was a problem. For instance, one night I had 175 people in summer clothes dancing in a salsa number. It was only twenty-eight degrees outside, yet not one of the dancers ever complained. The number was shot at night on the street, and my crew and I were all bundled up in our winter clothes. Again, I felt bad for the kids who were dancing, but what could I do? My partner Bruce Lewin and I were cursing Florida by this point, but we were stuck with no other possibility. So somehow, we plodded on and finished the shoot. Thanks for hanging in there with me, Bruce!

My choice of Christina and Jenni was a really good one, and I decided, then and there, that I want them to be a part of any pictures I make after this one. In this day and age, loyalty is very hard to come by, and they stood by me every second of the way. Without them, I couldn't have finished this picture. Thanks, guys!

Finally, we finished shooting, and Alan and I went back to the editing room and put our baby together. Then I decided to have two preview screenings of the picture, the first at Gulf Coast State College and the second at Arnold High School, both locations we had shot at in Panama City Beach. We did a questionnaire for the audience of 1,600 people, and the reaction was better that we could've ever expected. We received a 9 out of 10 for liking the film and recommending it to a friend, and 9.43 out of 10 for liking the dancing. Wow! What a response! Life was good! No—*very* good!

So we knew we had a film that pleased the audience, and now the problem was: How do we get it in the theaters so that a wide family audience can see it and enjoy it? Putting it out on DVD would be easy, but getting a theatrical release in the States is very difficult, and getting harder by the day. Actually, it's almost impossible, and it costs a bloody fortune. Having gotten this far felt really good to me, as I had now been working on this film for almost four years.

A serious David doing his thing on set during production

Will Time Be on My Side?

Yet another chapter in my life was about to begin, a crucial chapter...my life story. I silently pleaded that it would not dissolve so rapidly before my misty eyes. The fight—my fight—was on.

This next chapter is about life and death and the turmoil within that can have a most devastating impact. Now I write the script for my survival.

I was more than thrilled with the completed film, yet my work was not finished; there were still more details to consider, so I couldn't sit back and relax. I don't know how to relax, anyway. I'm always moving, and my mind is always spinning with thoughts of what is next. But now I felt something wasn't right.

My breathing began bothering me more and more, so I went to see a cardiologist in Panama City Beach at the Bay Medical Center. He did some tests, putting a catheter down my throat near my heart for an ultrasound, and told me I had a serious heart problem. He referred me to a surgeon who subsequently put a catheter up my groin and into my heart. The next day after this procedure, Jenni and Christina (who were with me throughout this) and I went for a meeting with the surgeon. I was stunned when he told me I had less than one year to live unless I had a triple bypass and two heart valves replaced. He said I could die within a month or six months or a year at best. Damn it, *just* what I needed to hear!

It did not take a brain surgeon to tell me that this is probably one of the most serious operations anyone can go through, and it scared the living daylights out of me. I had done some research before the meeting and asked him if he could do a less invasive surgery. But he said, "There is not a doctor or surgeon in the entire country who would do that to you in the state that you're in." I told him that, with this being a matter of life or death, I wanted to get a second opinion. He then told me, if that was the case, he was not going to speak to me anymore. I was in total shock when I heard him say this, as were the girls, and I immediately decided that this was not the surgeon for me. I needed someone without such a huge ego. But as I left the hospital one thing kept ringing in my ears: "You have less than one year to live." Pretty scary. No—*incredibly* scary. Thank goodness for the support of Jenni and Christina during this time. I don't know what I would've done without them.

I called my partner Bruce, who is a very well-to-do guy with lots of contacts worldwide, especially in NYC. He said he would ask around for recommendations of the top medical people in the country. At the First Presbyterian Hospital, which is ranked the number-three hospital for heart disease in America, he got contact information for the doctors who had done bypass surgeries on people such as Bill Clinton, David Letterman, Larry King, and other celebs. These doctors suggested that I come to New York City to see them. I thanked Bruce, but I really wanted to stay in Florida because there was still a lot of work to do on the picture, and I was afraid that if I left, we wouldn't ever finish it. Also, the cold weather in NYC could have been a big problem for me. So he got a local recommendation from each doctor, and as unbelievable as it sounds, they all recommended the same surgeon—Dr. Joseph Lamelas, head of cardiac surgery at Mount Sinai Medical Center and Mount Sinai Heart Institute in Miami Beach. I went on the internet to check him out and found that he had performed over 7,000 heart surgeries, more than anyone else on the planet. He is on the cutting edge of heart technology and has the best cardiac surgery survival rate in Florida. Wow, that was *some* recommendation! Thank you, Bruce!

The girls called Mount Sinai and made an appointment for me to see Dr. Lamelas, and they drove me all night for ten hours from

Panama City Beach to Miami Beach for the appointment. When I entered his office, the first thing he did was to show us a heart and explain it to us in layman's terms. Even though my medical records said that my arteries were eight-five percent blocked, he wanted to probe into my arteries with a new catheter device, which he created, that can actually measure each artery separately, before deciding what to do. This was music to my ears. Here was a guy who was being extra cautious before he said or did anything with my heart.

Dr. Lamelas also introduced me to Dr. Todd Heimowitz, a wonderful young cardiologist. A couple of days went by, and then it was time for Dr. Heimowitz to do the procedure. Afterward, he came running into my hospital room saying, "Good news, David, really good news." He said that my arteries were only fifty percent blocked, and I didn't need to have the triple bypass and valve replacement that the other surgeon in Panama City Beach had insisted that I undergo. All that needed to be done was to replace one valve, and Dr. Lamelas could do that with the less invasive surgery from the side of my chest, not the front. I was so happy that I had made the decision to come to Miami Beach to see these doctors.

The day for surgery arrived, and I asked them to put me out totally. My least favorite thing is getting stuck with a needle, and, boy, have I had enough of them. Sometimes I feel like a pincushion. So they put me out, and when the operation was complete Dr. Lamelas told me it was successful. However, he wanted to monitor me for the next week and make sure that all was well.

While I was in the hospital, I started to have trouble breathing again, and when the nurse came in my room she seemed to be at a loss as to what to do. She told me that my heart was dying, and she froze up and just stood there. At that moment, a young resident doctor walked into my room, saw what was going on, and said I had very little time left to live. He told the nurse to get an exterior pacemaker and hook me up to it immediately. After she did so, my breathing seemed much better and my heart stabilized. I looked up at the timer, and the doctor told me that I had twenty-five seconds left before I would have been dead! I'm so thankful to that doctor, that he happened to come into my room just at the right time. Life is so fragile!

Dr. Lamelas was out of the city doing a seminar that day, so one of his associates, Dr. Angelo La Pietra, came into my room and said they would probably have to put a pacemaker into my chest in a day or so. After calling Dr. Lamelas, he came rushing back into my room to tell me that Dr. Lamelas said I had to get it done now. So arrangements were made, and I was wheeled up to surgery yet again, where Dr. La Pietra inserted a pacemaker into my chest, which has been keeping me alive ever since. Today's medical technology is so amazing. If not for it, I would not be here. I've seen my x-rays and I have all of these wires in my heart, going all over the place. Medically speaking, the future is truly here! My pacemaker is supposed to last at least seven to ten years, and then they can replace it for another ten years. I don't know if I want to live that long. I guess I do as long as I'm not an invalid and can get around and enjoy life to its fullest as I always have. Before I was discharged from Mount Sinai Hospital, their press department asked if I would do some media interviews regarding my experience there, and I was more than happy to oblige, resulting in an article which appeared in the Miami and Southern Florida newspapers.

Having lived through this mind-boggling experience, I would like to say a few words regarding Dr. Lamelas, Dr. Todd Heimowitz, Dr. La Pietra, and the rest of the incredible Mount Sinai staff. We as artists just entertain. These doctors are true heroes, saving lives day after day. Having been a recipient of their gift of life, I am forever grateful for each and every day onward. Thank you for my life, Dr. Lamelas, Dr. Heimowitz, and Dr. La Pietra! Because of you, I exist and the world in general is a much better place! You all are my heroes!

Monday, June 30, 2014—While I cannot remember the last time I produced, directed, or acted in a sequel, this past week Dr. Heimowitz, my cardiologist, wrote his own script to the sequel of "My Heart Beats" or "What Can I Stick into You Today?" and cast me in the lead role! And I was simply brilliant!

On what I thought to be a routine visit to his office in Miami for a simple ultrasound procedure, within minutes, I found myself traveling on a clattery gurney into surgery for a cardiac catheterization. The lights went out, and I woke up in what felt like moments later in yet another recovery room with a whole new cast of actors around me.

Did I doze off or is the procedure over? What the hell happened? After a few lucid moments, I realized I had been cut in the groin. I felt a bit apprehensive, a little discomfort, but overall much better than before I "dozed off."

"How are you feeling, Mr. Winters?" echoed a voice.

"Not sure… What happened?" I responded.

"Well, Mr. Winters, during the catheterization, your doctor saw another problem and decided to insert two stints in your left artery," said the voice.

Two hours later, I was taken upstairs to a plush private room on the eighth floor with a great view of the Miami harbor. I asked for a "Do Not Disturb" sign to be hung on the door, and I proceeded to block out all notion that I was in a hospital with other very ill people around me. But not for long… They told me my heart was only working at twenty to twenty-five percent of capacity.

Then I was in and out of surgery over a dozen times. During one of these sessions, they implanted a defibrillator in my chest to help the pacemaker. If my heart starts to fail, it should shock me back to life. Although it kind of sticks out of my body and feels like a watch with dials and all sorts of things, at least it is keeping me alive. So now I am *bionic*!

Recently, I also had two operations on my right ear to remove cancer and another cancer operation close to my left eye and my brain. Man, when I do it, I do it totally! The last procedure was *really* scary because I thought I might lose either my eyesight or sustain permanent damage to my brain. Did I want to gamble and take the chance? You might think I'm crazy, but before I went ahead I spoke to my dear departed mother and prayed a lot. These procedures were performed by Dr. Arthi Kruavit at Bumrungrad Hospital in Bangkok, Thailand, rated the ninth-best hospital in the world. Dr. Kruavit did a magnificent job, as I have no eye or brain damage at all. He never even gave me any anesthesia during the surgery, in which he took out what looked like mini-donuts from my head. Some people think of Thailand as a third-world country; it's anything but! Thanks, Doc!

There were many times when I was in the emergency room or having an operation that I would be back in the editing room a few hours later, trying to complete my film, *"Dancin'–It's On!"* It seemed like I was always going between the two. I had to finish my film—that was the driving force that kept me going through this nightmare and gave me the strength I needed. The show will go on!

Upon release from the hospital, I rented a condo in Miami Beach, just a five-minute drive from Mount Sinai. It was a lovely place right on the Inland Waterway, and convenient to everything. When I felt a bit stronger I moved up the coast to beautiful Fort Lauderdale, where many of my friends live.

The great view from my Miami Beach condo, a good place to rest and recover

My Ft. Lauderdale view

EPILOGUE

The last curtain... but not for me–the show MUST and will go on!

Where do I begin? Where do I end? As I said, the curtain does not fall. "There's such a lot of living to do," to coin a phrase and song title from *"Bye Bye Birdie."* (Geez, one show I wasn't involved in... Wonder why?)

The response to *"Dancin'–It's On!"* was extraordinary, especially following the ordeals I went through. So now it was promotion, promotion, and more promotion. We got very busy as we made the cross-country red-carpet circuit, with premieres in major cities including Los Angeles, New York City, Boston, Minneapolis, Hialeah, Las Vegas, Hollywood (Florida, that is), and, of course, Panama City Beach. There were interviews and more interviews. I was feeling the pressure of achievement.

I also felt the squeezing pressure in my chest once again. I felt my life slowly draining away following the Panama City premiere, and I was so frightened. I almost collapsed in the men's room right after the screening. How could such a thrilling personal moment turn around so rapidly? My four assistants took me to the nearest hospital, where after a couple of tests, the doctors suggested that I stay for surgery the next day. For me, a hospital stay in Panama City was not an option, so we traveled again all night long to South Beach and yet another ten-day hospital stay.

With the theatrical release of *"Dancin'!"* in cinemas all over America, there was no stopping us as three- and four-week holdovers continued to impress the masses. How exciting! The video release followed, selling out in a week at over 400 Walmarts across the country. Next came its highly successful release on Netflix.

There are still many challenges I have to overcome, and as the sun sets, I'm thankful every day to live the dream life I've led. I have eighteen new and exciting projects in the works. Only time will tell...

While I no longer live in Florida, during 2016 and 2017, I visited quite often as I needed to check up on all my health issues, especially my heart and cancer. One day, I was called by Joey Dedio and Dennis Grimaldi, two producers who were filming a documentary about the performers still living who had appeared in the original production of the Broadway show *"West Side Story"* sixty years ago. As it turned out, Joey is also a very accomplished actor and Dennis has won three Tony Awards as well as the Pulitzer Prize and many other awards. They told me that Martin Charnin, who played Big Deal in the original Broadway production and went on to write and direct the hugely successful musical *"Annie,"* would be directing the film. They also told me that Lincoln Center in NYC was involved in its financing. It all sounded great to me, and I told them to count me in.

Other actors and creative artists from the show who are still alive today are super Broadway star Chita Rivera, winner of two Tony Awards and nominated for ten of them (To this day I still call her Chita-Bita.); Carol Lawrence, who played the leading ingénue, Maria, in the show; also my good buddy Tony Mordente, whom I still call Arabina because he played A-rab in the show; Grover Dale; Ronnie Lee; Jaime Sanchez; George Marcy; Liane Plane; Marilyn D'Honau; Reri Grist; Jay Norman; Noel Schwartz; Carole D'Andrea; producer Hal Prince; and writer Stephen Sondheim.

Joey and Dennis wanted to film an interview with me, so they sent a crew of eight to Miami Beach, where we did just that. They also mentioned an appearance in NYC on Broadway at St. Luke's Theatre sometime later plus numerous other personal appearance events that they'd like me to attend. The first interview went very well, after which they told me they planned to release the film in many cinemas in 2018 and would like me to be at some of the major city openings. I agreed without hesitation.

Right after that interview, I heard about Irma, the category-five hurricane that had demolished many islands in the Caribbean just off the coast of Florida. Every day, the news showed Irma getting closer and closer to land—heading, of course, just where I was staying. The after-waves were anywhere from six to nine feet high, and cars were being thrown about like they were toys. The situation appeared ominous, and I decided to leave the city since I was living on the first floor and was sure I'd be flooded out.

A friend of mine had an offer from a friend, Sonny Roshan, to go to Bradenton, Georgia, during Irma and stay in his mansion. He asked if I'd like to join him there. Thankful for the offer, I packed as little as possible into my car, and he drove his pickup truck. The ten-hour drive was pure madness! There were no hotel rooms available along the entire route and no gas as all the stations were sold out. I guess everyone else had the same idea: to escape. The highways were chock-full of cars creeping along.

As I was driving, I found it increasingly difficult to keep my eyes open. The highway was hypnotizing me since I hadn't driven in so long, and it was nighttime, which made it even harder. I actually fell asleep at the wheel three times that night. Each time I woke up, I was moving erratically on the highway, and I could see other drivers screaming at me and trying to get out of my way. It was an absolute nightmare, but somehow, luckily for me and everyone else, I never hit anyone. I called my friend, who was driving ahead of me, and told him what had happened. So at about 2:00 a.m. we pulled into a motel parking lot and parked our cars. He suggested we sleep in our cars for a while and then get up early in the morning and continue the trip. When we woke up, we grabbed a bite at a nearby restaurant and then actually found a gas station that had replenished its supply. By this time, it was just about daylight, and so back to the highway and all the traffic.

Without realizing it, I found myself falling asleep again, even in the daytime. I wound up falling asleep another three times. Can you believe it? The last time, my friend called me and told me that he had been watching my car in his rearview mirror and that I had gone from one side of the highway right across to the other side. He said the cars around me were swerving, trying to stay away from me, and that I was lucky to still be alive. He insisted I pull over, and he found a private airfield where he arranged for me to park my car with the understanding that I would pick it up on our way back. The people in Georgia are so sweet and hospitable. Even under these trying circumstances, they tried their best to make us feel at home.

Once we got back to Fort Lauderdale, it was time for a very special event. It was September 26, an auspicious day, the same date that *"West Side Story"* had opened on Broadway. Because of my heart, I decided not to fly to New York but to have my buddy drive me instead. So we took off again, this time for the Big Apple!

I was shocked to learn that St. Luke's Theatre was totally sold out in just two days after the *"West Side Story"* event was advertised. It was wonderful, and I had a great time seeing all my old buddies after sixty years. Don't forget, I was still the youngest of them all. The theatre filled up, and by the time the show began, they had to add more seats in the aisles—the crowd was amazing! I guess I had forgotten how popular the show was and that *"West Side Story"* has millions and millions of fans all over the world, especially in New York City. The audience asked us questions, and everyone seemed to have a terrific time.

The entire cast of the original Broadway show *"West Side Story"* on stage for the documentary. I am on the far right.

After the event, Joey and Dennis had arranged a party for all of us at Sardi's, *the* spot for Broadway show performers. More interviews, and eventually, as all things do, the evening came to an end. *"West Side Story,"* the original Broadway stage show and the movie version of it, have been an enduring influence in my life. What a wonderful way to come full circle with my involvement in this classic show! Sixty years later—wow! And back on Broadway! I felt truly blessed to still be alive to participate in and enjoy this event. It caused me to look back at my life and give thanks to God for all the close calls I had through the years and how I somehow avoided them all so that I can be here today writing about it. Thank you, thank you, thank you!

I am being interviewed at the famous Sardis in New York City

They say a cat has nine lives; well, I think I've probably had more. So here I am after over fifteen years of writing down my memoirs. Now on to my next adventure. My story will continue forever and a day; from day to day, night into night, hour to hour, minute to minute, second to second.

May I repeat several song lines from *"West Side Story"* to reflect upon? They are true to my feelings.

"Could be, who knows?
There's something due any day;
I will know right away,
Soon as it shows...

Something's comin';
Don't know when,
But it's soon.
Catch the moon—
One-handed catch...

Something's comin';
I don't know what it is,
But it is gonna be great...."

Thank you, fans! Thank you, friends! I couldn't have done this without you. You are the story of my life, and that is why...

Tough guys do cry!
Tough guys do love!
Tough guys do live on!

And tough guys do dance!

AWARDS & NOMINATIONS

27 award nominations, 16 wins
Winner of Best Director—WideScreen Film Festival
Winner of the Peabody Award
Winner of the Christopher Award
Winner of the Paris Film Festival
Winner of the Mumbai Film Festival
Winner of the Golden Scroll Award
Winner of the Bangkok Film Festival
Winner of the Houston Film Festival
Winner of the Charleston Film Festival
Winner of the Sitges Film Festival
Winner of the Star Entertainment Award
Winner of 3 World Television Awards
Winner of the Grammy Award
Nominated for 6 Emmy Awards

FILMOGRAPHY

Producer

2014: *"Nicholas Jingle"* (producer) (pre-production)

2014: *"Dancin'–It's On!"* (director/producer/writer)

2005: *"The King Maker"* (producer)

2004: *"Devil's Harvest"* (executive producer)

2003: *"Welcome 2 Ibiza"* (director/producer)

2003: *"Rhythm & Blues"* (executive producer)

1995: *"Body Count"* (producer)

1995: *"The Dangerous"* (producer)

1994: *"Raw Justice"* (executive producer) (producer)

1993: *"Night Trap"* (executive producer)

1993: *"Double Threat"* (executive producer)

1992: *"Blood on the Badge"* (executive producer)

1992: *"Armed for Action"* (executive producer)

1992: *"Center of the Web"* (executive producer)

1991: *"Cop-Out"* (executive producer)

1991: *"Dark Rider"* (executive producer)

1991: *"Maximum Breakout"* (executive producer)

1991: *"That's Action"* (video documentary) (producer)

1991: *"The Last Ride"* (executive producer)

1991: *"Presumed Guilty"* (executive producer)

1991: *"Raw Nerve"* (executive producer)

1991: *"The Lost Platoon"* (executive producer)

1991: *"Firehead"* (executive producer)

1990: *"Deadly Dancer"* (executive producer)

1990: *"The Bounty Hunter"* (executive producer)

1990: *"Lock 'n' Load"* (executive producer)

1990: *"White Fury"* (executive producer)

1990: *"The Final Sanction"* (executive producer)

1990: *"Invasion Force"* (executive producer)

1990: *"Fatal Skies"* (video) (executive producer)

1990: *"Future Zone"* (executive producer)

1990: *"Born Killer"* (executive producer)

1989: *"Shooters"* (executive producer)

1989: *"The Revenger"* (executive producer - uncredited)
1989: *"Time Burst: The Final Alliance"* (executive producer)
1989: *"Future Force"* (executive producer)
1989: *"Rapid Fire"* (executive producer)
1989: *"Hell on the Battleground"* (executive producer)
1989: *"Deadly Reactor"* (executive producer)
1989: *"Jungle Assault"* (executive producer)
1989: *"Order of the Eagle"* (executive producer)
1988: *"Dead End City"* (executive producer)
1988: *"Space Mutiny"* (producer)
1988: *"Operation Warzone"* (executive producer)
1988: *"Phoenix the Warrior"* (executive producer)
1988: *"Rage to Kill"* (executive producer)
1988: *"Death Chase"* (executive producer)
1988: *"Night Wars"* (executive producer)
1987: *"Codename: Vengeance"* (producer)
1987: *"Deadly Prey"* (executive producer)
1987: *"Mankillers"* (executive producer)
1987: *"Killer Workout"* (executive producer)
1986: *"Mission: Kill"* (producer)
1982: *"The Last Horror Film"* (producer)
1982: *"Yoga Moves"* (producer)
1979: *"Racquet"* (producer)
1977: *"Young Lady Chatterley"* (producer)
1976: *"The Lisa Hartman Show"* (TV movie) (producer)
1976: *"Once Upon a Girl"* (executive producer)
1975: *"Alice Cooper: "Welcome to My Nightmare,"* (producer)
1975: *"Linda Lovelace for President"* (producer)
1973: *"Old Faithful"* (TV movie) (producer)
1973: *"Saga of Sonora"* (TV movie) (producer)
1973: *"Dr. Jekyll and Mr. Hyde"* (TV movie) (producer)
1972: *"Timex All-star Swing Festival"* (TV movie) (executive producer)
1972: *"Half the George Kirby Comedy Hour"* (TV series) (exec. producer)
1972: *"The Special London Bridge Special"* (TV movie) (producer)
1971: *"Story Theatre"* (TV series) (producer)
1971: *"Rollin' on the River"* (TV series) (producer)
1971: *"The 5th Dimension Traveling Sunshine Show"* (movie) (producer)
1971: *"Once Upon a Wheel"* (documentary) (producer)
1970: *"Sonny & Cher: Nitty Gritty Hour"* (TV special) (producer)
1970: *"The George Kirby Show"* (TV movie) (executive producer)
1970: *"The "Barbara McNair Show"* (TV series) (executive producer)

1970: *"The Darin Invasion"* (TV movie) (executive producer)
1970: *"Raquel!"* (TV movie) (executive producer)
1969: *"The Leslie Uggams Show"* (TV series) (producer)
1969: *"The Spring Thing"* (TV movie) (producer)
1968: *"The Ann-Margret Show"* (TV movie) (producer)
1966: *"Lucy In London"* (TV movie) (co-producer)

Actor *(43 credits)*
2014: *"Dancin'–It's On!"* - Hal Sanders
2013: *"Dragonwolf"* - Brutus
2012: *"Teddy Bear"* - Scott
2008: *"Hanuman: The White Monkey Warrior"* - Stephan
2006: *"Blackbeard"* (TV movie) - Silas Bridges
2003: *"Welcome 2 Ibiza"* - Uncle Sam
1982: *"The Last Horror Film"* - Stanley Kline
1967: *"Love on a Rooftop"* (TV series) - Augie
1966: *"Out of the Unknown"* (TV series) - The Eye
1966: *"The Crazy-Quilt"*
1965: *"Burke's Law"* (TV series) - Special Agent James Martin
1964: *"The New Interns"* - Hood
1964: *"Breaking Point"* (TV series) - Frank Boyd
1964: *"Death at the Stock Car Races"* (TV movie) - Ralphie Linden
1963: *"Captain Newman, M.D."* - patient
1963: *"Perry Mason"* (TV series) - Chick Montana
1963: *"Take Her, She's Mine"* - coffeehouse patron Lester
1963: *"The Greatest Show on Earth"* (TV series) - Tig
1963: *"Stoney Burke"* (TV series) - Lip
1961–63: *"The Dick Powell Theatre"* (TV series) - Chino inmate/Richie
1963: *"Going My Way"* (TV series) - Charlie
1961: *"Bus Stop"* (TV series) - Omar Kelsey
1961: *"77 Sunset Strip"* (TV series) - Speed Minton
1961: *"The Detectives"* (TV series) - Billy Joe Temple
1961: *"West Side Story"* - A-rab
1961: *"The Law and Mr. Jones"* (TV series) - Shadow
1959: *"The Last Angry Man"*- Lee Roy (uncredited)
1958: *"Naked City"* (TV series) - Marty Nemo
1956: *"Rock, Rock, Rock!"* - Melville
1955: *"The Elgin Hour"* (TV series) - Glasses
1954: *"Roogie's Bump"* - Andy
1954: *"The United States Steel Hour"* (TV series) - Morning Star (1954)
1953: *"The Web"* (TV series) - Like Father (1953)

1953: *"Atom Squad"* (TV series) - Charles West

1953: *"Jimmy Hughes, Rookie Cop"* (TV series) - Henry Benaris

1953: *"Lux Video Theatre"* (TV series) - Stu Morgan

1953: *"Listen, He's Proposing!"* - Stu Morgan

1953: *"The Plymouth Playhouse"* (TV series) - Jamie (1953)

1952: *"The Red Buttons Show"* (TV series) - Red's nephew

1952: *"The Philco-Goodyear Television Playhouse"* (TV series)

1952: *"Campbell Summer Soundstage"* (TV series) - Herman

1951: *"Love of Life"* (TV series) - Spike

1950: *"Studio One in Hollywood"* (TV series) - Tom Boyne (uncredited)

1949: *"The Big Story"* (TV series) - Bobby Dagoras

Choreographer *(34 credits)*

1981: *"Blame It on the Night"* (choreographer)

1980: *"Diana"* (TV movie) (choreographer)

1979: *"The Big Show"* (TV series) (choreographer)

1978: *"Roller Boogie"* (choreographer)

1977: *"The Star Wars Holiday Special"* (TV movie) (choreographer)

1976–77: *"Donny and Marie"* (TV series) (choreographer)

1976: *"The Island of Dr. Moreau"* (creative consultant)

1976: *"A Star Is Born"* (choreographer)

1975: *"Alice Cooper: "Welcome to My Nightmare"* (choreographer)

1975: *"Alice Cooper: The Nightmare"* (TV movie) (choreographer)

1972: *"The Special London Bridge Special"* (TV movie) (choreographer)

1970: *"Raquel!"* (TV movie) (choreographer)

1969: *"Ann-Margret: From Hollywood with Love"* (movie) (choreographer)

1969: *"The Spring Thing"* (TV movie) (choreographer)

1968: *"Monte Carlo: C'est la Rose"* (TV special) (choreographer)

1967: *"The Steve Allen Comedy Hour"* (TV series) (choreographer)

1967: *"Movin' With Nancy"* (TV special) (choreographer)

1966: *"The Swinger"* (choreographer)

1966: *"Lucy In London"* (TV movie) (choreographer)

1965–66: *"Hullabaloo"* (TV series) (choreographer)

1966: *"Made in Paris"* (choreographer)

1965: *"Billie"* (choreographer)

1965: *"Tickle Me"* (choreographer)

1965: *"Girl Happy"* (choreographer)

1965: *"Bus Riley's Back in Town"* (choreographer)

1964: *"The T.A.M.I. Show"* (documentary) (choreographer)

1964: *"Pajama Party"* (choreographer)

1964: *"Kitten with a Whip"* (choreographer)

1964: *"Shindig!"* (TV series) (choreographer)

1964: *"Send Me No Flowers"* (choreographer)

1964: *"Breaking Point"* (TV series) (choreographer - 1 episode)

1964: *"Viva Las Vegas"* (choreographer)

1964: *"The Hollywood Palace"* (TV series) (choreographer)

1964: *"The Ed Sullivan Show"* (TV series)

Director *(22 credits)*

2014: *"Nicholas Jingle"* (pre-production)

2003: *"Dancin'–It's On!"* (postproduction)

1988: *"Welcome 2 Ibiza"*

1988: *"Space Mutiny"*

1987: *"Rage to Kill"*

1986: *"Codename: Vengeance"*

1986: *"Thrashin'"*

1985: *"Mission: Kill"*

1984: *"Girls of Rock & Roll"* (video)

1984: *"That Was Rock"* (video)

1982: *"Steadfast Tin Soldier"* (TV movie)

1979: *"The Last Horror Film"*

1975: *"Racquet"*

1973: *"Alice Cooper: "Welcome to My Nightmare"* (documentary)

1972: *"Dr. Jekyll and Mr. Hyde"* (TV movie)

1971: *"The Special London Bridge Special"* (TV movie)

1970: *"Once Upon a Wheel"* (documentary)

1969: *"Raquel!"* (TV movie)

1968: *"Ann-Margret: From Hollywood with Love"* (TV movie)

1968: *"The Ann-Margret Show"* (TV movie)

1967–68: *Where the Girls Are"* (TV movie)

1967–68: *"The Monkees"* (TV series) (2 episodes)

Writer *(5 credits)*

2014: *"Dancin'–It's On!"* (writer)

1988: *"Rage to Kill"* (writer)

1986: *"Mission: Kill"*

1982: *"The Last Horror Film"*

Soundtrack *(2 credits)*

1965: *"Hullabaloo"* (TV series) (performer - 1 episode)

1957: *"West Side Story"* (performer - "Gee, Officer Krupke!")

Music *(2 credits)*

1967: *"Roller Boogie"* (stager: musical numbers)

"Easy Come, Easy Go" (stager: musical numbers)

Other Appearances as Himself *(6 credits)*

1970: *"The Tonight Show" Starring Johnny Carson* (TV series)

1968: *"Monte Carlo: C'est la Rose"* (TV special documentary)

1967: *"Movin' With Nancy"* (TV special)

1965: *"Hullabaloo"* (TV series)

1964: *"The T.A.M.I. Show"* (documentary)

1952: *"The Milton Berle Show"* (TV series)

For more info on Mr. Winters please log on to: Wikipedia or www.IMDB.com (known as the show business bible).

David and his son, actor Alexander "Alex" Winters

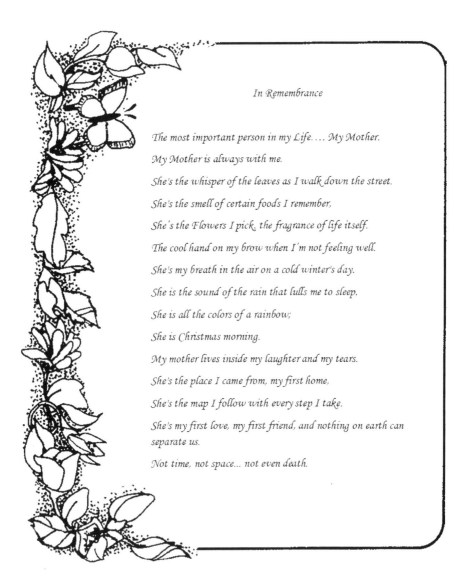

In Remembrance

The most important person in my Life.... My Mother.

My Mother is always with me.

She's the whisper of the leaves as I walk down the street.

She's the smell of certain foods I remember,

She's the Flowers I pick, the fragrance of life itself.

The cool hand on my brow when I'm not feeling well.

She's my breath in the air on a cold winter's day.

She is the sound of the rain that lulls me to sleep,

She is all the colors of a rainbow;

She is Christmas morning.

My mother lives inside my laughter and my tears.

She's the place I came from, my first home.

She's the map I follow with every step I take.

She's my first love, my first friend, and nothing on earth can separate us.

Not time, not space... not even death.

Acknowledgments

I'd like to give a big thanks to the following people who helped me with my book:

Larry Barsky: cover design

Dona Kay Waterman

Sean Casey

Alexander "Alex" Winters

Alexander Zilo

Dan Vega

Hamishe Randall

Bobby Dunaway

Georgette Green

Jay McCall

Justyn Newman

and, of course, Mom

Made in the USA
San Bernardino, CA
25 July 2018